SUSAN McKAY

Bear in Mind These Dead

faber and fa...

Leabha... ath

D0231973

First published in 2008
by Faber and Faber Limited
Bloomsbury House, 74–77 Great Russell Street
London WC1B 3DA
This paperback edition first published in 2009

Typeset by Faber and Faber Ltd
Printed in England by CPI Bookmarque, Croydon

Cover photograph: Eight-year-old Joseph McCloskey at the funeral of his grandfather,
also Joseph McCloskey, in Belfast, 1994. Photo by Brendan Murphy
p. ix: from John Hewitt, *The Selected Poems of John Hewitt*, Eds Michael Longley
and Frank Ormsby (Blackstaff, 2007), reproduced by permission of Blackstaff
Press on behalf of the Estate of John Hewitt.
p. 51: Eric Bogle, 'My Youngest Son Came Home Today'. Words and music by Eric
Bogle. © Larrikin Music Publishing Pty Ltd. International copyright secured. All
rights reserved. Used by permission of Music Sales.
p. 67: Padraic Fiacc, extract from 'Crucifixus', from *Missa Terribilis* (Blackstaff, 1986),
by kind permission of the author and Blackstaff Press.
p. 122: Louis MacNeice, extract from 'Autumn Journal XVI', lines 1–8
(Faber and Faber, 1998).
p. 352: Siegfried Sassoon, extract from 'Suicide in the Trenches', © Siegfried
Sassoon, by kind permission of the Estate of George Sassoon.
p. 362: Derek Mahon, extract from 'Rage for Order', from *Collected Poems* (Gallery
Press, 1999), by kind permission of the author and The Gallery Press,
Loughcrew, Oldcastle, County Meath, Ireland.
p. 362: Paul Muldoon, extract from 'Lunch with Pancho Villa', verse 2, lines 11–18,
from *Mules* (Faber and Faber, 1977).
p. 363: Paul Muldoon, extract from '7 Middagh Street', lines 8–12 of WYSTAN,
from *Meeting the British* (Faber and Faber, 1987).
p. 366: extract from Bobby Sands' poem beginning 'The men of Art . . .' taken
from *Bobby Sands: Writings from Prison*, © The Bobby Sands Trust, 1983.
Reprinted by kind permission of Mercier Press Ltd, Cork.
p. 370: Alan Gillis, 'Progress', from *Somebody, Somewhere* (Gallery Press, 2004), by
kind permission of the author and The Gallery Press.

A CIP record for this book
is available from the British Library

ISBN 978–0–571–23698–5

2 4 6 8 10 9 7 5 3 1

To my lovely mother, Joan, and in memory of my
endlessly kind father, Russell

Contents

'Bear in mind these dead:
I can find no plainer words.
I dare not risk using
that loaded word, Remember,
for your memory is a cruel web
threaded from thorn to thorn across
a hedge of dead bramble . . .'

John Hewitt,
'Neither an Elegy nor a Manifesto'

Map of the North of Ireland showing some of the places referred
to in the book

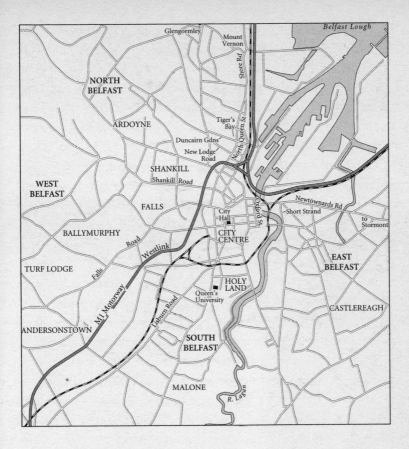

Map of Belfast showing some of the places referred to in the book

Introduction

'I now think, said Austerlitz, that time will not pass away, has not passed away, that I can turn and go behind it and there I shall find everything as it once was . . .'

W. G. Sebald, *Austerlitz*

This book is about the legacy of the events known as the Northern Irish Troubles, or the conflict in the North of Ireland, for those most profoundly affected by them, the families and friends of those who were killed, as well as some who narrowly survived. It was written during a time of great change, with old enemies sitting down together in government, the killings at an end. The relief of peace, at last.

Almost 4,000 people were killed between 1966 and 2005 in a conflict that was essentially about the sovereignty of a very small place. A British place, according to most of its Protestant unionist majority, who call it Northern Ireland, Ulster or 'the Province'. An Irish place to most of its Catholic, nationalist or republican minority, who call it the North or the Six Counties.

Former British prime minister Tony Blair went from attending the swearing in of the new executive in Belfast in May 2007 to a visit to British troops in Basra. Martin Amis, who accompanied him to both places, points out that the entire death toll for the Troubles was 'the equivalent of one bad month in Iraq'.[1] While this is true, it is worth recalling Sir Walter Scott's 1825 comment: 'They have such narrow ground to do their battle in.' Less than 2 million people live in Northern Ireland. If conflict on a comparable scale had occurred in the United Kingdom, almost 150,000 would have died.

During the conflict, however, we became adjusted to that sort of thinking. Full of foreboding, we'd switch on the radio in the morning to hear the news from Northern Ireland and then think, 'Not a bad night, only one dead.' But what if that person was your father? Your neighbour? Your milkman? We were relieved that 1973 wasn't as bad as 1972: only 263 dead compared with 497. That hardly anybody died in 1999 – only seven. It was a sign that we had been damaged in our souls.

I wrote this book because I believe the dead should not be forgotten and that they should be remembered, above all, in the words of those who loved them. I also believe that those who contemplate the use of violence for political ends should think first of the devastating pain that is visited on people who are bereaved as a result.

* * *

In his great meditation on history and memory, *Austerlitz*, the writer W. G. Sebald considers the possibility that 'the border between life and death is less impermeable that we commonly think'.[2]

This is a story that Gerard McGurk told me.

Gerard was fifteen when loyalist paramilitaries put a bomb in his father's small pub in Belfast in 1971. His mother, Philomena, and his only sister, fourteen-year-old Maria, were killed, along with thirteen other people, one of them Gerard's uncle and another his schoolfriend. Gerard was injured, as were many others, including his brothers. The pub and the family home above it were reduced to a heap of rubble.

Thirty-five years later, in 2006, Gerard brought his thirteen-year-old daughter, Emma, to visit his father. Patsy McGurk was by then living in a Belfast nursing home. When he saw Emma coming, the old man's face lit up. 'Och, Maria,' he said. 'Where have you been all these years?'

There are strange silences among those who lived in Northern Ireland during the Troubles. I grew up as a Protestant in Derry and left to go to Trinity College in Dublin in 1975. I met and became friends with Gerard McGurk. We were part of a circle that spent a lot of time in pubs, holding forth about Keats, angst, the price of a pint and the North. It was just four years since Gerard had lost his mother, his sister, his uncle, his friend and his neighbours in a horrific sectarian massacre. But we never spoke about it.

The friend who introduced me to Gerard had known him for years. Recently, he told me about trips they'd make around Belfast in the early 1970s to pubs in the most dangerous areas.

Gerard had a car. One night they drove down the loyalist Shankill Road, madness for a group of young Catholics. They crashed into a taxi, were pursued, got back to the nationalist Falls Road and were stopped by the British army. The windscreen of the car was broken and the boys had obviously been drinking. The soldiers laughed at them and let them go.

I lost touch with Gerard after we left Trinity and only met him again after I contacted him to ask if he'd talk to me for this book. He spent a long time deciding. He finally agreed, though he said it would be very hard for him. We met in Dublin in 2007. 'It was a very long time ago, a different age,' he said. 'People didn't talk about emotional things.'

He had a sense of 'terrible inevitability' about what happened. He hadn't talked much about it, even privately, he said, and he and his family had said very little in public. 'We kept a dignified silence. My own twin girls are fourteen now, the same age as Maria was. It is only in recent years I've realised the missed potential. I feel sad that Maria missed the opportunity to enjoy life.' His daughters had got very interested in 'Auntie Maria' and had a photograph of her on their bedroom wall. They would soon be older than her. Gerard's father died in 2008.

I have talked with other Northerners who are amazed at the way we lived blithely through events which, looking back, make the blood run cold. Partly, it must have been fear. Where possible, you kept your head down. The place was full of people listening in, gathering information, setting people up. You could put yourself in danger, or someone else. This coexisted with a sense of fatalism combined with the irrational belief that you personally and all those belonging to you were, as one man put it to me, 'bullet-proof'.

For my generation the end of childhood coincided with the start of the Troubles. Like many of my peers, I couldn't wait to get away. But it isn't so easy to leave a war behind, and I returned in 1981. The IRA hunger strike had just ended, and the sign for Belfast on the platform in Central Station had been smashed, so that it now read, 'Fast Central.' I felt compelled to get involved politically, and I helped to set up, and then worked in, a Rape Crisis Centre. The political violence masked a shocking level of violence against women.

I lived for a time with a man whose name and garrulous ways obviously revealed him to be a Catholic from the Republic. We lived on the edge of a hard-line loyalist area, the flat having been chosen for its view across the park to the mountains. An old man in the local pub warned us about 'bad boys', a euphemism for paramilitaries. One morning, 'Taigs out' had been painted across the road outside the house. We didn't move.

I think there was also a collective sense that if things were too horrific to contemplate they had better be ignored. No wonder Northerners, when they ventured outside of Northern Ireland in those times, often appeared manic to others. I visited Mostar in Bosnia not long after the second war ended there in 1994 and felt the same demented energy as I'd known in Belfast in the 1980s.

The African writer Alexandra Fuller compares people who grow up in war with clay pots fired in an oven that is over-hot. 'Confusingly shaped like the rest of humanity, we nevertheless contain fatal cracks that we spend the rest of our lives itching to fill.'[3]

People were always looking for transformations and miracles. The pubs were full. There were queues for days along the Falls Road outside the house of a woman who claimed she'd seen the face of Christ in the stone of her fireplace.

By the time I left Belfast in the mid-1980s, I had got scared and depressed by the violence. I'd glance up an alleyway and see a body dumped against the wall, then realise it was a black bag full of rubbish. In the days before I left, I walked for miles through the city. I passed an empty house that had been daubed with 'Get out or burn out.' I moved south to Sligo, which was only an hour's drive from the border but which kept a wary silence about the killings.

I moved back north to Enniskillen not long after the IRA's bombing at the cenotaph there in 1987. The bomb site was screened by plywood and the phone box which had been on the wall of the old reading rooms where the bomb exploded had been restored. I walked past it nearly every day. The phone seemed a potent and sad symbol in a place where so many voices had been brutally silenced.

My job was to work with rural community groups on the border. One woman who became a friend took me to see the lovely stone house she was going to move into when her son got married and took over the family farm. It had been empty since her late husband's cousin, a member of the Ulster Defence

Regiment (UDR), was murdered there, along with his wife, by the IRA. After I left Fermanagh, I learnt that another woman I was friendly with there had lost her husband years before I knew her. He was an IRA man, and after he was murdered, by loyalists, his body was put into the fridge in his butcher's shop. These two women later became good friends.

Republicans, mainly the IRA, killed more than half of those who died in the Troubles. Loyalists killed about a third. The rest were mostly killed by the security forces. Well over half of the dead were civilians, and almost twice as many Catholics were killed as Protestants. North and West Belfast were the most dangerous places, along with the 'murder triangle' in Armagh and Down.

But no one was really safe, and the sweat of terror could visit anyone. Most people tried to live normal lives, and to keep their families safe. Some were 'involved', as paramilitaries, police-men, prison officers. Their silences were the deepest. Others were exposed to the realities of Troubles deaths by their work, among them firefighters, doctors, priests and journalists.

From the early 1990s on, I covered the North as a reporter. I met many bereaved people, often in the immediate aftermath of a murder. We journalists would record the harrowing stories told by heartbroken wives, parents and children in the first throes of their grief, and then we'd leave. It was extraordinary work, priv-ileged and damaging. Soon after my younger daughter was born in 1994, I interviewed the husband of a woman who had been shot dead while heavily pregnant, in front of her five small children. Her husband had been in the IRA, and loyalists in the area had begun killing women in such families.

I returned to my mother's house, held my lovely baby in my arms and felt a sudden shaft of bleakness, as if I had no right to that happiness. The wife of one of my relatives was visiting the house that evening. I told her about talking to the widower, his children around him, shocked and quiet. No family deserved to have to go through such horror, I said. 'Och, I dunno,' she said, dismissively. 'He was a Provo, wasn't he? He probably did as bad himself.'

A colleague who works in television told me about covering the aftermath of the 1998 Omagh bomb, in which twenty-eight people were killed. Part of what he had to do was edit footage to cut out material that was deemed too graphic to be shown on the news. He spent his time in Omagh doing his work, expertly and diligently, because he had a strong sense of the need to do right by the people of the town. All the time he was longing to be with his wife and children. 'Your defences were down. You realised, surrounded by all that death and destruction, that being with the people you love is what really matters,' he told me. As soon as he could, he raced off home, driving far too fast, but when he got there he found that all he could think about was work and getting back to his colleagues in Omagh.

Sometimes we knew a person who was killed, and some journalists lost close friends or family. But mostly the murders touched us briefly, in passing. Those close to the murdered person had been plunged into horror. We were workers with a job to do, a job we'd chosen. Often, by the time our reports of a murder were published or broadcast, the ghastly story of the Troubles would have moved on and there would be another door to knock. The story of how the families and friends of the murdered person managed to survive and continue their lives was only just beginning and was rarely told.

I remember asking a woman if she found the anniversary of her husband's murder hard. 'Yes,' she said. 'But a rainy afternoon in April can be just as bad.'

Some people made astonishing recoveries. Love played a powerful role. I met a man and his wife who decided against being interviewed for this book but who told me how she had succeeded in getting him to walk again after he suffered horrific injuries in a gun attack.

Initially, he said he would never be able to leave the wheel-chair. She couldn't even persuade him to try. Then she got a foal. At first, she looked after it, aware of him watching from the house, but later she told him she could no longer manage it alone and it would have to go. Her husband began to wheel himself out to the stable. She'd watch him from the house, talking to the horse, starting to work with it. He was still in the chair but reaching up all the time, until one day he put his arm across the horse's neck and pulled himself up. It didn't take long after that, the horse patient by his side, the man's faltering steps getting stronger all the time.

In the worst days of the Troubles, some murders got only the most cursory of mentions in the news. When I arrived to interview one woman in West Belfast about the murder of her son, she told me she'd met an old man on the street earlier that day and had told him I was coming. He told her that no one had ever come to talk to him about his son, who had also been murdered. Some families were never visited by the police or contacted by anyone in authority to tell them if there had been developments in the murder inquiry.

I met some people who were so hurt and angry about the distortions and lies in the way their story was presented in books or newspapers that they had decided never to speak out about it again.

During the Troubles, some people were bereaved more than once, and some many times. One woman lost her husband in a sectarian assassination, married again, and saw her second husband murdered in the same way. Another heard her husband had been shot dead, went into labour and gave birth to still-born twins. One man lost his wife, his daughter and his grandchildren in a bomb. Another went out to phone relations to tell them a child in the family had been killed by loyalists and was shot dead by the IRA on his way to the phone box.

Often when people would ask what I was writing, and I told them, they would relate stories about their own experiences. A woman spoke about sitting her finals at Queen's University in the 1970s, with everyone aware of the empty seat of the friend who had been abducted and murdered while he hitched back to Belfast from his family home after the weekend. A man told me he'd been impressed by a display of Celtic football club memorabilia in a pub in County Armagh but had wondered why it ended abruptly at a certain point. The barman told him a brother of the owner had collected it, and he'd been shot dead. A friend of a friend in London told me the father of her child had killed himself. She thought it was because he had witnessed a murder and couldn't get over it.

I have heard people speak about thirty-year-old grief with the raw pain of one bereaved yesterday, and I have heard people say, sometimes bitterly, sometimes with resignation, that nobody wants to hear about it. A former British soldier who had a brutal comment made to him after he was overheard talking about how he was almost killed in Northern Ireland said he never talked about it now. 'None of my neighbours know why I'm in this wheelchair,' he said. 'They've got far more important things to think about – like the colour scheme in their kitchen.'

The writer Primo Levi has described the pain of the 'unlistened-to story'. While in Auschwitz, he repeatedly dreamt that he was back among his family and friends and telling them about his horrific experiences in the concentration camp. He was intensely happy in the dream but gradually began to realise that those around him were not paying attention, that they were indifferent. 'A desolating grief is now born in me,' he writes.[4] He learns that his friend and others had the same dream.

Sometimes people chose silence out of discretion. One man who killed another in self-defence said he felt it would be hurtful to the dead man's family if he talked about himself as a survivor. Others felt they had no right to speak, for they weren't the real victims: those were the people who died. Others still didn't feel quite safe. This was particularly the case with former members of the security forces, some of whom had retained habits of vigilance that had been a survival tool for decades.

A lot of the parents and relations of people killed in the early years have since died. They are lost witnesses. Others are elderly. They lived through the Troubles with their own grief, seeing others forced to embark on the same sorrowful paths year after year. They were terribly neglected.

The dead are lost, but not gone. The North is full of people searching for them. An old woman feels a lift in her heart when she sees a red-headed boy on the street. She runs to greet her youngest son, but when the stranger turns she remembers once again that thirty years ago her boy was massacred with his brothers at her home, and she feels the stab of pain.

Another woman wonders how anyone can laugh on the street in the village where her daughter was blown up. A sense of loyalty to someone killed in a war can make the peace which comes when the war is over extremely painful. Some people live with a sense that they have betrayed the person who was murdered.

In some places, like North and West Belfast and South Armagh and East Tyrone, the killing was intense and nearly everyone lost family, friends, colleagues or neighbours. However, many people who lived in Northern Ireland through the Troubles suffered very little beyond the inconvenience of bomb scares and roadblocks and bad news on the radio. Many in the Republic were oblivious, and many in Britain seem to have seen what was happening in Ireland, if they thought about it at all, as some sort of tribal feud into which their soldiers had inexplicably been flung.

A few years ago, a Dublin editor responded to my suggestion that I write a report on a commemorative event in Derry with an impatient, 'These bloody Northerners. The Troubles are finished. Will they never just get over it?' I went to the meeting anyway, and was moved to hear an elderly man quoting from a poem by Maya Angelou: 'History, despite its wrenching pain, cannot be unlived, but, if faced with courage, need not be lived again.' He was, I learnt afterwards, a doctor who had tended some of those who were lying dying or injured on the street after the British army went on the rampage on Bloody Sunday in 1972, killing fourteen civilians.

John Hewitt called it 'our ghost-haunted land'. The past refuses to go away, however we try to banish it. Every journey through the North brings you past places where atrocities were committed. Sometimes you see a withered wreath in a ditch, sometimes a monument, sometimes nothing at all marking the spot where blood was spilt, for Ireland or for Ulster or for pure hatred dressed up as politics.

Primo Levi wrote about the impact brutality had on relationships between people in the concentration camp. It was not black and white, he said. There was a 'grey zone' which we needed to try to understand, 'if we want to know the human species, if we want to know how to defend our souls ...'[5]

We have much to learn from those who bore the brunt of the small war in the North of Ireland: how they suffered, how they survived and what they need now. Some would love to learn how to forget; others feel they cannot rest until they know the full truth about why the person they loved was murdered, who did it and who ordered them to do it. Some crave justice. Some have forgiven the killers; others want revenge. The generosity of spirit in the former amazes and impresses us, but the bitter and raging have as much right to be heard.

Neighbours set up and killed neighbours; families were divided by conflicting loyalties. In many hundreds of cases, no one was ever convicted. Slaughter was met with slaughter. Children were used as killers, children were killed, parents were killed holding their child's hand. People were murdered at weddings and funerals. One man shouldered the coffin of a dead comrade in the morning, visited his wife and their newborn baby in hospital at lunchtime, and was shot dead that evening. Another was kidnapped and brought to a house where he knew he was to be killed, escaped through a window and ran to another house, only to be brought back by the people who lived there. He was murdered.

Murdered bodies were used as booby traps to kill others. Killers celebrated. Their supporters jeered at those mourning their victims. A killer who knew he was not going to be convicted saw the parents of the boy he killed at the swimming pool and swam in circles round them like a shark. There was a shocking level of hatred.

The Troubles ended fitfully. The people were worn out with war, and the British and the IRA knew that neither could defeat the other. Long-term negotiations behind the scenes led to ceasefires by the IRA and the main loyalist paramilitary armies, the UVF and the UDA, in 1994, followed by the political settlement known as the Good Friday, or Belfast, Agreement in 1998. The first assembly set up under its terms collapsed in acrimony in 2002.

Politically motivated murders continued at a low level for

several years. The IRA gave up its arms in 2005, but loyalists refused to do so. It was 2007 by the time a legislative assembly with the support of all the main local political parties, as well as the British and Irish governments, was established in Belfast.

The magnificent *Lost Lives* includes the stories of all those who died in the Troubles. It is a huge book, but of necessity the stories are told only briefly. In this book I have chosen to tell a far smaller number of stories more fully and to concentrate on the experiences and thoughts of people who survived the deaths of their loved ones and of some who were almost killed themselves. The first section of the book is chronological. The second explores themes identified by the bereaved and by others deeply affected by the killings.

Listening to the brave, hurt voices I often thought of the bleak, humane wisdom implied in Samuel Beckett's lines: 'I can't go on. I must go on. I'll go on.' People put themselves through considerable anguish to tell me their terrible memories and thoughts. One man said he and his family had decided to talk to me because a book would be a sort of memorial to his murdered brother. I hope that I have done justice to his and all the other stories.

PART I
The Killing Years

1

Dragon's Teeth

In 1966, a *Belfast Telegraph* editorial warned that Ulster was 'in danger of being thrown back into a dark past by sectarian forces which have too long been winked at by many who should know better'. It said that Protestants should have 'nothing to do with those who have been sowing dragon's teeth' and that they could now see 'how terrible the harvest can be'.[1]

This followed the murder of an elderly Protestant woman by loyalist extremists who had set out to kill Catholics. 'This house is owned by a Taig – Popehead – Remember 1690' had been daubed on the wall of the pub beside her home. The gang had already murdered two young Catholic men.

'Remember 1690.' It is a tribal injunction to all Protestants in Northern Ireland. This was the year of the Battle of the Boyne, when King William of Orange defeated King James. A key event in unionist history, it was seen simply, and simplistically, as a victory of Protestantism over Catholicism. Two years before it, thirteen Protestant apprentice boys had shut the city gates against King James in the siege of Derry. Unionism is a defensive politics, and until 2007, when he sat down in government with Sinn Féin, the leader of the DUP, the Reverend Ian Paisley, would routinely end speeches with the cry, 'No surrender!'

After he agreed to share power with his old enemies in the

North and to cease regarding the Irish Republic as a hostile state, the diplomatic gesture chosen to demonstrate how things had changed was a visit by Paisley to the site of the Battle of the Boyne in the Republic as the guest of the Irish Taoiseach, Bertie Ahern.

Both loyalists and republicans claim a proud historical lineage for their struggles and have invoked dead heroes in their support. Led by a former military policeman, the gang which started the 'Troubles' killings was modelled on the Ulster Volunteer Force. This was formed in 1912 by the Ulster unionist leader, Lord Carson, to fight against Home Rule for Ireland. Again, this was framed as a religious battle to save Protestantism. 'Home Rule is Rome Rule' was the warning, and Ulster would resist it. The First World War saw Carson's men joining up instead, and thousands of them died at the Somme. Afterwards, unionists believed Britain owed them.

If 'Remember 1690' was the battle cry of the loyalists, 'Remember 1916' was its equivalent for republicans. The Easter Rising of 1916 was meant to expel the British and establish an Irish republic. One of its leaders, Padraig Pearse, invoked an earlier phase of the rebellion against British rule in Ireland when he declared, 'The fools, the fools, they have left us our Fenian dead. Ireland unfree shall never be at peace.' The Easter Rising was swiftly put down by the British. However, when they executed its leaders, the British created martyrs whose ghosts would be summoned up by the IRA during the conflict that began fifty years later.

Ireland was partitioned in 1920. The six northern counties, where a majority of the country's Protestants lived, remained British. A civil war followed in the remaining twenty-six counties, after which they became the Irish Free State, and in 1949, the Republic of Ireland. Its constitution laid claim to the Northern counties, and in the 1950s, the IRA launched a brief and unsuccessful 'border campaign' to 'free' the North.

The unionist majority in Northern Ireland ruthlessly ensured that nationalists would have no power. The first prime minister, James Craig, boasted that he ruled a 'Protestant parliament and a Protestant state'. Another minister, later to serve for forty years as prime minister, warned against employing Catholics, claiming that they were out to destroy the state: 'I have not one about the place.' Government ministers were drawn from the anti-Catholic Orange Order, and most judges were former unionist politicians. The heavily armed police had the backing of the auxiliary B Specials, described by poet Seamus Heaney as 'neighbours with guns'. There were two policemen per Catholic family and they had extensive 'special powers' which they did not hesitate to use.

Catholics were largely excluded from the North's big industries and from all but the lowest ranks of the civil service. They were denied houses and many lived in overcrowded slums. A system of gerrymandering ensured that unionists always got elected, even in areas where there was a Catholic majority. Many seats were not even contested. Britain washed its hands. There was a convention at Westminster that Northern Ireland would not be discussed.

Minority resentment simmered. In 1963, the newly elected prime minister, Terence O'Neill, began a programme of tentative reforms. The Reverend Ian Paisley immediately declared that a sell-out was afoot. O'Neill was a traitor, ready to sell the Protestant people 'down the river'. Paisley also launched a newspaper which published intensely anti-Catholic propaganda, including, once, a letter referring to Catholics as 'two-legged rats'.

The poet John Hewitt wrote about the influence of 'that noisy preacher' in his fine poem 'The Coasters', and about the danger of those who refused to say outright that they supported him but who would nonetheless confide in the club, 'You know, there's something in what he says.' Many of the early members of the UVF had in the 1960s attended rallies at which Paisley made his dire predictions. After republicans commemorated the 50th anniversary of the 1916 Easter Rising, there were warnings that this presaged an invasion from the Republic. The scene was set for the killings of 1966.

* * *

By 1969, to quote Hewitt again, 'the fever was high and raging' and 'the cloud of infection' was hanging over Northern Ireland.[2] Unionist reforms introduced by O'Neill were too little, too late, and were resisted by too many Protestants. Nationalists took to the streets to protest. Unionists called them the IRA by any other name, and the RUC lit into them with batons. Some responded with stones and petrol bombs.

Soon, fierce rioting was a feature of life in parts of Belfast and Derry. The police made no secret of their allegiance, and many of the loyalists who brutally ambushed a student march for civil rights in 1969 were B Specials. The first child to be killed was nine-year-old Patrick Rooney, who was in his home in the Divis Flats on the Falls Road in Belfast when it was hit by heavy machine-gun bullets fired by the RUC, a killing which a government commission found to be 'wholly unjustifiable'. There is a reference to the child's death in Michael Longley's poem 'Wounds'. The poet describes the death of his own soldier father – 'at last, a belated casualty' of the Battle of the Somme – and his burial more than half a century later. Beside him, he buries some of the early casualties of the Troubles and emblems of their lost lives, including 'the Sacred Heart of Jesus/Paralysed as heavy guns put out/The night-light in a nursery for ever.'[3]

The RUC was overwhelmed. The British sent in the army 'in aid of the civil power'. The IRA had been largely dormant since its failed border campaign. Its Dublin-based leadership was attempting to transform it into a Marxist revolutionary organisation. When loyalist mobs burnt down Catholic streets in Belfast, graffiti appeared: 'IRA = I Ran Away.' In the summer of 1969, 1,500 Catholic families and 300 Protestant families fled their homes to seek the safety of ghetto areas.

Angry Northern IRA members protested that the organisation had descended into ignominy and had to start defending beleaguered Catholics and retaliating for attacks on them. There was a split. The 'Provisional' IRA was founded and swiftly began to arm its volunteers for gun and bomb attacks. On 27 June 1970, after loyalists attacked nationalist areas in North and East Belfast, the IRA returned fire, killing five men. Although the 'Official' IRA did get involved in the violence in the North, it was overshadowed by the more militant 'Provos', who quickly demonstrated that they would be brutal and merciless.

Loyalists had a crude strategy at this time of carrying out acts of violence that were then blamed on republicans, a tactic that led to the defeat of Terence O'Neill, who was not seen by unionists to be doing enough to defeat the IRA. Resigning in 1969, he said he had been 'blown out of office' by loyalists.

By the end of 1970, the death toll seemed high, at around fifty. The following year, it surged upwards, with 180 people killed in bombings, riots, gun battles and assassinations. In February 1971, O'Neill's replacement, Sir James Chichester Clark, had declared war on the IRA but was quite unable to stem the violence. He was replaced soon afterwards by Brian Faulkner, whose response to the steadily intensifying conflict was, on 9 August, to introduce internment without trial. That morning, soldiers swooped on hundreds of Catholic homes across Northern Ireland, lifting three hundred men. Faulkner had a list which was meant to be of IRA suspects, but many of those arrested had no such connections.

There was chaos in Belfast, with families fleeing their homes, gunmen on the streets, young people throwing up barricades against enemy incursions and intense riots in Catholic areas. Reports of the torture of internees were soon fuelling the fire.

* * *

Ordinary life went on, even in the most troubled parts of Belfast, and Alice Harper, for one, was happy. The eldest of Bella and Danny Teggart's thirteen children, Alice lived with her husband and young baby in the new estate of Turf Lodge, not far from her parents. She had just found out that she was pregnant with her second child. When her father came over that day, 9 August 1971, she told him the good news. He had come to ask her if his brother, her uncle, could come and stay with her for a while. 'His house was right beside the army barracks and there were bullets going right through it,' Alice said. She told her father it was fine for her uncle to come and stay.

Danny went home, told his wife Bella the news that they were to have another grandchild and asked her to put the kettle on. He said he was just going down to tell his brother to go to Alice's house. That was the last time Bella Teggart saw her husband. She was worried when he didn't come back that night, but there was shooting and rioting going on in the streets and she was afraid to go out looking for him. Like most working-class families at the time, the family had no phone. In the morning, she went to get Alice.

They started off asking people if they'd seen him. They heard about stone throwing around the base and that there had been shooting. The IRA was shooting, the British were shooting and so were the loyalists. People had been killed. A priest had been shot dead by the army while he held up a white Babygro to show he was unarmed. But there was no word about Danny Teggart.

They phoned all the hospitals, including ones across the border. Then Alice went to the sentries at the nearby army base. 'They said, "We haven't effing time for arresting, only killing,"' she remembered. 'I walked away. I was crying. We were out of our minds distracted. A man came over to me and he said, "Alice, never mention my name, but I can tell you he was shot."'

The man told Alice that her father had been talking with a group of people on the street when the shooting started. He was shot in the thigh, and the man had tried to make a tourniquet for him from his shirt. A Saracen had then backed out across the road, and soldiers had lifted Danny Teggart and other injured civilians and taken them into the barracks.

Alice returned to the barracks. 'They said, "There's an effin unidentified body lying in the morgue. Why don't you try there?" There was a car parked outside and it was a journalist. He said he'd take me. As soon as I walked in, I knew it was my father. He was riddled with bullets,' she said. 'We believe it was a massacre in that barracks.'

Among the others killed along with Danny Teggart that night was a mother of eight children. Two of her teenage daughters had gone out to see what was happening in the streets, and she had gone out to look for them and bring them home. She found the girls, but then a crowd of loyalists surged down the road. The soldiers fired CS gas, and in the confusion that followed they became separated again. Danny Teggart, this woman and others were standing near the barracks when the army opened fire.

Eight of Alice's brothers and sisters were among the hundreds of Belfast Catholics who were brought on a long journey south through the night to makeshift refugee camps in the Republic, where they stayed for several months. The children of the woman who was shot alongside Danny Teggart were also sent south. Two days later, they saw a news bulletin from Belfast which mentioned the funeral of their mother. That was how they learnt for certain that she had died.

One headline from the *Belfast Telegraph* of 10 August 1971 conveys the horror: 'Fifteen bodies are found.' The following day, it was: 'Death toll in 2 days of bloodshed rises to 17 – another night of gunfights in Belfast.' The article recorded that while the killing continued, 'the pitiful exodus of terrified families from riot areas continues'.[4] Another article reported that British soldiers had smashed every ground-floor window in a street on the Falls Road.

There was so much trouble going on it took Alice Harper four days to get her father's body home. She said that when she went to the barracks to get his clothes back, the soldiers were singing a pop song to mock her: 'Where's your papa gone, chirpy chirpy cheep cheep . . .' They directed her to a big chest full of bloody clothes. Alice said that at the inquest, a year later, they made a 'complete fool' of her mother, claiming that bullets were found in the pocket of a donkey jacket which he had been wearing. 'He never even had a jacket like that,' she said.

The British army had initially been welcomed in nationalist areas of Northern Ireland. Although it had been sent in to support the beleaguered unionist government, it was preferable to the RUC. The British Labour government appeared to recognise at last that nationalists had legitimate grievances and that unionists were incapable of addressing them. Cups of tea were famously served to soldiers, but not for long, as the army soon gave every appearance of being on the unionist side, watching as loyalists attacked Catholic homes. It was also responsible for a lot of killings at this time – forty-five in 1971 and seventy-nine in 1972 – and many of its victims were Catholic civilians.

Alice Harper's parents' marriage was a mixed one. Her mother was a Protestant who 'turned' after she met Danny. 'As a matter of fact, my father went to his grave with a scar on his forehead from when they told my mother's father they were going to get married. He was none too pleased a daughter of his was to marry a Catholic. He had a shovel in his hand and he let it fly,' said Alice. 'But they became the best of friends. We used to go to the Twelfth of July.

'My parents' first home was a one-bedroom flat. Nine of us and the two of them shared that room. Later on, my father squatted a house. My mother dedicated herself to looking after us. Politics was never talked about in our house. My father was a good and a loving man, and he was terribly missed.'

Her Protestant relations came to her father's funeral, but as the Troubles went on, the family would meet on the neutral ground of the city centre rather than visiting each other's areas. Belfast was fast becoming a segregated city.

* * *

The alienation of Northern nationalists was intensifying. Unionism had rejected reform and met protest with force. The British army had proved brutal in its defence. The British government's reaction to the McGurk's Bar massacre in 1971 suggested that it was employing the sort of counter-insurgency tactics recommended by Brigadier Frank Kitson, who was then serving in Northern Ireland. Kitson had written extensively about ways to suppress rebel forces which went far beyond the use of military might. One tactic he had successfully employed in Kenya against the Mau Mau was the use of 'pseudo gangs' to carry out atrocities which would then be blamed on the anti-state rebels, causing public opinion to turn against them. In Northern Ireland, that meant using loyalist paramilitaries to carry out acts which would be blamed on the IRA.

It was about 9 o'clock on a Saturday night in December when an eight-year-old boy who was out delivering the *Belfast Telegraph* on North Queen Street saw a car pull up just down from the pub. There were four men in it and there was a Union Jack sticker on the back window. The child stopped and watched what followed. A big man in a long coat got out of the car. He had a mask on his face and he was carrying a large parcel wrapped in plastic. He carried it into the hallway of the pub, lit it with matches, then ran back into the car and the car drove off. The child was afraid. He didn't know if the man had seen him or not. He saw another man walking along the street towards the pub and shouted at him: 'Mister, don't go into that bar, there's a bomb there.' Then he ran, and was lifted off his feet by the force of the explosion.

Gerard McGurk, his friend, Jimmy, and Gerard's ten-year-old brother, John, were playing table football in the living room above the bar. Gerard's mother and sister had gone to Mass at the local Catholic church. His brother, Patrick, was having a bath and his father, Patsy, was serving in the bar downstairs. It was a small, family pub with a regular clientele of local people, most of them middle-aged men or pensioners.

'There was an intense, thunderous sound,' Gerard told me. 'Then it was like one of those pull-away shots in a Hitchcock film where you are being pulled above the table. Then all I remember is being buried in rubble and a mouthful of dust and shouting out, "Help."' He woke up in hospital, where someone was asking him his name and his religion. 'I always remember that,' he said. 'Here I am having survived a horrible attack motivated by religion and the hospital staff are concerned to establish my religion.'

He had a broken arm and toe and lacerations. The next morning, there was a radio on in the ward and the news came on. 'It said that among the fifteen dead in the McGurk's Bar explosion were the wife and daughter of the owner. That was how I learnt that my mother and Maria were dead. It turned out they had just got back from church and they were in the hall when the bomb exploded. My mother's brother was also killed, and my friend Jimmy, who had been about a foot away from me.'

The building had collapsed into a heap of rubble through which ambulancemen, police, soldiers and local people clawed with their bare hands in an effort to find survivors. At fifteen, the death toll was the highest in any single incident in the Troubles at that time, and would be for many years to come.

One man who had been in the bar remembered that everything was normal until he caught a strong smell, like a stink bomb. He glanced at the door, saw a surge of light from the hall and the bar collapsed around him. It emerged that a man who said he was from the 'Empire Loyalists' had phoned a local newsroom to claim responsibility for the bomb.

Despite this, the authorities immediately briefed journalists that this was an 'IRA own goal', that the forensic evidence suggested that the bomb had been under construction on the premises and had exploded prematurely. 'The bomb was on Saturday night. By Monday morning one of the unionist newspapers was reporting that a strange man and woman had been seen in the bar and that it was assumed they were there to collect the bomb,' said Gerard.

Within hours of the bomb exploding, Gerard's father, Patsy, did a television interview in which he called for there to be no retaliation. He said he had been praying for those who carried out the attack; it didn't matter who they were. 'What's done can't be undone,' he said. 'I've been trying to keep the bitterness out of it.'[5]

Ten days after the attack, a confidential Ministry of Defence memo to the prime minister and others said that the army felt it was important to put into the public domain the evidence that the bomb was being made on the premises. This was disinformation. There was no such evidence. 'The Minister for

Home Affairs, John Taylor, said in Stormont it appeared that the bomb had been well inside the building. It was put about that this was an IRA bomb factory,' said Gerard. 'There wasn't a shred of evidence for this, and in fact these people chose to ignore the eyewitness evidence which was available and the warning from the loyalists. But it was shocking the alacrity with which the Protestant establishment media took up the story put about by the army and the unionists.'

It seems likely that the loyalist bombers were intent on attacking another bar further up the street known, according to Gerard, as a place where republican sympathisers would drink. But there were men standing around the doorway of that pub, so it was obviously decided that McGurk's would do. 'Everybody knew our bar wasn't an IRA bar,' said Gerard. 'We were very much a religious working-class family with no political affiliations. When it came to elections, we voted for the Catholic candidate.

'I knew every single one of the people who were killed. None of them was in the IRA. No paramilitary organisation put death notices in the paper. There were no paramilitary funerals. They called us bomb makers. Who were they accusing? A friend of my dad's? An old lady in a headscarf? My sister? It was a malicious lie and they knew it. It was very personally hurtful. They didn't want it to be seen that the murderous violence was emanating from more than one side of the community. This had Kitson's tactics written all over it.

'We lived right across the street from one of the biggest police stations in Northern Ireland,' Gerard remembered. 'In those days cars were rare enough in working-class areas. You played football on the street. There had been an IRA escape from Crumlin Road prison round the corner the day before and there was a heavy security presence in the area as a result. The army was scouring the streets. Yet these loyalists felt sufficiently confident that they could drive in with a bomb, plant it and drive out again. They had to have a *laissez-passer* from the security forces.' Perhaps this was the meaning of the Union Jack the paper boy saw in the car. 'It meant you had no confidence that any justice was going to be sought,' said Gerard. 'It was obvious they weren't going to look for the perpetrators.'

Patsy McGurk and his surviving children were left homeless and with their means of income destroyed. They moved to a house close to one of Gerard's aunts. 'She became a sort of surrogate mother to us. She cried every day,' Gerard remembered. His family's attitude, he said, was one of 'quiet stoicism'. 'I knew something terrible had happened, but I don't think I realised the magnitude of it. You're fifteen. You have a short emotional appreciation of time and the value of family relationships.' He went back to school a couple of weeks after he got out of hospital. 'There were sincere but cursory expressions of regret, but the matter wasn't discussed. The whole idea of meeting strong feelings head-on was alien to most people,' he said.

The IRA ignored Patsy McGurk's appeal for there to be no retaliation and responded in sectarian kind with a revenge bomb attack aimed at Protestants. A week after the McGurk's bomb, when the Shankill Road was crowded with people out shopping for Christmas, it detonated a bomb at a busy furniture store. There was no warning, and four people were killed, two men and two infant children. A photographer took what would become one of the most famous Troubles photographs: a fireman carrying the body of one of the tiny children, wrapped in a blanket. He holds it gently, the way you would hold a living baby, but its head is covered.

The adoptive father of one of the children said on television that although he and his wife had always felt sorrow for others, until it happened to them and they lost their one beloved child, 'you don't really realise how much it is going to hurt'. This could happen to anyone in Northern Ireland, he said. There were people who were too willing to dwell on the past. It was time for the politicians to sit down and resolve the conflict.

2

The Worst Year

'Is there a life before death?'
(early 1970s graffiti in
nationalist West Belfast)

'Nineteen seventy-two was the worst year,' said Anne Larkey. 'All you did was go out in the morning to work and hope you'd get home that night. There was that many being killed you used to buy the paper and think, "Dear God, let it not be anyone I know the day."' It was, by far, the worst year, with a death toll of 497, more than half of them civilians. What is more, the swell of anger caused by some of the atrocities committed that year swept recruits into the ranks of both republican and loyalist paramilitaries.

On 30 January 1972, British paratroopers, blooded in West Belfast, had launched an attack on a civil-rights march against internment in Derry, the North's second city. Thirteen unarmed civilians were shot dead on the streets and others were injured, including one man who died later. The events of the day were shocking enough, but the British army then claimed that all of the dead had been gunmen and bombers. Nationalist Ireland was outraged. The British embassy in Dublin was burnt down.

The Irish Minister for Foreign Affairs said that from that point on, 'my aim is to get Britain out of Ireland'. The leader of the SDLP, John Hume, said that the feeling in Derry in the aftermath of the massacre was 'a united Ireland or nothing'. Young men and women queued up to join the IRA. Provisional IRA spokeswoman Maire Drumm said in Derry that if people who were calling for an IRA ceasefire were later murdered, they would deserve their deaths.

The Official IRA's 'revenge' for Bloody Sunday was to bomb an army base at Aldershot in England. The supposedly socialist wing of republicanism succeeded in killing five cleaning women, a gardener and an army chaplain. Brian Lynch, then working as a journalist, wrote a poem about this atrocity. It describes an exultant sub-editor who roars, 'The paratroops have got/Their answer now!' It goes on, 'The newsroom rang with howls of joy./They'd murdered us. We'd murdered them./And I joined in, a roaring boy/Who cheered the Butcher's requiem.'[1]

The British prime minister, Edward Heath, wrote in his memoirs that as the violence escalated, he feared that 'we might, for the first time, be on the threshold of complete anarchy'.[2] In March, the British suspended Stormont and brought Northern Ireland under direct rule from Westminster. This was regarded as a victory by the IRA, which saw it as a prelude to British withdrawal.

Meanwhile, the unionist Minister for Home Affairs, William Craig, had formed the Vanguard movement and was holding a series of 'monster rallies' around Northern Ireland, at which he menacingly advocated building up 'dossiers' on those who were a threat to the state. When the politicians fail us, he said, 'it may be our job to liquidate the enemy'. Loyalists were rallying to the cause: the UDA had about 25,000 members by this time, and rallies attended by ranks of masked men in dark glasses and parka jackets became common, as did roadblocks on street corners. Loyalists were getting ready for civil war, using random sectarian assassinations to spread terror among nationalists.

Anne Larkey's family was from the Ardoyne area of North Belfast, a tight enclave of straight, narrow terraced streets which were built to house millworkers in the nineteenth century. Her sister, Sally, had married a Protestant, who had died when their son, David, was small. Sally McClenaghan had then met another Protestant man and was living with him in Stockport Street in the River Streets area, where his family lived. This was one of those small working-class loyalist areas in North Belfast which has long since been demolished in slum clearances.

Anne Larkey still lived in Ardoyne, with her husband and ten children. It was only a few minutes' walk from the River Streets, but it was not a walk that Catholics would take. 'It was a no-go area for Catholics. There was a right few taken in there and killed, and given terrible deaths they were,' she said. She feared for her sister. 'I used to say to her, "Are you mad? You can't live there. It isn't safe. You should leave, now."'

Sally had three children. Her eldest son, David, was a big, strong fourteen-year-old, but he was intellectually disabled and had a mental age of about five. 'Sally used to say, "Sure with David the way he is, who would touch us?"' said Anne. 'I said, "Do you read the papers? Do you live in the same world as me?"' Anne knew a Catholic man who'd lived on Southport Street until loyalists captured him one day and tried to hang him from a lamp post. He fled the area immediately.

But Sally wasn't for moving. She was a millworker, and her late husband's aunt, Dot Day, who lived near Southport Street, looked after David when he wasn't at school. 'Dot Day was a good woman,' said Anne. 'David was a handful. She used to say to me, "If I die, you look after David."' Anne and her nephew were very close. He was anything but streetwise. He used to belt out 'The Sash My Father Wore', and then he'd follow it with 'The Soldier's Song'. That the first was a loyalist anthem and the second the anthem of the Irish Republic, and that to sing either indicated the taking of a strong political position, meant nothing to him.

Sectarian violence had flared in North Belfast during many earlier periods of unrest. Between 1920 and 1922, a gang from the Royal Irish Constabulary (the pre-partition police force) had murdered Catholics in the River Streets. Often the spark was lit during the season of Orange Order parades. Louis MacNeice's 'Autumn Journal' refers to childhood memories from the 1930s, of expecting to hear shooting in the evening: 'And the voodoo of the Orange bands/Drawing an iron net through darkest Ulster,/Flailing the limbo lands . . .'[3]

The Eleventh Night was bonfire night for loyalists in towns and villages across Northern Ireland. It was the night before the 'glorious twelfth', when the Orange Order celebrated the victory of William of Orange over King James in 1690. It was a night of frenzied partying around huge fires on which effigies of the Pope or flags with 'Kill all Taigs' painted on them might be burnt. Extreme drunkenness characterised such gatherings, and in Catholic places like Ardoyne children were got in early and doors were locked.

That night in 1972, Sally McClenaghan's younger children stayed with Dot Day, while she and her partner took David around the bonfires in the streets near their home. He loved the big blazing fires and the coloured bunting and the wild atmosphere, and didn't feel its vicious edge. They were all asleep in bed when, in the early hours of the twelfth, someone fired three shots into the house. Sally's partner went downstairs. He told her it was just drunks messing around, and the couple went back to sleep. 'Never, to my dying day, will I understand why she did that,' said Anne Larkey. 'That will haunt me. Shots fired into the house and you go back to sleep?'

I'd been brought to meet Anne by her old neighbour, Doreen Toolan. In her seventies and with fifteen children reared, Anne was tired and not in the best of health. She hadn't known we were coming, and when Doreen explained that I wanted to ask her about the events of that night, she immediately became distraught. 'I don't talk about it,' she said. 'I just don't talk about it.' I said if she didn't want to talk, that was all right. She called her husband, Tom, and asked him what he thought. They decided it was right for them to tell the terrible story. 'For David,' Anne said.

Two hours after the shots had been fired, a gang of men kicked in the door of Sally McClenaghan's house. Her partner went downstairs, and Sally watched in a mirror as he spoke with the men. Several of them were masked, but one, with a gun in one hand and a bottle of wine in the other, was not. 'That meant no one was getting out of there alive,' said Anne.

Sally watched as her partner went to a sideboard and got out his Orange sash, the proof that he was Protestant; Catholics aren't allowed to join the Order. After that, one of the men punched him on the chin. 'And then he [Sally's partner] left,' said Anne, angrily. 'He left.' During the court case which followed the horrific events of this night, the barrister for the prosecution told the jury, 'You may well think that he had come close to death here.'[4]

However, Anne Larkey felt that by leaving the house at this point, the man had abandoned her sister in her hour of need. 'After that, they had a wonderful time,' she said, bitterly. 'One of them said to Sally, "You are a Taig." She said, "I am not. My husband Lindsay McClenaghan was a Protestant, and me and David are Protestants, too."' But they insisted Sally was a 'Taig' and that she had guns in the house.

Then one of them turned to David. 'Go and get your mummy's rosary beads,' he said. Sally tried to get David to stay where he was, but he went and got her handbag. They found the beads there, the proof that she was a Catholic.

In the hour that followed, they broke David's leg, grabbed him by the throat and burnt his fingers. They raped Sally. 'She told me they were out-and-out animals,' said Anne. 'One of them bit her on the breast, and she took breast cancer after it. I am sure that David squealed and yelled. There must have been neighbours heard the commotion, but nobody came.'

Then they made David lie down beside his mother on her bed. She begged them not to hurt him any more. During the trial, she told the court that she had pleaded with them to leave him alone 'because he was retarded and he looked so afraid'. The gunmen ignored her. They shot her son in the throat, twice. She screamed and threw herself over her child to protect him, and they shot her. They left her for dead and ran out of the house. They did not have to go far. Two of them were neighbours of Dot Day.

David was dead. The British army arrived at the house, and Sally told Anne that the big soldier who carried the boy's body down the stairs was crying. 'He said to her, "What sort of people are they?"' While Sally was in hospital recovering from gunshot wounds to her arm and leg, her brothers and Anne's husband, Tom, set about finding her a new place to live. 'Houses were like hen's teeth in those days, but they moved heaven and earth and they got one,' said Anne.

After getting the new place for Sally, her brothers and brother-in-law went down to Tennent Street police barracks to ask if they could have the key of the house in Stockport Street so they could move her stuff, but the police said they couldn't let them have it. The house was a crime scene. Anne's husband, Tom, told this part of the story. As the men walked down the road from the barracks, they passed a parked van. 'Next thing these boys jumped out with masks on and guns,' he said. The gunmen pursued them and succeeded in hitting one of Sally's brothers with a pickaxe. He kept running.

The terrified men ran back to the barracks and asked to be brought home to Ardoyne. The RUC refused, but a military policeman who was there sent out a radio message that the van of loyalists was operating in the area, again, and gave them a lift to the edge of their area. 'Much as you mightn't like the army, that was a decent man,' said Anne.

Anne began to prepare her house for David's wake. She said she was in such a state that she was 'like a zombie'. She was also heavily pregnant with her eleventh baby. Her old friend Doreen Toolan lived across the road, and she came over to help. The women covered all the furniture with white sheets, drew the blinds and stopped the clocks.

*   *   *

Meanwhile, Doreen's husband, Terence, was tending the thirty rose trees he had grown in his small front garden. He was putting new soil round them, which he'd got from the gardens of the burnt-out Protestant houses round the corner. The biggest exodus of civilians in Europe since the Second World War was happening in Belfast at this time, and Protestants living in the streets near the Toolans were among those on the move – some of them burning their houses as they left to stop Catholics getting them.

Doreen and Terry Toolan were childhood sweethearts. They'd met in Belfast but went to live in England for a while after they were married in 1959. She came from Hull. Her father was Protestant and in the British army, as was Terry's Catholic brother. The couple came back to Ardoyne in the early 1960s. She was a hairdresser; he was an electrician.

Terry was one of those who worked on the big crane, Goliath, in the shipyards. In the 1930s, there had been purges of Catholics from the shipyards, and by the 1970s they were in a small minority. Doreen said her husband got on well with his workmates. 'His closest friend was a reserve policeman, Artie, and once a month me and Terry and Artie and Winnie would go to a dinner dance together. Winnie was a hairdresser, too. I love to dance.'

Doreen came home from helping prepare Anne Larkey's house for the wake to make her family's dinner. She got the children to bed and was sitting patching Terry's work trousers when she and her husband heard shooting. 'Terry was a vigilante – he was meant to look after people in the area when there was trouble. He said he'd go and investigate,' she said.

According to Brendan 'Bik' McFarlane, a former IRA man and a friend of the Toolans, the Ardoyne area was 'under massive attack' that week, with constant gun battles going on involving loyalists, British soldiers and the IRA.[5] There were four separate gun battles raging that particular night.

Doreen asked her husband to check on her aunt and uncle, who lived near by and whose son had been shot dead by the army the previous year. Terry asked Doreen to wait up for him. The sky was lit up with flares and tracer bullets. 'Then word came that Terry was shot. The house filled up with people and I was screaming. A woman came down the street shouting, "Two dead!" The other one was an IRA man.' McFarlane remembered the moment when Doreen was told. 'I heard this unmerciful scream from the house . . . a heartrending scream of anguish and sadness.' In her own account of that night in *Ardoyne, the Untold Truth*, Doreen said the British army raided her house before her husband's remains were brought home. 'I went berserk,' she said. She was restrained by relations.

'They literally wrecked the house. They pulled electric fires out of the walls in the bedrooms and tore off the built-in wardrobe doors. They lifted nearly every floorboard in the house . . . it wasn't bad enough they murdered him and just left me there like an old floorcloth, like I was nothing or nobody and with six children to rear.'[6]

The soldiers said they were looking for 'evidence and

weapons', Doreen remembered. The next day, word came from Dublin that Terry was to be given an IRA funeral. This has remained a bone of contention for Doreen. 'My husband was not in the IRA,' she insisted to me. McFarlane described him as being 'involved in the struggle'. He said he 'played a significant role in defending this district against loyalists, Brits and the cops'.

Before the start of the Troubles, the IRA largely consisted of a small core of people who came from traditional IRA families that had been involved in the Easter Rising of 1916, the war of independence in 1921, the civil war which followed, and after partition, in the border campaign of the 1950s. The goal of the IRA was to put Britain out of Ireland. Those who joined the IRA after 1969 and who saw its immediate and primary role as being to defend Catholics from attack were known as 'sixty-niners'. Brendan Hughes, who went on to become a leading IRA figure, was typical of the sixty-niners. He described his rationale to journalist Ed Moloney. 'At that time it was simply, "Here we are being attacked by Loyalists, by B Specials, by the RUC, by the British army," and there was a need to hit back.'[7]

The journalist Malachi O'Doherty, who grew up in West Belfast, dismissed this view as 'nonsense'. 'You don't feel defended – that is, made safer – when neighbours with guns are shooting at army patrols and retreating into your garden,' he wrote in his autobiographical account of 1972. 'Inevitably, with so much daytime shooting in residential areas, bullets would fly astray into the wrong bodies.'[8]

* * *

While Doreen was struggling with the death of her husband, her friend Anne Larkey and her mother-in-law went down to see the Protestant side of her nephew David's family to talk about arrangements for his funeral. It turned into a terrible row. 'When we got there, they turned on us. Dot Day began to scream at us that it was the IRA that killed David and not loyalists,' said Anne. 'She said David was to be buried from her house. I said he would be buried from mine. I said, "Can you guarantee that we'll be safe here?" She said, "No." I said, "Well, I can guarantee you'll be safe in Ardoyne."

'This was bad territory for us, as Catholics. There were men walking on the other side of the street with what looked like pickaxe handles, and they stopped and stared over. My mother-in-law said to me, "Can you run?" I said, "I don't think so."' Anne was due to give birth any day. 'She said, "I think you better," and we ran.' Anne was moved, however, by the fact that Dot Day had prepared her house in exactly the same way as she had: the sheets on the furniture, the blinds drawn, the clocks stopped. She decided that the best plan was for David to be buried from the neutral ground of a funeral home, so that both sides of his family could see him, and that was what she arranged.

Doreen Toolan's life went off into a blur of grief and drugs after Terry's death. 'I can't remember the funeral,' she said. She told me she vaguely remembered being led up for Communion by her husband's mother. 'We had to get permission for Artie and Winnie to come into the area for the funeral,' she said. Permission from the IRA.

She used to go to Terry's grave three times a week and leave a spray of fresh flowers there. Her brother-in-law stopped it, she said. Fresh flowers were a luxury that could not be afforded. 'I lived in hell, drugs morning, noon and night. I swallowed antidepressants like Smarties. I had injections to get to sleep. I never knew the rearing of my six children. I never brought one of them to school. My mother reared them, and she reared them well. I had to sell my house and move in with her. I was just dead. I lost all my hair. My teeth rotted and fell out. I was down to four and a half stone. I never went out. I must have looked like something out of Mars. I took a nervous breakdown and wrecked the house. I cried sore to get into Purdysburn.'

Purdysburn is Belfast's main mental hospital, and Doreen spent several extended periods there. 'If it wasn't for the nurses in there I would have killed myself,' she said. In *Ardoyne, the Untold Truth* she recounted being shown a video made of her in Purdysburn by hospital staff. 'I watched this woman in her pants and her bra in a padded cell on a mattress with foam flying out of her mouth. I couldn't believe it was me. It was like that scene in *The Exorcist*.'[9]

*   *   *

On 21 July 1972, a week after Terry Toolan was murdered, the IRA placed more than twenty car bombs in the centre of Belfast. They then phoned hopelessly inadequate warnings to Belfast newsrooms. All the bombs exploded within a period of just over an hour. Journalist Kevin Myers was in an office block overlooking the city centre. He said that to witness it was 'like seeing the hand of a terrible god, whose wrath was unquenchable and his means inexhaustible'.[10] The emergency services were overwhelmed. Utter carnage resulted.

Nine people were killed and more than a hundred injured. Terrified parents herded their children through the streets, not knowing if they were getting away from danger or moving into it. Police and emergency services personnel afterwards described horrific scenes: a head stuck to a wall; seagulls diving onto a ribcage on a roof; a body with no arms or legs. The dead included bus drivers, women and children. I remember watching the news on television with my family in Derry. The young newsreader broke down and bowed his head briefly before resuming the terrible catalogue of horror. The day would become known as Bloody Friday. Many young men from loyalist areas would join the paramilitaries in its wake.

The IRA claimed the British had deliberately failed to act on bomb warnings. Years later, while making a documentary about one of its leaders at this time, Joe Cahill, I saw footage of him defending the car bombings and blaming the British. They had started all this, it was up to them to end it, he said. He looked like a man wallowing in blood. The clip was edited out of the documentary, much to my regret. Gerry Adams would later be accused of having led the IRA in Belfast at this time. It was clear that post-Bloody Sunday, the resurgent IRA had gone on the offensive.

Car bombs were supposedly aimed at causing economic damage by wrecking towns and villages and thereby pushing Britain into deciding that it could not afford to hold on to Northern Ireland. Inevitably, however, they killed civilians. The IRA parked their bombs in busy streets and often gave no warnings. The Abercorn Cafe bomb killed two and caused horrible injuries to many others. Two weeks later, another bomb killed seven. Two days before Bloody Friday, a bomb killed a five-month-old baby.

The day after Bloody Friday, ten days after the rape of her sister and the murder of her nephew, Anne Larkey gave birth to her daughter, Anne Marie. Two hours after the birth, she walked out of the hospital, leaving the baby behind, and went home. 'I didn't know what I was doing,' she said. 'How are you supposed to survive these things?' Her husband, Tom, went back to collect baby Anne Marie. 'The doctor was a black man and he was shocked at what I had done,' said Anne. 'He said to Tom, "I thought I was in a civilised country. What sort of people walk away from their newborn baby?"' She laughed at the memory of his indignation.

Anne fell out with her sister Sally McClenaghan after the murder of young David and the rape of Sally. 'Me and her had words,' she said. She was furious with Sally's partner, and with Sally for continuing to see him. 'I said to her, "Why is he here and David is in the graveyard?" I said he wasn't man enough to stay that night. I said to him, "You call yourself a man – why did you leave that night?" He said, "They hit me." I said, "They didn't hit you half hard enough."'

Anne didn't go to the trial of the men who had killed her nephew and raped her sister. She and Sally were still estranged, and anyway, she could not face it. 'I couldn't,' she said. 'I wanted revenge – I wanted them in jail – but I couldn't face that.' Anne said Sally had reproached her about this afterwards. She told her that while she limped across the hall of the courthouse on the crutch she had had to use since the attack, relatives of the accused men jeered at her and called her a liar. 'They gave her terrible abuse until a big policeman came over and told them to be quiet,' said Anne. 'Sally said to me, "I had nobody."'

The barrister leading the prosecution told the jury that although the people of Belfast had become hardened, this case would create a new dimension in their minds. 'The restraints of civilisation on evil human passions are in this case totally non-existent. It is said that violence begets violence, and you may well think that in this case we have reached the lowest level of human depravity.' The man who shot David and raped Sally got a twenty-year sentence. The judge said that even the most extreme person must regard these crimes with 'utter revulsion'.[11]

One of the loyalists jailed got beaten up by other loyalists in prison. Anne said it wasn't for killing a Catholic boy, as that was no disgrace. It was for the rape. 'They thought he'd let the side down,' she said, angrily. Sally didn't recover from the events of that night in July 1972. 'She went off the rails. She'd change like water. She was adrift,' said Anne. 'She was between worlds.'

* * *

No one ever admitted responsibility for the Claudy bombs of July 1972, but nobody doubts that it was the IRA. A small village in the foothills of the Sperrin mountains, and a few miles from Derry, Claudy was religiously mixed. It had scarcely been touched by the Troubles, though it was close to Burntollet Bridge, where loyalists including B Specials had attacked a civil-rights march. There had been sporadic rioting in Claudy itself. 'Once, after a civil-rights march, they rioted and they threw bottles at our shop,' said Merle Eakin. 'Civil rights meaning IRA,' she added, bitterly.

Merle and her husband, Billy, were Protestants. Many others in that community shared the belief, promoted by unionist politicians, that the civil-rights movement was just a front for armed insurrection. They had been warned since the Northern state was set up that Catholics were not to be trusted. If Catholics complained about injustice, it was just an excuse to try to destroy Northern Ireland. When they were killed by loy-alists or by the security forces, and their relatives protested their innocence, many Protestants harboured the suspicion that there was no smoke without fire.

Merle and Billy had lost their only daughter, eight-year-old Kathryn, in the bombing of the village. 'Kathryn was standing on the street outside our shop,' said Billy. 'The boy parked the car and got out of it and walked away.' In the north of Ireland, 'boy' is often used to mean a man, usually a stranger, about whom there is an implied wariness or hostility. 'If he'd only shouted at her, used bad language to her, she'd have run inside.' Instead, the man just left, the bomb exploded, and Kathryn lay dead on the footpath. Thirty-five years later, imagining the cal-lousness that allowed the bomber to see the child and walk away, Billy drew back his arm as if to punch the man in the face. Then his own face shook and he wept.

Billy and Merle ran a small shop and hardware store on the main street. Billy was from the town and had taken the business over from his father. Merle had come to Derry from the Republic to work in the bank, and the couple had met at a dance. They had two children: Mark, who was twelve in 1972, and Kathryn.

'Kathryn was a child you'd have said was here before,' said Merle. She meant that the child seemed wise beyond her years. 'She had the teachers tortured – she had a book read in no time and she was very studious.' She was looking forward to learning to play golf when she was nine and old enough to join the junior club. She was ambitious. 'She was going to be a brain surgeon,' said Billy, smiling.

The family had just returned early that morning from the caravan they kept beside the beach at Castlerock, a small seaside village on the north Derry coast, less than an hour's drive from their home. As they drove into Claudy, they noticed four cars parked at the top of the village. 'We thought maybe someone had died and these were visitors to their family,' said Merle. 'We knew we'd hear about it later on.'

Billy got ready to open the shop, which was at the front of the family home. 'Kathryn wanted to bake,' said her mother. 'She used to bake with Granny Duffy, our next-door neighbour, a Catholic lady, and she loved it. I was getting the mixer out, and her Granda Eakin came and said he'd pay her to clean the front window of the shop.' Kathryn was a helpful child: her family has a photograph of her on the wall. She is putting potatoes into bags at the front of the shop, her small face concentrating, blonde hair tucked behind her ears.

Billy had walked past Kathryn and around the side of the house and had just knelt down to fix a pipe. 'There was an unmerciful explosion, and when the slates stopped falling around me, I ran round to the front of the house. There was

Kathryn lying on the pavement. There was a wee bit of blood on the side of her head.' Billy cried, pointing to the spot on his own head. 'I tried to carry her down to the surgery but I got wobbly. A fellow called Devine took her from me and carried her.'

There were three bombs, each meant, the Eakins said, for a Protestant business in the town: one for the garage at the top of the street; one for their shop and the post office across the road from it; and one for the Beaufort Arms Hotel. 'They wanted to take the heart out of the village,' said Billy. 'They couldn't get parked at the garage, so they left the first one outside McIlhenny's fuel pumps.' He paused. 'I saw Mrs McIlhenny's body.' He covered his face briefly at the memory. 'It was just incinerated.' Thirty people were seriously injured, some of them losing limbs. The street was filled with flames. People were screaming in agony.

Inside the house, Merle's shoe had been blown off. She does not remember much about what followed, except that she realised neither of her children was in the house. She ran down the street through scenes of devastation. She learnt that Kathryn had been taken to the Altnagelvin Hospital in Derry in a car. Merle's father-in-law told her he had been with her 'at the end', Merle said. 'I said, "The end of what?" He said, "It's over."' At that point, Merle became hysterical.

A friend of the family who was a photographer had just driven through Claudy on his way to film Operation Motorman, a huge deployment of British troops charged with removing the barricades around 'Free Derry'. Local people and IRA volunteers had erected barricades around the Bogside and other nationalist parts of the city, and these were known as 'no-go' areas for the authorities. Unionists had been pushing for them to be taken down and for 'order' to be restored. The photographer heard the bombs and turned back to Claudy. When the Eakins told him they couldn't find their son, Mark, he took their family dog and searched until he found the child, who was safe.

The bombers had headed up the road to Dungiven, where they went into a chemist's shop and tried to phone a bomb warning. 'It was already too late,' said Merle. 'The bombs had gone off by then, and anyway, the phones weren't working because the IRA had blown up the exchange a fortnight before.'

James Simmons wrote a fine ballad about this attack, in which nine people were killed and the village was wrecked. The poem has the wrenching line: 'And Christ, little Kathryn Eakin is dead.'[12]

Martin McGuinness, who had declared himself the deputy leader of the IRA in Derry not long before Bloody Sunday, issued a statement saying none of his volunteers had been involved. 'I think the IRA was ashamed because Catholics were killed,' said Merle. Of the nine who died, five were Protestants and four were Catholics. The Catholic Church shortly afterwards transferred Father Jim Chesney to a parish across the border in Donegal. From the start, it was rumoured that he was involved.

Their daughter dead and their home and business ruined, Billy and Merle went to stay with friends in England for a few weeks. 'The first day home in Claudy, I heard someone laughing in the street,' said Merle. 'I thought, "How can you laugh here?"' She could not walk, and has never walked since, on the pavement outside the shop and her home. 'I couldn't walk where my child was murdered. Hallowed ground,' she said.

Billy tried to rebuild the business, but after ploughing his few life savings into the effort he took his bank manager's advice and gave up. 'He called me in and said it was no good and I was going to kill myself trying to make it work,' he said. 'I sold it then, and we got a bad price. Ah now, it is a sad day.' Their son could not bear to live in Claudy, and the family moved to Castlerock. Merle and Billy said there was no getting over the loss of Kathryn. 'No matter where you went you thought you should see her,' said Merle. 'It was hard to watch the other kids playing. It is just something you had to learn to live with. Your heart is just torn out of you.'

The year ended as badly as it had begun. In December, the IRA abducted a thirty-seven-year-old mother of ten children from her home in the Divis Flats complex on the Falls Road in West Belfast. Jean McConville was born into a Protestant family on the other side of the city but had become a Catholic when she got married. Her husband had died a year before the abduction. Divis was a tough, poor area, and life was difficult for Jean. She had attempted suicide more than once.

She had also run into trouble with the IRA, for reasons that are the subject of dispute. Some of her children believe that her crime was to comfort an injured British soldier. Ed Moloney, the author of an acclaimed history of the IRA, maintains that she was a low-level informer against the organisation, a claim her family angrily reject. Four women came for her. Her small twins clung to her legs, but she was dragged away, never to be seen alive again. It would be many, many years before her family recovered her body. Jean McConville had been 'disappeared'.

* * *

Anne Larkey couldn't settle after the murder of her young nephew. 'I decided that Ardoyne was like a prison,' she said. Doreen Toolan agreed. 'It was like there was a curse on it,' she said. Half of the killings in the Troubles were in Belfast, and most of those, nearly 1,300, were carried out in the swathe of Belfast that lies to the north, including Ardoyne, and the west, including the Falls and Shankill Roads. As Padraic Fiacc described it in 'More Terrorists', 'The prayer book is putting on fat/With in memoriam cards.'[13] Catholic civilians were the most likely victims.

'The way they looked at us was, we were all terrorists. We were less than human. It didn't matter which of us you killed,' said Anne. She and Doreen reminisced about the seemingly endless stream of deaths, and it was obvious how this close-knit working-class community had been ravaged.

Less than two weeks after Terry Toolan's death, loyalists shot dead a family friend and left him in the boot of his car, which had been set alight. Doreen witnessed the shooting of an elderly neighbour by the British army in 1973. Another neighbour, Patsy Crossan, was a popular bus driver who had been named in a threat on a pirate radio station broadcasting from the loyalist Shankill Road. He stopped the bus when two men flagged it down on the loyalist Woodvale, at the top of the Shankill. They were UFF gunmen and they shot him. He was one of three to die that day.

After his death, his widow relied a lot on his brother, Frankie, who used to help her with the children. Both brothers had been involved in community work, including organising cross-community holidays for children. Loyalists picked him up one night as he walked home from a local hall, beat him up and cut his throat before leaving his body in a doorway.

The women talked about an electrician they'd known. Loyalist gunmen from the UDA entered a workmen's hut at Ligoniel in North Belfast, stole the wages of the men there and then told the Protestant men to kneel down. They proceeded to rake the Catholic workers with gunfire, killing three of them.

Doreen introduced me to a neighbour whose grandmother and ten-year-old nephew were burnt to death in their house after gas cylinders were attached to their front door. The house went up like a furnace, the woman said. An uncle of this woman had already been shot dead by soldiers in Ardoyne. (Though Doreen and her neighbour didn't mention it, a few days before the arson attack the IRA had killed a ten-year-old girl, along with her UDR father. The Ardoyne killings were assumed to have been revenge.)

Doreen spoke about a woman who had taken her child out of school to bring him to the dentist and was walking along holding the little boy's hand when a bomb exploded, killing him. And of another whose baby was caught in crossfire and killed while her daughter was pushing the pram. 'An awful lot has died,' she said.

3

'My Youngest Son Came Home Today'

The Scottish-Australian singer and songwriter Eric Bogle has a haunting anti-war song about a mother describing the funeral of her son, a young man shot dead in the Irish Troubles. It includes the lines: 'An Irish sky looks down and weeps/At children's blood in gutters spilled/In dreams of freedom unfulfilled/As part of freedom's price to pay/My youngest son came home today.'[1]

In the Troubles, as in most wars, young men were the most likely both to be killers and to be killed. More than a quarter of all of the dead in the Troubles were men under the age of twenty-four. In the early years, the British army and both republican and loyalist paramilitaries enlisted teenagers in their youth wings to fight. The book *Ardoyne, the Untold Truth* includes one entry for a sweet-faced child who was accidentally shot with IRA comrades and is described as 'OC [officer in command] of na Fianna Éireann (Cubs)'. Teenage boys rioted, too, recklessly taking on armed soldiers and police. More than one died in this way after escaping through windows, forbidden by their parents to leave the house.

Many of the young men who died were not involved in anything other than being young. Some, like David McClenaghan, were intellectually like young children. It was no protection.

It was a dark, cold November night in 1973 when fifteen-year-old Gerard Teggart arrived at his mother's door, crying and incoherent in a coat that wasn't his. Bella Teggart was struggling to raise her large family alone, since the British army had shot dead her husband, Danny, two years earlier.

Bella tried to calm him, but he was inconsolable. She had to get her eldest daughter, Alice. 'We were at a wake and my mother came in and said, "Could you come round to the house? Gerard's in a terrible state and I can't make head nor tail of what he is saying,"' Alice told me. Alice had suffered a further bereavement after her father's murder: the baby she was carrying died shortly after he was born. She called him John Pearse.

She hurried home with her mother, and they tried to calm Gerard. 'He kept saying, "Bad men came and took us away in a black taxi."' Gradually, the women gathered that Gerard was saying that these men had forced him and his twin, Bernard, to come with them, and that they'd taken them to several different houses and through an army checkpoint in parts of the city the boys didn't know.

At the last house there were women, too. They left Gerard downstairs and took Bernard upstairs. He could hear his brother screaming and the people beating him. After a while, one of the women came down. She put a coat around Gerard's shoulders, gave him money to get the bus and told him to go home and say nothing.

Gerard and Bernard were identical twins and exceptionally close. Once, when they were small, Bella went to take a bath and left them in the living room. Gerard burnt himself on the fire, but didn't appear to feel it. It was Bernard's screams that brought Bella rushing back and Bernard whom she found rolling around the mat in agony. The doctors were able to take skin grafts from Bernard for his brother.

Alice said that you would have known when you met Bernard that he was childish for his age, 'even from the way he spoke'. Mentally, he was about nine. He used to sing 'How Much Is That Doggy in the Window?'. There was no special school available, so he went to the normal school with Gerard. The twins hated it. Their father, Daniel, had, until his death in 1971, walked them to the front gate of the school in the morning; they'd wave goodbye to him and head straight out the back. By 1973, they had been sent, for this truancy, to St Patrick's Detention Centre, which was run by the De La Salle Brothers. They were allowed home at weekends.

It was a weekday night, the night Gerard turned up distraught at his mother's house, so Alice rang St Patrick's. Gerard was in such a state she wasn't sure about his story, so she asked the Brother who took her call if Bernard was still there. He said he didn't know and someone would ring back, but they never did.

It was half past two in the morning when British soldiers came to the house and banged on the door. 'One of them said, "Can I come in?"' said Alice. This was unusual in itself – the preferred army method of entering Catholic homes in this part of Belfast at that time was to break the door down. 'He put his arm around Mummy. He was only about eighteen and he was crying. She said, "What's wrong with you, son?" He said, "I have very bad news for you. You have been through enough without what I have to tell you."'

The soldier told Bella that a UDR foot patrol had found Bernard. He was lying on the steps of the Floral Hall, an old dance hall in the north of the city, near the zoo. The child was dead. His hands and feet had been tied and he had been shot in the back of the head. His killers had hung a cardboard sign around his neck with the word 'tout' – meaning 'informer' – written on it.

Her mother, Bella, had been 'doing fine', Alice said, after her husband's murder, but she became suicidal after the murder of her son. 'She said to me, "Your daddy was my husband and my best friend and my soulmate, but Bernard was my son. He was part of me. I carried him for nine months,"' said Alice.

There were a lot of rumours about why Bernard was killed. There were stashes of IRA guns all over the place, and it was said that he had found some. Then a man who had been working as a doorman at a pub came to see Alice. He told her that he had seen the incident that must have led the IRA to kill the boy. Though they had to go back to St Patrick's that night, the twins had the day off for Princess Anne's wedding, and Bernard had been to Alice's house to watch it on the television. He was walking to his mother's house and had reached the top of the Whiterock Road when he saw a man putting a gun to the head of the driver of a drinks lorry. He rushed over and said to the gunman, 'Hey mister, leave that man alone. I'm going to tell on you.'

'Just the way a nine-year-old would do,' said Alice. 'The doorman heard our child.' The army had, in fact, witnessed the attempted hijacking, and soldiers had surrounded the area and arrested the gang responsible. Bernard had never told anyone. He went back into St Patrick's that evening. 'Around 8 p.m. these ones in a black taxi went to the school and took the twins. They couldn't tell them apart so they took them both. The priests never told us,' said Alice.

'When we brought Bernard's body home, it was terrible in the house. Every time you turned around, Gerard was lifting the body out and holding it in his arms. He couldn't sleep. We had to put pills in his food and then we'd carry him up to bed. One day, we were walking through an army checkpoint, me and him, and he went white, as if he'd seen a ghost. He started to run, and the soldiers cocked their guns. I think he'd seen one of the IRA ones on the street that took them away that day.'

Three priests, including two who would later become prominent peacemakers, Father Denis Faul and Father Alex Reid, issued a statement: 'What kind of an organisation would feel threatened by a boy with a mental age of eight? What kind of justice did this boy receive . . .? We are asking people to stand up and say they will not tolerate an environment which does not respect the vulnerability of children.'[2] The poet Padraic Fiacc wrote about Bernard's murder: 'Glory be to, so/Much for, salute/All us "armies of/The people" who/Drag away/A "backward boy".' The poem describes how they torture a confession from the child, 'And crucify him with/Bullets for nails/Up by the zoo.'[3]

A few weeks after Bernard's death, Alice was out shopping, and when she came back home, she saw a fellow lying on the ground surrounded by IRA women with guns. They were about to kneecap him. 'For a second I thought it was our twin. I started squealing and screaming. One of the women slapped me on the face and told me to go home and shut my mouth. The fellow got away in the commotion,' Alice said.

'Around that time as well there was a person lived down the street and he was in the IRA and he was a tout and he got put out of the country. I started shouting at them, "Do you have to be in the IRA to be let go?"'

Alice was too busy looking after others in the aftermath of the murders in her family to take much care of herself. About a year after her brother was killed, she and her husband had been out at a wake for another sixteen-year-old boy who had been shot dead. When they got home, Alice wrecked the living room. Telling me about this, she made a sweeping gesture towards her mantelpiece, covered with family photographs and ornaments. 'My husband didn't know what to do. He rang his mother to come. She told him to let me be. She knew I needed to do it. I'd had no chance to grieve. No chance to grieve for my father. No chance to grieve for my baby, John Pearse. No chance to grieve for my brother.'

* * *

At sixteen, Henry Cunningham knew next to nothing about the Troubles. He'd spent his childhood in the most northerly part of Ireland, the Inishowen Peninsula, in Donegal. Inishowen juts out into the Atlantic and had suffered economically from being cut off from the rest of the Republic when the border was drawn in 1921. Mountainous, beautiful and poor, there was little employment. Henry had left school at fifteen and had trained to be a plasterer. He and his brothers were among many local people who had to travel into Northern Ireland for work.

He had a date on 9 August 1973: he was to meet his girlfriend at the Lilac Ballroom in Carndonagh, near his home. That summer, he and a team which included several of his brothers were working on a site in Glengormley, on the northern outskirts of Belfast. They set off as usual that morning, but Henry never made it to the dance. At six-thirty that evening, the van in which the Donegal men were travelling home was ambushed by gunmen. Henry was shot dead.

His brothers, several of whom now have children older than Henry was when he died, still live on Inishowen. They've done well and live in fine houses they have built themselves. They have no photographs of Henry: the large, struggling family didn't have a camera in the 1970s. Their parents hadn't talked much about the murder, and it was only after their deaths that Henry's brothers had begun to broach the subject. 'Ninety-nine times out of a hundred, it would have been me sitting in the passenger seat,' Henry's brother, Robert, told me. 'But I was to play in a country band that night so I was having a lie down in the back.' He wept. 'I always think I put Henry into my seat.'

There were six men in the Bedford van; some days, there would have been eleven. One of the other men received a serious facial injury. The others were splashed with blood. Another of the Cunningham brothers, Herbert, probably saved five lives by managing to keep driving the van through the hail of bullets. One grazed his arm. 'We passed a slipway and I saw three men up on the flyover ahead of us,' he said. 'Next thing I heard a noise like a shower of hail and I could see the flames coming flying from their guns. Henry cried out, "I'm hit," and he went very white and fell down over me.

'I kept driving towards the gunmen. There didn't seem anything else to do. At the next flyover, there were two men in a car pulled over and they were leaning out, looking at us. I thought, "Oh no, this is it." I was out of my mind with fright. I was sure they were coming after us.' The tyres of the van were punctured and Herbert stopped soon afterwards. They flagged down a car, and its driver agreed to report the attack to the police. They knew Henry was dead.

That night, Robert and Herbert gave statements to the RUC in Antrim. Some of the family drove over to collect them there. The journey was difficult. 'We had to go home a long way. It was the anniversary of the bin lids – what do you call it . . . internment – and there were riots in Toome,' said Robert. The next day, they brought Henry home.

Henry's funeral was one of the biggest for many years in Carndonagh. 'We're Presbyterians, but there were Protestants in the van that night and Catholics, too. We were always a mixed crowd, and we still are and always will be. We have the best of Catholic neighbours,' said Robert. 'We're nothing to do with Paisley's crowd, by the way.' By Protestant he meant Church of Ireland. Paisley's crowd were the Free Presbyterians, his fundamentalist breakaway church. The majority of the population in Donegal, as in the rest of the Republic, is Catholic. The local Catholic priest organised a collection and brought £100 to the bereaved family.

Henry was, his brothers agreed, a 'happy-go-lucky sort of young fellow'. The Cunninghams were a law-abiding, 'good living' sort of family. There were eight boys and five girls. The youngest, Ruby, was ten when Henry was murdered. 'My father was a small farmer and he also worked in the alcohol factory. He would always hire a car on Sunday to bring us to church,' said Robert. 'He was strict – if you came home from school and said the master strapped you, he'd say, "Well, it wasn't for doing your lessons."' In summer, the family would be 'out to the hill to work at peats' – in other words, turf cutting on the bogs. The boys all left school to work as soon as they could.

Derry is less than an hour's drive from Carndonagh, but, says Robert, 'We never thought anything of the Troubles. We'd nothing against anybody.' The brothers had worked in Creggan in Derry when it was a 'no-go' area for the security forces. 'We had to go through the army checkpoints to get in, and the IRA used to be training across the road from us. The day the police came in, we went and sat down on the road in protest along with everybody else. You had to. I remember so well, the foreman said to us, "You're wasting your time. This'll be going on for twenty-five years."' That was on 31 July 1972.

On 1 January 1973, loyalists murdered a young Catholic couple at Burnfoot, not many miles from the Cunninghams' home. The Gardaí criticised the RUC for failing to co-operate in the investigation. 'People round here were really stunned by those murders,' said Herbert. 'Things were very bad at that time. But we never saw any danger. When the company we worked for moved to Glengormley, we went. We'd been working there three months. If anybody had approached us and said, "You shouldn't be here," we wouldn't have been there.'

A month after the ambush, the family was called to Belfast for the inquest. 'We were terrified on the journey,' said Robert. 'Every flyover we were getting flashbacks to what happened. I would say my father had never been further than Derry in his life.'

'We were like dummies in the court,' said Herbert. 'We just sat there. We had no say.' An open verdict was returned. Nobody explained to the family that this was routine in cases that had not come before the courts. Nobody told them anything about the police investigation. The compensation hearing was similar. 'We sat in the canteen, and someone came out and told us Herbert and I would get £300 each and Henry's funeral expenses,' said Robert. 'Nobody asked us our opinion. My parents were the kind of people who wouldn't want a fuss. If they'd been told we were getting nothing, they'd have gone away.'

And that was that. The RUC never contacted the family again. Nor did the Gardaí or the Irish government or any of its agencies. 'From the day Henry was killed it wasn't too long before my father took ill with his nerves. He never talked about it, but he never got over it. He died not long after,' said Herbert.

The family had no idea who was responsible for the attack. 'Ninety-nine per cent of the family thought it was the IRA, but we never blamed anyone or got bitter. I think my parents were afraid of bringing more trouble to our door,' said Robert. 'They never knew anyway where you would go looking for answers. My mother always thought it was loyalists. Others round here might have had suspicions but they didn't want to blame their own. That is what it comes down to.'

* * *

Terence Griffen was mad keen to join the British army, so keen that he persuaded his father to give his written permission for him to join up early, at fifteen. It was a family tradition to serve in the forces. He was based at Catterick in Yorkshire in 1974.

The IRA's war, it maintained, was against the British, but most of its violence in the early years of the Troubles was carried out in Northern Ireland. The families of British soldiers worried about them when they were sent there, but not when they were at home. However, the IRA was keen to avoid the waves of public revulsion that followed the mass slaughter of civilians in the North of Ireland. It began to target police and soldiers more, and to strike in the UK, where deaths would have less impact at home and potentially more influence on the British.

Mo Morton was driving to her work in Lancashire when she suddenly got a horrible feeling of apprehension. Noticing that she was passing an undertaker's, she wondered if she was going to have an accident and be killed. She knew something was wrong. When she got into the office, the women she worked with asked her whether she had heard about the coach bomb on the M62.

Mo went straight to the phone and rang her father. Her brother Terence Griffen had been at home in Lancashire for the weekend and had gone off to Manchester to get a coach back to Catterick the night before. He'd brought a friend home with him, and he, too, was on the coach. Mo rushed to her parents' house.

All morning the family huddled round the television. The IRA had put a bomb in the boot of the bus, and there had been multiple casualties. The Griffens kept ringing the emergency numbers on the screen and kept being told there was no news about Terence.

Then, at lunchtime, the television cameras zoomed in on the scene of carnage on the M62. The family saw with horror some of Terence's belongings. He'd taken some of his LPs back, and they could see the album sleeves. Some of the journalists were commenting that one of the songs was about little children, and little children had been killed in the blast.

'My father said quietly to my mother, "He'd have rung now if he was OK,"' Mo said. 'Later that day, his battery commander came onto the phone and said that he was terribly sorry,

Terence had been positively identified. Minutes later, he was named on television.'

Nine soldiers died in the explosion, including one whose wife and two children, aged five and two, were also killed. Terence's friend was also among the dead. His family found out when a newspaper reporter called at their door.

The army chaplain came, along with Terence's commander. 'They said he would have known nothing,' said Mo. 'I often wonder, do they tell you that only to pacify you? My father, being a military man, wanted a military funeral. My mother wanted to bury her son. He persuaded her. He said the MOD would look after the grave, which they didn't. On the day of the funeral, someone with an Irish accent phoned and said the funeral wouldn't get through the cemetery gates "because we are going to blow you sky high". We kept it from my parents.'

For a long time, Mo was afraid every time she heard an Irish accent. The family was pleased when, a few weeks after the coach bomb, the police arrested a young drifter called Judith Ward. She was later jailed for involvement in the bombing, though the conviction would later be held to be unsafe. The IRA had launched an onslaught on England: later in 1974, it bombed pubs in Guildford, Surrey, killing four, and in Birmingham, killing twenty-one people, many of them Irish, and horribly injuring many more.

Mo said her mother was strong. 'She kept it within herself. She joined groups and art classes. She got on with things. She kept herself going. She kept the family going. It was different for my father. He blamed himself for letting his son join up so young. He grieved and took ill. He stopped eating. Being a military person, it was the stiff upper lip. He didn't talk, but it was obvious he was suffering from extreme, untreated depression. He died two years later, at the age of fifty-five.'

* * *

Vera McVeigh was eighty-one when I met her. I knew her son, Eugene, a BBC cameraman, and when I asked him if I could meet her, he said he'd tell her I was a friend of his and to expect me. 'You'll have to take her as you find her,' he said quietly. 'She has had several strokes and she can get very, very angry.' Vera's youngest son, Columba, Eugene's brother, had disappeared in 1975.

She lived in a small council house in the village of Donaghmore in Tyrone. When Vera opened the door to me and heard my business, I thought she might send me packing. 'I'm the mother,' she said. 'It is thirty-two years too late for you to be coming to my door, thirty-two years since that bunch of murdering bastards took him away. What is the use of me talking to you, daughter?' But she softened and let me in, and talked to me while she prepared a mug of porridge. There were two pictures in the kitchen: one of Padre Pio and one black-and-white photograph showing Columba striking a pose, doffing his hat, flicking a cane, a rakish smile on his young face. He'd been in a youth-club talent show, Vera said, smiling fondly at her boy.

She had been relieved when, in 1975, Columba, aged nineteen, moved to Dublin. The news every day in the North was full of death and destruction. Vera had encouraged him to go – she wanted him out of harm's way. He'd had a brush with trouble already.

The McVeighs were a working-class family. Vera had been born not many miles from Donaghmore in 1925, the last child in a large Catholic family. She had left school early to work in the fields. The area was mixed, and Vera's memories of her girlhood included going to Twelfth of July parades and dancing to 'The Sash', the Orange song that celebrates the Williamite victories over the forces of King James. All her brothers and sisters emigrated. She got a job as a barmaid and met and then married Paddy, a weaver at the linen mill in Castlecaulfield. They had four children, Eugene, Oliver, Columba and Dympna, and when they were young, Vera worked part-time in a local laundry. They were an ordinary family, trying to keep their heads down as the Troubles raged.

Columba had left school early and worked in a local hatchery until the IRA blew it up. He was arrested in 1974 by the RUC on what the family believe were trumped-up charges of possession of ammunition. He spent a short time on remand at Crumlin Road prison. Eugene told me the RUC was probably trying to use him to get low-level information about the local IRA. This was common practice throughout the Troubles. 'But anyone who ever met Columba would know he wasn't involved and knew nothing,' he said. 'He was a very innocent, almost simple sort of fellow.'

He disappeared in 1975. Eugene didn't think there was anything sinister about it at the time. 'You have to remember, this was the '70s,' he said. 'He was nineteen, a young fellow who might have easily just gone off and then lost touch.

'My career as a cameraman was just taking off. I had left home and I wanted to get as far away from the place as possible. I was living in Dublin, beginning to travel the world. I got a call to say Columba was coming to Dublin. I arranged to meet him, and when he jumped into the jeep with me and another RTE guy, he was whistling a republican tune to try to impress. I said, "Columba, give it a rest." I think I gave him some money. He was restless. I left him down to his house near the canal so that I'd know where he was. That was the last time we ever met.

'There was no phone in his house and the one in my house was really only for emergency use. At that time there were no mobiles, no texts, no emails. If you wanted to stay in touch, you had to write a letter. Some time after that I remember being up home and my mother saying he had left and couldn't be found. I thought there had probably been some row. Then I was busy and abroad, and then months later I was home and my parents were worried. I wasn't. It was really the Christmas after that, in 1976, when he hadn't been in touch, that I began to be concerned. I went to the Gardaí. Their attitude was, this happens. If he gets into trouble, we'll hear about him.'

Two months after Columba disappeared, the IRA abducted a nineteen-year-old neighbour of the McVeighs. He was taken at gunpoint from a garage where he was working, shot in the head and his body dumped near by. The IRA put it about that he had given information to the RUC, but it is widely suspected that he was murdered because his father had been in the British army.

Vera told me that Columba used to write to her regularly before his disappearance. She knew he was living with a girl and that he was working as a window fitter. 'He was one man who never forgot me,' she said. 'I came down every day looking for a letter with his writing on it on the mat. I thought when we heard nothing from him he was away with some lassie. His father was a bit strait-laced of himself, and I maintained that was why Columba didn't come home. I waited for every van or car or bus that passed here to stop. His dog Dusty never left the pavement outside there watching for him. The day that dog died, I cried, but it was a double cry because I knew whose dog it was.'

Vera and her husband continued to buy birthday and Christmas presents for Columba, and when he didn't come, Vera stored them for him. They didn't go on holidays in case he came back while they were away. And that was how life went on for them, because Columba never came back and it was to be twenty-three years before Vera found out what had happened to the boy she remembered as 'the apple of my eye'.

* * *

Doreen Toolan talked about people being 'Shankill Butchered', a verb from a terrible time. Robert 'Basher' Bates was one of the Shankill Butchers, which was led by a notorious thug called Lenny Murphy. A disruptive and violent child, Bates left school at sixteen and had his first conviction for assault by the time he was seventeen. A police mugshot from the mid-1970s shows him glowering out, heavy set, bearded and with long, lank hair.

Often using a black taxi owned by one of the gang, the Butchers would cruise the streets of North and West Belfast with their jagged, invisible sectarian boundaries looking for a victim whose route suggested he was a Catholic. Loyalists called this 'hunting for a Taig'. This was the politics of the Butchers, even though they occasionally used loyalist magazines to dress their sectarianism up in grandiose claims about taking on the IRA.

They'd bundle their victim into a car, where the torture would begin. Typically, they would then take him back to the Shankill and murder him using butcher's knives, nooses, hammers, wheel braces and blow torches. Their trademark was to cut the throats of their victims back to the spine. The Butchers did not operate with the full approval of the UVF, which has claimed it removed their guns. However, on occasion they did have firearms. The violence was excessive and prolonged; it appeared they enjoyed what they did.

Bates was a part-time barman, and his gang hung around various UVF pubs and clubs on the Shankill Road. He was part of the UVF's 'Brown Bear' unit, named after a pub. Their violence was often fuelled by alcohol, followed by alcohol and even paid for by alcohol: in one statement after an atrocity, Bates told police two men who took part in the attack were paid with a large bottle of vodka.

Although he was already a young criminal in the mid-1960s, Bates told his grandson, also called Robert, that he had got involved in the UVF to avenge an uncle who was blown up by an IRA bomb on the Shankill Road in 1971. 'He was in a bar and he ran up to where the bomb had been and found bits of his uncle. It made him angry and vengeful. He said he was standing in the pub up to his ankles in blood,' said Robert Bates junior. 'It was just a really bad era.'

The IRA didn't claim it, but it was assumed to have been responsible for the no-warning bomb attack on the Four Step Inn. Two men, Basher's relative, Ernest Bates, and Alexander Andrews, were killed and almost thirty people were injured. People dug in the rubble with their bare hands searching for survivors, and an angry crowd gathered. More than 50,000 people attended the funerals. The Northern Ireland Civil Rights Association called the bomb the work of madmen and said it was obviously meant to stir up sectarian hatred. Loyalist paramilitaries presented themselves as avenging their beleaguered community; attacks like that on the Four Step Inn gave them succour.

'Its retributions work like clockwork/Along the murdering miles of terrace houses,' writes Tom Paulin in 'Under the Eyes'. The poem explores the balancing out of 'an exact revenge' in a city 'built on mud and wrath'.[4]

Republicans have been reluctant to admit that the IRA engaged in such tit for tat sectarian violence, but the pattern is clear, particularly during the 1970s. It was Ardoyne IRA men who planted the no-warning bomb on the Shankill after the loyalist attack on McGurk's Bar in 1971. In 1975, the IRA embarked on a ceasefire but warned that it might sanction 'retaliations'.

It was Doreen's friend, Brendan 'Bik' McFarlane, along with other Ardoyne IRA men, who that year attacked the Bayardo Bar on the Shankill Road. They shot two men outside, left a no-warning bomb in the doorway of the crowded pub, killing two, and then, for good measure, fired at women and children standing at a taxi rank as they made their getaway.

Discussing this incident in a later book, former IRA man Richard O'Rawe berates the British 'gutter press' for branding McFarlane sectarian for his role in this bombing. The IRA thought the pub was being used for a meeting of UVF leaders, he writes; the attack was an attempt to stop the bloody onslaught on the Catholic community. 'Unfortunately IRA intelligence had got it wrong . . .' he noted.[5] The random shooting at the people at the taxi rank, however, fits inconveniently into the story.

Loyalist sectarianism was visceral, full of loathing. In one of the most disturbing books about the Troubles, *The Shankill Butchers*, Martin Dillon describes the excesses of the Butchers and other 1970s loyalist gangs. One man was hung from a beam in a lock-up garage and stripped. 'A knife was used on his body much in the manner a sculptor would chip away at a piece of wood or stone,' Dillon writes.[6] The man, a nightwatchman called Thomas Madden, had 147 stab wounds and finally died from slow strangulation. In the early hours of the morning of his murder, a woman reported hearing a man screaming, 'Kill me, kill me.' It is believed that this murder was carried out by elements of the UDA.

Police said the Butchers were sadists and psychopaths who would keep on killing till they were caught. They had up to thirty victims, and inspired Padraic Fiacc's relentlessly violent poem 'Crucifixus': 'In all the stories that the Christian Brothers/Tell of Christ He never screamed/Like this. Surely this is not the way/To show a "manly bearing"–/Screaming for them to "Please stop!"–/And then, later, like screaming for death!' The poem ends: 'Poor Boy Christ, for when/They finally got around to finishing him off/By shooting him in the back of the head,/The poor Fenian fucker was already dead!'[7]

* * *

At nineteen, Thomas McErlane had followed in the footsteps of his elder brother, John, when he went to work in the Belfast Meat Factory. The McErlanes were Catholics, and the factory was in an industrial estate near the loyalist Mount Vernon housing estate, an area which had a very active UVF unit. But Thomas had no fear about going there. 'John was doing well – he was nearly management,' said his brother, Gerard. 'It was a large, mixed workforce, and the two of them were friends with everybody. We weren't brought up to be bitter.'

The McErlanes were from the Short Strand, a small enclave of working-class terraced houses, a Catholic area separated from the city centre by the River Lagan and with largely Protestant East Belfast all around it. The main thoroughfare onto which its narrow streets open out is the Newtownards Road, which by the mid-1970s was one of the heartlands of the UVF.

The family had lived in 'the Strand' for generations. 'It was a great community and we loved it,' said Gerard McErlane. 'It was very close-knit – everybody knew everybody else and looked after everyone else. Each and every family looked after the area, as it was always under attack. The people depended on the IRA – there was no one else to defend us.'

It was a fierce gun battle in the grounds of St Matthew's Church on the edge of Short Strand in June 1970 that many people believe established the IRA's credentials as the defenders of beleaguered Belfast nationalists. Loyalist gunmen attacked, and neither the RUC nor the British army intervened. That was left to the IRA.

Thomas still lived at home with his parents. John was married and living with his wife, Rosaleen, and their little daughter, Seaneen, in the suburb of Glengormley. He didn't drink but loved a game of cards. Some of his workmates kept asking him to come and play with them in Mount Vernon. 'In those days you wouldn't go into a Protestant area, with the Butchers and everything,' said Gerard. John refused, but his workmates persisted until eventually he agreed. They finished work at lunchtime on Fridays, and since everything seemed OK, John took to spending his Friday afternoons playing cards in one of the flats in the multi-storey blocks on the estate. These were routinely festooned with UVF banners and Union Jacks.

Thomas was wary, and he wasn't keen on card games anyway. The men from Mount Vernon kept asking him to join them, and he kept saying no. 'Eventually, after a few weeks, a trust had built up, and Thomas gave in,' said Gerard. They went to the card school. Gerard told me the address in the flats and named the couple who were living there at the time. 'There was an ice-cream van watching their arrival. The door was kicked in. Two gunmen were there. They told everyone to lie down and shot John and Thomas twice each in the back of the head.'

A few hours later, John's wife saw a newspaper billboard in the city centre stating that two brothers who worked at a meat plant had been shot. She knew. She ran to her mother's house. 'We got about seventeen seconds of coverage on the television,' said Gerard. 'Footage of the two bodies being carried out of Mount Vernon and then the two coffins being taken out of St Matthew's chapel during the funeral. That was it.'

Rosaleen found out a few weeks after John's murder that she was pregnant again. Her two-year-old daughter was called Seaneen, after the Irish for John. She would call her new daughter Noeleen, because John's middle name had been Noel. Gerard said that when it came to the compensation hearing, Rosaleen had got very little. The judge told her she was a young, attractive woman and he was sure she would marry again.

4

Goya by Moonlight in South Armagh

The British had no great desire to run the province they'd ignored for so many years. They had been forced to take control after the unionist government proved incapable of reforming to meet nationalist demands for equality, but from the start the aim was to get a local settlement, get the troops home and leave the locals to it. Years of talks, including secret meetings between the British and the IRA, led to the Sunningdale Agreement. This was an attempt to bring the 'middle ground' into a power-sharing executive, with the belief that the 'extremes' would then wither away.

The IRA rejected the deal, still confident it could get the 'Brits Out'. The SDLP, led by John Hume, supported it, though it was unhappy that Dublin had not been given a stronger role. Unionism was split. Unionism was always split. Prime Minister Brian Faulkner, who had looked like a hard-liner under Terence O'Neill, was now, like O'Neill, facing the wrath of Paisley, who warned the Protestant people that this would spell the end of their beloved province. Faulkner was unhappy that Dublin had been given a role at all, but this had been the price of getting the SDLP on board.

Paisley won. He did so because most unionists, including most of Faulkner's party, were not ready to compromise. Above all, he won because unionists were willing to let the loyalist paramilitaries use their muscle to wreck the initiative.

The Ulster Workers Council Strike began on 15 May 1974. With the encouragement of Paisley and the compliance of other senior unionists, loyalist paramilitaries were soon manning roadblocks all over the North, intimidating workers and shutting down power stations. The British army decided that dealing with this was a matter for the RUC, but the still almost entirely Protestant RUC was disinclined to do so.

Two days after the start of the strike in the North, down south in Dublin fourteen-year-old Derek Byrne was feeling good. He had no interest in the North or in politics of any kind. He'd left school and was working as a petrol-pump attendant at a garage in the north inner city, near his home. He'd been paid before lunch and had bought a new pair of football boots. 'We were heading to Liverpool the following week to play a tournament,' he said.

At around 5.15 p.m., he was serving petrol to a man. 'There was an almighty bang,' he remembered. 'I remember waking up in what I found out later was the morgue,' he said. 'I got up and screamed.' Derek had been pronounced dead, along with twenty-five others, after a series of no-warning bombs around the city centre. He learnt later that the man he'd been serving at the garage had been killed in the blast.

Twenty of those killed were women and two were babies. One woman was due to go into hospital to have a baby that night. Another was about to get married. One entire family was wiped out – a husband, wife and two baby girls. The young woman was only able to be indentified by a broken earring. Eight more people were slaughtered in bombs in the border town of Monaghan.

Morgue staff rushed Derek to hospital, where he was again

pronounced dead on arrival. The *Irish Press* listed him among those who died that day. A journalist went to his parents' home and interviewed his mother about the loss of her son. It was a Jesuit priest who brought the news that he was still alive the following day. Derek's jugular had been lacerated, one of his hands was badly damaged and he had shrapnel wounds to his face and body. He couldn't feel any pain immediately after the bomb but has been in constant pain since.

After months in various hospitals, Derek was allowed home to the one-bedroom flat he shared with his eight brothers and sisters and his parents. 'I was the second youngest. It was like casualty at night with all the fold-down beds,' he said. 'After the bomb, it was like being in prison. The worst thing was having to give up sport. I was into soccer, athletics and boxing. You'd go out to football matches and you'd want to be out there playing.

'I'd bottle it all up and then I'd lash out at my mother, God rest her, or someone else in the family. My father died the following year. My mother tried to protect me – I think she was afraid I'd get involved in the IRA or something. The bombs weren't talked about. The government hid a lot from the people, and so did the media. It was a case of out of sight, out of mind.'

Dozens of loyalists were arrested in the aftermath of the bombs and some were accused of several sectarian murders of Catholics which followed, but none were prosecuted. Stung by British prime minister Harold Wilson's attack on 'spongers' and 'bully boys' in Northern Ireland, the UDA denied involvement, claiming that the British SAS was behind the shootings and the bombs. 'When this is established beyond a doubt, it will give the lie to the claim that the people supporting the Ulster Workers constitutional stoppage include thugs and bully boys,' it said.[1]

* * *

The SAS claim was regarded as far-fetched, and there was no doubting that the strike relied on loyalist bully boys. However, it was soon rumoured that the bombs in the Republic had been planted by loyalists from the County Armagh town of Portadown, in the heart of what was known as the 'murder triangle'. Catholics in this part of mid-Ulster had suspected for some time that the loyalists and members of the security forces might be closely linked.

It was the British Secretary of State, Merlyn Rees, who, in 1975, dubbed South Armagh 'bandit country'. It was one of the IRA's heartlands, and the IRA's deadly effectiveness in the area was greatly enhanced by the fact that the Irish border zigzagged crazily through its mountains and bogs. It was easy to escape into the Republic across a network of roads as intricate as the cracked glaze on an old plate.

Portadown, on its northern edge, was known among unionists as 'the Orange citadel' and it had a militant, paramilitary edge. South Armagh, by contrast, was overwhelmingly nationalist and related more to the border town of Newry and towns just across the border in the Republic, like Castleblayney and Dundalk, than to Portadown. Protestants from its minority community lived, according to some accounts, contentedly enough. Others, like Margaret Frazer and her son, Willie, claimed that their lives had been made miserable by constant threats and attacks when they lived in villages like Whitecross and Newtownhamilton. 'I never lay down,' Mrs Frazer told me. 'I'd have come home from work and sat and slept in the chair, but at the edge of dark I got up again.'[2] She described her husband, Bertie, firing out of the window at Catholic neighbours who had come to burn the family out. His gun was legally held: he had been in the B Specials, and when that force was disbanded in 1970 he had joined the UDR.

Catholics who lived in the area said people were kind to the few local Protestant families. However, the UDR was deeply disliked. 'They would take your private letters out of your handbag at checkpoints and read them and sneer at you,' said one woman. A man said a local UDR man had, one night, taken a hatchet and smashed up Catholic graves in a cemetery near Whitecross. It was rumoured that Bertie Frazer and other local UDR men were also in the UVF. His son, Willie, would later say that his father and other members of the local security forces were working covertly to support the British SAS. He denied his father was in the UVF.

Between 1974 and 1976, there was what appeared to be a brutal spiral of tit for tat killings in South Armagh. From the start, it was apparent that members of the security forces were involved with local loyalist paramilitaries. In the summer of 1975, a gang consisting of UVF and UDR men who were also in the illegal organisation set up a checkpoint and stopped the van in which the Miami Showband was travelling home to the Republic after a dance. During a botched attempt to load a bomb onto the van, the UVF shot dead three members of the band, while two members of the gang were killed when the bomb exploded prematurely.

In August, the IRA murdered a local RUC reservist. Nine days later, two local Catholic men returning from a Gaelic Athletic Association (GAA) football match in Dublin were stopped at what appeared to be a UDR checkpoint and murdered. Six days after that, the IRA murdered Bertie Frazer as he was driving off after taking his sheep to a field. Two nights later, using Frazer's car, the IRA shot up a meeting of local Orangemen in Tullyvallen Orange Hall, killing five men. An armed off-duty policeman who was a member of the lodge fired at the gunmen.

In December, a bomb exploded in a pub in Dundalk, across the border in the Republic, killing two men. Hours later, there was a gun and bomb attack on a pub in Silverbridge in South Armagh. A fourteen-year-old boy was killed, along with two men, one of them an Englishman, Trevor Brecknell, who had married a local woman. A caller to the BBC said the Red Hand Commandos were responsible. This was one of the *noms de guerre* used by loyalists. Later that month, the INLA bombed a pub in the village of Gilford, killing three Protestants.

* * *

It was Oliver Reavey who found the bodies of his brothers. He came home through a heavy, icy fog on a Sunday night in January 1976 to find the bodies of John Martin, twenty-four, and Brian, twenty-two, lying in their blood on the living-room floor in the small cottage that was their family home in the village of Whitecross. A trail of blood led out the front door. 'He got some shock,' said his brother, Eugene. 'Oliver never spoke for twelve months. Not one word.'

I met Eugene at his big, comfortable farmhouse on the edge of Whitecross. He showed me photographs of the old house, which had been demolished. They were disturbing photographs, obviously taken by the police in the immediate aftermath of the shootings. There were bloodstains and bullet marks. The house was tiny. The small bedroom the boys shared had five beds, each with a cardboard box beside it for personal belongings. There were a couple of girlie posters on the walls and photos of football teams.

'I tell you, that was a bad night in this country,' said Eugene. Six other members of the large family were out visiting their mother's sister. The key was in the door. John Martin, Brian and their younger brother, seventeen-year-old Anthony, were watching television. The gunmen sprayed the room, killing John Martin instantly. Brian made it as far as the bedroom and was shot dead there.

Anthony tried to hide under the bed, but one of the men dragged him out by his legs and shot him several times, leaving him for dead. After they left, he managed to stagger past the bodies of his brothers and up the road to a neighbour's house to raise the alarm.

Anne McKeown had grown up with the Reaveys and knew them as 'lighthearted and full of fun, innocent as the flowers of May'. She and her husband, Gerry, both teachers, had moved from Whitecross to nearby Newry a few years before this, but they were staying with Anne's family in the village that weekend.

'That night, nearly everyone who had anywhere to go left Whitecross,' said Anne. 'Everyone was terrified they'd be back to kill more.' The choice of large Catholic families made it obvious that the assassins were loyalists. The following morning, the news reported that about half an hour after the murders of the Reaveys, gunmen had launched a similar attack on the home of the O'Dowd family in Gilford, a few miles away, killing three of the family and seriously injuring another.

Anne met one of the neighbours on the street in Whitecross the following morning. 'I recognised her coat, but I didn't recognise her. People were so traumatised they didn't look like themselves.' That day, the father of the murdered brothers, Jimmy Reavey, was interviewed for the television news. He called for there to be no retaliation.

* * *

Anne and Gerry McKeown were driving from a hospital visit in Belfast back to Whitecross with their small children that evening. They were hurrying because Gerry wanted to get back to Newry for the removal from the hospital of the bodies of John Martin and Brian Reavey. The tradition is for family, friends and neighbours to pay their respects as the coffins of the dead are either brought home or taken from home to the church at which the funeral service will be held the next day. The McKeowns found a lorry stopped on the narrow road and a Mini turning to go back the way they had come from. The driver of the lorry told them not to go up the road – something had happened. But Gerry did. The first thing he remembered seeing was a plastic lunchbox lying on the road. Then he looked around. 'I realised I was in the middle of something awful,' he said. Gerry McKeown had happened upon the scene of one of the most notorious massacres of the Troubles.

It was the end of an ordinary working day for the workers from the linen mill at Glenanne, South Armagh. The talk on the bus home was, as usual, of football. The men on board were Joseph Lemmon, forty-six; Robert Freeburn, fifty; John Bryans, forty-six; James McWhirter, fifty-eight; Robert Walker, forty-six; Kenneth Worton, twenty-four; John McConville, twenty; the Chapman brothers, Reginald, twenty-five and a talented footballer, and Walter, twenty-three; Richard Hughes, fifty-six; Alan Black, thirty-two; and Robert Chambers, at nineteen the youngest worker.

Alan Black had only been working at the factory for a few months. 'Football was the big thing at the mill. I supported Liverpool, and Richard Hughes was Man United. There was a good mix. The Protestant–Catholic thing didn't really come into it. The money was bad but the craic was mighty. I loved going to work.'

That evening, though, the men were a bit subdued, especially as the bus passed through Whitecross. There had been horrified talk in the factory earlier of the murders of the Reaveys and the O'Dowds. When they saw the red light of a torch in the road signalling the bus to stop, they would have thought little of it. The Glenanne UDR base was not far away, and you would expect the soldiers to be out in the aftermath of the shootings.

All but one of the men on the bus were Protestants, so they hadn't the same fear of the UDR as a group of Catholics approaching a checkpoint might have.

When they heard an English accent, they would have assumed it was the British army. They could see that men in combat jackets with their faces blackened were surrounding the bus. This was odd, and a couple of the men exchanged worried glances. The Englishman shouted, 'Everybody out of the bus,' and they all filed off and stood at the side of the narrow country road, next to the crossroads at Kingsmills. Then things got sinister. The Englishman told them to put their hands on the top of the minibus and started shouting, 'Who's the Catholic?' He repeated the question over and over, getting more and more aggressive.

Richard Hughes was the Catholic. Because of what had happened the night before and the times they were living in, the men thought their colleague was in danger. The two young men on either side of him, brothers Reginald and Walter Chapman, each put out their hands to try to hold him back, to protect him, to keep him among friends. But one of the gang pulled Hughes out and told him to run, running after him and shouting at him to keep going. Then the shooting started. Some of the men screamed, but within seconds there was silence. Nine men lay dead on the road.

Alan Black remembered lying there in agony, blacking out and then coming round, knowing that he was gravely wounded, freezing and lying among the dead. He remembered that a man came out of the darkness, a man who was distraught as he walked through the bodies, praying aloud. The man heard Alan's groans and knelt beside him. This was Gerry McKeown.

'I could hear moaning and I ran and got my wife, Anne. We both knelt down beside the man. I said, "Give me your hand." He gripped my hand. I said, "Tell me your name." He said, "Alan Black." I was glad I didn't know him,' said Gerry. 'I know that

sounds terrible. He said, "Pray for me." I said an act of contrition, and he said it after me. He said, "Tell my wife to look after
the children." He said, "What about the others?" I said, "Och,
they seem to be all right."' Anne put her hand under Alan's coat
to feel his wounds. 'He was riddled with bullets,' she said.

Alan remembered the man praying at his side, but he told me
he didn't repeat the act of contrition, simply because it was a
Catholic prayer, and as a Protestant, he didn't know it. 'I was
glad someone was praying for me anyway,' he said.

Anne then ran to the nearest house where they knew there
was a phone. At first, the people wouldn't open the door. They
were Catholics who had bought a farm that had always been
Protestant before, and there was tension about it. They'd been
threatened and had left for a while. They'd only just returned,
after getting assurances from the local police that they'd keep
an eye on the place.

Eugene Reavey and other mourners for his brothers were
caught on the other side of the road blocked by the massacre,
and he was among those who got out of their cars to direct others to go back. Eventually, the family used a different route to
get to Daisy Hill hospital to collect the bodies of John Martin
and Brian and bring them home.

'When we got to the hospital, it was mayhem,' said Eugene.
'Ambulances, police, people roaring and screaming. Someone
told me it was the families of the people that were killed on the
bus. I went into the room where they were and I said I was
Eugene Reavey from the Reavey family and I wanted to express
our condolences.'

Then the Reaveys got into their cars to follow the hearses carrying the coffins of Eugene's murdered brothers. 'The army and
the police stopped us out on the road. We had the boys' clothes
in the back that they'd been shot in. They threw the clothes on
the road and they danced on them. One of them put a gun

against my back and shouted, "Have you only one ear? Where's your other ear?"'

As he told me about this, in his home a short distance from where the old family place had been, Eugene became distraught. He got up and walked around the kitchen, sobbing and waving his arms. Then he came and stood behind my chair. 'They got Mummy and Daddy out of the car and they were saying to Mummy, "It is well for you, Mrs Reavey. We had to come over here to this hellhole,"' he said.

Then Eugene grabbed my ears and pulled them, followed by my nose. I felt the momentary invasion, a shocking glimpse of the bereaved woman's humiliation. 'That is what the soldier was doing to my mother,' he said. 'That haunts me. Mummy reared eight big strong fellows, and in her hour of need none of us was fit to protect her.' His mother was given pills by the doctor, and continued taking them. After that, he said, the UDR and the army never gave his family peace. 'One night they made me walk into the river up to my nose and they put a gun to my head and said, "Who shot the people at Kingsmills?"'

The McKeowns went back to work the day after the massacre. 'You never thought of doing otherwise,' Anne said. They were never interviewed by the police.

Shortly after the Reavey murders, the RUC officer investigating them told Eugene and his father the names of three men who had, he believed, been involved. Two were in the police and the other was in the UDR. All were local. He also said they had been involved in previous violent incidents, including the murder of three people at Donnelly's Bar in 1975. An officer of the Royal Marines had also come to the Reaveys' house with information. Eugene's father told him not to disclose any of this.

Immediately after the Kingsmills massacre, there was a debate in the British Parliament about the worsening violence in the north of Ireland. A Tory MP suggested trading a swathe of South Armagh for part of County Monaghan in the Republic. The government did, in fact, contemplate this, but decided against it partly because it believed the government of the Republic would not, as Prime Minister Harold Wilson put it, be enamoured of such an offer, and partly because it would move the border closer to Belfast. What Wilson did do was to announce that he was designating County Armagh as a 'special emergency area' and that he was sending in undercover units of the SAS 'to stamp out cross-border banditry and murder'.

The IRA, for its part, did not admit responsibility for Kingsmills, which it claimed instead using the *nom de guerre* 'South Armagh Republican Action Force'. A senior IRA man articulated a commonly held view. It was the loyalists who'd killed the Reaveys and the O'Dowds that were to blame, he said. 'It was sad those people [at Kingsmills] had to die but I'll tell you something: it stopped any more Catholics being killed.'[3]

In fact, it seems likely the Kingsmills atrocity was planned at a meeting in Dundalk on New Year's Eve, four days before the murders of the Reaveys and the O'Dowds. Such thinking is in any case folly. One local Protestant teenager in the area at the time was called Billy Wright. He claimed that it was Kingsmills that filled him with a desire for revenge. He learnt his trade and went on to become one of the most depraved loyalist killers and gang leaders in the history of the Troubles.

* * *

A few days after he was admitted to Daisy Hill hospital, Alan Black decided to die. 'I mind I was lying in bed with all these tubes in me, and I was thinking about the boys and I decided I was going to die, too – it wasn't worth living. I let myself drift. I was going down and down, drifting, a lovely feeling coming over me . . . I was smiling to myself. I was saying, "Bye bye, I'm away,"' he said.

The team looking after Alan had high hopes for his recovery. A bullet had skimmed his head and he had multiple injuries, but it looked like he was going to make it. But now nurse Ann Carlin, who had been assigned to look after Alan, saw that his vital signs were plummeting. She shouted for the doctors, and they rushed to his side, helpless as he slipped away.

Alan was almost gone when he heard Ann's voice calling urgently to him: 'Alan. Alan, come back. What about Karen, Alan? How is she going to cope without her daddy? Come back.' Karen was Alan's two-year-old daughter, and Ann knew he doted on her. He was laughing as he remembered the incident. 'I said to myself, "Fuck you, Ann," but I knew that I had to come back. Ann was the difference between me living and dying. She knew the magic words.'

Alan was in hospital for weeks. He got to know young Anthony Reavey, who was in the ward next door. Anthony was in a wheelchair. He'd come into Alan's ward and they'd talk. 'We talked about everything under the sun except the shooting,' said Alan. 'He was seventeen. I had an apprentice, Robert Chambers, so I could relate to him. He was around the same age. Robert had me tortured to teach him to drive.' Robert Chambers had been killed in the massacre. 'We had something in common, Anthony and I: we'd both survived. But we never talked about it.'

He got to know Anthony's family, too. They would always call in to see Alan when they came to visit Anthony. 'Nicer people you couldn't meet than the Reaveys. They'd bring in presents for my kids. I struck up a friendship with the mother and the sisters after that. We'd meet at fundraising charity events in a pub every Thursday.'

Weeks after Anthony got out of hospital, Alan heard he had been readmitted. 'The next day, I went in to see him. When I asked what ward was he in, I was told, "Anthony's dead." It was like being hit with a hammer. A young man with his life in front of him.' Anthony Reavey had died of a brain haemorrhage. Remembering the loss, Alan bowed his head.

The horror in the area continued. Later that year one of those suspected of UVF involvement, local UDR man Robert McConnell, was murdered by the IRA. At the time of his death, he was the family breadwinner for a brother with cancer and a disabled sister.

Seven months after the murders of the Reavey brothers and the Kingsmills massacre, a young nurse called Alice Campbell went to the graveyard at Ballymoyer, near Whitecross, with members of the Reavey family. It was a particularly sad occasion. She should have been going to the church instead of the graveyard – it was to have been the day she married Brian. Instead, she laid flowers on his grave.

Twelve-year-old Majella O'Hare was on her way to the church at Ballymoyer for confession that day, along with some of her friends. Her father was cutting grass in the graveyard when he heard a shot and saw one of the children fall. He raced out onto the road, saw that it was Majella and gathered her up in his arms. She had her hand in her hair as if her head was hurting and she was bleeding profusely. Her father was shouting and screaming.

Soldiers appeared, and after learning that he was the child's father, one of them told him to 'Close your fucking mouth.' Alice Campbell tried to approach the child, but the soldiers held her back and one of them said to her, 'This is the fucking Provos for you.' In fact, Majella had been shot by one of the soldiers. An army helicopter arrived, and the nurse said the soldiers threw the child roughly into it. She was allowed to accompany the child to the hospital at Newry, where Majella was pronounced dead. The British army claimed at first she had been caught in crossfire, then that the soldier whose shot killed her had seen an IRA gunman and had shouted a warning before he opened fire. Local people said there was no crossfire, no gunman and no warning. The soldier was acquitted of manslaughter.

* * *

It was hard for Alan Black to live in Bessbrook after the Kingsmills massacre. Most of the men who died were from the village. When he was taking his boys to school in the morning, he'd see their wives and children. He imagined the children thinking, 'Why is that man walking about and my daddy is dead?' He'd get home from school and go to bed and stay there, weeping, all day. 'My head wasn't the way it should have been,' he said.

The doctors prescribed antidepressants, which kept him 'on a level path' but would lead to a serious dependency. The family moved to Scotland, to a council flat in Galashiels. On the anniversary of the Kingsmills massacre, a reporter and a photographer turned up at the door. Alan asked them to leave him be. He didn't want people knowing who he was. They'd have to move if they were identified in the paper.

'They were under orders that they had to get the story. They were decent enough. They took a photo of us from behind down at the River Tweed. I got Karen a new coat and we threw it away afterwards.' He laughed. 'The next day, the headline in the paper was "The Fugitives". To this day, I call Karen the Fugitive! I was in the club that night and one of my Scottish friends was looking at the paper, and he said, "Look at that poor bastard. That's one of your countrymen."'

Alan's wife never settled in Scotland. She was homesick, and he'd come home from work to find her crying. After two years, they decided to come home to Bessbrook. Before leaving

Scotland, Alan came off the antidepressants. 'I flushed them down the toilet and went through three weeks of torture. It was nearly worse than being shot.'

Back home, he was seeing the relatives of his dead colleagues again. 'You always have a sort of guilty feeling. Apparently it's normal,' he said. 'They are all very glad for me and they want me alive. A lot of people have said to me, "You were spared for a reason." But it isn't that. It is just they didn't get me. They didn't intend anyone to stay alive.' He touched his head where the bullet skimmed him. When nurse Ann Carlin removed the scab from his head, she told him, 'That's the one was meant to finish you.'

Singer and songwriter Tommy Sands wrote a song about the Kingsmills massacre. Poets Michael Longley and Paul Durcan both wrote elegies in the aftermath of the massacre. Durcan's is full of rage and disgust. He calls it 'the height of obscenity' and refers to Queen Macha, the legendary figure who gives Armagh its name: 'The green clad lady/For whose liberty/We butcher.' After this atrocity, Durcan writes, 'Liberty in Ireland/Is a corpse.'[4] In a later poem, he describes the IRA as 'Having photocopied Goya by moonlight' and includes a savage attack on the complicity of southern Irish nationalists in the IRA's carnage. The narrator of the poem speaks to his father about the slaughter, and he replies: 'Teach the Protestants a lesson.'

Longley's poem 'The Linen Workers' has a more mournful tone, with a comparison to the crucified Christ and a reference to Communion in the lines, 'When they massacred the ten linen workers/There fell on the road beside them spectacles/Wallets, small change and a set of dentures:/Blood, food particles, the bread, the wine.'[5]

Alan had joined the Northern Ireland Peace Movement, set up by Mairead Corrigan, Betty Williams and others in 1976 after a terrible incident in Belfast, a few days before the shooting of

Majella O'Hare in South Armagh. Anne Maguire was walking with her five young children near her home in the west of the city when a car smashed into them, killing six-week-old Andrew, two-year-old John and eight-year-old Joanne. Anne was seriously injured. The driver of the car was dead. Danny Lennon was an IRA man and he had been shot by British soldiers, who had been pursuing his car.

Alan had a phrase for extremists from either side: 'out and outers'. He liked Bessbrook, he said, because it was a mixed village with good relations and not too many 'out and outers'. The Peace People, as they became known, held rallies all over the North. Alan was at a rally in Newry, a few miles from Bessbrook, when it came under attack by a republican crowd. 'We were saying the prayer for peace and the stoning started – it was out and outers from Newry,' he said, and then he laughed. 'An old lady said to me, "Never you mind them, son, just you say your prayers."'

5

Into the Hunger Strikes

By the late 1970s, the British and the IRA had both realised that they were each facing a formidable enemy and that they were in for a long war. Both had also realised the importance of propaganda. The British were losing too many soldiers. They had been rebuked by bodies like the European Court and Amnesty International for ill-treatment of detainees under internment. They needed to challenge the international perception that the Irish problem was essentially a colonial one. For its part, the IRA had killed too many civilians in careless slaughter; it needed to recover its martyr status.

In 1976, the British removed the 'special category status' which politically motivated prisoners had been granted in 1972. It was part of a policy of 'Ulsterisation', whereby the IRA would be dealt with as a local criminal problem by the RUC and the UDR. The local security forces and the prison service were overwhelmingly Protestant, so Ulsterisation helped make the Troubles like a civil war, with Britain as the honest broker caught between the warring factions. In the early years of the Troubles, the British army had borne the brunt of the IRA attacks on the security forces. In 1976, four times more local soldiers and police were killed than British soldiers.

The IRA embarked on a series of protests against criminalisation. The most popular song in republican clubs and bars at the time was the ballad which included the lines: 'I'll wear no prison uniform/Nor meekly serve my time/That England might/Brand Ireland's fight/Eight hundred years of crime.'[1]

Lord Louis Mountbatten was, it seemed, the symbol of everything the IRA detested. He was an earl, the Queen's cousin, mentor to Prince Charles, a much decorated former British naval commander, a former chief of defence staff and the last viceroy and first British governor general of independent India. He was also something the IRA liked very much – an easy target. Mountbatten had been bringing his family to Classiebawn Castle at Mullaghmore on the west coast of Ireland every summer for thirty years. The tiny fishing village was in the Republic, not far west of the border.

During the intensely violent year of 1972, Mountbatten had asked the British government to advise him on his safety. He was told that experts felt the risk was 'one which can reasonably be taken'. The Gardaí did provide a level of surveillance, but Mountbatten found their presence irksome and would not allow them onto his small fishing boat *Shadow V*, which was moored in the harbour.

In the summer of 1979, Mountbatten asked young Paul Maxwell if he would take a holiday job as his boat boy on the *Shadow V*. The fifteen-year-old was thrilled. 'He was fanatically keen on boating and very fond of the water,' said his father, John Maxwell. 'I used to take him out fly fishing for trout on the lakes. He was good.' The Maxwells, who lived in the lakelands near Enniskillen, County Fermanagh, had a cottage at Mullaghmore and used to spend the summer holidays there. It was only a short drive from home, across the border.

Paul got on well with Lord Mountbatten's twin grandsons, Nicholas and Timothy Knatchbull, who, at fourteen, were just a year younger than him and were spending the summer at Classiebawn. Paul's summer job with the family included serving dinner in the castle at night. 'He loved it,' said John. 'He was a very independent sort of child. At home, he used to go down to the market to help a guy who sold radios.' I asked John if it had ever occurred to him that his son might have been at risk. 'I suppose it must have,' he said. 'But Mountbatten spent a lot of time pottering around the harbour on his own. I suppose I would have thought that if the IRA wanted to get him, they had plenty of opportunity. They didn't need to kill other people.'

Summer was ending, and Paul was due to go back to Portora school to start into his 'O' level year in a few days. The morning of 27 August was hot and sunny, after a bad, wet summer, John recalled. 'Paul went out at about eleven. Soon after that, I went down to the harbour to buy a paper, and I saw him out on the deck of the boat. I waved at him, and he waved back.' John was sitting in the sun at the cottage when he heard the explosion.

Full of fear, he jumped into his car and drove to the cliffs. Out on the sea he could see a churned-up area in the water and debris floating in circles around it. He felt that no one could have survived. Down at the harbour, a crowd had gathered. It was a Bank Holiday Monday. John got a fisherman he knew to take him out in the boat. No one spoke as they headed out, and then the man told John it was too late and turned back.

By this time, some of the injured had been brought into the harbour in boats. John ran around frantically asking about his son, and eventually a man told him Paul had been brought to the Pier Head House Hotel, just across the road. He was injured, the man said, but alive. John was elated. He ran into the hotel and was shown a fair-haired, badly injured boy. It was not Paul. It was Timothy Knatchbull, whose twin, Nicholas, had been killed in the blast.

Devastated, John ran back to the harbour, where a fisherman

told him he had Paul's body on his boat. He jumped on board and gathered the body of his child into his arms. 'I thought he might have been still alive, because he was still warm,' he said. 'He didn't have his shirt on; it must have been blown off. His femur was sticking out. His face was covered in pockmarks. He was missing a thumb.'

He rocked Paul in his arms. Suddenly completely full of rage, John began to shout, denouncing the IRA as cowards, demanding to know what they thought they were doing, killing their own people. 'My son was a better Irishman than you,' he yelled. At that moment, he said, he wanted to kill the people who had killed his son. As quickly as it had come, the rage departed and the pain surged in. 'There are really no words to describe such pain,' he said. 'It was utter desolation and loneliness. I thought, "No one should ever have to feel like this."'

Someone brought a blanket, and between them John and the other men gently wrapped Paul's body in it. It felt, he said, broken. Ambulancemen took it away, but John did not go with them. He felt it was useless to do so but it also felt like desertion. Wandering around the harbour, he met a friend from Fermanagh who hadn't heard about the explosion. The man greeted him and said, 'Isn't it a lovely day?' John didn't try to explain.

Later, another man brought John to the mortuary in Sligo to identify Paul's body. He stroked his son's hair, sticky from seawater, and his cut face. Overcome by a sense of sadness, love and loss, John began to cry. 'I felt as if I could never stop,' he said. He smiled, a handsome man in his seventies who looked a lot younger. 'For a week or more afterwards, the only thing I could eat was fruitcake. My sister-in-law kept me supplied with it.'

Three other people had died in the explosion. Lord Mountbatten and his grandson, Nicholas Knatchbull, died at the scene. Lady Doreen Brabourne, who was eighty-three, was injured and died the next day. Her son and his wife, Mount-batten's daughter Patricia, were seriously injured. In her account of the day, Patricia described how, before they set off, her father had been reading a book about the last days of Adolf Hitler. Lord Mountbatten had served in both world wars. The family had discussed the state of their boat and had decided this was probably the last summer it would be seaworthy.

The mood on the boat was happy, she told journalist Alf McCreary. She remembered her mother-in-law saying, 'Isn't it a beautiful day?' Then she heard the explosion. It was while she and her husband were in intensive care in Sligo Hospital that she learnt that her father, her son and her mother-in-law were dead. She struggled with feelings of guilt because her grief for her child overwhelmed her grief for her father, but she came to accept her feelings. Her father and her mother-in-law were old and had enjoyed long and full lives, she said. 'But Nicky, only fourteen years of age, so bright and so lovely, was on the threshold of life. There's nothing you can say to yourself which makes that any easier.'[2]

Patricia told McCreary that she hadn't felt bitter. Maybe, she said, it was because she didn't regard those who carried out the attack as fellow human beings. 'The terrorists seem to be sub-human, a race apart,' she said. She added that she had no anti-Irish feelings either. She said that when she and her husband were transferred to hospital in England, Irish nurses told her they had felt so 'desperately ashamed' about what their fellow countrymen had done that they were reluctant to come and nurse the couple. 'We tried to reassure them that we loved Ireland and that the people who had done this could not be regarded as representatives of their country,' she said.[3]

John Maxwell said he didn't want anyone using his son's death as the excuse for further violence. He knew a lot of the people of Mullaghmore and knew they were horrified by the attack. In a radio broadcast a few days later, he was at pains to say this and to say that he knew the killers were not local to Mullaghmore. However, when I mentioned what Patricia Knatchbull had been quoted as saying, he told me he was unable to share the view that the IRA was 'a race apart'. 'They obviously had considerable support,' he said.

* * *

The twenty-seventh of August 1979 had been a good day for the IRA. Within hours of the Mountbatten bombing, eighteen British soldiers – sixteen of them from the hated Parachute Regiment – had been blown to pieces in two co-ordinated ambushes at Narrow Water on the shores of Carlingford Lough, not far from Newry. The first bomb killed six. The second killed twelve of those sent in to rescue survivors.

The weekly *Republican News* celebrated in its 'war news' columns. These events would remind the English people that Ireland was an occupied country, it said. 'We will tear out their sentimental imperialist heart.' As for the murder of Mount-batten, 'The execution was a way of bringing emotionally home to the English ruling class and its working-class slaves that their government's war on us is going to cost them as well.'[4] The loy-alist UDA held a news conference claiming it had drawn up a 'death list' of republicans and carried out a typical 'doorstep killing' in North Belfast.

In his book *Blanketmen*, former IRA prisoner Richard O'Rawe recalls the news about Mountbatten's death and, later, about the death of the soldiers coming into the Maze prison. There was 'euphoria' among the prisoners over Mountbatten and 'elation' about the soldiers. O'Rawe remembered the behaviour of the paratroopers on internment day and uses the phrase, 'The measure you give is the measure you get.' He describes hearing others talking about their memories of

Bloody Sunday. The 'paras' were 'bloodthirsty killers of inno-cent people'. He writes that he personally felt the killing of Paul Maxwell and the two members of Mountbatten's family was morally unjustifiable.

O'Rawe discussed this day's work by the IRA with leading IRA man Brendan Hughes, who said the 1975 ceasefire had almost defeated the IRA and the Mountbatten attack showed that the new leadership, including Gerry Adams, were 'brilliant strategists'. Overall, the view was that 'the war had taken a turn for the better for the IRA' and that it could be won. Morale in the H-Blocks, where the prisoners were in the throes of a des-perate battle with the British authorities over criminalisation, was lifted.

One of the IRA prisoners was twenty-four-year-old Laurence McKeown, from County Antrim, who had been jailed in 1976 for the attempted murder of a policeman and causing explo-sions. He had not washed for three years and lived in a blacked-out cell, wrapped in a filthy blanket and spreading his excrement on the walls. The maggots the prisoners didn't flick under the doors to annoy the 'screws' turned to flies. He paced the cell for ten hours a day. He was on what the IRA called the 'no-wash' protest and the prison authorities called the 'dirty protest'.

The stench, another prisoner told me, was 'unbelievably hor-rendous'. He compared the prison with a Nazi death camp. 'The only thing missing was the gas ovens,' he said. Republicans fre-quently compared themselves with Hitler's victims. 'SS RUC,' was chanted during confrontations with the police. Unionists angrily pointed out that the IRA prisoners had not been jailed because they were Catholics but because of their own campaign of violence.

There was intense hatred between the prison officers and the prisoners. The IRA had killed ten officers, including the deputy governor of the Maze with responsibility for the H-Blocks, in 1979 alone. The prisoners claimed the officers brutally and routinely beat them, a claim the prison officers deny. When Bobby Sands used to recite his poem 'Crime of Castlereagh', his fellow prisoners applauded wildly and banged their 'piss pots' in appreciation when he got to the epitaph for a prison warder, 'Here Lies a Stinking Screw'.[5]

One officer told me that staff found working on the H-Blocks horrific. 'You were wading in urine. Your eyes would be streaming. The stench was nauseating,' he said. 'You were liable to be killed at any time. Your family had no life.' When news came in of the murder of a prison officer, the IRA prisoners would cheer and gloat; when the fatality was an IRA man, the prison officers returned the compliment.

In 1980, the prisoners embarked on a hunger strike. It ended in confusion and recrimination. As Richard O'Rawe put it, 'Sean McKenna was snatched from the jaws of death.'[6] Months later, in 1981, the IRA's officer in command in the Maze, Bobby Sands, embarked on another one, vowing that he and his comrades would die rather than accept being designated as criminals. The hunger strike was to be phased. As one prisoner died, another would replace him.

This was an ambitious strategy. If the British could not be defeated in armed conflict, they could be broken in a grand moral confrontation. There were, at this stage, more IRA men in prison – around eight hundred of them – than at large.

The prisoners volunteered for the hunger strike but were selected only if they were deemed 'media friendly'. Bik McFarlane was the officer in command of the prisoners, but it was decided that it would be a PR disaster to put him on the strike because he was in jail for killing Protestant civilians.

Bernadette Devlin McAliskey, who as a student civil-rights

leader and then Britain's youngest ever MP had proved herself a brilliant orator, was a leading figure in the 'H-Block committee'. The UDA, which had already assassinated several members of this committee, launched a gun attack on her and her husband at their home, the circumstances suggesting that the British army was well aware of the plan. British soldiers were in the vicinity of the house, which is up a lane in the countryside, but only intervened to arrest the UDA gang as the gunmen left. McAliskey heard one of them say, 'Fuck this for a double-cross.'[7]

She remembered the time of the hunger strikes as agonising. 'The stress was relentless. People were destroyed by the trauma. Most of us survived by being in collective denial of the absolute enormity of what we were part of. People were dying, a minute at a time,' she said. 'Imagine what that was like for their families. Sixty busloads of people went from Tyrone alone down to a hunger-strike march in Dublin. That is how intense it was. The more it went on, the more it seemed like madness. It was a surreal game of poker, and the stakes were people's lives.'[8]

Sands was elected as a Westminster MP, defeating a leading unionist and marking the start of a move towards politics for the republican movement. Laurence McKeown was exhilarated. However, Prime Minister Margaret Thatcher was not for turning. On 5 May, after sixty-six days of starvation, Sands died. A priest brought the news to Laurence and the other prisoners. The mood was sombre, he said, subdued. 'The issue then was his replacement.' Laurence would start his fast in June. According to O'Rawe, 'a light of inspiration had been extinguished, but an eternal flame of valour had been lit'.[9]

Thatcher did not see it in those terms. 'Mr Sands was a convicted criminal,' she told the House of Commons. 'He chose to take his own life. It was a choice his organisation did not allow to many of its victims.'[10] More than 100,000 people attended Sands' funeral in West Belfast.

Bernadette Devlin McAliskey said she always believed Sands would die but had assumed he would be the 'ritual sacrifice' and that Thatcher would then relent. It was quickly apparent that this was not going to happen. The second hunger striker to die was Francis Hughes, from Bellaghy, County Derry. He had been described by the RUC as the most wanted man in the North. He had survived several shoot-outs during which policemen were killed and was responsible for numerous shootings and bombings in South Derry. To the IRA, he was a legend, skilled, disciplined, ruthless and selfless. He had spent years on the run, often moving on foot through the night and sleeping rough in fields and ditches. According to a 2006 eulogy, he 'regularly dressed in combat uniform, openly carrying his rifle, a handgun and several grenades, as well as food rations'. To Protestants, he was a ruthless murderer whose crimes, it was suspected, included murdering a ten-year-old girl, along with her father, a UDR soldier. In revenge for this, loyalists burnt a house down in North Belfast, killing two people.

The poet Seamus Heaney was at a grand event in an Oxford college days after Hughes died and admits he was thrilled to learn he was to sleep in a room belonging to a former Tory government minister. However, he would afterwards write that because of 'ties of memory, affection and community', his thoughts kept turning to the 'corpse house' in Bellaghy where his neighbours, the Hughes's, were holding a wake for their son. His feelings were complicated. Even if he had been at home in Dublin, he would not have gone to the wake or the funeral. 'I would have been susceptible to the traditional sense of obligation, but I would have been wary of the political implication of attendance,' he wrote. 'Suffice to say that the handling of the

1981 hunger strike by the British government of the day had created a moment of entrapment for everybody.'

It was 'intensely emotive' to watch men die because their total willingness to be victims had been met with the total intransigence of Margaret Thatcher. To express support for the prisoners would have been seen as an endorsement of the IRA's violence, but as the deaths continued, the scruple which prevented him showing support for the prisoners' demands began to feel 'unseemly'. Silence began to seem, by default, like support for the 'triumphalist, implacable' government.[11]

I was still living in Dublin at the start of the hunger strike. By this time the slight glamour which had gone with having a Northern accent in the South in the early years of the Troubles had dissipated. We were no longer regarded as quasi-refugees but as reminders of a very dirty conflict. The country was decked out in black flags by supporters of the hunger strikers. Northerners seemed to make people uneasy. There was a perceptible distancing, but sometimes strangers would accost us and launch into angry tirades. The whole country was afflicted.

By the time Laurence McKeown was moved to the hospital wing of the Maze, nine of his comrades had died in the protest. He remembers an orderly, an elderly Protestant man called Bobby, who was kind to the hunger strikers. 'He was what became known as an "ordinary decent criminal" to distinguish them from the "terrorists". Once, one of the screws had confiscated Bobby Sands' tobacco and was boasting about it. The orderly spoke up and said when the tuck shop opened that night, he'd replace it. I remember walking down the corridor with my arm around his shoulder and his arm around my waist when I was too weak to walk alone.'

There was also the novelty of being able to read newspapers and listen to the radio, but Laurence's eyesight was failing. He sat weakly in a chair in the sunshine of the hospital yard and listened to the inhuman sounds that another of the hunger strikers was making as he entered his last days.

'He must have been hallucinating,' said Laurence. 'You could hear this high-pitched gibberish and then deep, low moaning and sobbing. I knew he was in pain. I could hear his mother trying to comfort him, speaking softly at his bedside.'

The families were under intense pressure, Laurence said, from the media and the Church. Their sons had instructed them that they were to let them die, but the Church was encouraging the families to use the power of attorney which passed to them when the prisoner fell unconscious to instruct the authorities to feed them. Several mothers had already done this.

Laurence had discussed this with his mother. He said he wanted to go on to the death. 'She said, "You do what you have to do, and I'll do what I have to do." My family wasn't republican. They would have been SDLP voters. My mother's biggest crime was smuggling tobacco into the prison for me. But she stood by me.'

In August, Mickey Devine died. He had joined the hunger strike after Laurence. 'The focus was on me then,' said Laurence. 'There had been a sense of hope but there came a point when you knew nothing was going to happen. It was a very lonely time. You get used to people dying. I was physically exhausted. I'd done sixty-eight days. Bobby died after sixty-six. The doctors said I could die any time. My sense of smell was heightened, and they used to leave the food in the room with you, breakfast, lunch and supper. My eyesight was gone.

'I used to lie and listen to country-and-western music. The only music I don't like is country and western, but it was all I could listen to then. I'm six foot two and I was seven stone. I knew my family was around me but I don't remember them coming in . . .' Laurence said that his next memory was of waking up and realising 'fairly quickly' that he had been moved and that he was no longer dying. He was in the intensive care unit of the Royal Victoria Hospital in Belfast. 'I was neither happy to be alive nor sad to be alive,' he said. 'I knew I existed.' When he had lost consciousness, his mother had instructed that he be saved.

Laurence was returned to prison to serve the rest of his sixteen-year sentence. 'It was different then, because we had made it different. We had won,' he said. This was not a widely held view at the time. Indeed, the hunger strike was seen as a defeat for the IRA in the sense that the British did not concede political status; however, in the eyes of the world, the prisoners did gain such status, and within weeks of its ending Sinn Féin strategist Danny Morrison was articulating a radical change of direction for the republican movement. 'Who here really believes we can win the war through the ballot box?' he asked delegates at the 1981 Sinn Féin Ard Fheis. 'But will anyone object if, with a ballot box in one hand and an Armalite in the other, we take power in Ireland?'

*   *   *

People were dying on the streets, too. There were intense riots in nationalist areas. A fourteen-year-old Protestant child was killed while helping his father on his milk round. Rioters protesting after the death of Bobby Sands stoned their milk lorry in Belfast and it crashed. His father died soon afterwards.

The RUC and the British army fired more than 31,000 plastic bullets in the three months after Sands' death. The use of the ammunition was controversial. The bullets were meant to be non-lethal and to be used to quell riots. They were supposed to be fired at the legs, but most of those who were killed by them had been shot in the head or upper body. Following unwelcome international publicity, the British had taken to calling them 'baton rounds' instead. Seven people were killed that summer, including three Catholic children, none of them involved in the rioting.

In the early hours of 8 July, hunger striker Joe McDonnell died at the Maze prison. Riots immediately broke out and a sixteen-year-old member of the IRA's youth wing was shot dead during a confrontation between youths with petrol bombs and soldiers on the Falls Road at around eight in the morning.

At around the same time, thirty-three-year-old Norah McCabe set off from her sister's house in one of the side streets off the Falls Road to go to the corner shop for cigarettes. Her marriage to Jim McCabe was volatile, and the couple were living apart for a while after a quarrel. 'We were chalk and cheese. It was a silly argument,' Jim told me. 'I'd gone to my mother's in a huff. She had the children.' Paul was six, Jim junior was two and Aine was three months. Jim said he and Nora were republicans. 'We supported the hunger strikers,' he said.

Norah passed a group of women who had gathered to say the rosary in memory of McDonnell. When she came out of the shop, the group had dispersed and just one woman remained on the street. Suddenly, Norah must have heard the screech of brakes as an RUC Land Rover tore into the street and came to a halt about ten feet behind her. She half turned, there was a bang and she fell to the ground, fatally wounded. She had been shot in the back of the head by a plastic bullet fired by a policeman in the Land Rover, which immediately reversed back out of the narrow street and sped off up the Falls. She died in the Royal Victoria Hospital the following day. 'They told me she would have been a vegetable if she'd survived,' said Jim, bleakly. 'Her skull was shattered.'

Jim had been managing a bookmaker's shop before his wife's death, working six days a week, sometimes late into the evening. 'I was a distant father,' he said. 'That time, in this place, life was all about surviving. We lived in a sort of semi-darkness, surrounded by military activity, the IRA, the British army, the loyalists in the streets. So many people were being killed. You just kept your head down and hoped your turn wouldn't come. So many young people were getting involved around you, climbing down into battle and never coming out. At night you might go to the local shebeen and drink. Night after night, drinking and drinking and drinking.

'You didn't reflect. That would have been a luxury. I think we as a community grew shells. Violence was just part of life. It went over your head. You thought your own family was bullet-proof. But when it visits your own home, when someone points a gun at your wife's head and pulls the trigger, it is a different matter.'

After Norah was murdered, Jim rented a new house and became a full-time parent. His mother became the primary carer for baby Aine. 'People used to stare at a man out looking after children,' he said. 'Nights were the worst time ever. The loneliness. I'd been brought up in a family of twelve and I'd always dreamt of having a room of my own. But you can only take so much silence.'

Jim was full of anger about the killing of his wife but he did not, at first, feel there was anything he could do about it. 'I was occasionally taken out of my little box by certain politicians and journalists and used as an exhibit as to how bad things were. Then I was put back,' he said. 'As well as that, it was 1981 and I was living on the peace line. I was very close to the murder of two people. The loyalist murder gangs were about and they could easily escape across Lanark Way into the Shankill. It would have been dangerous to raise my head above the parapet.'

In November 1982, Jim attended the inquest into his wife's death. He heard several RUC men, who remained anonymous, claim that they were in the area to quell a serious riot and to disperse petrol bombers who had set up a barricade. They denied firing into the street on which Norah McCabe was shot. A named chief superintendent backed up this evidence. Jim said the policemen were laughing and at ease throughout the hearing. The only witness who demurred was the woman who had been at the prayer group. She said the street was quiet when the Land Rover sped in and that she saw the gun, heard the shot and saw sparks before Norah fell. She told Jim afterwards that she began to wonder if she was the one who was lying – the police seemed so confident.

However, unknown to the RUC, Jim's solicitor, Pat Finucane, had a devastating piece of evidence. Shortly after the killing, he had been approached by a Canadian film crew which had been filming reaction to the hunger striker Joe McDonnell's death that morning. The crew handed over a video of the incident; it clearly supported the civilian eyewitness's account. When Finucane produced the video, the court was adjourned, and an RUC inspector was despatched to Canada to interview the film-makers.

A year later, the inquest was reconvened. 'The RUC inspector had done his duty as a responsible policeman should,' said Jim. 'He had thoroughly investigated the video and he told the court it was genuine.' The jury found that there was 'no clear evidence to suggest that there was a legitimate target to be fired at in that street' and that 'neither is there evidence to suggest that the deceased was other than an innocent party'.

Jim was elated. He expected murder charges to be brought against the police, as well as perjury charges for lying to the coroner. What happened next shocked him. 'I was informed that the Director of Public Prosecutions had decided not to bring any charges,' he said. 'After that, I started to live in the real world. I realised these people were intent on killing and that the system would allow them to get away with it.'

Advised by Pat Finucane, Jim sued the chief constable of the RUC. He also took part in a Yorkshire Television documentary about his wife's death, after which seventy British MPs called on the British home secretary to hold a public inquiry. The SDLP leader asked the attorney general to reopen the case. Both were refused. However, in 1984, Jim was awarded compensation, and a lawyer for the police said the RUC accepted that Norah McCabe had been an innocent passer-by. Jim said it was not good enough. He wanted justice: the killer to be brought before a court to explain why he had done it.

'My children kept asking me, "Why did they shoot our mummy?"' he said. 'I didn't have an answer for them.' One day, Aine, still a toddler, was sobbing at her granny's house, and when Jim asked her what was wrong, she said, 'I just want my real mummy back.' Not long after this, Jim became one of the founder members of the Campaign Against Plastic Bullets. 'I was no longer isolated. I was with people who didn't assume that my wife must have been doing something wrong to get shot, people who didn't use that hateful expression, "She was in the wrong place at the wrong time."'

6

Dying for the Queen

In March 1981, when Bobby Sands was embarking on his hunger strike, John Moore was a twenty-year-old British soldier on the night boat to Belfast, about to start a tour of duty in South Armagh. He was with his friend, Gavin 'Deano' Deane. He had joined the army three years earlier in honour of his grandfather, who had told him stories about his own service in the First World War. John and Deano had guarded Buckingham Palace together.

They were stationed in Bessbrook Mill, round the corner from the village where Alan Black, the survivor of the 1976 Kingsmills massacre, lived. 'It was cramped and filthy and packed with a hundred soldiers and police, with naked women wallpaper,' said John. He also spent time in a base at Crossmaglen, known to the army as XMG. 'When we were out on patrol, people looked through us. We were like ghosts in a movie. There was a sense of waiting – hate-filled eyes watching us with loathing, waiting for us to make a fatal error,' he said. 'Yet all this was happening in lovely country like the Yorkshire Dales.'

He showed me a photo of his patrol group company, sixty or so soldiers on a mountain slope, a helicopter hovering above them, with heather and blue skies and smiles. 'Slieve Gullion was like a campsite in France, except for sleeping with rifles and the army-issue spades used to create our toilets!' Michael Longley has written a poem about watching a soldier 'as he sweats up the slopes of Slieve Gullion/With forty pounds of history on his back'. The poet and the soldier 'pass in silence'.[1]

On 19 May, the IRA detonated a landmine from across the border in Louth and blew up a British Saracen as it passed through close to the railway line near Camlough and to the home of hunger striker Raymond McCreesh. John Moore was one of those sent out to form a cordon to bring the bodies back. 'Four Green Jackets and a driver were killed. That had a profound impact on me, on all of us. We'd been playing cards with them the day before. I knew most of them.'

The attack was seen as a gesture of solidarity with McCreesh. 'On our way back through Camlough, local boys came out and bricked us,' said John. 'They were singing that Queen song, "Another One Bites the Dust".' The soldiers killed were aged between nineteen and twenty-seven. McCreesh, who was twenty-four, died in the Maze prison two days after the ambush.

'We were camped out on the hillside overlooking Camlough. Some of our lads found the guns fired over his coffin. At the time, I thought, the more of them committed suicide, the better. At least he had a choice. Squaddies are strange people – we say things in the heat of the moment that are too macho. The yellow card doesn't mean that much to aggressive, heavily armed soldiers either.' The yellow card outlined the rules of engagement and stated that it was forbidden to shoot someone unless that person was seen to be using or threatening to use a weapon first. Soldiers were also meant to give a verbal warning before opening fire.

John's tour of duty was due to finish on 28 July. 'I'd met a girl on R and R [rest and recreation] at Peterborough station and we'd agreed we'd meet in a bar, both wearing pink carnations.

We had one really big mission left to do. We'd been told the IRA were mounting illegal checkpoints along the border and we were told to stop them, either by arresting them or by shooting them – whatever it took.'

John's platoon of about twenty men was told to assemble covertly around a farm and scrapyard close to a border crossing the army knew as 'Hotel 24'. ('Hotel 25' was on the farm belonging to the then IRA leader, Slab Murphy.) 'We knew it was a pretty intense area. A rough area,' said John. They were taken to their positions in unmarked vans under cover of darkness. They were split into bricks – teams of four, although John's brick had only three in it.

'The three of us were friends. There was a Dexy's Midnight Runners song popular round that time called "Geno", and the soldiers used to sing it with "Deano". The photo he had beside his bed was of his seven-year-old sister,' said John. Deano was the brick commander. They were positioned in a derelict van. 'We did our stags – lookouts – one man off, two on. Conditions were very cramped. Cold rations and water. It was hot. There was a packet of melting Rolos in my pocket,' said John. 'We were bored rigid.'

All new young soldiers in Northern Ireland, known as NIGs, were warned it would be 95 per cent pure boredom and 5 per cent sheer terror. They had to look out for dogs – a barking dog could be fatal, and soldiers had, on occasion, killed them. 'We watched a blackbird going in and out of a tiny gap in a small green bush. I wasn't wearing my good-luck charm, a necklace of beads given to me by an old girlfriend. It was broken. We weren't wearing flak jackets either – too bulky.'

At one stage, John was on stag when a man walked along the narrow road. The soldiers had their guns at the ready, and then they saw that he had a child with him. 'We came that close' – John indicated inches with his hand – '. . . to shooting them. We eyeballed the guy but we didn't know if he'd seen us. We gave him the benefit of the doubt – that is probably why I'm here in this wheelchair,' he said.

'It was like a deadly game of hide-and-seek. On the third night, another corporal further along the border was sounding alarm bells. He thought he'd been dicked and he was about to bug out. Then everything fell quiet. It was about half nine. The radio fell silent. It was really eerie. I went on stag at ten o'clock. Moments later, the silence was broken by heavy machine-gun fire.' Describing these moments, John made shooting noises. 'Our 5 per cent of terror had begun. I was almost frozen with raw fear.

'Deano had just lain down to rest. He got up and he got hit, twice, close to his heart and under his armpit. I shot back at where I thought it was coming from. Deano fell next to me. My Armalite ran out of ammunition, so I picked up Deano's SLR [self-loading rifle] and blatted back. I got hit in the head then by a bit of the van, which I still have.' He wheeled himself out to his bathroom and opened a cabinet, coming back with a plastic tube containing two tiny bits of metal.

'I got hit again then. I knew I'd been zapped seriously. It felt as though my body was lifting into the air. Apparently it happens to a lot of people when they get spinal injuries. Although I wasn't fortunate enough to have any religious beliefs, I yelled out to my new instant best friends, God and Jesus. I thought I was dying and going to heaven. A surreal calmness enveloped me.

'I tried to send a message on the radio: "Come and fucking help us, we're in the shit." I am sure the IRA was enjoying my screams for help. I imagined gunmen coming to finish us off or dragging us away and slowly and sadistically torturing us to death just for the sheer fun of it. I thought about Captain Nairac [the IRA murdered Nairac, a British soldier engaged in undercover operations, but his body was never found].

'An intense longing to be at home overwhelmed me,' continued John. 'I called out for my mother and my girlfriend. Deano was lying next to me. The other guy was in the back – he got hit by shrapnel but not seriously. Deano was dying. I could see blood coming out of his mouth like that . . .' He mimed a fountain surging up from his own mouth.

'Some of our lads and our colonel arrived then. There were helicopters and the Gardaí arrived on the other side of the border, but they were too late, weren't they? The lads had got away. We were right on the border, so the IRA had the upper hand. The helicopters took us away, I said, "Look after Deano." They brought us to hospital in Belfast, and that is where my memory finishes for a while. I'd begged for morphine and I'd been given it. Some of us carried it round our necks. Within seconds of taking it you were on cloud nine.'

He pulled up his shirt and showed me the groove where a bullet exited. 'Feel the dent,' he said, which I did. John was put on a life-support machine. 'It was close,' he said. The day after the incident he was flown to a military hospital in Woolwich. While he was in intensive care, he was strapped into a special bed, a sort of metal casket in which he was suspended and which turned every few hours to prevent sores developing on his paralysed body. His father came. He told him that Deano was dead. He'd died just as the helicopter carrying the injured soldiers reached Belfast.

'I remember him telling me,' said John. 'I was looking out through this slit in the frame, upside down. I could hear and see my tears hitting the floor. Deano was twenty-one and one week. My dad had gone to the funeral. I think he was cremated. I am sure the locals in Crossmaglen must have been delighted – another Brit killed on their hallowed soil. He was the 2,348th person to be killed.

'It would have been the same the other way round. If I'd

killed someone, I would have been the toast of the regiment. I'd have felt very good. And the sons and the daughters of the IRA man I'd killed would have been even more determined to kill British soldiers.' Former soldier Jimmy Johnson writes that when he heard 'the Paras had shot 13 Paddies' in Derry in 1972, 'we were all chuffed . . . all the lads in the squadron were cheering'.[2]

'It was another dreadful waste of a young life,' said John. 'Deano would have been briefly mentioned on the news in between the gossip and the looming royal wedding.' That summer in London, Diana Spencer was about to marry Prince Charles. 'Deano was dead, but what had he died for?'

John Moore spent almost a year in hospital. 'The Falklands injured started arriving soon after I got there. Mrs Thatcher came to see them, and Prince Charles. All I got was the padre in intensive care! The Falklands lads were seen as somehow superior to the Ireland lads.' He showed me a photo of him with Simon Weston, the Falklands veteran.

'One night while we were at Woolwich, we were out in a pub, and a crowd of us were talking about our injuries. This woman came over and said to me in a strong Irish accent, "I wish it had been your fucking head." Then she walked out.' After that, other than in his home, John stopped talking about Ireland.

Getting his first wheelchair was 'like Christmas and a funeral all rolled into one – you are excited and yet it is this grotesque thing'. A doctor told him he'd never walk again. He was an incomplete paraplegic – the bullet nipped rather than severed the spinal cord.

Although he was totally paralysed for a while, he recovered some feeling within months. 'If your sensation from nipple line down is 100 per cent, mine would be 5 per cent,' he said. 'Once our regiment came back from South Armagh, a lot of them went funny in the head or took to the drink. The army flew me over to meet them many months later in Aldergrove, but it wasn't the same. I met Deano's mum and dad at a wedding of one of our friends. It was awkward. I didn't know what to say. But I kept in touch with his mum.'

*   *   *

Those who were in the local security forces, the RUC and the UDR, were particularly exposed. They lived in the community. Ulsterisation put them in the front line – but it was a line that could lie anywhere. Most were picked off singly. Being off duty, or having resigned or retired, was no protection, though the IRA did occasionally issue statements after a murder claiming that the victim should have told them he was no longer a serving member of the security forces.

On the last day of July 1981, RUC man Bill Harpur and his family were getting ready to go on holiday to Portrush on the north coast. They had their cases packed, he told me, and he was in the bath when the phone rang. His wife came and told him it was for him. 'A woman's voice said, "We've shot your brother." Then she hung up,' said Bill. He lived at Sion Mills, a small village in Tyrone a few miles from the depressed and troubled town of Strabane. 'I phoned Strabane station. A sergeant said, "Yes, there is someone shot, but we don't know who it is. Come in on duty." So I went in, and they sent me up to the housing estate where it had happened.

'There was a pad [path] up through the garden and on either side of it there were . . . well, I'll call them people. They spat at me and clapped their hands and cheered. My brother Thomas was lying there with blood all around him. He had left the RUC after twelve years. It was dark. I left. I had to go and tell my father and mother.

'It was the INLA [Irish National Liberation Army] shot my

brother, and they said they'd attack the cortège. We had to go seven miles around the town to get to our family burial plot. We were advised not to put a green mat over the grave but to fill it in ourselves. The police had word they were going to do something to the body. The day after the burial, me and two of my brothers went to see everything was OK. The headstone, my grandmother's, had "scum" and "orange bastards" scrawled on it. The wreaths had been thrown away. We could see them along the road.'

Bill said that the day after his brother was murdered, he was 'summoned' by members of the CID. 'They told me they'd the names of the boys that shot my brother. They offered to give them to me. I said no. If you got someone to do a shooting – someone in an illegal organisation – the next time they wanted someone killed, you'd have to do it for them. I wasn't getting into that,' he said.

Bill had been in the UDR before he joined the police in 1977. He lived just yards from the border outside Strabane, but later moved into Sion Mills for security reasons. He had joined the UDR when it was set up, in 1970. 'I was nineteen, and I'm the fourth generation of my people who fought for my British heritage,' he said. 'My grandfather served in the First World War and three of his brothers are lying in a graveyard, killed at that time. My father was a B Special for fifty years. But, of course, they understood nothing – they did away with the B Specials.' This was a source of grievance to many Protestants who believed the B Specials 'knew who was who' and should have been allowed to shoot the IRA from the start.

'In 1978, I was attempted to be murdered,' Bill said. 'The person who tried it got fourteen years. He was in the same pigeon-racing club as me. They hid the gun in the wall to shoot me, but it all went wrong on them. Information led to the finding out of the plot. Life for me in Strabane stopped then. I felt everyone just hated me. The rest of the club members rallied round, I must say. But I felt a wild bit of hurt. It put a great bit of fear into my family.'

He had been just fifty yards from the first UDR man to be shot in the Troubles. 'Strabane was on fire. They wouldn't let the ambulances through to him. The next day, four serving RUC men didn't come back,' he said.

His home was like a fortress, with bulletproof windows and doors. There were constant threats. At Christmas, a card would arrive with a black coffin on it. Bill used to put it in the front window for people to see. 'We were a British family and very bitter people hated us,' said Bill. 'My children wouldn't know what it was like to play in the garden. The steel door couldn't be opened.' He would come home off duty at four in the morning, and his wife would get up to let him sleep. Someone was always awake.

'Known IRA men would rhyme off the registration number of your wife's car to you. They'd say they were going to get me, and I'd say back to them, "Well, I have made arrangements, and if I go, you'll be coming after me a couple of weeks later." Your personal weapon was at your side. Home life was on the edge. The hidden victims were wives. When you were together with a group, there was so much tension you might stay at work for a few drinks.'

The police barracks in Sion Mills was blown up several times. Bill had another lucky escape. 'Me and my comrades entered the base for duty and there was a football lying there. I thought the army had left it and I kicked it. It was full of Semtex and six-inch nails. It didn't explode.'

Bill spoke about his terrible memories. He'd seen a soldier blown up. 'His intestines were hanging on a hawthorn hedge which the magpies were eating.' He witnessed another bomb attack. Something hit him on the neck. As the smoke cleared, he saw his colleague. 'He has no head, just a few strings. His brains are on top of the car. It was his teeth that hit me. I look for my other colleague. He is crawling on the road. He has lost his leg and an eye. Meanwhile, a hostile crowd has gathered. They throw pints of beer into the car and spit at the man who lost his head.'

He survived four murder attempts. 'It is very hard to mind it all,' he said, with a heavy sigh.

* * *

The ballot box part of Sinn Féin's post-hunger strike strategy had already got first Bobby Sands and then his former election agent, Owen Carron, elected as MP for Fermanagh. This prompted unionist MP John Taylor to state that Protestants in the area were living among '30,000 accomplices to murder', and Paisley to say that the IRA had been given a mandate for genocide.

The Armalite claimed another victim in November, when the IRA ambushed an off-duty part-time UDR man in County Fermanagh. Thirty-two-year-old Cecil Graham's wife, Mary, had given birth to their first child, Darren, five weeks earlier. The baby was premature and needed round-the-clock attention, and Mary was unwell. Cecil was a hard-working man. As well as his duties as a UDR private, he had a job in a local factory and he ran the small farm he had inherited from his father. He was also building a bungalow on the farm to replace the caravan in which he and Mary had been living.

Mary and the baby were staying with her parents. Her family was Catholic, though she had 'turned' Church of Ireland when she married Cecil. Her parents lived in a housing estate in Donagh, a village on the Fermanagh border with a strong republican element.

The Graham family was a 'security-force family': Cecil's

father had been in the B Specials for many years, and after it was disbanded, moved into the new UDR. Three of the Graham boys and one of the girls also joined the regiment. The family all lived around the lakes.

Cecil would have been acutely aware of the dangers he faced. The IRA had murdered his elder brother, Ronnie, a part-time UDR man, five months before, while he was delivering coal to a house on the shores of Lough Erne. One of those involved was a thirteen-year-old boy who had been recruited into the youth wing of the IRA by one of his schoolteachers, a woman. (The writer John McGahern, who lived across the border in Leitrim, not far from the Fermanagh lakelands, wrote a television drama about a fanatically nationalist teacher from an earlier period – and was denounced in the republican newspaper *An Phoblacht* [known in English as the *Republican News*] for it.) Another of Cecil's brothers, James, had survived an attempt on his life the previous year.

Cecil varied the times of his evening visits to his wife and baby. However, he was obviously being watched. As he went to drive away from the house, he was shot sixteen times. There was silence in the village. The neighbours stayed in their houses as he lay dying in the street, and he had to drag himself back to the house of his parents-in-law. He was airlifted to hospital but died two days later. At the inquest into his murder, in 1983, his father-in-law said that he was 'a bit upset' that in the intervening two years, 'none of the neighbours had extended sympathy or even mentioned the murder of his son-in-law'.[3]

This was completely contrary to the normal unspoken code of neighbourliness which prevailed in rural Northern Ireland at the time of a bereavement. But this was war, and normal civilities had been abandoned. An RUC man described the housing estate as a 'hard-line republican area', and the coroner said that 'its inhabitants must have felt to some extent terrorised'.[4]

However, this wasn't the full story. There was no love lost between the UDR and the wider nationalist community. A Fermanagh man I knew who had been in the UDR for many years told me that he believed that the IRA could have been defeated if he and his men had been allowed to shoot civil-rights marchers. In 1972, a UDR man was ambushed and murdered by the IRA in the Fermanagh lakelands. Two days later, in what appeared to be a revenge attack, British soldiers stabbed two local Catholic men to death in a frenzied attack. One of them had been prominent in the civil-rights movement in the area. The writer Eugene McCabe has several stories about such killings. One of his characters reasons, 'If we don't do it to them, they'll do it to us, and that's the story to the bitter end.'[5]

In 1980, the SDLP had warned that the UDR had an appalling record: 'Former members . . . have been convicted in the courts of (inter alia) sectarian multiple murder, sectarian pub bombing . . . sectarian arson, sectarian assault, sectarian intimidation, arms theft of their own weapons, conspiracy to pervert justice, arms offences and common criminality of all kinds.' The regiment was known to be 'seriously infiltrated' by loyalist paramilitaries. It was 'identified among the minority community more as a menace to than a support for law and order'.[6]

The IRA had no qualms about killing in the proximity of the newly born. In 1980, it shot dead a British soldier after he had gone to comfort his wife at her family home in Derry after she suffered the stillbirth of their baby. Former IRA man Eamon Collins wrote about his own suggestion that the IRA could ambush and kill an RUC man whose wife was in the maternity ward at the same time as Collins' own wife, Bernie.

'He could be got handy.' Eugene McCabe has one of his characters use this succinct Fermanagh turn of phrase to describe the ease with which people could be set up for murder. A

Fermanagh friend told me that after the IRA killed one UDR man on a particular border road, they put up flags at the bottom of the lanes leading to the homes of several others, 'to show them they were next'.

My friend said that after his brother Cecil was murdered, James Graham used to 'half jokingly' say to people, 'Sure, I'm only living on borrowed time.' In 1985, the IRA caught up with him. A school-bus driver, he was an easy target. He was ambushed one morning as he was about to drive schoolchildren from the Catholic village of Derrylin to the swimming pool in Enniskillen. He was shot more than twenty times in front of the children. The local curate later spoke about hearing the gunmen as they made their getaway. He described their wild howl: 'Yahoo! Yahoo!'

Hilary, the sister of Cecil, Ronnie and James, was also in the UDR and was knocked down and seriously injured when a car burst through a checkpoint at which she was working. She never recovered fully and died young. Author Colm Tóibín records a story told to him in a pub in the village of Brookeborough in 1985. The man said that the fourth brother in the Graham family, who wasn't in the UDR, used to drink in the pub and that someone had recently said to him, 'as a joke, as a throwaway line, something like: "If you don't finish that drink, I'll kill you."' The man told Tóibín that the Graham brother had replied: 'Sure, you've killed my three brothers, you might as well kill me.'[7]

7

The Mother of a Son, the Son of a Mother

'I do not grudge them: Lord, I do not grudge
My two strong sons that I have seen go out
To break their strength and die, they and a few,
In bloody protest for a glorious thing,
They shall be spoken of among their people,
The generations shall remember them,
And call them blessed . . .'
                    Padraig Pearse, 'The Mother'[1]

On a dark, miserable night in December 1984, Nora MacBride was far from her home in County Derry, attending a meeting in County Kildare in the Republic. It was a reunion of pilgrims and helpers who had taken handicapped children to the shrine at Lourdes in France. Her eldest son, Tony, was meant to be at the meeting as well, but hadn't turned up. 'I was talking to a priest there and had this thought,' said Nora. 'It was just a calm, clear thought that came into my head: the next time I talk to you it will be to tell you that Anthony is dead.' She was right.

Tony MacBride was in a remote part of Fermanagh that night, on the border with Donegal in the Republic. In a long black Crombie coat over a pinstripe suit, he was walking along a country road through sleet and fog. He had been called in at the last minute to drive a van for a four-man IRA unit. Tony was walking from the van. The operation had already gone wrong.

The IRA had planted hoax firebombs at a hotel frequented by police personnel and had planted a landmine under the road the police would use to get to the hotel. However, the landmine had failed to explode. The two men who planted it had escaped, running across the border to the Republic.

Tony was walking towards the spot where two of his armed comrades were hiding in the ditch. They could hear his foot-steps as he approached through the swirl of fog and wet snow. He would have seen a car parked on the road outside a house. Suddenly, the IRA men heard other boots on the road and an English voice ordering Tony to halt and demanding, 'Where's your fucking gun?'

According to the IRA, Tony put up his arms and said he had no gun. According to the SAS, which was responsible for the ambush, a soldier had fired at the fleeing IRA man, who, as he fell, had made as if to reach for a weapon. The soldier said he shot him again, as did another soldier also in pursuit.

The IRA version of what followed is that while the wounded Tony MacBride lay on the ground, the soldiers began beating and kicking him. The volunteers in the ditch opened fire, fatally wounding a soldier, Alistair Slater. They also put up flares. More SAS soldiers arrived in another car, which skidded and spun on the icy road. Then there was blue light in the snow as an ambu-lance arrived, called by the soldiers. According to the IRA, a burst of shots and then two single shots were heard: the SAS had shot Tony in the back as he lay handcuffed and seriously injured on the ground. The coroner at Tony's inquest con-cluded he had been unarmed but that he was shot in the chest. 'The soldiers said they knew he was an IRA man by his boots,' said Nora. 'But Anthony was wearing fine black boots.'

On the night of the ambush, Nora drove back to the North through the cold and the snow, with only her premonition to indicate that anything was wrong. 'Before I lay down it was on the news that a soldier and a civilian had been shot dead in an incident in Fermanagh. It connected in my mind with the thought I'd had, and I was going to wake my son Lughaidh to tell him, but I didn't. In the morning he came and woke me. He said, "Don't cry and get upset. Anthony is dead."'

Tony MacBride had, it seems, decided to join the IRA when he was still a boy. His parents, Frank and Nora, brought their family of six children up in a terrace house in predominantly Protestant East Belfast. Nora remembered loyalist vigilantes at the end of the street.

The house was stoned, then petrol-bombed, and then, in 1972, gunmen came. They shot Frank and fourteen-year-old Tony. Some of the boys had first-aid training and saved their father's life, but within a year his arteries burst and he died, aged sixty-two. Tony became the father figure and the family moved to predominantly Protestant Newtownards. 'From the frying pan into the fire,' said Nora. The older boys got bad sectarian beatings. Tony would go out, a sixteen-year-old with a brush handle, and take on a gang.

Nora said her son had become politicised at his grandmother's knee. 'It was circumstances and my mother between them. She used to be telling him stories about how they were raided by the Black and Tans in the 1920s.' This was a British auxiliary force notorious for its brutality.

By the time they moved to South Derry in 1976, Tony and his brothers were Sinn Féin activists, putting up posters in support of the 'blanket men' in the Maze prison, with broken glass in the paste to cut the hands of the UDR men who tried to tear them down. Tony's brother Oistin says they took pleasure in finding blood on the posters. 'It sounds terrible now, but that's the way things were.'

This was the heartland of Willie McCrea, one of Ian Paisley's right-hand men, a well-known preacher, an implacable opponent of republicanism and a gospel and country-and-western singer. He used to organise prayer meetings at the same time as the MacBrides organised republican rallies, and there were frequent disturbances.

Tony MacBride joined the IRA. He campaigned for the

prisoners, he quite probably killed, he went on the run for long periods, he went on speaking tours for Sinn Féin, he went to jail. Oistin described him as being 'like a republican priest, an apostle of the republican faith'. Nora said he was very religious. He would not eat on Good Friday and he would spend a lot of time in his room with a candle lit, reading the gospels. 'He always carried his rosary beads and a miraculous medal,' she said.

'Anthony joined the Irish army when he was seventeen, the year after his father died. Looking back, I can see he did it for the military training. He was very disciplined. He told me that he didn't like fighting, but we couldn't just let our people be murdered. I used to think, at times, there must be a better way, but I didn't know what it was. I was sympathetic – I knew the abuse people were getting. I was in the relatives' action committee when he was in jail for gun smuggling. I just prayed and prayed. After Bobby Sands died in 1981, I thought they won't let any more die. I remember after Thomas McIlwee died I was in Lourdes and I couldn't imagine how Mrs McIlwee would cope. I little thought it would come to my door.'

When the body was being returned to the family home, there was a heavy police presence along the way and in Magherafelt. 'Some policemen turned their backs on the coffin, but one older policeman saluted,' said Nora. 'I thought, "Good for you, to show respect for the dead."' The funeral was mayhem. Riot police surrounded the house, and Nora had to ask them to move the Land Rovers back to let mourners through.

Oistin said they'd beaten people up at the house and on the way to the graveyard and rammed his car with a jeep. There were scuffles and fights and arrests. A lot of relatives were too scared to come; few of his classmates from school did, and no one from his university year in Belfast. Gerry Adams, Martin McGuinness and other leading republican figures were there. 'The boys put a tricolour on the coffin,' Nora said. 'The police charged. I said, "Link arms and stand your ground. We will bury my son with dignity."'

Once Tony had been killed, the family's status in the locality changed. It was out in the open that they had IRA connections. Tony was described in media reports as a 'well-known terrorist'. 'There was a lot of hurt,' Nora said. 'I was called a murdering granny. Women would spit at me and people pushed trollies at me in the supermarket. There were friends who crossed the street so as not to be seen talking to me.' She said she was comforted by letters from priests who said Anthony had been a 'good Christian' and a 'committed soldier'.

Oistin MacBride took photographs of ugly scenes at funerals, some of them occurring when the RUC moved in to try to arrest IRA colour parties that would fire shots over the coffins of dead volunteers. The Church had decreed that there were to be no paramilitary displays on church property. 'We used to say the rosary every night for the hunger strikers at the church in Magherafelt,' said Oistin. 'Then they locked us out. The priests denigrated us from the altar.' The Pope, John Paul II, had come to Ireland in 1979 and begged the IRA to give up its violence.

Boots kept featuring in the MacBride family history. One of the photographs Oistin published in his book *Family, Friends and Neighbours* shows a pair of work boots sitting on a kitchen chair. Their owner was dead, and Oistin said the house had been abandoned. 'The life had gone out of the house; the boots were like a ghost.' The caption explains that they belonged to an IRA volunteer who was killed when a booby-trap bomb he was planting under an RUC man's car had exploded prematurely. He was still alive and conscious, though with appalling injuries, when the RUC arrived. Oistin reports with obvious indignation that the IRA man was 'dragged from beneath the car and viciously questioned'.[2] He makes no allowances for the fact that this bomb had been intended to kill a colleague of these policemen.

Oistin had written a speech which he delivered at a family memorial event that perhaps explains his attitude. A young SAS soldier was killed during the ambush in which Tony MacBride also died. Tony 'wanted so much to live for Ireland, not die on a cold road beside a foreign soldier who was the same age and also single,' he wrote. 'Their blood may well have mixed on the tarmac but there for us the commonality ends.'[3]

It reminded me of lines from Louis MacNeice's 'Autumn Journal': 'Nightmare leaves fatigue:/We envy men of action/ Who sleep and wake, murder and intrigue/Without being doubtful, without being haunted/And I envy the intransigence of my own/Countrymen who shoot to kill and never/See the victim's face become their own/Or find his motives sabotage their motives.'[4]

There were nine IRA volunteers killed between December 1984 and February 1985, when the IRA killed nine RUC officers in a mortar-bomb attack in Newry. 'You were very exposed,' Oistin said. 'You had no time to wallow. You had to be strong and defiant and keep fighting for the others. A soldier dying in battle isn't normal; your grief is tinged with patriotism and pride. You were public property. You had to keep up an image of strength and dignity.

'Some people put you on a pedestal – it was Ra-Ra this and Ra-Ra that. You were a local icon; you were ruthlessly exploited by the republican movement. The first anniversary of Tony's death was a big affair with band parades and commemorations.'

Nora lost not just her son but the man who had replaced her husband as the male head of the household. 'He was very thoughtful. When he was away he would come back with a bag of fruit and maybe a gas cylinder,' she said. 'With his military training he always made sure everyone had shining shoes.'

* * *

Peggy Whyte had no time for violence and was determined that none of her eight children would get mixed up in it. She and her family lived on Belfast's University Street. 'It was a wonderfully bizarre area to grow up in,' her son, Jude, said. 'We had Women's Aid on one side and the Lutheran church on the other. In the '60s, Queen's was the centre of the universe.' This was the area celebrated by Padraic Fiacc. 'Our Paris part of Belfast has decap-itated lampposts now,' he writes.[5] Once the conflict started, Jude knew they were conspicuous, a big Catholic family with seven boys of an age to be 'involved'.

Peggy was a member of the middle-of-the-road Alliance Party, said Jude. 'The only thing you could get smacked for in our house was for saying something that could be taken as con-doning sectarianism. Half the family had gone to London. My sister Ann went there with Edith from the Shankill – they were lesbians. They died in a car crash. My mother used to say to my father, "Don't wallow in your grief."'

I'd met Jude often in 1982, when I shared a flat with a mutual friend around the corner from University Street. We had a lot of parties, and Jude would come, a witty, emotional man with a bit of a temper.

In April 1983, the Whytes were woken one night by an explo-sion. Peggy rushed out and found a young man lying badly injured in front of her house. He had been planting a bomb and it had exploded prematurely, blowing off his arm, his ear and part of his face. 'My mother went out and put a pillow under his head and comforted him,' said Jude. 'I thought that because she had done that it would get us off the hook.'

He went to the trial of the 'failed' bomber. The court was packed with loyalists, many of them from the Donegall Road area, not far from the Whyte family home. 'A rough crew,' Jude said. The bomber got a seven-year recorded sentence; he was not sent to jail. 'His life was ruined anyway. I often wondered how he felt about what he'd done.

'After the first bomb, I had pleaded with my mother on bended knee to leave University Street. But the family had lived there since 1911. She loved it. I was her blue-eyed boy, her favourite. Jim, she called me.' A devastated look crossed Jude's face. 'I should have made her move,' he said.

A silence. 'What am I talking about? She wouldn't listen. She was a cantankerous rascal when I think of it, a fiery wee woman. My kids were the first grandchildren and we lived just round the corner. Anyway, she thought she was cut from a wee bit finer a cloth than to live in one of the completely Catholic areas down the road.'

Jude might well have considered himself at risk, too. 'I had myself convinced they wouldn't know where I lived,' he said. Belfast was odd, that way, during the Troubles. People who lived a couple of streets away from hard-line areas under paramilitary control would tell you that their street was safe, as if there were invisible lines protecting them.

The second bomb came a year after the first. Jude was woken at half two in the morning by the sound of the front door being kicked and his brother shouting for him to come down. His brother told him his mother had been badly hurt, along with a young policeman. 'We walked through the doors of the City Hospital, and this stunningly beautiful middle-aged woman said, "I am very sorry, we couldn't do anything about it,"' said Jude. 'Daddy was lying on a trolley, disorientated. He had been behind Mummy when it exploded. He only had minor injuries. In the waiting room the family of the policeman, Michael Dawson, were sobbing quietly. He was dead, too.'

Peggy Whyte was a part-time taxi driver. Jude thinks the UDR tipped off the UVF about her hours. 'The UDR had the

Catholics in that area tortured,' he said. She'd been out working and arrived home in the early hours to see a sports bag on the windowsill. She went inside and rang the police, who arrived within minutes. As the two policemen walked up the drive and she walked out the door, the bomb exploded.

'There had been that many bombings and killings around then,' says Jude. Ten people were killed that month. Four days before his mother's murder, the IRA had shot dead a twenty-two-year-old woman, in the nearby Malone Road area, as she and her family left Mass. Their intended target was her father, a magistrate. He would later say that the look he had witnessed on the face of the gunman was 'out of hell itself'.

'After Mummy died there was a massive outpouring of grief,' said Jude. 'She was a grandmother. That made it different. The day after, I went to Braniel, to the home of the policeman's parents, with a wreath. That led to a lot of "United in Grief" headlines. I was very naive. I had no idea that would overtake the murders as a story.'

The reality was, as usual, more complex. 'I went into the house and there were a lot of Protestant ministers. The family was polite and we were served tea in china cups, but there was something unspoken, a poisonous atmosphere almost. They couldn't fathom why we were there. Then one of them said, "Why did you come over here? You can't undo what the IRA has done."'

It soon became obvious, though, that the bomb was loyalist rather than republican, but the UVF never did claim it – probably, Jude believed, because while killing a Catholic was fine by their supporters, they had killed a policeman as well. Jude said that the police seemed to assume that his family was in the IRA and that the unfortunate policeman had been the only innocent victim. Peggy's funeral was huge. 'All the great and the good were there – except the RUC.'

Jude also wrote to Michael Dawson's widow. 'I said I was very sorry about the death of her husband, who died protecting my family.' He handed the letter in for delivery to Mrs Dawson at Donegall Pass RUC, marked 'Private'. He was upset when he learnt that the police had opened the letter.

'Michael Dawson's parents rang me a couple of months later; they had clearly seen the letter. We had a long and very emotional conversation. He was around the same age as me. If I'd been born and reared in Braniel, I might have joined the police, too.'

The explosion had wrecked the family home. 'Home had gone with her,' Jude said. Jude left his own house that night and never returned to it. There was nowhere to bring his mother's body home to; she was buried from a funeral parlour. Jude and his wife and children moved in with a friend. His father moved in with one of his brothers, and later with a sister.

'There was something taken away that night,' Jude said. 'Leaving the area was nearly like a death in itself. I moved to West Belfast, and my employer relocated my job. It was a totally different place, a monocultural wilderness. In lucid moments, I felt safe. But overwhelmingly the feeling was of self-destruction and mental breakdown.

'I began to be paranoid. I think I became intolerable to live with. I changed my driving routes all the time as if I was being watched. I used to sleep with a knife under my pillow.' He picked up a knife from the table where we were sitting, an ordinary dining knife without even a serrated edge. 'A knife like that,' he said, shaking his head at the madness of it.

'I was afraid of everything. My wife used to say, "You are only imagining things." Grief makes you selfish. My marriage broke up in 1987. I was a very angry man in those years.'

8

The Darkness Before the Dawn

'Now I know us plain folks don't see all the story
And I know this peace and love's just copping out
And I guess these young boys dying in the ditches
Is just what being free is all about
And how this twisted wreckage down on main street
Will bring us all together in the end
And we'll go marching down the road to freedom . . .
Freedom.'

Paul Brady, 'The Island'[1]

On Remembrance Sunday 1987, without warning, the IRA detonated a bomb at the cenotaph in Enniskillen. Ten people were killed and others horribly injured. 'There seemed to be a deathly silence, then all hell broke loose . . .' one survivor remembered. They had gathered to commemorate relatives who had been killed in the First and Second World Wars. The IRA also placed a bomb at Tullyhommon, a border village where a large number of children – Girl Guides and Boy Scouts – were taking part in a commemoration. It failed to go off. After the bomb in Enniskillen, the IRA tried to blame the British army. To most observers, though, the evidence was clear: this was a sectarian massacre.

It was a tragedy for Enniskillen and a deeply shocking event for a population which had seemed inured by years of carnage. The then British Secretary of State for Northern Ireland visited the critically injured Jim Dixon in hospital. Mr Dixon told him he had 'hands dripping with the blood of the Protestants of Ulster'.[2]

His rage was widely felt. Unionists had been shocked and

deeply angered in 1985 when the British prime minister, Margaret Thatcher, signed the Anglo-Irish Agreement with the Irish Taoiseach, Garret Fitzgerald. The Agreement gave the Republic a formal consultative role in Northern Ireland and marked a significant shift in relations between the two governments. It signalled that the focus had shifted from the territorial argument over the North's sovereignty, Irish or British. Instead, both now regarded the North as a common problem requiring a co-operative approach. Ian Paisley claimed that the Agreement was a disaster and that Protestants would resist it 'to the very death', and said Thatcher would 'wade knee deep in the blood of loyalists for this document of treachery and deceit'.[3]

There were disturbances and protests in Protestant areas all across the North, with graffiti loudly declaring, 'Ulster Says No.' In late 1986, Paisley was the key speaker at a meeting at which it was announced that the 'Ulster Resistance' was to recruit 'men willing and prepared to take direct action'. The following day, thousands of men in paramilitary gear and with red berets paraded in County Down. There was widespread intimidation of Catholics, and loyalists also turned on the RUC.

The Agreement appeared to be having the effect desired by the two governments when support for Sinn Féin dropped in the 1987 elections, though the party's president, Gerry Adams, retained the West Belfast seat he had won in 1983.

The Enniskillen bomb was a PR disaster for his party. The 'ballot box and Armalite' strategy was seriously undermined. The parish priest for Enniskillen, Monsignor Sean Cahill, condemned the bombing as an evil act which could not be morally justified. There was 'no longer any room for romantic illusion'. Those in the Catholic community who helped the IRA in any way shared in 'the awful crime of murder'.[4]

There were fears that the bombing might unleash a horrific

loyalist response. However, there was to be a small voice of peace, and it captured the imagination of people around the world. Days after the bomb, Gordon Wilson, who had been injured, gave an interview to BBC journalist Mike Gaston. He spoke in a quiet, heartbroken voice about the death of his daughter, Marie, in the blast.

He himself had been buried under the rubble, and he said that he found Marie's hand as he lay there. He asked her several times if she was all right, and she said yes; then, the fifth time he asked, she replied, 'Daddy, I love you very much.' Wilson said those were the last words she spoke. (I remember reading an article by a British journalist in which he said that this version of events was complete nonsense and that it couldn't have happened. I was shocked. It seemed almost sacrilegious.)

The words for which Gordon Wilson became famous were: 'I have lost my daughter and we shall miss her, but I bear no ill will, I bear no grudge. Dirty sort of talk is not going to bring her back to life . . . she's in heaven, and we'll meet again.' He said her death was part of God's plan, and that if he didn't believe that, he would commit suicide.

During a US concert in U2's Rattle and Hum tour, lead singer Bono launched a scathing attack on Irish Americans who talked about 'the glory of dying for the revolution' in Ireland. Against the background of the song 'Sunday, Bloody Sunday', a protest against Britain's actions on that day in 1972, Bono demanded: 'Where's the glory in bombing a Remembrance Day parade of old-age pensioners . . .?' He ended his tirade with a passionate 'No more!'[5]

People thought Enniskillen was a turning point. Playwright Frank McGuinness ended a powerful article in the *Irish Times* with a reference to Yeats's poem about Easter 1916. Yeats's lines 'All is changed, changed utterly/A terrible beauty is born' are echoed in 'All Is Changed after Enniskillen'.[6] Sadly, while change was coming, it was coming slowly, and the bloodshed was very far from ending.

* * *

In 1990, the IRA kidnapped Patsy Gillespie from Derry. They tied him into a van and forced him to drive a bomb into the middle of a British army checkpoint at Coshquin, near the border with Donegal. The IRA then detonated it, killing Patsy and five British soldiers. Patsy had been used as a human bomb. His wife, Kathleen, was under IRA guard at the family home a few miles away in the city when she heard the explosion.

'Patsy wasn't perfect but he was as near perfect as a man could be,' she told me. 'He was full of life.' They had met when she was sixteen and he was eighteen, and had been married twenty years. Their first child was stillborn in 1971. They had three more children, Patrick, Ciaran and Jennifer. 'That is all I ever wanted in life, to get married and have wains,' said Kathleen. Wains are 'wee ones'.

I met Kathleen in a chilly hotel beside the walls of Derry on a snowy winter morning in 2007. She had been furious with me because I had botched a previous arrangement we'd made, stupidly failing to ring her when I'd said I would. She'd rearranged her plans to fit me in and felt I'd shown her no respect. The interview was off. 'Full stop,' she said.

I felt ashamed. Kathleen Gillespie deserved to be treated with respect. I wrote and apologised. It took a while for her anger to subside, but she did relent, agreeing to give me another chance. She swept into the hotel, an elegant woman with short blonde hair and big expressive eyes. We got coffee and she began to talk. She talked for four hours.

Patsy had his own business, selling fruit and vegetables from a van. He didn't drink, but when he went bankrupt, Kathleen realised he had a gambling problem. 'I got that under control and I managed our finances,' she said. She worked two nights a week on the checkout at a supermarket. They bought the house Patsy grew up in and rebuilt it.

He got manual work on a naval ship that was docked down in the quays, and in 1973, he was offered redundancy or work in the kitchens at the army base, Fort George. He had left school early and he had no training, and jobs were hard to come by for Derry Catholics. He took the job on the base. 'The first bother we had was in 1986,' said Kathleen. 'There were a lot of warnings from the IRA about civilian workers for the army. Patsy said he wasn't going to let anyone threaten him out of a job.'

Gunmen came to the house one night that year and took the family hostage. Thanks to his job, Patsy had clearance to drive through British army checkpoints, so the IRA made him drive into Fort George with a bomb in the car. He had time to jump clear and shout a warning. The army carried out a controlled explosion and disabled the bomb. No one was hurt.

'We were offered a move to anywhere we wanted. Patsy maintained he wasn't moving. He wasn't letting the IRA dictate his life. The memory fades. You think lightning never strikes twice. You think everything will be all right,' said Kathleen. 'The actual night it happened, it was obvious they'd been watching us. They knew our routine.' On Tuesday nights, the couple usually visited friends who lived, as it happened, down near the Coshquin checkpoint. Their eldest child, Patrick, was in London, working to save up for a car. It was his eighteenth birthday the next day and he rang to say his friends were taking him out on a pub crawl.

'Oh God, looking back at all that. This doesn't get any easier, no matter how many times I tell it. Every time you remember something different. I find it very hard to tell you this part. His daddy said to him, "Don't be getting drunk and making a fool of yourself." And those were the last words he ever said to him.'

Jennifer was twelve. Her parents usually left her with Ciaran, who was sixteen, but he hadn't arrived back that night, so at a quarter to ten they decided they would go down to their friends' house just for a short while. They told Jennifer not to open the door or answer the phone, but when they got to Coshquin, Patsy was worried about her, so they didn't stay long.

'When we got back to the house, there was a key in the door. A figure came up the hall with a mask on. I thought it was Ciaran playing around and I said, "That's not funny." Then I could hear Jennifer crying. I went into the living room and she was cowering in a chair. This other boy in a mask in the room said to me, "We haven't touched her, missus."

'I cuddled Jennifer and I said to them, "Take the car if you want it."' There were five IRA men, all masked, one of them obviously the leader. The first time this had happened to them Kathleen had realised afterwards that she hadn't been very observant, so this time she noticed everything about the men: their height, their clothes, their voices. The leader said that if the Gillespies did what they were told, nobody would get hurt. 'He said they were waiting for a phone call on our phone and when it came they would be gone.

'Ciaran came home then with his girlfriend. The men took Patsy out of the room and into our bedroom. When they brought him back, he sat on the arm of the chair and put his arms around me and Jennifer. He said, "Don't worry, girl." He always called me Kate or "girl". "Everything will be all right. It will be just like the last time." I was stupid enough to believe that. I said, "Watch yourself, I'll see you soon." Then they took him away in our car.' In a newspaper report at the time, Kathleen was quoted as saying that once they took her husband away, she knew she would never see him again. 'No, that's wrong,' she told me.

Kathleen kept questioning the ones who stayed behind about

what was happening. About an hour and a half later, the men who had taken Patsy came back in the Gillespies' car, without him. At about five to four in the morning, the phone rang. 'The man in charge, whose identity I believe I know, said, "Give us half an hour and your husband will be back,"' remembered Kathleen. He pulled the wires out of the receiver of the phone in the living room, and then the gang left, taking the Gillespies' car again.

'I watched them go down the street, and then, later on, the explosion happened. I said, "That's the bomb. Your daddy will be home soon." I rang Fort George from the bedroom phone, and they said they were very busy, there'd been a terrible explosion and they couldn't talk to me. I said, "No, listen." I told them what had happened. Then I rang my friends at Coshquin whom we'd been visiting. They said they'd seen our car parked across the road.'

The IRA had parked the car across the road which led to the bomb site, presumably so that the authorities would suspect it was booby-trapped, thus delaying the rescue.

'I went out down the road to see would I meet Patsy coming back,' said Kathleen. 'There was an army checkpoint set up at a Land Rover, and I asked them did they know where Patsy was? They must have thought I was mad. I came home again, and then my friend Mary Bradley arrived and said it was all in the news: five soldiers dead and one civilian missing, presumed dead.

'My priest, Andy Dolan, came and stayed with me all day. He went out at one point to see what the news was, and when he came back he asked me did Patsy have anything with a grey zip? I said he did have a grey sweater with a zip but it was in the bedroom. I frantically searched for it, but it was gone.'

Kathleen stopped and there was silence for a moment. She was very pale. 'That was how Patsy was identified. A piece of a grey zip with a bit of flesh attached. At the morgue, I still didn't get it. I said to Andy, "Do I have to go in and identify Patsy?" I said, "I have to see him." Andy said, "Kathleen, there really is nothing to see." How can you accept someone is dead when you don't see them?'

The IRA had chosen Patsy again because he had clearance to enter army installations without the full security checks to which other drivers had to submit. This time, though, the plan required him to die. 'They got him to drive across the border in our car to a safe house in the Republic,' said Kathleen. 'To go through the checkpoint on the way down, they had to remove their masks. From the minute they did that, Patsy had to know he was going to die.'

The route was the same as the one he and Kathleen had taken to visit their friends at Coshquin earlier that night. At the safe house, he was chained into a van containing a huge bomb and told to drive it back to the checkpoint. The explosion killed three soldiers instantly. Two others died before they reached hospital. Patsy was gone.

It was a huge story, one of those that could still bring the cameras in from around the world. The bishop of Derry, Edward Daly, said the IRA had crossed 'a new threshold of evil'. Once again, the ballot box and the Armalite strategy had shown that violence had a ruinous potential to alienate those voters who had lent their support to Sinn Féin but who did not support the IRA.

In 1986, the IRA had issued a list of all those it claimed were to be 'treated as collaborators', in other words, regarded as 'legitimate targets'. They included civil servants, suppliers of vending machines and British Telecom workers. It had already threatened those working in any capacity for the security forces and had killed several building contractors and their workers. Speaking at a republican commemoration that year, Martin McGuinness said that this 'posed serious problems for the British government'.[7]

However, the use of an ordinary working man, from the city where Bloody Sunday had taken place, as a bomb to kill soldiers posed serious problems for the republican movement. The murder of Patsy Gillespie shocked people who felt that a new threshold had already been crossed with the Enniskillen bomb.

Kathleen Gillespie was worried that her son Patrick would see the television news about the Coshquin bomb in London and notice his family's car. She rang him and asked him to come home; she didn't want to tell him on the phone. But he insisted she tell him what was going on. 'I said, "They've killed your daddy,"' she said. 'He started to scream. "Those bastards, I'll fucking kill them . . ."' Kathleen cried as she recounted this part of her story. 'I was so afraid my boys would do something stupid. But they didn't.'

She did a lot of media interviews around the time of the murders. 'People used to say to me, "You are very outspoken – are you not afraid?" I said, "No, they'll not touch me. They've done what they wanted."'

'I went through the funeral in an almost comatose state,' remembered Kathleen. 'I hadn't slept for days. They had to take me away from the house because the place was swarming with media. I never cried once during the funeral. I didn't want them to see what they had done to me. I never went out since without my make-up on, for the same reason.

'After the funeral, my family wanted to make up my bed with clean sheets, but I insisted I wanted to sleep on the sheets that Patsy lay on. There is a climbing rose around my bedroom window. A few weeks later I heard scratching at the window. I thought, "It's Patsy. He wants to get in and the rose is stopping him." I got up and went out and cut the rose to its roots. I had myself convinced Patsy had escaped the explosion and run away, because if they'd caught him, they'd kill him. Every time the phone rang, I'd think it was him. He'd be ringing to say, "I'm in Australia, bring the wains and come."

'My head knew Patsy was dead but my heart didn't want him to be, so this was my fantasy, that a new life was going to open up. I loved Patsy so much, and I know he loved me. I could never imagine living without him.

'There was constant laughing and carrying on when he was around. Friends used to say to me, "Whatever you are doing, you are doing it right." We'd have gone to dances and he'd have got up and danced and hoolied all night with the old ladies. They loved him. He was a great cook, and when he'd had a couple of drinks he'd have cooked for the whole of Derry. When I went to my friends' houses, their husbands would go to the pub. When they came to mine, Patsy would cook for us, wash up and then drive my friends home.

'My state of denial lasted two years until the inquest. Father Andy came with me. It came out in the soldiers' evidence that Patsy had saved a lot of lives,' she said. 'He shouted out to them, "Run! Run! I'm loaded with a bomb here." Then it was the turn of the detectives. I was OK until they started talking about numbered body bags. I realised they were talking about Patsy. I left then and collected Jennifer from school and we drove up to Malin Head.' Malin is the most northerly point of Donegal, a beautiful, wild place where a friend of Kathleen's was living.

Kathleen and Patsy had talked about what would happen if one of them died. 'He said, "If I go first, don't be on your own. You weren't meant to be alone. Find someone else." I said, "See if I go first and you meet someone – I'll haunt you for the rest of your life!"

'He has come back to me three times. I used to get nightmares. They showed Patsy all put back together but in the wrong way – with his head coming out of his hip, and . . .' She shuddered. 'Just all wrong. One night I'd been out and I couldn't face going home to bed. I called at the parochial house, but Andy wasn't there so I just drove around for hours.

'When I finally went home and went to bed, I was sitting up reading and I sensed something. Patsy was standing inside the bedroom door. He was wearing the grey zip-up cardigan. He had his full black beard and his lovely long thick eyelashes. He said to me, "Look, I'm all right, girl, and I'm happy so long as you are all right." I blinked and he was gone.

'Then there was a healing service at the chapel, and the sermon was all about the last day and how we would all be together. I felt the priest was talking to me and telling me Patsy was all right and not the way I'd seen him in those nightmares. It gave me the shivers.

'Patsy used to spoon me or I'd spoon him in bed. Another night I felt the bed go down and the warmth and I got wrapped around.' She smiled. 'Maybe it was just wishful thinking, but it was so strong.'

* * *

In 1989, the British Secretary of State, Peter Brooke, admitted that the IRA could not be defeated militarily. Sinn Féin president Gerry Adams warned IRA volunteers that they had to be 'careful and careful again'. The following year, Brooke declared that Britain had 'no selfish strategic or economic interest in Northern Ireland'. Adams announced that Sinn Féin's position was one of 'critical support' for the IRA and it shouldn't be required to defend everything the IRA did.

The peace process was under way. The British banned the UDA in 1992; astonishingly, it had remained legal through more than two decades of sectarian killings. The SDLP's John Hume was central to a complex network of talks between the various parties, including, behind the scenes, Sinn Féin and the IRA. The process survived the IRA's mortar-bombing of 10 Downing

Street in 1991, which narrowly missed the prime minister, John Major, and bombs in Protestant towns across Northern Ireland and in Britain. Unionists were incensed at what they saw as the appeasement of the men of violence. Their own men of violence, the loyalist paramilitaries, threatened 'all-out war' and launched a new wave of killings. Unionist MP John Taylor predicted civil war.

During the summer of 1993, I interviewed a large party of leading UDA men in rooms above Frizzell's Fish Shop on the Shankill Road in Belfast. Desmond Frizzell was a born-again Christian and gospel singer who would slip biblical tracts to his customers as he handed over their parcels of fish. He rented his shop from a landlord. The rooms above it were rented out to the UDA, which, employing a cover name, used them for weekly meetings.

I knew who most of the dozen or so men in the room were and shook their hands politely, feeling it was the right thing to do, but felt my palm burning throughout the interview. They had just killed Damien Walsh, the sixteen-year-old nephew of one of my friends. I asked them about this, and they claimed they had information that the place where he was working was used by the IRA. They boasted that they were about to unleash a ferocious wave of violence against the IRA and the people who sustained it. After the meeting, I went straight to a cafe and washed my hands over and over.

On a Saturday morning in October 1993, Alan McBride drove his wife Sharon to work at Frizzell's. Desmond, the owner, was her father. Two-year-old Zoe was in the back seat. She and her dad were going to go cycling along the towpath on the River Lagan. Saturday was the busiest day at Frizzell's and Sharon and her sister took turns to help out. It was meant to be her sister's turn that day, but they'd swapped.

Alan was a butcher on the Shankill, the shop where he worked just a block away from his father-in-law's. Sharon was doing well as a junior manager in the health service. The young couple were also born-again Christians and their lives revolved around the Baptist Church on the Antrim Road. They'd met at a youth club when Alan was an officer in the Boys' Brigade. She was his first serious girlfriend. They fell in love, married and had Zoe. 'It was just normal,' Alan told me.

As Sharon was getting out of the car, Alan asked her if she'd remembered to set the video. He had asked her to record a soccer match he wanted to see that afternoon. 'Oh no, I forgot,' she said. Telling me this, Alan's eyes filled with tears, but he made himself say it. 'My last words to her were harsh,' he said.

For Raymond Elliott, that Saturday started in a normal, cheerful sort of way. His wife, Doreen, was to get the bus from the Shankill Road to visit relatives, and the couple decided to set off early from their home on the Highfield estate and have a big Ulster fry at the Rose of Sharon cafe, just up the road from Frizzell's.

After breakfast, Raymond saw Doreen off and headed for the bookies to check his football teams. He heard a bang, and suddenly the road was full of smoke and dust and people covered in blood were running and screaming. Raymond ran towards the scene.

He had coached young boxers. Blood didn't upset him and he knew how to dress wounds. Staff from the chemist's along the road handed out bandages and first-aid stuff, and Raymond set to work along with others. By the time the ambulances arrived, he was covered in blood, and an ambulance man tried to usher him into one of the vehicles. 'I'm all right, it's not my blood,' Raymond told him.

It was just after this that Raymond spotted there was a hole where the roof of Frizzell's had collapsed. He climbed in.

'That is where the slaughterhouse began,' he told me.

He was standing where the bomb had exploded. Bricks were still falling from the gable wall. He could feel them hitting his back. He lifted one off the rubble on the ground and found something bloody. 'I thought it was a wee dog. It was a scalp,' he said. Beside him, an ambulanceman or fireman vomited. Someone handed him a hard hat with 'Doctor' written on it. He went up for air, and someone gave him body bags. 'Then they brought shovels in,' he said.

A fireman, addressing him as 'doctor', asked him to put anything with blood on it aside for the police. 'We made a wee pile. I found a wee child's leg, then an arm. We set them to one side. Then, how would you describe it . . .' Raymond proceeded to go into a lot of bloody detail. He was convinced that he could hear someone groaning. He groped around where the central beam of the building had collapsed. He saw a body. He heaved the beam off it, with a strength he still doesn't understand. 'This is the part that really haunts me,' he said. 'There was this girl.'

The bomb was planted by Thomas 'Bootsy' Begley and Sean Kelly, both IRA volunteers from the Ardoyne area of North Belfast. The IRA plan, it would afterwards claim, was that Begley and Kelly would plant the bomb in the shop, then shout a warning to those buying and serving fish. The bomb would be set so that there was time for those on the ground floor to leave, and it was directed upwards, so those upstairs would be blown up.

Michael 'Minnie' Morrison, his partner Evelyn – both in their twenties – and their seven-year-old daughter, Michelle, were in the shop buying crab sticks for Michelle. Leanne Murphy, who was thirteen, had left her mother in the shop next door and gone into Frizzell's for a tub of whelks. Sharon and her father were serving. Kelly and Begley, dressed in white coats and carrying fish boxes, walked in and set down the bomb. It exploded instantly. All of the above, except Kelly, were killed, along with sixty-three-year-old George Williamson and his forty-nine-year-old wife Gillian, who were passing the shop, out to buy curtains. Wilma McKee, who was thirty-eight, was seriously hurt and died a day later. The nine civilian dead were all Protestants.

Kelly was seriously injured but survived and was placed under guard in hospital until he could be arrested and charged with the slaughter. There was widespread revulsion after the attack, and outrage when Sinn Féin leader Gerry Adams shouldered Begley's coffin.

After the ambulances had taken away all the survivors, and the body bags with the remains of the dead had been taken to the morgue, Raymond and others realised that there could be nobody else left alive in the ruins of Frizzell's. He had been digging in the wreckage for what must have been a couple of hours. On the street, still wearing his hard hat, he was approached by a policeman. 'Well done, doctor,' the man said.

In a daze, Raymond set off walking up the Shankill in the direction of home. A taxi driver saw him and gave him a lift. In his house, Raymond took off his bloodied clothes and put them in the bin. Then he had a bath. When Doreen got home, she asked him whether he had heard about the bomb on the Shankill. 'What bomb?' he said.

When Alan McBride and Zoe got home in the afternoon, one of Alan's friends was waiting for them. He told Alan there had been a bomb on the Shankill. Alan doesn't remember much of what followed, but he knows he was brought over to the Mater Hospital. Sharon's mother was there; she had left the shop minutes before Begley and Kelly entered it. The waiting areas of the Mater were full of panicking and grief-stricken relatives. Sharon and her father were the last of the dead to be identified. Her sister was the one who went to the morgue.

Zoe woke up that night crying for her mummy. 'The hardest thing I ever had to do was to tell her,' he said. 'I said, "Mummy's going to be with Jesus for a while."' Some republicans jeered at mourners during one of the funerals for the Shankill dead, but Alan said that nationalist shops near the church where Sharon's funeral was held closed down for several hours as a mark of respect.

The next few weeks and months were traumatic for him. He couldn't go back to work. He couldn't go to church. He couldn't go home. He was consumed by an anger so fierce he felt it was going to destroy him.

One night when he was visiting his mother, who lived near Ardoyne, where Begley and Kelly came from, he went for a walk with his dog. 'I walked into Ardoyne and just walked around in a blur. It was pissing rain. I had all this anger in me and I didn't have a violent bone in my body. My life had gone to pieces.'

He spent a lot of time at Sharon's grave, alone, writing journal after journal about the turmoil of grief and rage he was experiencing. Christmas morning was awful, thinking of the joy that would have been on Sharon's face when Zoe ran into her parents' room to show them her presents.

In the weeks after the bomb, Raymond got used to meeting people who boasted of their involvement at the scene in the aftermath of the bomb. He knew they hadn't been there, but he just looked away. 'There is no glory in seeing that there,' he told me. In late November, a few weeks after the bomb, Raymond broke down. 'I finished up in a secure unit on the psychiatric wing of the Mater hospital,' he said. 'I didn't know what was happening to me. They let me out on Christmas Eve but I asked to go back in again. I didn't feel safe outside.'

In January 1994, Alan wrote to the *Irish News*, the Belfast daily read almost exclusively by nationalists. 'I needed to tell my story. I wanted Catholics to know what my Christmas had been like,' he said. He also wrote – nine times, he thinks – to Gerry Adams. The last letter was an attempt at Irish, and Adams replied. Alan had to get the Irish bits translated. In the state schools in which Northern Irish Protestants are educated, Irish is not taught.

'He said, "You know, Alan, we understand your hurt, but no one is working harder for peace than Sinn Féin and the IRA,"' Alan recalled. Soon after this, the IRA planted a bomb under the car of a man who worked as a cleaner at an RUC station in Lurgan, County Armagh. His family was in the car with him when the bomb exploded, killing him. His wife was seen to run screaming and covered in blood from the wreckage with one of the children in her arms. She and her nine-year-old son were not badly hurt, but her three-year-old daughter was so seriously injured that she was not expected to survive. Thankfully, she did.

Alan rang the BBC's *Talkback* phone-in programme during an interview with Adams and tackled him on air about this murder. How could Adams tell people he was working for peace? he demanded. He also joined Families Against Intimidation and Terror (FAIT) and confronted Adams with a placard that said, 'Gerry Adams carried the coffin of the man who murdered my wife.'

The UDA threatened that there would be 'a heavy price to pay' for the Shankill bomb and launched a brutal attack on the Rising Sun Bar in Greysteel, County Derry, the following week. It was Halloween, and one of the gunmen who entered the quiet country pub shouted, 'Trick or treat,' before spraying the bar with gunfire. Seven people died, bringing to thirteen the number of people killed by the UDA since the Shankill bomb – a settling of scores.

Paradoxically, the horror and revulsion that people felt after all of these atrocities undoubtedly gave momentum to the secret talks then going on between SDLP leader John Hume and Gerry Adams and the diplomatic contacts between the British and Irish governments. Hume wept openly at the Greysteel funerals. The then British prime minister, John Major, wrote in his memoirs that he believed the peace process would have broken down 'had not the Shankill and Greysteel tragedies intervened'.[8]

The bloody year ended with the signing of the Downing Street Declaration by the British and Irish governments. The future of Northern Ireland would be decided by its people, it stated. Sinn Féin would be accepted into negotiations, provided there was an IRA ceasefire.

* * *

Loyalist violence proceeded relentlessly. 'I was the blue eye, the first grandson,' Joseph McCloskey told me. 'I was named after him.' He was speaking about the murder of his grandfather in 1994. Joseph McCloskey senior, who was fifty-two, had just come in from a night driving his taxi and, as usual, had left the front door open. Some of his children, young adults by then, were out socialising. Loyalist gunmen let themselves in and shot him eleven times.

'I remember I was half asleep in bed and I heard someone frantically banging on the door. Then I heard all this screaming and shouting downstairs,' said Joseph, who was eight at the time. 'I pulled the covers over my head and tried to go back to sleep. I wanted to feel safe in my bedroom.'

The next morning, he and his younger brothers were brought to a neighbour's house. 'Leeds were playing on TV,' he said. He vaguely pieced together that his grandad was dead, that bad men had come to his door and shot him. He remembered going back to school and everyone coming over to him saying how sorry they were. 'I didn't like it, I was shy,' he said.

Joseph was living in England but had come home to Belfast for his twenty-first birthday when I met him at his parents' house in North Belfast. He still seemed a shy person, quiet and thoughtful. His father, whose father was Joseph senior, sat on the sofa in the small front room while Joseph talked. He looked close to tears. His wife, Joseph junior's mother, brought in an album of all the press cuttings she'd kept about her father-in-law's murder.

'I was close to my granda,' said Joseph. 'He and my granny lived two doors up from us. They looked after me when I was small. My daddy said when I was a baby my granda used to reach out his arms for me when they brought me into the house. I used to go up on a Friday to collect my pay. I used to go and sit there and twiddle my thumbs, and then he'd come over and pat me on the head and slip me 50p. He was more like my mate. He knew the way children get on.'

By the time Joseph McCloskey was to be buried, there had been another murder. The priest spoke of it at the funeral. Among those who had come to pay their respects to Joseph at his wake was his friend, James Brown, a forty-eight-year-old ex-docker and trade unionist who ran a corner shop in the docks area. He called his shop 'Margaret's', in honour of his wife. The talk at the wake had turned to the number of people who were being killed at that time – Joseph was the ninth that month. 'I wonder who will be next,' said James. Two days later, he was opening his shop when UVF gunmen arrived. They shot him ten times in the head and body.

As his grandfather's cortège moved up the New Lodge Road, Joseph broke away, striking out himself in front of the funeral car and the rest of the mourners in his Christmas jacket and polished shoes. His mother whispered to an uncle to call him back, but his father said to let him go on. He caught the eye of press photographer Brendan Murphy. 'There he was, ahead of the rest, kicking his heels and lost in his own wee thoughts,' recalled Murphy. 'You wonder what goes through a child's mind.'

Joseph remembered what was in his mind. 'I remember feeling so guilty,' he said. 'You know, when you are that young, you think you are Superman, you think you can do anything. But now this had happened and there was nothing I could do. You kind of see how small you are in life. I felt lucky, too. I could have been at my granda's. It could have been me that was dead. I was disgusted and I felt bitter, too. I couldn't believe anyone could do this to my granda. This was the first bit of proper evil I'd seen in the world.'

Joseph said that in the weeks and months that followed, he kept his feelings to himself. 'Your mum and dad are crying and you try to be strong for them and say, "It'll be all right." I used to go up to my room and cry my lamps out, but if anyone came in and said, "Were you crying?" I'd say no. You hold things in, keep things to yourself. I take after my granda – I'm quiet.'

Before the murder, Joseph used to watch the older boys in the area rioting across the peace line with the boys from the Protestant side of Duncairn Gardens. 'It wasn't as bad as people said it used to be, but it was still bad,' he said. 'You'd watch them and you'd think, "Is this what you have to do when you are older?" I couldn't wait to join in.'

After the murder, Joseph didn't wait any longer. He joined in. 'They used to be shouting, "UDA scum, UVF scum," at the Protestants, and they were the people that shot my granda, so I was in there and I'd throw anything I could get my hands on. I was very bitter, even though I was so small.'

When he was ten, Joseph started being involved in cross-community exchanges at school. These had been introduced into the largely religiously segregated school system to try to promote understanding among Catholic and Protestant children. Joseph decided to thwart these events. 'I started to wear a Celtic top just to wind up the Protestants,' he said. He'd go on that way for a while.

Loyalists also slaughtered eight men in a bar in County Down in 1994. They included the oldest person to be killed in the Troubles, eighty-seven-year-old Barney Green. In turn, the IRA killed several prominent loyalist figures. Old enemies from within the republican movement were believed to have been responsible for the murder of one of the most notorious figures of the conflict, Dominic McGlinchey, as he walked with his son near his home in the Republic. McGlinchey was a former South Derry IRA man who, following his expulsion, had gone on to join the Irish National Liberation Army, soon becoming its leader. In 1983, he had boasted in a newspaper interview that he had been involved in thirty killings. He said his targets were mostly members of the security forces. He admitted providing a gun that was used in a notorious attack on the congregation at Darkley gospel hall in South Armagh in 1983, in which three men were shot dead as the congregation sang, 'Are You Washed in the Blood of the Lamb?' However, McGlinchey claimed he had provided the gun in order to kill a UVF man and said he abhorred the murders of innocent civilians.

At his funeral, Bernadette Devlin McAliskey was one of those who carried the coffin. She delivered a fierce tirade against the media, which had dubbed her friend 'Mad Dog'. He was 'the finest republican of them all', she said, and it was journalists who were 'curs and dogs . . . May every one of them rot in hell.'[9]

A significant number of victims at this time were women. Some were killed by the UVF, presumably in order to put pressure on male relatives who were republicans. One was an elderly Tyrone woman who lived with her sister and was well known in the area for her kindliness and her sewing. Two of her nephews, who lived near her, had been in the IRA, an organisation she herself did not support. After she was murdered, the family found British army surveillance cameras trained on the lane that passed her home, but the army claimed it had no record of the events surrounding her death. Another victim was heavily pregnant and surrounded by her small children when the gunmen struck.

The mid-Ulster UVF gang leader, Billy Wright, was believed to have been involved in the murder of these women. His henchmen would drive him around nationalist areas, and even reports that his long, pale face had been seen staring out would be enough to strike fear in those who heard them. Loyalists from the UDA in Belfast also killed a young Protestant woman they mistook for a Catholic. They dumped her body in a bin. For its part, the IRA killed a young Belfast mother they claimed was an informer. It was suspected that this was the settling of a personal grudge.

Then, suddenly, it seemed to be over. At the end of August 1994, the IRA announced a 'complete cessation' of military activities. In October, the UDA and the UVF followed suit, with Gusty Spence, one of the first killers of the Troubles, offering 'the loved ones of all innocent victims over the past twenty-five years abject and true remorse'.

9

Drumcree Warriors

'Southern tree, bears a strange fruit
Blood at the leaf, and blood at the root . . .'
Abel Meeropol, 'Strange Fruit'

On 11 July 1997, the Morgan family, from Castlewellan, County Down, did what thousands of Catholic families did during the loyalist marching season and left for their holidays in the Republic. Philomena Morgan said that when the family drove south through Newry it was 'like Beirut', with burnt-out buses and lorries across the road. 'I was so glad we were getting away.'[1]

That night, around bonfires in Protestant housing estates in towns and villages across the North, 'Kill all Taigs' banners were hoisted, as the killing went on. On the twelfth, Ian Paisley declared that 'fascism is a child of Romanism' and that the 'entire pan-nationalist front has united in seeking this reincarnation of the beast of fascism'. The pan-nationalist front meant the Catholic Church, Sinn Féin, the SDLP and the GAA – Catholics, in other words. Two days later, in the village of Aghalee, near Portadown, a Drumcree loyalist murdered a fifteen-year-old Catholic girl at the home of her Protestant boyfriend.

The murderer's brother had, the summer before, used the same gun to murder a Catholic taxi driver called Michael McGoldrick in support of the Orange Order. The Order demanded the right to march from the Church of Ireland at Drumcree through the Catholic part of Portadown during its annual commemoration of the Battle of the Somme.

Progress towards a peace settlement had foundered. Drumcree had become a focus for unionist discontent, with Paisley the loudest supporting voice. The UVF was on a ceasefire, and the small political party which had emerged from it, led by David Ervine, was talking about socialism and claiming that working-class loyalists had been exploited by unionist leaders.

The Orange Order had, since its formation in the eighteenth century, promoted ethnic solidarity among Protestants, and talk of social class was anathema to it. The Drumcree murders were carried out by a new breakaway faction of the UVF, the Loyalist Volunteer Force (LVF), led by Billy Wright. Wright believed in traditional loyalist values and dismissed Ervine as 'well nigh a communist'. His organisation formed links with British National Front supporters and with anti-ceasefire elements of the UDA. It existed to kill Catholics.

In 1996, after the murder of Michael McGoldrick, the LVF succeeded in getting the RUC to change its mind about banning the parade; the chief constable said that, otherwise, more Catholics might get killed.

There were elections in May 1997, and the DUP warned after Sinn Féin won the mid-Ulster seat from it that nationalists would 'reap a bitter harvest'. The LVF went on to murder Sean Brown, a highly respected Gaelic Athletic Association official, in Bellaghy, County Derry. Loyalists also beat to death a young Catholic man in Portadown and a policeman in County Antrim.

In Ballymena, loyalists protesting about the banning of another parade put a blockade on Harryville Catholic church on Saturday evenings. It would go on for forty-two weeks, until the Mass was suspended. Protesters painted sectarian slogans, grunted like pigs as people arrived and left the church, petrol-bombed homes and tried to burn out the priests.

Republicans were infuriated by the perceived lack of commitment to talks by the British and Irish governments, and the IRA dramatically abandoned its ceasefire with huge bombs at Canary Wharf in London and in Manchester's city centre. It also murdered two community policemen in Lurgan, County Armagh.

However, the Morgan family had left all this tension behind, and hundreds of miles away, in the south-west of the Republic, in Kerry, sixteen-year-old James Morgan was having a ball. He had been working with his father on a building site in Newcastle, County Down, so he had plenty of money. 'He was a millionaire for that week,' his mother told me. 'He was at every disco. I'm so glad he had that time.'[2]

She remembered that someone in Killarney, hearing their Northern accents, had remarked to them that it must be terrible to live in the North. James said that no, it wasn't. It was actually very quiet where they lived. Then the family heard on the news that the IRA had restored its ceasefire. 'We thought we were going home to peace.'[3]

When they got home, James headed over to his best friend's house. He'd brought Nathan Elliot a bottle of Givenchy aftershave. 'Well, half a bottle, actually,' Nathan told me. 'He'd used the rest.' James told Nathan he'd missed him. Nathan was going to his aunt's house in Dublin the next day, and James asked him to bring him back a silver ring. They saw each other every day. James would arrive and tap on the window of Nathan's bedroom, Nathan would open it, and James would climb in.

They made plans for James to come to Dublin for a couple of days later on, and they played one of their epic battles on Super Nintendo late into the night. Nathan didn't know what time his aunt was going to call for him next day, so they left it that James would call in the afternoon in case his friend was still around. Then he set off home across the fields, as usual.

Nathan's aunt came in the morning. In Dublin, they went to an art gallery and then out for dinner, and it was late when they got back to her house. There was a message on the answering machine from Nathan's mum, Jane. Was James with Nathan? He hadn't come home. First thing in the morning, Nathan rang home. When he learnt that James had vanished, he knew something bad had happened. 'James would never just go missing,' he told me. 'He was very strong with his family.'

When James didn't come home that night in July 1997, his parents had at first assumed he was up at Nathan's house. 'James was like a streak of lightning,' his mother, Philomena, told me. 'He'd flash through the house and away again. He was always on the go, and always a smile on his face and a twinkle in his eye.'[4]

They rang the Elliots. When they heard Nathan had gone to Dublin, they hoped against hope James had gone too, though they knew in their hearts that he would not have done so without telling them. When they heard from Nathan the next morning that he wasn't there, they were deeply worried.

Unbeknownst to them, that morning Norman Coopey, a milkman from Newcastle, County Down, had rung the RUC in the seaside town. He confessed that he and another man had killed a boy. He said he had been out of his mind on drink and drugs, and that he had been afraid of the other man, a notoriously violent local loyalist who was suspected of having been involved in several sectarian murders. The two had been cruising the area in a silver Toyota car. Coopey was driving; the other man was hiding on the back seat.

Coopey said that as they drove on the road between Annesborough and Newcastle, he saw a teenage boy hitching a lift. He pulled up beside him. Once the boy got in the car, the other man revealed himself and produced a hammer. They found out the boy's name and that he was a Catholic. The other man then set about beating him with the hammer, and Coopey 'finished him off' from behind.

He told the police they had driven the dead boy to the outskirts of the village of Clough, where the other man lived. They had poured petrol over him and set him alight. Then they buried him in a pit of animal carcasses dumped by local farmers. Coopey brought the police to that grim place, where they recovered a knife.

Nathan came back to Castlewellan and joined the Morgans in a frantic search of all the places James frequented: the homes of friends, the discos in Newcastle, the beach, the campsite, the slopes of Slieve Donard where he and Nathan used to light campfires and sit out at night. The area is extraordinarily beautiful, with forests and lakes and a skyline dominated by the crags of the Mourne mountains.

That evening, a detective from the RUC called at the Morgans' house, on the edge of the village of Castlewellan in County Down. He asked if anyone in the family was missing.

The police had sealed off the field with the stinking animal pit in it. On the Sunday, the Morgans watched the lunchtime television news and saw a hearse being driven slowly down a lane through foxgloves to the field at Clough. Soon afterwards, the police came to the house with the local priest.

Even then, Philomena told me, they kept looking out of the window, hoping to see James coming up the path. 'Hoping,' she said. 'Knowing right well, but hoping.' Hope ended that night when the body was identified. James had been so badly beaten that he could only be identified from dental records and a fingerprint. His coffin was brought home closed.

James's funeral was huge, with hundreds of teenagers following the cortège up the steep road that connects Annesborough with Castlewellan. One of the Morgans' relations, who cried his eyes out in the church, was the owner of the bar in Lough-inisland in which loyalist gunmen had shot dead six Catholic men in the summer of 1994.

The priest said James's was the saddest funeral he had ever conducted. After the singing of the Psalm 'The Lord Is My Shepherd', he quoted from it: 'The Lord is my shepherd. There is nothing I shall want. He maketh me to walk in green pastures . . .' Then he went on, 'Those words haunted me last Sunday as I walked down green pastures in lovely sunshine to the place where . . . a child had been battered and thrown into a pit.'[5] There was a profound silence in the church, where grandfathers and grandmothers sat beside their children and their children's children, defenceless in the knowledge that a lovely boy, James, had been selected for murder simply because he was a Catholic.

The mood among loyalists had been ugly all of that summer. In Castlewellan, a local nationalist residents group had succeeded in getting a local Orange parade banned. Philomena Morgan had no doubt this was behind the sectarian murder of her son. 'They didn't get marching and this was a spin-off,' she said.

The family was at pains to stress that they didn't hold Protestants in general responsible. A neighbour who was in a flute band had come home from his holidays to carry the funeral wreaths in his car. 'That'll tell you all you need to know,' said the boy's father, Justin, who was on the board of a local integrated school. 'We have had so many Protestants telling us they feel ashamed,' Philomena said. 'They have no need. The ones who did this weren't Protestants. They weren't Christians.'[6]

The violence against James was frenzied, far in excess of what was required to kill him. Justin shuddered as he spoke about it. 'All we can hope is that the first hammer blows to his head killed our son,' he said, his gaunt face eloquently conveying the horror that such a statement entails.[7] He and Philomena were worried about the impact of what had happened on their remaining children, three sons and a daughter, and on the wider circle of children and young people who knew James.

I had met Nathan after the funeral. I was writing a newspaper report about his friend's murder. He couldn't stop crying. He said he kept waiting to hear the tap, tap on his bedroom window that used to mean James was there. They had known each other since they were eight years old, but their friendship had really blossomed when they became teenagers. 'We did everything together,' he told me.

'He was fiercely loyal to me, and I to him. He had his own wee slant of logic on things. We used to get chairs and sit out in the field looking out at the stars and talking. One night we saw the cows lying and we decided to roll them over.' Nathan's home is on the wooded grounds of a big old house, now used as an outdoor pursuits centre. It faces across sloping fields to the mountains.

The boys used to keep an eye on the busloads of schoolgirls arriving to do their Duke of Edinburgh Awards scheme challenges at the big house, and then they'd make an appearance and try to chat up the ones they fancied. James announced to Nathan one night that he'd 'got off with the second best Irish dancer in Ireland'. He told him he wanted to meet 'everyone interesting'.

They climbed mountains, threw stones at targets, lit bonfires. They'd pool their money, hitch to Newcastle and try and win enough money on the seafront slot machines to buy bottles of cider. 'There was nothing we couldn't say to each other,' said Nathan. They had no interest in politics. James was a practising Catholic and went to a Catholic secondary school, while Nathan, whose parents' marriage is mixed and whose family didn't practise any religion, went to an integrated school in Belfast.

After they heard James was dead, Nathan and his brother, Jerome, went out and sat and stared into the night sky until they found a constellation to name after their lost friend.

Then Nathan went off the rails. He told me about this when we met again, ten years after James's murder – a man of twenty-seven now but still, when he speaks about his friend, like the seventeen-year-old lost in horror I'd met before. 'It was like being in a scary movie,' he said. 'I guess there was a big culture here of desensitisation. When me and James were kids, you'd hear about deaths all the time, but it wouldn't be real to you. You'd be caught up in bomb scares and controlled explosions, but you just took it for granted.

'Then all of a sudden it was your best friend's face that was on the news. A wee bird flew into the house at the same time. It froze. I lifted it and let it go. I walked for miles out towards the mountains, still not believing it. You don't believe it. Up to that, the worst violence we'd known was a few punches.

'A couple of times I thought I heard his knock on the bedroom window. It freaked me out. James had been in my room constantly. I had a real desire to get out. I had mad ideas of how I'd kill the people that did it. I remember carrying a big hunting knife. I don't know what I was thinking of, what I was going to do with it. I was all over the place,' he said. He dropped out of one 'A' level, but did two. 'All I wanted was to get out of the country. I had a real good girlfriend. She helped me through a lot.'

He and his girlfriend went to Holland for a while. They camped, worked in factories and then came home. Nathan had no idea what he wanted to do. They got a flat in Newcastle, County Down, and he got work doing the nightshift in a fish factory. He could put the murder out of his mind, but then, he said, 'It would creep up on you and you'd spin . . .'

Norman Coopey, who had confessed to the murder, almost immediately retracted his statement. The other man he'd named was questioned and released without charge. The car had been scrubbed clean of forensic evidence. While on remand awaiting trial, Coopey was attacked by other inmates in jail and soon asked to be transferred to the LVF wing, where he joined Billy Wright and others.

* * *

The LVF followed in bloody footsteps. Like the Shankill Butchers of the mid-1970s, it was led by a particularly vicious egotist who cultivated his menacing image. Billy Wright was said to have charisma; I had interviewed him several times over the years and found no trace of any such quality. His followers were devoted, however, and the LVF's first killing was said to have been a birthday present for him.

As Wright's new gang began its murder campaign in 1996, the old Butcher, Bobby 'Basher' Bates, was being released from prison. He began work with the Ex-Prisoners' Interpretive Centre (EPIC), an organisation for ex-UVF prisoners, which was based at the top of the Shankill Road. Nine months later, Bates was shot dead there one morning as he unlocked the front door.

It was at first assumed the IRA had carried out the murder, thus breaking an unwritten rule that ex-prisoners would not be targeted. However, it quickly emerged that the killing was carried out in revenge for the murder of another loyalist twenty years previously.

There was considerable anger over Bates's release. Some of the relatives of those he had murdered pointed out that the judge who jailed him in 1979 had said he should never be released. One man said that Bates didn't belong to the human race.[8] Another, a brother of one of Bates's victims, spoke of his 'barbarous atrocities' and said 'cannibals wouldn't have done it on people'. After Bates's death, the man said he wrote to his sister to say, 'The wheels of God grind slowly but surely.'[9]

Community worker Marion Weir worked as a research co-ordinator at EPIC, and when she was told by her boss that Bates was to be released and was coming to work at the centre, her first thought was that she would have to leave. 'I couldn't bear the thought of it,' she said.

She had been a Protestant child living in Glencairn at the top end of the Shankill Road during the 1970s, when the Shankill Butchers were at large. 'On our way to school we used to see the police visiting crime scenes. You were terrified to think you might pass someone in the street who had done these things. You were terrified that they were out there,' she said.[10]

However, she stayed. 'When you work for an ex-prisoners' organisation, you try not to be judgemental. He [Bates] came along and he was this wee old man with glasses – though he was actually only in his forties. All he did was laugh and smile – he was very jolly. He couldn't have done enough for you. He was always making tea.

'I told him how I'd felt. He said that back in those days it was like cowboys and Indians. Everybody had guns. He said if they were in a bar and they didn't like the music, they'd shoot the jukebox. Most of the work he did at EPIC was with young people. He'd tell them violence was wrong and it had ruined his life.'

Marian was just parking her car when the gunman shot Bates, who was opening the front door of EPIC. 'I was devastated by his death – I had become really fond of him,' she said. Later on that day, when she told her family, one of them said, 'What goes around, comes around.' A thousand or so people attended Bates's funeral, the service conducted by Ian Paisley.

Bates had undergone a prison conversion. Twice. The first time was soon after his conviction in 1979. His wife went to see the detective in charge of the investigation. She told him Basher didn't want any of his children 'to follow in his footsteps' and gave him a biblical tract. According to the author Martin Dillon, Bates, having lost the status he had enjoyed as part of a gang of killers, had become 'vulnerable and open to new emotional experiences'. Dillon believed this conversion to Christianity was short-lived.

Bates briefly shared a cell with IRA man Brendan Hughes, who felt Bates had 'mouthed political slogans but never understood them'. He said Bates became quite loyal to him and said he was protecting him from other loyalists in the prison. He also said Bates had a 'loose tongue' and gave away plenty of information about other loyalists which was of use to the IRA.

Bates was certainly suggestible. Other loyalists encouraged him to kill a child abuser, and Bates duly set off, knife in hand, for the man's cell. It was his new friend, Hughes, who stopped him. On another occasion, however, Bates wrapped an iron bed leg in a newspaper and attacked a republican who had tackled him roughly during a football game.

He had written about finding God in prison in *The Burning Bush*, a fierce bimonthly newsletter published by Free Presbyterian minister the Reverend Ivan Foster. 'The Testimony of Bobby Bates' had first appeared in 1989, and Foster reprinted it after Bates's murder in the hope, he said, that it might show others that Jesus saves.

'Thank God I can say I am forgiven,' Bates wrote. 'I'm covered by the precious blood of Christ.' He said the judge had told him he should never be freed, but it did not matter now because 'Christ has set me free.' His 'wee wife, Carol' had been the instrument God used to bring about the first conversion, in 1980. 'I gave my life to Christ . . . I felt the dirt being drained out of me and the power of his Holy Spirit coming into me and cleansing me.'

However, Bates was to 'backslide' a year later. He reverted to being Basher. 'Men feared me once again and that was good for my ego,' he wrote. His word was law. For seven years his gods were 'the UVF and Glasgow Rangers'. Then, in 1988, he learnt that his little granddaughter had a potentially fatal illness. He read Psalm 40 and was saved again. 'My battle cry is no longer "No surrender" but "Full surrender",' he wrote.

Prison was a 'battlefield', he said. 'The devil tries his utmost to take men to hell, and if they are not saved and covered in the precious blood that is where they are going.'[11] Some relatives of Bates's victims were unimpressed by this conversion. One said it was hypocrisy and that he had never heard Bates apologise for what he had done.

Billy Wright, who had also claimed to have been saved at various times, was himself murdered in prison that November. INLA men shot him as he went to the visitors' area to see his girlfriend. The circumstances were extraordinary: the killers had guns in the high-security prison, had been able to cut through a rooftop fence, and the watchtower which overlooked the scene was unmanned when they struck, its cameras not working. His henchmen wreaked terrible revenge, and a spate of murders followed. One of the victims was a young Belfast community worker called Terry Enright.

* * *

When most people see a gaggle of teenagers hanging around drinking cans of beer on a street corner late at night, they cross the road. Terry Enright was different. He was a youth worker with a brief to make contact with the most marginalised young people in Turf Lodge in West Belfast.

It's a tough area, and by the mid-1990s a generation was growing up with parents who were suffering the aftermath of the Troubles. Alcoholism and prescription-drug addiction were rife among adults. The RUC had not been tolerated in the area, which was policed instead by the IRA. There were gangs of young 'hoods' who defied the IRA. Some of them had been 'kneecapped' – shot or battered in the knees – more than once for activities such as joyriding – or death-driving, as some of the victims of this wild racing of stolen cars have insisted it should be known.

The teenagers Terry was looking out for were the ones who were always in trouble, the ones who were barred from the youth clubs. He saw them not as anti-social but as at risk. He'd go around graveyards and parks and the streets looking for such young people. He'd approach them, get talking to them. In time, he'd get to know them.

'Everyone would be telling them they were shit,' said Terry's father, Terry Enright senior, when I visited the family home in an estate high up on the slopes of the mountains in West Belfast. The room was full of sporting trophies won by the Enright boys. Their parents, Mary and Terry senior, are both long-time community activists.

'Terry used to say to me, "Da, all these want is a bit of respect. I have to start to get them to believe in themselves,"' remembered Terry senior. 'He had a vision of all the things these kids could do – climb mountains, cycle, abseil . . . and he'd gradually get them to do it. He just had this charisma with young people.'

Terry, who was twenty-eight, loved to be out in the mountains or at outdoor pursuits centres or on GAA pitches with the young people, and he never counted the hours he worked. He wasn't very well paid and had taken on extra work as a door-man at a nightclub in the centre of Belfast. He needed to make some money to do up the kitchen of the home he shared with his wife and two little girls.

On the night of 11 January 1998, Terry was working at the club. He wasn't meant to be on duty that night; he was doing it as a favour for a friend. His parents, Terry and Mary, weren't keen on it. The club scene was associated with drugs – anathema to them and to Terry. They also felt their son was already working too hard and that he was exhausted. 'He worked night and day,' said Terry senior. 'From October to Christmas he'd dealt with four hundred kids.' He'd reassured them that the job at the club was only for another couple of weeks.

Two gunmen drove to the front of the club that night, and while one pointed his weapon at the doormen, the other got out and started shooting. Terry had been chatting to the owner of the club and they were both running away when he was shot in the back. He was able to tell the owner he'd been shot.

Terry senior and Mary had just come home from a night out when a man they knew came running to their door. He said Terry had been shot but he was all right; they were to go to the Mater Hospital. 'We thought, "Terry is a tough guy, he'll be all right,"' Mary recalled. They were brought into a room, where, soon afterwards, a surgeon came and told them that their son was dead. 'A million things went through my mind, but mostly it was, "I'm his father, but I can't sort this out the way I normally do,"' said Terry.

'I'll never know if he called out for me. I met an elderly peeler [policeman] in the corridor in the hospital, and he told me if it was any consolation to me, there was a priest with my son when he died.' As Terry said this, Mary listened intently. 'You never told me that,' she said. Another policeman told Terry senior that his son did not suffer.

Mary said she was in shock for a long time. She doesn't even know how long. She couldn't talk about it, and still can't talk about that time. 'I went through the motions, but it was sometimes like I wasn't there and it was someone else doing these things,' she said. 'Maybe that is how you cope. I was concerned as a mother as to how my children were coping.'

They knew Terry had been popular, but they were amazed

when there were queues of people at their door wanting to give their condolences. He had made a deep impression even on people who only met him briefly. A man who'd met Terry and his baby daughter in the mountains behind West Belfast and had had a chat with him saw his photograph in the paper and came with ice cream for the children.

People said the funeral was the biggest in Belfast since the hunger strikers' funerals in 1981. Mary said she asked a young girl that day what had been special about Terry. The girl replied, 'You don't know my family, but Terry did. He kept on saying to me, "Can do, can do – you can do it." He made me believe in myself.'

Among those to pay tribute was PUP leader David Ervine. He said that Terry had been 'a fine and reputable young man with a vision for the future, murdered brutally by people without a vision for the future'. Ervine was himself under threat from the LVF at the time. He said the LVF was out to destabilise the peace process and accused 'seemingly respectable politicians' of backing it.

Within two days of their son's death, the Enrights had been told, by reliable sources within loyalism, of the names of the killers. One was a well-known LVF man and drug dealer, and the other was a Catholic drug dealer. At first, the police told Terry's wife that they were hopeful of making arrests and that they had forensic evidence. But no one was ever charged. Later on, the Enrights heard rumours that the LVF man was working for the RUC's special branch.

'People used to say to me, "Obviously you'd want the people who did this dead,"' said Mary. 'I'd say, "Why? It is not going to bring Terry back." Those people who killed him had nothing to offer – Terry had so much.' Terry senior agreed. 'Revenge would be irrelevant,' he said.

After the Deluge

'In the end they traded their tired wings,
For the resignation that living brings . . .'
Jackson Browne, 'After the Deluge'[1]

On 10 April 1998, lengthy, fraught negotiations between the British and Irish governments and the political parties in the North produced the Good Friday Agreement. The DUP did not take part in the talks, which, Ian Paisley warned, would not bring peace but war.

The Agreement proposed a power-sharing government and sweeping reforms of the policing and justice systems. However, although it was overwhelmingly endorsed by Catholics in the referendum which followed, approximately half of the North's Protestants rejected it. The Ulster Unionist Party, then the dominant unionist party, supported it, but with deep reservations. The DUP called it a deal 'with the men of blood' and 'a prelude to genocide'.

There are gracious words in the Agreement for the victims of the Troubles. The 'participants', that is to say the political parties and the governments, acknowledged their suffering and agreed it must be addressed 'as a necessary element of reconciliation'. The Agreement went on: 'It is recognised that victims have a right to remember as well as to contribute to a changed society. The achievement of a peaceful and just society would be the true memorial to the victims of violence.'[2]

However, there was no proposal about how to deal with the

past in response to the needs of victims, and there were other provisions in the Agreement that were less soothing. Some four hundred paramilitary prisoners were to be given early release. The reaction of one victim gives an idea as to how painful this was for many: 'You are a disease in my bones and the only cure is justice. To say I hate you doesn't even begin to describe how I feel.' This was what Michelle Williamson wrote in an open letter to the Shankill bomber, Sean Kelly, in 1998.[3] Her parents had been killed in the bomb, five years earlier. When he gave Kelly nine life sentences, the trial judge had described the bombing as one of the most outrageous atrocities of the Troubles. Michelle had tried to handcuff herself to a turnstile at the Maze prison when Kelly was getting out on parole.

Other victims, however, called on people to vote for the Agreement. Alan McBride, whose wife and father-in-law were killed by the Shankill bomb, decided that if it was the price of peace, he could live with it. Even so, there were times when he had to struggle with difficult feelings. One night in 1999, he was visiting his mother, who lived near the Catholic Ardoyne area. He heard the sounds of a street party and suddenly realised it was to celebrate Kelly's release from prison. 'That hurt,' he told me.

Many families of the security forces were furious. More than two hundred members of the UDR and its successor, the RIR, had been killed, along with just over three hundred police. Now the RUC was to be replaced. Relatives talked of sacrifices made in vain and wasted gallantry. I heard one old man say at a meeting of the Patten Commission on the future of policing that the RUC had been thrown out like the rubbish.

The Loyalist Volunteer Force was still killing in 1998 and took the DUP line of opposing the Agreement. However, to exploit the terms of the prisoner-release scheme, it declared a ceasefire in 1999.

Justin and Philomena Morgan voted 'Yes' in the referendum on the Agreement. In 1999, they travelled to Armagh for the trial of Norman Coopey. The milkman from Newcastle, County Down, had initially confessed to murdering their son, James, in 1997, but on remand in jail Coopey had changed his mind and claimed he was innocent. Just before the case came to court, he changed his plea again and admitted his guilt.

Justin and Philomena wept on the steps of the court. They said they were 'glad it is now all over'. It wasn't, though, because Coopey had aligned himself with the LVF. Within eighteen months of going to jail, Coopey was freed. His crime had been defined under the Good Friday Agreement as a politically motivated act. Philomena was horrified. She knew the killers of her son had been motivated by a deep sectarian hatred. 'Even after they had James killed they couldn't leave him alone. They just set him alight,' she said.

However, she said that even after the shock of Coopey's release, if she had her vote to cast again, she would still vote for peace. 'We can't forget the past but we have to move on for the sake of the rest,' she told the BBC. 'We can't leave James behind. He's there with us every day, every morning.'[4]

Their son, Joseph, James's older brother, was a twenty-one-year-old student in 1998. He told the *Irish News* that while his parents had accepted the release, he had not. Coopey had killed as a member of the Orange Order, not the LVF, he said. He'd only joined that organisation in jail. 'It hasn't come as the biggest blow because we've been expecting it, but it is silently annoying everybody.'[5] The Orange Order had not expelled Coopey; on the eve of his trial he was asked to resign.

James's friend, Nathan Elliot, said he had felt a 'huge sense of injustice' after the trial, which was 'one of the worst experiences ever'. He'd thought the killers would be brought to justice, but Coopey was only the accomplice, and it turned out the man who instigated the whole horrible attack wasn't even going to be tried. 'There wasn't any reason he should have got away with it. Everyone knew he did it,' said Nathan.

Seamus Heaney was widely quoted in the strange, euphoric days after the Agreement: 'History says, Don't hope/On this side of the grave./But then, once in a lifetime/The longed for tidal wave/Of justice can rise up,/And hope and history rhyme.'[6] In Nathan's view, though, there had been no tidal wave of justice. A settlement had been reached, but at the cost of denying the injustice done to his friend.

He felt that James's murder wasn't given the public attention it deserved because the focus was on the peace process and on moving on. 'There was this great wave of optimism. It was all, "Vote for the Good Friday Agreement – vote to get the prisoners out!" Coopey got out after less than two years. If anything would alienate you from politics here, it was that. It undermines any sense you might have of justice. I have no romantic notions of allegiance to my country. I feel just completely negative about all that.'

Alan Black, who survived the IRA's Kingsmills massacre, didn't have to watch those who tried to kill him walk out of prison, because they had never been jailed. It was the same for the families and friends of a majority of those killed in the conflict. Alan said he had mixed feelings. 'I didn't agree with the release of those butchers from jail, but it has brought a kind of peace.' All the same, things were being 'airbrushed out of history', he felt. Murderers were being presented as role models and turned into leaders.

'There are homes all over this country full of people grieving all because some bastard said, "You are a Protestant so you have to die," or "You are a Catholic so you have to die." Jesus, when you think of the actual mechanics of the things that were done, the shootings and the stabbings, dragging people up mountain roads and stripping them, blowing people up . . . How can you ever be a good guy after doing something like that to an innocent person? How does anyone live with themselves after that?'

* * *

'. . . history creaks on its bloody hinge
and the unspeakable is done again.'
John Montague,
'A Response to Omagh'[7]

The marching season had been a volatile and dangerous time since the start of the Troubles, and the summer of 1998 showed that some of the killers had not finished yet. Drumcree once again became the focus of unionist opposition to a settlement. Ian Paisley claimed that the security forces had better allow the parade through Portadown before the twelfth of July because that day would be 'the decider'. On the night of the eleventh, following a UVF roadblock at which Orange sashes were worn, loyalists petrol-bombed the home of Christine Quinn, a young Catholic woman in Ballymoney, County Antrim. Three of her four young sons, all under the age of ten, died in the blaze that followed.

The republican violence wasn't over either. Although most former IRA members backed Sinn Féin and supported the Agreement, a significant rump did not. They included the organisation's former quartermaster, Michael McKevitt, who was married to Bernadette Sands, a sister of the hunger striker and IRA icon, Bobby Sands. Their 32 County Sovereignty Movement was widely seen as the political wing of the so-called Real IRA, whose answer to the Agreement was the Omagh bomb.

The bombers parked their car on the main street of the Tyrone town and walked away. A woman would later give evidence that one of them looked at her as he did so, and that he grinned. Their accomplices phoned a warning, but it was too late and in any case they gave a wrong location, so that police were rushing people towards, rather than away from, the bomb. When it exploded, it killed twenty-nine people. The dead included men, women and children, Protestants and Catholics, Irish people and Spaniards on a school exchange visit.

One family suffered particular devastation. Mick Grimes lost his wife, Mary, who was sixty-six. The couple had twelve children. One of their children, Avril Monaghan, aged thirty, was also killed. She was married with four children under the age of seven, and she was heavily pregnant with twins. One of her children, Maura, aged eighteen months, was also killed.

Avril and Maura Monaghan's funeral was conducted in St Macartan's Catholic church in Aughadarra. In 1979, at the same church, the IRA had lain in wait for a wedding party to emerge. When a brother of the bride came out, holding his three-year-old daughter's hand, the gunmen shot him dead. He was a prison officer. One of the mourners at the Monaghan funeral was a Protestant neighbour of Mary Grimes. His daughter, an RUC woman, had been blown up in an IRA mortar-bomb attack in Newry in 1992.

* * *

After the Omagh bomb, a former IRA man called Eamon Collins called for the internment without trial of the Real IRA, many of whom were his former colleagues. He named names and denounced the dissident leader, Michael McKevitt. He also agreed to give evidence against Thomas 'Slab' Murphy, who was suing the *Sunday Times* for libel after it called him an IRA commander. Collins told the court in Dublin that 'If Tom Murphy decided I should be killed, I would be killed. That's the power he had at his fingertips.' Murphy lost his case. The newspaper gave Collins a reported £1 million.

From the 1970s on, Collins had played an active part in the

Troubles himself. He had set up murders and made all the necessary arrangements to ensure the gunmen escaped to kill again. He'd seen himself as one of 'history's vengeful children', paying Britain back for centuries of wrongs done to Ireland, fighting the injustices experienced by the Catholic people stranded in the Protestant state of Northern Ireland.

But his commitment to the 'armed struggle' had given way to doubt and despair. In 1985, while under arrest, he broke down and gave RUC detectives enough information on bombings and assassinations for them to arrest fifty IRA men. He changed his mind again in prison, was promised an amnesty by the IRA and retracted his evidence. He also managed to get himself acquitted on five murder charges.

After his release, in 1987, the IRA put Collins through an aggressive and protracted debriefing, eventually banishing him to the Republic. He was told by a leading figure: 'You are an embarrassment we can't afford to have.'

He was supposed to stay out of the North on pain of death. However, he began to return quietly for weekends, and after several years in Dublin, the Aran Islands and Scotland, he returned to live in Newry in 1994. He believed that his 'case' had been 'pretty much forgotten with the passage of the years'. This was also the year the IRA went on ceasefire. The peace process was gathering momentum.

Collins felt driven to speak out about his past, about what drove the armed struggle and why he'd left it behind. He took part in a television documentary in which he excoriated the IRA, and published a book, *Killing Rage*, which laid bare the squalor of political violence and charted his own descent from aggressive enthusiasm into soul-destroying disillusionment.

The artist Rita Duffy had been a friend of Collins, and she gave me a phone number for his widow, Bernie. She was not eager to talk. 'I have real difficulty in remembering those years,' Bernie told me. 'I suppose there was so much trauma. I look back and I think, "How did I ever do that?"' She had moved with their four children to a big modern house overlooking the town and the mountains of Mourne. There were a lot of Duffy's paintings on the walls, crowds of harrowed-looking people in black and white. 'They were Eamon's,' she said. 'He loved them.' She shivered. 'They're very dark. A bit bleak.' On a table there was a smiling colour photograph of her husband.

At the end of his book, Eamon Collins had written about his plans to return with Bernie and the children to his old family home in Camlough, in South Armagh. By September 1998, the house was ready and its empty rooms, full of light from the new windows, were freshly painted. The family was about to move from their house on the Barcroft housing estate in Newry.

'We were really looking forward to it,' said Bernie. 'Then that September the house was burnt. After that, the graffiti over the whole town became a nightly event.' The graffiti, big, ugly letters, sometimes two feet high, said with brutal simplicity: 'Eamon Collins, Tout.'

While her husband was in exile, Bernie and the children would visit him: 'A baby, a toddler, a three-year-old, a five-year-old, a baby walker, a pram and our bags, all packed into a wee Mini Metro.' When Eamon would come to Newry for clandestine weekends, they would be terrified. 'It was intense, a cloak-and-dagger life. You didn't know if someone was going to come and riddle the house.'

'There was no sort of normal life after he came back to live. He was never supposed to be back. He was tolerated but he still had to not have a big presence. When he started doing articles and things, we'd have disagreed, not over the content but about him doing it. The book was a catharsis for him. He just felt the need to tell it as it was.'

They refused to consider leaving the area. 'Maybe it was naivety on our part,' Bernie said. 'Our families were here, and family was very important to us, family and roots and the place you belong. The children were settled, too. I thought I could keep things stable and right. The house in Camlough was lovely. It had sunlight till eleven at night in the summertime. We had very happy memories from when the children were small and we'd visit Eamon's mother there.'

Bernie had threatened to divorce her husband in 1985 when she learnt that he had become a supergrass and was about to turn Queen's evidence and name his former comrades. 'There was a definite rift then,' she said. 'I thought he had taken leave of his senses. He was in a completely disorientated state. I don't think I ate for three weeks. I was down to six stone.'

In *Killing Rage*, Collins described her reaction. '"You fucking bastard," she said. "If I had a gun I'd shoot you myself . . . you've ruined our lives . . . only scum do this and if you do it you'll be scum forever in my eyes."'[8] He knew her view of him would be widely shared. 'I was now an ally of this Protestant militia in a Protestant state – a collaborator, a traitor, a tout.'

Bernie's loyalties had been violently torn. She was deeply involved with Sinn Féin in Newry at the time. However, she made up her mind: her husband came first. She took him back when he was released, and when he was exiled, she disengaged herself from the republican movement. 'At the end of the day, he was my husband and I was standing by him,' she said. 'You get married and you have a family, and that is what life is about.'

Bernie was in her final year of training as a social worker and was on placement with a social-work team in Portadown, the tough loyalist town fifteen or so miles away from Newry, in

County Armagh. This was during the fierce years of the events known as Drumcree, the annual battle over the Orange Order's demand for the right to march through the Catholic part of town.

'Every different aspect of your life had a fear and a pressure attached to it. There was very limited opportunity for conversation. There was all the normal stuff of trying to manage the kids and all their activities, and then the other stuff. I'd get up at the crack of dawn and try and paint out the graffiti between our house and the school,' she said. 'Then I'd get the kids out and I'd drive to Portadown. I hated that road with a vengeance. It was difficult at work. No one knew my past or my background. You were working with people in situations that were themselves intense, in very loyalist areas. You had to show your competence. There were assessments to write up at night. You'd be driving home late at night through UVF places, hoping your old car wouldn't break down. You would be wondering, "Am I going to get home and find the house surrounded by police, and it a murder scene?"'

Eamon Collins supported the peace process and applauded the efforts of Sinn Féin president Gerry Adams. In the winter of 1998, he wrote an open letter to Adams, asking him to use his influence to end a 'reign of terror' against him. 'The people who are carrying this out are former Provisionals, former Sinn Féin people, and are now playing dual roles,' he wrote, accusing them of being tied in with both Sinn Féin and dissident republicans.[9]

On the night of 26 January 1999, two men spent the evening painting graffiti around the estate. 'I was out till about half one in the morning and I'd painted out most of it,' said Bernie. 'When I got home, I said to Eamon that I hadn't got all of it, and he said he'd go out early and finish it. He went out at about half four or five to do that. He came back and got changed to take the dogs out for a walk.

'Later on, I was getting the kids ready for school and I saw the dogs running around with their leads on. The back door was open. There was a sort of butterfly in my stomach. There was no sign of Eamon, but I thought maybe he'd walked out to Camlough or maybe he'd gone to Mass.'

However, when she went out to drive the route he might have taken, she saw that the police had part of the road taped off. 'I drove around, and after about three times passing the police tape I stopped and asked what was happening. I said, "My husband is missing."

'The policeman told me to go down to the police station. I knew the reporter on the *Irish News* and I phoned him first. I asked him what was going on, and he said, "We think there's a body found." I said, "I think it is Eamon."'

His body had been found shortly after six that morning, but his face had been so badly beaten and slashed that he was unrecognisable. His assailants had battered him with a heavy iron bar and repeatedly stabbed him in the face and body, possibly with a bayonet.

'I just rolled from there,' said Bernie. 'I had a couple of really good friends, Protestants as it happens. One of them came round the schools with me to get the kids. The coffin was closed. I debated it at the time and I still do. I feel that when that is done you don't really get final closure, but I had to ask myself, would I let the children remember him as he was or see him with his face all cut up?'

Sinn Féin claimed it did not know who killed Collins. Martin McGuinness said he had no idea who killed 'that man'.

'A couple of the neighbours were exceptionally good,' said Bernie. 'But there was severe intimidation of the whole community. People felt they couldn't come to the house.'

They didn't come to the funeral either. Fewer than fifty mourners followed the coffin through the estate to the church.

'There weren't many came. A couple of republicans stood on the hill above the road and made their presence felt,' said Bernie. They made a video of those attending. 'I held my head high. This was my husband. He was a good father. He was a good person. I thought to myself, "We won't be stooping to the level you are at."'

In his time, Eamon Collins had stooped to appalling behaviour in the aftermath of murder – and he is unsparing of himself in *Killing Rage*. Having set up one RUC man to be killed, Collins went to his graveside to read the messages on the wreaths in case any of his police colleagues had left any useful personal details. Then he blessed himself and said a little prayer for the dead man's soul.

When he joined the IRA, he wrote, 'I had to descend into the darkest pit of amorality . . . Death had become my way of life, my everyday mission, my reason for living.' The local RUC commander described him as a 'psychopath'.

He'd joined the 'nutting squad', the unit that interrogated alleged informers, even though by the time he was invited to do so, his feeling that the armed struggle was futile was at an advanced stage. 'We were continuing to embrace death recklessly,' he wrote. 'The war was over; the only thing was that no one could call it off.' He was told, 'At some stage down the road you could find yourself executing touts.' He did not demur.

He had, he wrote, become 'a diminished, dehumanized being incapable of feeling for my victims . . .' Since 1984, when he began to be subjected to intense RUC harassment, he had been having premonitions of his own death. 'So what?' he wrote. 'Another pointless death to add to all the other pointless deaths I had been responsible for.'[10]

Bernie said that after her husband's murder, she was 'full of rage' and the longing for revenge. She went home after the funeral and washed all the windows in her house. 'I was full of nervous energy,' she said.

'There was a mission in town and I went to it a couple of evenings and spoke with one of the missioners. I remember telling him I hated God. I asked him how a human being was different from a cow. Didn't we rot in the ground the same way? I'd lost my faith, and I'd had a strong enough faith before.

'He was very good and down to earth and not a bit priestly. I began to realise I wasn't doing myself any favours. I'd lost a lot of weight. I wouldn't have gone to bed till three in the morning and then I had to get up early to get the kids to school. I had to get back to normal. I had four young children and I had just qualified as a social worker. I had bills to pay. I went back to work within three months.'

She vowed she wouldn't leave her home in Barcroft, but after a couple of years, she did move. 'It was just time,' she said. 'It was part of the healing process, moving on.'

* * *

There could be no healing for Vera McVeigh. She still did not know what had become of her son, Columba, who had disappeared in 1975. Her husband, Paddy, had died in 1997. The couple had continued to hold out hope that Columba might turn up; Vera had even taken to fantasising that he might appear at the door with his children. Then, one Sunday morning in 1999, she opened up a newspaper. There she read that the IRA had abducted Columba in 1975 in Dublin, taken him to the border and shot him dead as an informer. Columba had not gone missing; he had been 'disappeared'.

'Twenty-three and a half years of all hell let loose and then this was the end of it,' she told me. 'After he went away, I never left here, in case he would come home. Such a stupid thing to think.' She was disgusted by the claim that he had been an informer. 'Thank the Lord Jesus I have that consolation – he wasn't in the IRA. The fucking IRA. I'd rather what he is today than that. That was thanks to me preaching. He wouldn't have let me down. The only thing Columba was interested in was lassies.'

That year, under pressure from families, and from Father Denis Faul, the IRA admitted that it had 'disappeared' nine people, including Columba. A commission dealing with the location of victims' remains was set up. Those with information could give it without the risk of being prosecuted.

Eugene, Columba's elder brother, also read about what had happened to his brother in a newspaper. He remembered that his son was playing at his feet as he read the article. 'I remember feeling, sweet Jesus, I have sleepwalked through these years,' he told me. He said that when he went back to Donaghmore to see his mother after the truth came out, he had the feeling that the village was 'a nest of vipers'. It was clear local IRA men had been involved, had seen Vera's long anguish and had done nothing to relieve it. One of them had, during the years when Vera was waiting for Columba, served her Communion at Mass in the local church.

* * *

There was to be no healing for the Reavey family either. In 1999, the Reverend Ian Paisley stood up in the Houses of Parliament and claimed that Eugene Reavey was one of the IRA men responsible for the 1976 Kingsmills massacre, which was carried out the day after loyalist gunmen had murdered three of Eugene's brothers and three members of another Catholic family. When Alan Black, who had almost died in the massacre, heard what Paisley had said, he was shocked, he told me, because he knew it was not true.

'I met Eugene in a newspaper shop in Newry a couple of days

later,' he said. 'He was in an awful state. He said to me, "Alan, I had nothing to do with that." I said, "I know you didn't, Eugene.""

The two men were together as they spoke to me about this. Eugene had brought me to meet Alan. When we arrived at his house in Bessbrook, the pair had a long chat about country-and-western music before we began to speak of the terrible past. Alan's brother is a singer, and Eugene is one of his fans. 'I have no hesitation in saying that this man is innocent,' Alan said, very formally, for the record. They smiled at each other, and at me, as I wrote it down. Alan had made it his business to be seen with Mrs Reavey, too. 'It was all I could do,' he said. 'It was a bad thing that was done – it was character assassination.'

It was also a strange reversal of the strong stand Paisley had taken after the IRA murdered John Bingham in 1986. Bingham, an Orangeman, had been injured when a bomb he was making exploded prematurely in 1971, killing two other UVF men. He had been jailed as a UVF commander. He'd been convicted on weapons offences. UVF men posed for photographs holding guns aloft over Bingham's coffin, on which his UVF cap had been placed and which was draped with a UVF flag.

Despite all this, Paisley, who attended the funeral – to the consternation of the Catholic bishop, Cahal Daly – spoke in the Northern Ireland Assembly to protest about the fact that BBC Northern Ireland reporters had described Bingham's paramilitary background in their coverage of the murder. 'A man is innocent until proven guilty,' he said. 'The BBC has no right to destroy a man's character.'[11]

Paisley made the allegation about Eugene Reavey under parliamentary privilege. He said Eugene had set up the Kingsmills massacre and brought several other named men to the scene. He was a 'well-known republican'. Paisley spoke of the 'wild men' of the IRA who were free because the government had not been ruthless enough in putting down terrorism. He said his information came from security-force files. The claim reinforced loyalist rumours which had been put about that Eugene's brothers had been killed, not as innocent Catholic victims of sectarianism, but because they were IRA men.

It was a dangerous claim. A decade earlier, in 1989, a Tory minister, Douglas Hogg, had said in Parliament that there were solicitors in Northern Ireland who were 'unduly sympathetic' to the IRA. A few weeks later, a UDA gang murdered solicitor Pat Finucane at his home. It would later emerge that most, if not all, of that gang were security-force agents.

'It put me and my family in grave danger,' said Eugene. 'It was another terrible blow for my mother, after all that she had already suffered.' Eugene's father had died five years after his sons were murdered. 'He had to get through not only the murders of his sons but also the security-force harassment that followed and the whispering campaign against our family,' Eugene said. This continued even though at the inquest into the deaths of the brothers, the police said the family was not believed to have paramilitary connections.

'I grew up in a good time when there was no trouble,' said Alan. 'My own children grew up in the Troubles. My father used to say a decent man is a decent man and a bastard is a bastard. From an early age, I drummed it into my children that there would be no bitterness in our family, and there's not a bitter bone in any of them.' Eugene nodded. 'Not one,' he said.

'I'm not a great speaker,' said Alan, 'but when you look at what was done, you have to speak.' He shook his head in disgust.

After Paisley made the speech, committing the claim to Hansard, Seamus Mallon, the then SDLP deputy first minister in the new executive at Stormont, expressed outrage. Eugene went to the then chief constable of the RUC, Ronnie Flanagan, who assured him he had 'absolutely no evidence whatsoever' to connect him with the massacre. Nor was there any police file containing such an allegation. But Paisley refused to retract it.

* * *

In the same year that Ian Paisley made his claim, the suspicion among nationalists that members of the security forces had been party to the murders, by loyalists, of Eugene's brothers and dozens of other Catholics was dramatically corroborated – by a member of the paramilitary gang responsible. This man was former RUC sergeant John Weir.

In a thirteen-page affidavit which he provided for a journalist who was being sued for libel over a controversial book, Weir described extensive collusion between the RUC, the UDR and loyalist paramilitaries. Gangs consisting of this combination of forces, and using weapons owned by the state, had carried out assassinations and bombings, including the atrocity with the largest death toll in the conflict, the Dublin and Monaghan bombings of 1974 in which thirty-three people died.

As a young constable in Belfast in the early days of the Troubles, Weir said senior officers were well aware that police guns were being given to members of the UDA. He was sent to County Armagh to work in a specialist anti-terrorist unit called the Special Patrol Group (SPG). He 'quickly discovered' that many members of this entirely Protestant unit, along with other members of the RUC, the RUC reserve and the UDR, actively supported the loyalist paramilitaries.

After a murder in which information passed on by Weir had played a part, he met with other members of the Armagh SPG and agreed that 'the only way to stop the IRA murder campaign was to attack the Catholic community itself, so that it would put pressure on the IRA to call off its campaign'. The other RUC men told him they had already carried out the bomb and gun attack at the Rock Bar near Keady. The bomb had failed to explode, but one man had been shot and injured by another RUC constable.

Weir said he later learnt that a farmhouse owned by an RUC reservist at Glenanne called James Mitchell had been used as a base for many of the attacks. A UDR intelligence officer had provided the explosives for the Dublin and Monaghan bombings, and both the RUC and the UDR knew the identities of those who carried out these atrocities, possibly even before they were carried out.

The gang had carried out the murder of the two GAA supporters who were stopped by men in military uniform at a spurious UDR checkpoint on their way home from a match in Dublin and shot dead. It had carried out the gun and bomb attack on Donnelly's Bar at Silverbridge, killing two men and a teenage boy. Weir said his associates claimed this was in revenge for the IRA murder of a local UDR man. On the same night, it had carried out a bomb attack in Dundalk which killed two men.

The attack on the Reaveys was carried out by a gang of four, several of whom were in the police or the UDR as well as the UVF. The attack on the O'Dowd family on the same night had been co-ordinated with the attack on the Reaveys.

Weir learnt of several other terrorist attacks by the gang, both north and south of the border. He attended meetings at the farmhouse in Glenanne and observed armed men in camouflage parading in the yard. He said that at one meeting he learnt that the RUC and army intelligence had known about plans for a bomb attack on a pub the previous night, in which two people were killed. In fact, the farmhouse had been under surveillance, but the bombers had not been stopped. He also alleged that a loyalist group called Down Orange Welfare was manufacturing weapons which he and other RUC men transported to the farm at Glenanne, where they were sold on to the UVF.

In 1977, Weir had taken part, along with Constable Billy McCaughey and two notorious UVF men, in an attack which became known as the 'Good Samaritan murder'. William Strathearn ran a grocery store in the County Antrim village of Ahoghill and lived with his wife and seven children above the shop. After he was woken up in the early hours by someone knocking on the door downstairs, he called out the window to ask what the person wanted.

The man said he needed aspirin for a sick child, and the shopkeeper came down. They shot him dead on the doorstep. Because superior officers, special branch and army intelligence were well aware of the activities of the Glenanne gang and had given the 'green light' by their silence, Weir said in his affidavit that he did not think there was 'the slightest possibility' that he would be arrested or charged with the murder.

However, what did begin to rattle the group was the growing suspicion that British army captain Robert Nairac was playing republican and loyalist paramilitaries off against each other and feeding them information about murders carried out by the 'other side' with a view to provoking revenge attacks.

McCaughey had a breakdown, and while in a mental hospital, told the story of his activities with the UVF, including the murder of William Strathearn. He named the others. He and Weir were charged and tried. The other UVF men were not even questioned, for what a police witness called reasons of 'operational strategy'. Weir said he later learnt that one of them, Robin Jackson, 'was untouchable because he was an RUC special branch agent'. McCaughey and Weir both got life sentences. After his release in 1992, Weir said he had learnt that his details had been 'leaked' to the IRA. He moved to Nigeria.

Eugene Reavey drove me around the area and showed me the farm run by James Mitchell and the homes of others whom he believed had killed his brothers. One of them had a biblical tract over the door. Eugene knew Mitchell. He had worked as a poultry adviser in the 1970s and used to visit the Mitchell farm, which was down a steep lane just a mile or two from the Reavey family home. Eugene said people knew Mitchell was a loyalist and suspected he associated with paramilitaries. Friends used to joke to him, 'Watch yourself at Mitchell's.' After the murders, the police warned him against going there.

11

Corrupting Another Generation

The war was over but the killings were not. They continued after the ceasefires in 1994 and even after the Good Friday Agreement in 1998. The momentum had gone, though, and by the end of the twentieth century the Northern Irish conflict was all but over, though the paramilitaries continued to recruit young members. Most of the people who have died in Troubles-related violence since 2000 have been killed by loyalists.

Unionist support for the Agreement was shaky from the start, and it soon became apparent that the 'creative ambiguity' which had been woven around essentially unresolved issues would not survive the day-to-day business of running a government. The most contentious issue was IRA disarmament: unionists insisted it was a prerequisite for Sinn Féin going into government; Sinn Féin insisted it was not. The first executive, led by the UUP and the SDLP, was set up at Stormont in 2000 and, under pressure from Ian Paisley, collapsed in 2002.

The politicians who had emerged from the UDA and the UVF supported the Agreement, but it was not long before the UDA largely abandoned politics. One of its 'brigadiers', a big, hulking man called 'Grug', told me in 1998 that he'd gone back to seeing things Paisley's way and regretted voting 'Yes' in the referendum. The UVF seemed increasingly indifferent to the progressive ideas so eloquently espoused by the leader of its political wing, David Ervine, who appeared more and more isolated.

The loyalist paramilitaries had always been prone to feuds, often over territorial issues to do with racketeering or other criminal matters. Quite a number of leading figures killed by the IRA over the years had been betrayed to the republicans by their own former comrades. Feuds were dangerous for nationalists, as once the internal killings ended, there was often a spate of sectarian killings. It was as if this consolidated the new regime.

Loyalists had seen themselves as an unacknowledged wing of the security forces. The end of the Troubles left them demoralised, a situation well reflected in the plays of Belfast-born Gary Mitchell. In one of these, a paramilitary leader turned loyalist politician tells his deputy to get the men on the ground to change. They can't change, the deputy replies, 'We made them that way.' An intransigence based on decades of 'not an inch' and 'no surrender' politics will not yield readily.

* * *

In 2000, loyalists hacked to death two teenage Protestant boys from Portadown. David McIlwaine and Andrew Robb were the victims of a feud in which they had no part. Their killers took them after failing to find those they intended to punish. The pair had been at a local nightclub in the village of Markethill and had been asked to a party afterwards. They were taken away and killed with knives, their bodies abandoned on a country road and found by a young woman who was driving her small children to a dancing class the next morning. She told the children to look away, but one of them kept talking about the man in the road covered in blood. I asked a local businessman with a good knowledge of the paramilitaries in the area who he thought was responsible. He didn't know, he said. 'There's none of the boys round here would be capable of doing the likes of that. Not to Protestants, anyway.'

A year later, on Remembrance Sunday, sixteen-year-old Glen Branagh marked the day by getting together with about a hundred other Protestant teenagers from the narrow working-class streets of Tiger's Bay in North Belfast and setting out to start a riot. The police observed them heading purposefully down towards the interface with the New Lodge district; then sirens were sounded in both areas, the young Catholic males emerged, and within minutes, four hundred youths were hurling missiles and abuse across what used to be known as the peace line, now termed the interface.

This was the sort of activity that young Joseph McCloskey had got involved in after the murder of his grandfather in 1994, a little further along the interface. Joseph had outgrown it by now. A couple of his friends had got hurt: one of them had a blast bomb thrown at him, and another was shot at with an air rifle. The cross-community work Joseph was doing through his secondary school began to influence him. 'I was fed up being bitter,' he said. 'I decided to give Protestants a chance.' He also discovered a talent for football, and it became his passion.

The rioting went on, but by 2001 it had become routine. The then first minister, David Trimble, called it 'recreational', and community workers from both sides of the sectarian divide were trying hard to find ways of distracting this hard core of young people with more constructive activities. However, as one such worker, himself a former rioter, put it to me, 'It is hard to find anything that compares with the buzz you get from a riot.'

Glen Branagh was in a youth club, and one of the workers there told me he was 'exuberant, full of life, and with a lot of promise'. His photograph shows a grinning boy in a baseball cap with spots on his chin. His nickname was 'Spacer' and he was a bit wild – but not a bad boy, not a bully or a vandal, the youth worker said. However, by the time he was fifteen, Glen had been recruited into a very different sort of youth organisation: he had joined the Ulster Young Militants, the youth wing of the UDA.

The police had their own routine for dealing with these Sunday riots: they threw a barrier across the road between the New Lodge and Tiger's Bay and pushed the young nationalists back. On that Sunday in 2001, they were facing the young loyalists, at a distance of about fifteen metres, when they saw a masked youth run towards them. He was raising his arm to throw a device which was fizzing in his hand. It exploded. Glen Branagh's hand was blown off and he received terrible head injuries. He died shortly afterwards. Mandy Branagh had lost her son. Jonathan, Sam and Natasha had lost their brother.

The UDA's reaction to the death was to lie. Its spokesmen claimed their young foot soldier had died a hero. The pipe bomb that killed Glen had been thrown across from the nationalist side, aimed at Protestant women and children. Glen had bravely picked it up and was preparing to throw it out of the way so that it would not harm anyone. Privately, many loyalists admitted this was nonsense, and the police said they had closed-circuit television footage of the entire episode. But the UDA refused to relinquish its own version.

'So young and yet so brave,' said one of the cards tied to the wilting carnations on the railings which became Glen's shrine in the following days. 'We respect your commitment to loyalism,' said another, from the LVF. An Ulster flag had been laid out on the pavement to mark the spot where he fell, while a UDA flag hung from the lamp post above it. 'Tiger's Bay Young Gun' was spelt out in flowers on a wreath. Nearby graffiti spelt out the crude politics in which the teenager and his friends had been indoctrinated: 'UYM KATS', meaning Ulster Young Militants Kill All Taigs.

All that summer, the UDA had been sending its young out to plant pipe bombs at the homes of Catholic neighbours in mixed villages and housing estates. It had also been involved in the 'Holy Cross protest', during which loyalists blockaded the road along which nationalist parents brought their four- and five-year-old girls to school. The loyalists, who claimed they were under threat, threw bags of urine at the children and their parents and hurled sectarian abuse at them. They also threw a blast bomb. The PSNI said that, overwhelmingly, the summer's violence was emanating from Protestants.

All the old guns of the UDA came out for young Glen Branagh's funeral. The 'brigadiers' who, after thirty years of sectarian warfare, were still 'blooding' their young, joined the teenagers, who wore their UDA ties with obvious pride. Dark suits, white shirts, dark glasses. Thousands of men and boys on the march. On the footpaths, messages spray-painted in gold and silver remembered Spacer, and women and girls sobbed.

Across the road, blocked by the British army, a handful of young nationalists hung an Irish tricolour out of a high window. Others danced about on the street, hoping for a bit of action. It was clear that there was no respect for the dead in a place where there was little for the living. The funeral passed a pub with a plaque celebrating famous locals. They included actor Kenneth Branagh, a distant relative of Glen's, and Buck Alec, who was reputed to have kept toothless lions in his backyard. A redundant army marched through Tiger's Bay as, a week before his seventeenth birthday, Spacer lay dead.

* * *

Like Glen Branagh, Alan 'Bucky' McCullough was a Belfast boy who had joined the Ulster Young Militants when he left school at fifteen. By 2003, aged twenty-two, he was deeply involved in paramilitarism. He was a hard man. The heavy gold chain he wore around his neck had been his reward for playing a part in 'operations' which included murder. He had a tattoo on his leg of the Grim Reaper holding an Ulster Freedom Fighters flag. He wore a pendant round his neck which held a photograph of his father, William 'Bucky' McCullough, who had been murdered by republicans in the INLA after he was betrayed by his former comrades in the UDA.

That was in 1981, when Alan was just a baby, a few months old. His mother said he grew up idolising his dead father. He was twelve when the UDA called a ceasefire in 1994 and expressed remorse for its victims. His bedroom was decorated with the UDA flag which had covered his father's coffin, and a mirror with his own name on it, emblazoned over the figure of a masked gunman.

By the time he was seventeen, Alan was a 'military commander' in the UDA's 'C' Company on Belfast's Shankill Road. 'He always said he'd control the Shankill at a younger age than his father did,' said one woman who knew him. Once he'd joined the UDA, 'that was that', she said. 'He was a wee boy that got given a man's job.' His mentor was the local 'brigadier', Johnny 'Mad Dog' Adair, a vain psychopath who had been jailed for his part in more than twenty sectarian murders after he had boasted of them to an undercover police officer. Adair had emerged from prison under the terms of the Good Friday Agreement, pumped up with steroids and wearing a T-shirt with the word 'Replay' on it. He ran 'C' Company as a lucrative gangster business: shebeens, drug flats, brothels, extortion rackets, robberies, pipe bombings, grenade attacks, low-level violence against Catholics.

Adair's base was on a housing estate called Boundary Way, in a house known as the 'Big Brother house'. The big, bare field in the middle of the estate was known as 'Johnny Square' and was surrounded by murals celebrating his prowess. He controlled the bleak streets, using young men like Alan McCullough as his enforcers.

Alan, his girlfriend and their two-year-old daughter had moved into a flat across the road from his mother's house on the estate. They ran a small shop from a Portakabin out the back. Along with bread and milk, they sold cigarettes and painkillers. Alan did not smoke or drink, and spent hours every day in the gym perfecting the muscular physique favoured by Adair's set.

After decades of paramilitary dominance, in the early years of the new century the lower Shankill was a desolate place. A local research project showed significant mental-health problems, high rates of assault against children in their own homes and a level of educational attainment that ranked among the lowest in the UK. Less than 1 per cent went on to further education. Most, like McCullough, left school with no qualifications. At the turn of the twenty-first century, a group of teenagers was asked by a community worker what they would like to do with their lives. A majority said they'd like to be 'former paramilitary prisoners'.

Adair clearly saw himself as the natural successor to the late Billy Wright, known as 'King Rat', and was forging links with the LVF without the say-so of the UDA, which turned against him in 2002. He was in prison in February 2003, when his young acolyte, Alan McCullough, set up the murder of Brigadier 'Grug'. He was returning from a Rangers match in Scotland when he was ambushed and shot dead. Furious, the UDA moved into the Shankill. Most of 'C' Company surrendered, but a hard core of Adair's closest associates, including McCullough, were expelled.

They got the night boat to Scotland and got housed in Bolton in Lancashire, where some of them soon got involved in drug dealing and criminality. Adair beat up his wife in a park. UDA spokesmen said they would never be allowed back to Belfast. William 'Mo' Courtney, a leading figure who had defected to the mainstream UDA at the height of the feud, threw paint over one of the many murals of the bald-headed Adair, then took over. A spokesman said the UDA had to 'get back to basics and support the community'. Its broken ceasefire was to be restored.

'Alan was a home bird. He couldn't stay away,' one Shankill woman told me. His girlfriend came back first. McCullough negotiated with the UDA. It is understood his willingness to be loyal to the new Belfast regime was tested. He was asked to attack Gina, Mad Dog's exiled wife, and did so, shooting at her house in Bolton. McCullough may have been helping the UDA to lure some key figures from the Adair faction back to Belfast again – to their deaths.

He came back to his mother's house. On 28 May, he told his family he was going to a meeting with senior UDA figures. His mother asked him whether he trusted them. 'Two hundred per cent,' he replied. Courtney was one of those who called for him. They went into the territory formerly controlled by 'Grug' and had dinner at a hotel in Templepatrick. Alan McCullough never came home.

There was silence on the Shankill. People hurried away from reporters. However, I noticed that one house defiantly carried the PSNI's 'missing person' poster about McCullough's disappearance in its front window. Inside, women wept and a boy who looked to be about eleven sat in an armchair smoking and talking about revenge. The man of the house had been murdered during a previous loyalist feud in 2000. 'They're scum, the ones that did this,' one of the women told me. 'Johnny Adair got blamed for everything, but he kept this community together. The ones that took over has it destroyed. Open your mouth and you get put out. This place is like a ghost town now.'[1]

The body was found eight days after McCullough disappeared, following a tip-off from a member of the public who had seen suspicious activity around a derelict house in the rural hinterland of loyalist North Belfast. It had been buried in a shallow grave inside the house, which was near the ruins of a UDA brothel burnt out by Adair in 2002. The young man had been shot in the head.

Kenny McCullough, Alan's brother, called for there to be no retaliation. 'My brother is gone and I don't want another family to go through what we have been through,' he said. Alan's girlfriend was among about sixty women who protested on the Shankill Road on the Friday night after the body was found. They carried posters denouncing the UDA, which admitted the murder.

On Remembrance Sunday, Alan McCullough used to lay a wreath at the mural of his father round the corner from his home. The mural says Bucky McCullough was 'murdered by the enemies of Ulster'. Wreaths to his son were placed along the wall. One said, 'Murdered by traitors.'

Outside the McCullough home, a group of young men stood around. Neighbours came and went, comforting the family inside. Police in white Land Rovers watched, and there were armed soldiers on the corners. 'The wee lad was a good wee lad,' one of them told me. 'Did you ever hear of Billy Wright?' demanded another. 'He was the man. He was class. He was a prophet, you know. The RC [Roman Catholic] British government wanted rid of him because they knew he was going to lead a big Protestant uprising. He was a warrior.' There was a lot of madness in loyalism.

A young evangelical minister said something about 'blood sacrifice'. Then he went on, 'It is the orphan spirit. There are no fathers. No one is leading the way out of the quagmire. We need someone to envision the people.'

In 2006, Mo Courtney was acquitted of the murder of Alan McCullough. Although her son, like her husband before him, had operated a brutal system of justice that was outside the law, the dead man's mother said she was devastated. 'You have to ask yourself, is there any justice in the world at all?' Barbara McCullough said. Alan had been 'the baby of our house', but he had grown up 'listening to stories about his father' and had been brought into the UDA, only to be discarded. His murder, twenty-two years after the murder of his father, was 'history repeating itself', she said.[2]

She expressed her sympathy for Vera McVeigh, who had that week been photographed with Ian Paisley after he appealed on her behalf for those with information about the whereabouts of her son, Columba, to come forward. Barbara McCullough said she had been lucky to get her son back for burial. However, if the UDA had got its way, he, too, would have become one of the disappeared.

The Crown appealed against Courtney's acquittal, and in 2007, at his retrial, he dramatically changed his plea and admitted the manslaughter of Alan McCullough. He claimed he had brought the young man to the place where he was murdered, but that he had thought that what was going to happen was, at worst, a kneecapping. The trial judge said this would bring 'a measure of closure' to the McCulloughs. However, the family, which had been under the protection of police in riot gear during the trial, was unhappy at the verdict. 'Justice has not been done,' said the dead man's brother.[3]

'As the tide of terrorism abates, sectarianism re-emerges, oozing forth again to corrupt another generation.' These were the words chosen in 2005 by Mr Justice Coghlin as he convicted a Protestant man for the attempted murder of a Catholic man in Ballymena two years previously. The Catholic had saved his own life by pretending to be dead after a vicious beating. He had listened as the convicted man and his brother had discussed cutting up his body and disposing of it in a bin. While one of them had gone off in search of a saw, he had escaped.

These killers had been exposed to extreme Protestant fundamentalism. One of the brothers had been jailed before, for his part in the loyalist blockade at Harryville's Catholic church during the late 1990s. There he had heard a preacher instructing the mob one night that this was the 'ancient battle between the true church, Protestantism, and the Whore and the Beast and Baal worshippers within Catholicism'.[4] Despite the high death toll from internecine feuding among loyalists, those most at risk from their violence had always been Catholics.

Nobody knew what to say to seven-year-old Sean McIlveen after his big brother, Michael, who was fifteen, died in Antrim hospital in April 2006. He'd heard his mother's awful sobbing and screaming. He was there at Michael's bedside when the adults were all saying goodbye. He'd watched the photographer lean over the bed to take a picture. But what do you say to a little boy whose brother has been beaten and kicked to death?

His uncles and aunts gave him money and said he could go to the hospital shop for sweets. In the shop, all the newspapers had photos of Michael on them. He bought them all, and he bought a lot of lollipops, too. When he got back to the ward where Michael was lying, he laid the papers out and set a lolly on top of each of them.

Michael was born in 1991, so he was three when the ceasefires were called, and seven in the year of the Agreement, 1998. He was a Catholic, and it appeared that it was for being a Catholic that he was murdered in his home town of Ballymena, County Antrim.

It was a Saturday night. Mickybo, as all his friends called him, had been out with friends. He was attacked, but managed to make it back up the long hill to his home in the Dunclug housing estate, where most of Ballymena's Catholic minority lives. There his uncle spoke with him and saw that he was in a bad way. He called an ambulance. By the time he got to Antrim, Michael was in a critical condition and was put on a life-support machine. He died the following night.

His mother allowed a press photographer to take a photograph of him moments after his death and gave permission for it to appear the next day in the *Irish News*. After that, it was never to be published again, she said. In the photograph, the tubes from the life-support machine are still on his white face. His uncle is kissing his forehead. Other family members have placed their hands lovingly on his chest.[5]

In the days around his death, Mickybo's friends and enemies traded vicious insults on the web pages of the teenage chat room, Bebo. One young Catholic wrote: 'Did u c da pepers da day nice big pic of Michael on it the next pic we will be cing will be urs u wee scummy bastard hope u rot in hell!!!!?' A young loyalist defined himself in these terms: 'Hate all taigs Put one in the bck of there heads scum of da earth.' He listed his musical tastes as 'UDA' and his sports as 'rangers fc'. Under the heading 'scared of' he wrote, 'nuthin'.[6]

Michael's body wasn't released by the police for several days. All the young Catholics got 'Mickybo RIP' printed on the back of their Celtic shirts and walked around looking dazed. A lot of them told me they'd been attacked, too. They called the loyalists 'huns' and 'yoofers', from UFF, Ulster Freedom Fighters, the killing name of the loyalist paramilitary UDA. Not all Protestants are like that, I was told. 'Some of them are the best mates ever,' one boy said. 'They hate the yoofers, too.'[7]

Some of the boys clearly gave as good as they got. One said he'd been left unconscious after a beating with a wheel brace.

His mates 'caught one of the huns and hit him with a skirting board and left his eye hanging out', he said. One, a boy with a pit bull terrier straining at its lead, pulled up his shirt to show a belly criss-crossed with angry scabs. He said these lines had been carved on him with a knife. He was counting on his dog to protect him. 'Aye, he'd rip their arm off', he said.[8]

Michael's mother, Gina McIlveen, put up a shrine to her son outside the house, a big sheet of plywood covered with photographs from his brief life: chubby baby pictures, pictures of a little boy playing combat games, and one of a beaming Mickybo getting kissed on both cheeks by two blonde-haired girls. 'That's Michael with two wee girls from Ballykeel,' Gina told me. Ballykeel is a local Protestant estate. 'One of those girls had a brother died from an E tablet.'[9]

Gina was sitting on one end of a sofa that was snowed under with cards and letters. 'I am hurt and heartbroken. I don't think I'll ever get over it. Me and my son were very, very close. There is not one person in this town could say anything against Michael. He was just a happy-go-lucky child. He was a brilliant kid and I'm really going to miss him.' She said she had no bitterness towards Protestants. She explained that the father of her youngest two children was Protestant, and though she had separated from him, she was raising the children to know both faiths. 'I have had great support this last two days from people from both communities. There has been people here from the Shankill Road in Belfast. Even Ian Paisley has phoned. But something has got to be done to stop this madness.'[10]

She'd had her own experience of the madness before she lost her son to it. The previous Christmas, she and her sixteen-year-old daughter, who was heavily pregnant, were in a shopping centre in Ballymena. 'This girl was following us around and she came over and said, "I'll kick that Fenian baby out of you." She went for me outside Santa's grotto, and then this man ran out and cracked my face with his fist and broke my nose,' she said.[11]

She knew the man, a local big shot in the UDA. She said the police told her they couldn't guarantee her safety if she proceeded with the case, so she dropped it. Then, about a month before he was killed, Michael had been attacked near All Saints church. 'His mouth was ripped. I wanted to go to the police, but he said, "Don't, Mummy. What did they do for you?"'[12]

She spoke in the bleak monotone of a person who's been given strong tranquillisers for a broken heart. She said Michael used to make her laugh when she was worried about things. 'We'd have a wee dance. He was the sort of child would ask the grannies up to dance at a wedding. He got everyone going.'

Among the photos on the shrine were several of Michael in full army fatigues. 'He loved combat games,' Gina explained. 'He was a marshal in a cross-community combat group. He loved Celtic and he loved Man United.' Young Sean had been listening. 'He loved Liverpool, too,' he said. 'Liverpool's crap.'[13]

That night, there was a vigil in Gina's garden. I heard her tell someone that the rhododendron which was in full, red bloom was from her mother's garden and had just come into flower, though it had never flowered before. Sean was proudly showing his friends all the tributes to his brother. There was a message from the Celtic team.

The upstairs windows of the house were open and Gina kept playing a song over and over again. 'There Were Roses' is about two friends, one Catholic, one Protestant, and one gets killed in revenge for the killing of the other. Each verse ends with the line, 'And the tears of the people fell together.' The song was written by Tommy Sands and it is a plea for an end to hatred.

Gina also played the Tracy Chapman song about getting out of the ghetto and away to freedom. 'Take a fast car and keep on driving.' But Michael hadn't wanted to escape Ballymena, she said. 'He was born here, and after we moved to Stranraer in

Scotland, they all broke their hearts to get back to it, so we came back.' Gina wanted to move to Antrim after that, but Michael had said, 'Why would we leave Ballymena? All our friends are here.'

Michael had lots of friends. Down at the black basalt wall where he was beaten people left flowers and teddies. A little girl was there with her mother. 'A Protestant hit me when I was coming out of school,' she said. 'But I have Protestant friends, too.' Friends sprayed messages onto the metal casing of some electrical apparatus. 'Them wee bodies don't know how to grieve,' a young woman told me. She pronounced the 'o' in bodies to rhyme with toe.

On the morning of the funeral, hundreds of the 'wee bodies' gathered at the house. Gina was still playing 'There Were Roses'. I saw a face I knew in the crowd. 'You don't remember me,' she said, with a smile. I did. I'd interviewed her the day after loyalists had shot dead her husband in Ballymena in 1993. She'd told me that after the gunmen ran off, she ran for help. She didn't run to any of her neighbours, who were Protestants. 'I wouldn't put blood on her carpet,' she'd said, bitterly, of one of them. She meant she believed the woman would care more about the bloodstains than the dying man. Instead, she ran down the road to the nearest Catholic house.

I asked about her little girl, who was three when her dad was killed. Her mother told me she was one of Mickybo's friends and was somewhere in the crowd. She'd become a top young GAA player. 'I drive her everywhere,' said her mother. 'This town is terrible.' She remembered I was heavily pregnant at the time. 'I had a girl,' I told her. 'She's twelve now.' She called over a big tall man in motorbike leathers and introduced us. She hugged him. 'He's made me very happy.'

Michael's family began to load the wreaths and floral tributes into the funeral cars. It took half an hour, there were so many.

Silence fell as Gina emerged from the house, hardly able to stand, clinging to a relative. 'The Fields of Athenry' was played from the house, with its wrenching line: 'Michael, they are taking you away . . .' Then the men of the family carried Michael's white coffin down the path.

At the funeral, the Catholic bishop of Down and Connor told mourners that the name Michael McIlveen had joined 'the long sad litany of those murdered by sectarian hatred'.[14] He said that exposure to a culture of intolerance and sectarianism made a young person's heart 'a storeplace of hate'. Such exposure began when they had to listen to hate-filled words, he said, and quoted the Psalms: 'Their teeth are slings and arrows, their tongues sharpened swords.'[15]

The local priest pointed out that Michael had shared his last meal on earth, a takeaway pizza, with a Protestant friend. He spoke of the crucifixion as 'the world's darkest hour' and said that on the day of the 'wanton murder' of Michael McIlveen, 'darkness descended on Ballymena'. Michael had died 'a brutal and unjust death', he said, 'like his saviour'. Then he said that if Michael's death led to a new vision for Northern Ireland, he would not have died 'in vain'.[16] It was a sentiment that had been expressed hundreds of times at the funerals of victims of the Troubles.

Two months later, a loyalist gang attacked a group of young people who were tidying up after a summer party in a back garden in Derry. The party had been organised as a going away celebration for a young man who was going to teach English in Azerbaijan. Those attending were not only of mixed religion but of mixed race – but the house would have been perceived to be Catholic. A twenty-nine-year-old Catholic man was beaten up so badly that he was left in a coma from which he is unlikely to return.

PART II
Aftermath

1

The Damage Done

'For those who lived through it, war is never over . . . it stays with them like a mental hump, a painful tumour . . . [they are] possessed by the past, by the constant returning to what they lived through . . . the psychic and moral wounds were deep.'

Ryszard Kapuscinski[1]

'I can't believe I've lived sixteen and a half years on this earth without Patsy,' said Kathleen Gillespie. 'I can't believe I've managed that. He was the heart of the family. How did I live?'

Patsy was blown up by the IRA in 1990. Many of those who were bereaved by the Troubles had similar feelings of bewilderment. Looking back, it seemed impossible that anyone could survive such pain and loss.

When I interviewed them in 2007, it was thirty-five years since Merle and Billy Eakin's child, Kathryn, was killed in the IRA's Claudy bomb. 'Thirty-five years – a lot of hours,' said Merle. 'Your whole heart is just pulled out of you, it really is.' Billy agreed. 'Nothing is any good,' he said. It had been the couple's wedding anniversary the day before the bomb, and they'd celebrated it with their children. They have never celebrated it since. 'We have no heart in doing anything,' said Merle.

Many did not, in fact, survive. In some cases, people died many years later as a result of their injuries. A policeman from County Tyrone who was left paralysed and unable to communicate after being shot in the head by the IRA in 1973 died from his injuries twenty-two years later. One of his relatives said his death was all the more heartbreaking, coming as it did 'now that there is peace in the country'.[2] An Enniskillen headmaster who was critically injured in the IRA's 1987 bomb went into a coma from which he never recovered consciousness. His wife set up a nursing home and cared for him there until he died, thirteen years later.

Others died of less tangible injuries. Silence killed men in particular. Mo Morton's father stopped eating. He pined away and died within two years of the death of his soldier son, Terence, who was blown up by the IRA in 1974. Mo said the family believed he felt guilty because his son couldn't have joined the army as a fifteen-year-old without his consent. But he didn't talk much.

The father of Henry Cunningham, shot dead in 1973, also died soon after his son. His nerves went, said one of his other sons. 'He never talked about it, but he never got over it.' Silence was the outward sign of the pain that would kill Paddy McVeigh, too, whose son, Columba, disappeared in 1975. He lived until 1997, but according to his wife, 'He really died of a broken heart.' He never talked about it, she said. 'No, he'd have walked out of the house sooner.'

Broken hearts killed many, many people during the Troubles. Jude Whyte, whose mother, Peggy, was killed in a loyalist bomb attack in 1984, also said that although his father lived until 1996, 'really he died that night'. His father had idolised his mother and depended on her. 'After Mum died, there was no going back. He lost his spark . . .' He also took to drinking heavily. Jude said that one of his regrets is that he was intolerant of his father during those years. Jude himself suffered years of mental breakdown.

In 1992, a fifteen-year-old schoolboy was shot dead by the UDA in Belfast. His dying words were, 'Tell my mummy that I love her.' His mother became ill and died before two years were out. Her husband said the UDA had killed her, just as it had killed their son. 'The bullets that killed James didn't just travel in distance, they travelled in time,' he said. 'Some of those bullets never stop travelling.'[3]

Jim McCabe felt he had damaged his relationship with his children, because after his wife was shot dead by the RUC in 1981, he didn't talk with them about it. 'I was busy campaigning for justice for my wife. I didn't realise what they were going through.'

He had certainly harmed himself. 'The kids have grown up emotional and so affectionate, whereas I am known as Stoneface, or sometimes, the Silent Man,' he said. 'I don't let anyone get close to me. My daughter asks me, "What was mummy's favourite flower?" I say, "I don't know. I don't think she had one." They say, "Dad, you have got so hard." I tried to protect them from becoming bitter, but I have become a person who hates, and I know that has a way of coming back at you.'

It took eighteen years for John Maxwell, whose teenage son, Paul, was blown up with Lord Mountbatten in 1979, to realise that his grief was locked inside him and that he needed to learn to speak about it. When people tried to talk to him about it, he got upset and couldn't cope. He had learnt to avoid it, to deflect the conversation. In 1997, he went to a psychiatrist.

According to psychiatrist Oscar Daly, who has worked with people bereaved in the Troubles and people who survived assassination attempts, when a bereavement is traumatic, 'it is far more likely people will run into trouble'. He said 'survivor guilt', while it was mostly completely irrational, was common and was a symptom of serious depression. Anger, turned inward, could lead to suicide, he said. As for the many illnesses which people believe were precipitated by experiencing the violence, Daly said, 'There is no doubt that trauma can impact physically on people. There hasn't been enough good research done on these issues.'[4]

Broken hearts may take time to kill, but heart attacks have more immediate effect. There were deaths that were due to the shock of witnessing a murder or getting the terrible news that a loved one had been murdered. In 1973, the daughter of one Belfast man had to tell him that his son, and namesake, had been shot dead by loyalists. She described what happened next: 'He got down on his knees and beat the path and cried, "My son, my son, I loved my son."' He suffered a massive heart attack and died. He and his son were buried together.[5]

Laurence McKeown's mother endured the stress of watching her son starving himself to the point of death on hunger strike, while also coming under intense political pressure from the IRA, the British government and the Catholic Church. She had a heart attack during the prison protest and died of heart disease two years after she saved her son's life by taking him off the hunger strike. 'Probably it was the hunger strike killed her,' Laurence said.

When a sister-in-law of Martin McBirney heard that he had been shot dead by the IRA in 1974, she had a heart attack and died. In 1980, a UDR man was ambushed and shot dead by the IRA as he left a Fermanagh police station. He was not thought to have been the intended victim. His friend happened on the scene, had a heart attack, crashed his car and died. In 1972, a forty-eight-year-old woman heard that her policeman son had been shot by the IRA. She had a heart attack and died; her son, who was badly injured, survived. He said that as far as he was concerned, 'the IRA murdered my mother'.[6]

Some families suffered multiple bereavements. One seven-year-old child was killed when a UVF bomb exploded as a republican parade passed through West Belfast. His mother had forbidden him to go, but he had sneaked out. Then his great-uncle went out to find a phone box so that he could tell relatives in England about the child's murder and was shot dead by the IRA. The child's father would not let the family talk about his son's death. He became ill, had a nervous breakdown and developed agoraphobia. Ten years after his son's murder, he had a massive heart attack and died, aged forty-one. His wife, the child's mother, said in 2007 that she still suffered from very bad depression. 'I really think if it wasn't for my kids, I wouldn't be here. They are what keeps me going. I wouldn't get out of bed otherwise.'[7]

Other people simply could not survive the death of their loved one and killed themselves. Twenty-year-old student Julie Statham's boyfriend, Diarmuid Shields, and his father were shot dead by loyalist paramilitaries at their family shop in County Tyrone in 1993. Julie's family had tried to arrange for her to see a bereavement counsellor, but because of heavy demand, an immediate appointment was not available. Just under a month later, Julie wrote a letter. 'When they killed my darling, they killed me too ... I may be breathing and moving but what use is that when I don't have any emotions left in me? When two shots were fired my life ended. I may, at one stage, have had lots to live for, but 27 days ago everything that mattered was snatched from my grasp ... Let me also tell you, Mum and Dad – how very much I love you and how very sorry I am for the pain I've caused.'[8] Then she took an overdose. That day, someone from the counselling service rang to say that an appointment had been allocated to her.

Anne Maguire is probably the best-known Troubles suicide. The horrific incident in 1976 which led to the death of three of her children had inspired a campaign for an end to violence. According to the account of the incident written up on the Peace People's website, the young mother's mind was shattered. She was 'haunted by images of the three children she never saw again'. The family emigrated to New Zealand and had two more children. They later returned to Belfast.

In a 1997 article, Anne's sister, Mairead Corrigan, wrote that her sister suffered from psychotic depression. She had refused to accept that the children were dead, perhaps because she had never seen them buried, as she was too seriously injured to attend their funerals. 'She would often talk about seeing them playing in the garden . . . Anne became a troubled soul . . . she seemed to lock herself in a private world with her dead babies.'

Anne attempted suicide on several occasions, and finally, in 1980, three and a half years after the tragedy, she took an electric carving knife and slit her wrists. Her son found her dying. She left a note which said, 'Forgive me – I love you.'9

In 1974, a man's body was found in the canal at Newry, County Down. He had been suffering from depression since the British army had shot dead his twelve-year-old son the previous year. The circumstances of the child's killing were disputed: a judge refused to accept the army's claim that he had been shot during a riot, and the soldier who shot him was sentenced to prison for unlawfully killing the boy. However, he appealed, was released on bail a week later, and since the appeal was successful, was not returned to prison.

Mavis McFaul had attempted suicide after the murder of her partner, David Caldwell. He was one of the last to be killed, in 2002, when he picked up a Real IRA bomb at the army base in Derry where he was working as a labourer. 'Me and my daughter, Gillian, just don't seem to be moving forward,' she told me in 2007. 'It is like being in a whirlpool and you can't see the bottom and you can't see the top. People say there is light at the end of the tunnel, but what tunnel are we to go through to see a light?'

There was hardship, too. Because she and Davy were unmarried, the Ministry of Defence ruled that she was not entitled to his UDR pension. There was also constant vandalism of his grave. It wasn't sectarian, she said. It was done by people who hated her.

She believed the spirit of the man she'd lived with for nineteen years was still around her. 'Davy's an angel,' she said. On the morning before he died, Mavis told me, Gillian had been meant to go in to work with him to do some cleaning at the barracks. He had looked in on her and decided she was far too peaceful there asleep in bed to be disturbed. He'd straightened the quilt and left without her. 'His anniversary was there last week,' Mavis said, meaning the anniversary of his death. 'That morning, she woke up and the quilt was the same way as he'd left it on the day he was killed.'

Mavis didn't remember much about the day she tried to kill herself. 'I'd let everything pile into me,' she said. 'People say it is selfish, but that isn't right. It is the state your mind is in. I took all the pills in the house and I drove to the Foyle bridge and tried to drive over it. The police found me.'

The inquest was difficult, though she had been glad to meet the young policewoman who had comforted David as he lay dying. 'She is still very shook,' Mavis said. 'We had no idea about the extent of his injuries. He had a terrible death. His hand was blown right off him. God almighty. I find it terrible hard to live without him. It is like my own right arm is off me.'

*　*　*

In 1987, William Henry, the assistant governor of Magilligan prison in County Derry, shot himself dead while drunk. At the inquest into his death his wife said that he had become paranoid about his safety after receiving threats from the IRA. He had become prone to violent rages and excessive drinking.

'It was a life of twenty-four-hour intimidation,' said Dessie Watterson, who worked for twenty-five years in the prison service. 'And it was for life – they shot retired officers as well as serving ones.' He said he felt bitter towards the authorities for the way they had neglected the prison staff. 'The IRA was sending parcel bombs addressed to wives. A prison officer's wife couldn't even hang her husband's blue shirt out on the line. A hell of a lot of people just put the gun to the head. I knew at least twenty, and others who had their firearms taken because they were considered a risk to themselves. A lot took to the drink. Everything was just grey.'

There was a lot of anger among security-force families bereaved in the Troubles. There was a widespread belief that soldiers and police were sacrificed because the government refused to allow them to crack down on the IRA. Wreaths sent by the authorities were rejected, dignitaries were hissed at when they turned up at funerals, and letters from police chiefs and secretaries of state were torn up and sent back. The wife of one of the last policemen to be murdered by the IRA said she could never accept Sinn Féin's involvement in the police force.

The IRA and loyalist paramilitaries regarded prison officers, both on and off duty, as members of the hated security forces and therefore as 'legitimate targets'.

In 1992, an incident occurred which proved beyond doubt that there were dangerous levels of stress within the security forces. Allen Moore was a twenty-four-year-old police constable who had won a medal for bravery for pursuing and catching an IRA man who had attempted to bomb Moore's police Land Rover. By 1991, he was drinking heavily and attempted suicide. In February the following year, he attended the funeral of a colleague. He drank all day and returned to the graveyard that night to fire shots over the grave. He was arrested as he drove wildly away and examined by a police doctor, who said he might be a risk to himself. A gun was confiscated, but he had another at home.

Later that night, he made a series of calls to police colleagues, telling one of them that he was going to shoot named republicans. This man rang a local police station to warn them. Police gave conflicting versions of what followed, but the outcome was indisputable. Moore's second gun was not confiscated. In the morning, he rang the police station himself, said he was going to lose his job and added: 'Listen to the news.'

Later that day, the RUC did issue an 'armed and dangerous' alert, but nonetheless let him go when he turned up at a police station. Moore then proceeded to a Sinn Féin advice centre in Belfast, where he shot three men dead. Then he drove to the shores of Lough Neagh, phoned the police to admit what he had done, put the barrel of the shotgun in his mouth and killed himself. After his death, police found explosives in his bedroom.

At the inquest into his death, a psychiatrist said Moore had been 'a time bomb' and criticised the RUC for its handling of the case and for failing to face up to the fact that fifty-seven police personnel had killed themselves between 1978 and 1993.

Bill Harpur's mother died soon after his RUC brother, Thomas, was shot by the INLA. She hadn't been able to mourn at his graveside, Bill said, because it was constantly vandalised. Bill was full of rage. He had survived four murder attempts, and then in 1996, ready for a mental breakdown, he suffered two heart attacks. He also got skin cancer. 'That was the end of my working career,' he said. 'We are an embarrassment to the police now. I am speaking to you because in fifty years there will be no RUC men left to tell what it was like.'

He was disgusted by the power-sharing deal that has seen former IRA man Martin McGuinness installed as deputy first minister. 'I am a very bitter man,' he told me. 'I wore a uniform for my country and I suffered for it. All those years Ian Paisley stood up and shouted, "Never, never, never," and now to see him laughing and smiling with a republican terrorist by his side as his equal ... I will never accept this set-up at Stormont. It would betray the members of my family that died for their country.'

Bill still felt his life to be in danger. 'A relation of mine had a pipe bomb there at his house a few weeks ago,' he told me in early 2008. 'The Real IRA is just the same thing as the Provisional IRA, just wearing different clothes.'

He said he had suffered 'psychological trouble' for twenty years. 'I take eleven drugs in the morning and six at night. With my wife, marital life has ceased.'

In 1998, his soldier son, who had, he said, been under a lot of pressure, suffered a brain haemorrhage and died. Bill said he himself had considered suicide and that his life was a constant struggle. 'You never forget all the friends you carried on your shoulders. You'd turn around and say, "This will not be the last." I see every one of those men who's dead. I have buried them a hundred times. Some nights I don't sleep at all. I lie down and the demons come. Distorted faces. The wallpaper can make faces. They are sitting on my bed and looking out of my wardrobe. I think I am roaring out to my wife. And this has been my life.'[10]

* * *

Taking to the drink to deal with the stress of loss was an option easily taken in Northern Ireland during the Troubles, because excessive drinking was regarded as perfectly normal at all levels of society. One man lost a leg in a bombing, got compensation, spent it on drink and ended up a homeless street drunk. A man who knew him told me that when he got cold, he used to burn his wooden leg. He would get another one from the hospital. Eventually, he died on the street.

Gerard McErlane, whose brothers, John and Thomas, were shot by the UVF in Belfast in 1974, said that he 'hit the drink' afterwards. He ended up spending years in and out of psychiatric care, suffering from depression. 'I remember numbness. The psychiatrists couldn't come to any conclusion about what was wrong with me, other than that it was a delayed reaction to the murders of my brothers,' he said. 'I'd been numb for years but I'd have felt that if I blamed it on their deaths, I'd be letting them down.'[11]

The effect of the murders on his parents had been devastating, he said. A silence had fallen. 'From the day they were shot, the television was never on in my parents' house. There was never a birthday celebrated. My mother never spoke about it. She never mentioned my brothers by name. She hated Fridays, the day they died.'

His mother's whole focus was on her dead sons, Gerard said. 'My mother practically lived in the graveyard. She prayed for an hour every morning and then she went to the graveyard. She'd take a packed lunch and a flask, even in the rain and the snow. She did that every day for twelve years until her health got too bad.

'They could never find out what was wrong, but eventually they said it must be because of what happened to her sons. My father only lived eight years after they died. Four years ago, my mother found out she had cancer. She was happy because she knew she was dying. To be honest with you, I was at ease with her dying. She was in no pain. My sister always said she would die on a Friday, and she did. The pain of those twenty-eight years was released. I was happy.'

The loss of a twin is known to be a particularly traumatic bereavement in any circumstances. Alice Harper told me that after her brother Bernard's murder by the IRA in 1973, his identical twin, Gerard, could not be consoled. He didn't get better. The family ended up having to commit Gerard to a mental hospital for treatment. After he came out, they sent him to live with a sister in England. 'He has never slept in a bed since Bernard died. He'll just lie down. He doesn't eat,' Alice said. 'He is like a skeleton.'

Alice said she has tried to get him to talk about it, but he refuses. In 2006, aged forty-six, Gerard was back in Belfast to visit the family. He and Alice were at a garage near her home. Alice was paying for petrol. When she got back into the car,

Gerard said, 'Alice, don't look now. That is one of the men that took us away.'

Timothy Knatchbull, who was injured when the IRA bombed the boat he and his family were on with their grandfather, Lord Mountbatten, in 1979, has written movingly about the experience of losing his identical twin brother in the blast. He said he knew immediately that 'this was so calamitous for me that I must either get over it in that minute or I was never going to get over it'.

He then experienced 'a very strange period, perhaps an unconscious wish, of thinking that I had died and Nicky would wake up in the hospital bed'. Studies of bereaved twins have identified a sense in many of never feeling quite whole again. Timothy said he was helped by talking with Norris McWhirter, whose identical twin brother Ross had also been killed by the IRA. He, too, had experienced the sense of seeing himself dead.[12]

According to Eugene Reavey, whose brothers Anthony, John Martin and Brian were murdered by loyalists at the family home in Whitecross, County Armagh, in 1976, 'It isn't the remembering that is the problem; it is the reliving of it.' He said he was particularly afflicted at night-time, before going to sleep. His brother, who was the first on the scene of the slaughter, stopped talking for a year afterwards. Eugene's father had a series of heart attacks and died five years after the murders.

He said his mother's trauma was compounded by being sneered at and manhandled by the UDR as she accompanied the bodies of her sons home for burial. 'She was given tablets the night it happened and she was on them for years,' said Eugene. In 2003, Mrs Reavey had a breakdown. 'She kept saying she had murdered someone and she would have to go away.'

Like Mrs McErlane, Mrs Reavey found solace in being near the dead and the grieving. 'My mother is surrounded by candles,' said Eugene. 'She is praying for this one and that one, and if someone dies twenty miles away, she is off to the wake. She is always looking out for a funeral to go to, even for ones she hardly knew. If the funeral is at twelve, she will be at the church at half ten. That is just the way she copes. She found her own escape without ever knowing what a psychiatrist was. She has never cried, though, and she says she would love to.'

* * *

People talked about homes dying, too, after a murder. Jude Whyte spoke of it. After his mother was blown up on the doorstep, the family home was, literally, demolished, but so was the idea of home. 'Home was gone with her,' he said. I once interviewed the mother of a boy who was shot dead by the British army in North Belfast. She told me that at Christmas time, instead of having a tree in the house, she brought it up to his grave and had it there, all lit up in the darkness of the graveyard.

Jean McConville's children tried to manage on their own in their flat after she was 'disappeared' by the IRA in 1972, but they were taken into state care and split up as a family. Members of the family talked to journalist David McKittrick in 2003. 'It would have been a good family but it was a family split and ruined,' said Archie McConville. His brother, Michael, said, 'It was ripping the stomachs out of all of us, it was ripping us apart.'[13]

Sally McClenaghan's house was ransacked after she left it following the murder of her disabled son, David, in 1972. Her sister said that even the slates were stolen from the roof. It was done to show disrespect: it said that she'd been a Catholic in a Protestant house, one where only Protestants had a right to live. A teenage girl was murdered in 1997 by a loyalist who was a friend of her Protestant boyfriend's family. She was shot as she lay in bed in their house. Afterwards, the boy's mother told me, they could not bear to sleep upstairs in the house, and soon afterwards they sold the place for demolition. A block of flats was built on the site.

Several people spoke to me about rooms they couldn't go into because someone they loved had been murdered there. In 1971, the British army shot a young mother in Derry's Bogside. She died in her back garden, leaving a husband and young family. One of her daughters, who was eight at the time, told me, 'After that, our back garden was a no-go area.' This was the term that came to be used for nationalist areas that were barricaded in the early days of the Troubles so that the army couldn't enter. 'I never played there again.'

The loss of a family member can devastate relationships among those left behind. After his brother, Columba, disappeared, Eugene McVeigh said that his mother changed. 'It didn't make for easy living for the family,' he said. 'My mother became very detached from those of us who were alive. Selfishly, we wanted attention that she didn't have to give us. To be honest, she became unbalanced. She is my mother and I respect her and love her, but for all those years, she hasn't been the woman I knew. She lost her spark when Columba disappeared.'

Mrs McVeigh told me the pain she felt was 'the same as on the day he disappeared'. She spoke harshly about other people, but her voice softened when she spoke about Columba and she smiled.

One mother gave a moving interview to reporter Sharon O'Neill in 2006 about the murder of her son, Damien Trainor, a Catholic, along with his friend, Phillip Allen, a Protestant, as they sat together in a pub in the village of Poyntzpass. Phillip was soon to be married, and Damien was to be his best man. Mrs Trainor said, simply, 'I'm dead, darling.'[14]

She explained that she had never been able to cry. She didn't go to Mass and she didn't pray, but she did go to her son's grave. At the start, she asked Damien to pray for her, but she had stopped. 'I just go into the chapel, look at the crucifix and light three or four candles,' she said. She had attended the trial of her son's murderers and said one of them had menaced her family in the courtroom. 'He turned around like a bird, watching us,' she said.[15]

Mrs Trainor said she woke every morning in a cold sweat. Every day was the same, neither better nor worse than the one before. The newspaper published a photograph of her living-room wall. Above a crucifix there is a frame containing, against a background of bright flowers, a woollen bonnet and mittens that had been Damien's when he was a baby.

* * *

The Troubles still cast a long shadow over some of the places most affected by them. Ardoyne is a grim place, despite the valiant efforts of some of its residents, along with youth and community workers and some of the locally based Catholic clergy. There are murals on the gable walls insisting on remembrance: 'Remember collusion', 'Remember the hunger strikes', 'Remember 1916'. By day and by night, teenagers hang around the street corners smoking joints. Huge, barn-like clubs are full of men drinking, while women consume quantities of prescription tranquillisers of one kind or another.

When I arrived at one woman's house on the edge of the area, a tall young man, very pale and nervous, was standing in the kitchen. 'I'll go upstairs,' he said. She said it was all right, he could stay, but he shook his head and left. 'That's my nephew,' she said. 'He found his sister-in-law hanging in her kitchen two weeks ago. He can't go home since. He's afraid. Every time he closes his eyes, he sees her.'

North and West Belfast are now among the worst areas for suicide among the young. In some cases, entire groups of friends have killed themselves. In some families, more than one young person has died. Most of those affected were not born until the late 1980s to early 1990s.

The Troubles have ended, but there is a legacy of fear and depression. 'The amount of suicide since the ceasefires is shocking,' said Doreen Toolan, who lived in the area for many years. 'The young people have nothing to live for and a lot of the older ones have come through a lot of trouble. I have had a very hard life. I am just about living, and no more. I am just living for the day I die. Every day to me is a nightmare. I relive the night my husband was shot. I'm on tablets morning, noon and night. They hold back tablets on me – they'll only give me part of my prescription at a time. I think they think I'm suicidal. I don't know if I am or not. I'm a drug addict, I know that.' A worker at a victims' group that Doreen attended told me that one of the favourite subjects of conversation for the women there was their tablets.

Doreen smokes, too, constantly, and has a big electric air freshener pumping out industrial-strength pine scent to counteract the smoke in her kitchen. She regretted missing out on being a mother. 'I often look at my grandchildren now and I wonder, did my kids do that?' Doreen said she still spoke to her husband at night and was waiting to join him in heaven. 'If he's with some other woman, God help her when I get there,' she said, with her big, bleak laugh.

It was Doreen who brought me to meet Anne Larkey, whose house she was in on the afternoon before Terence was shot. Anne's young nephew, David, had been murdered by loyalists just days earlier. 'I don't like to talk about it,' Anne said, and began to cry. 'There was that many killed, wasn't there, Doreen? You wonder, where did we get the strength? How did we get through?' It was Anne who said that Ardoyne had been 'like a prison' during the Troubles.

The women remembered not being able to let the children

out for fear of them getting caught up in the trouble on the streets and a neighbour who used to complain about Doreen's children kicking their ball against her wall and into her garden. 'One day I went out,' said Doreen, 'and I took a sledgehammer and I smashed it into her wall and I said, "There's what I think of your fucking wall."' She laughed, loudly.

'People say, "I'd love to live my life over,"' said Anne. 'Not me. If you'd known what it was going to be like here, you'd have done yourself in.' Doreen nodded. 'No, I wouldn't live my life again,' she said. 'No, never,' said Anne. Her sister, Sally, who was raped and left for dead with her murdered son, had tried to commit suicide twice afterwards. 'She turned to drink, too,' Anne said. Sally died from the breast cancer her sister believes she got when the man who raped her and murdered her son bit her breast that night in 1972.

Anne had not really got over what had happened to her family, either. 'They offered me drugs after what happened, but I refused. I said, "This is reality. No use trying to get out of it with pills."'

She'd moved house several times to different parts of Belfast – no small matter for a couple with fifteen children – but had ended up returning to North Belfast. 'There is no use doing the gypsy,' she told me. 'It will follow you anyway.'

What she did regret was not leaving the North of Ireland right at the start of the conflict. 'I'd never have stayed here if I'd known what was in front of me,' she said. 'It was a waste of my young life.'

The British have always insisted that the Northern Irish conflict was not a full-scale war. 'Why were there British tanks on our street then?' Anne demanded. 'I mind the night the Protestants were burning the Catholics out of the street round the corner, and the wee woman up the road wanted us all to run up to the caves at Cave Hill and hide like they did during the Blitz.

The First and the Second World Wars only lasted a few years; this one lasted a lifetime.'

The Austrian philosopher Hans Mayer, who renamed himself Jean Améry, was tortured by the Gestapo for his work in the Resistance before he was deported to Auschwitz. 'Anyone who has been tortured remains tortured,' he wrote. 'Faith in humanity, already cracked by the first slap in the face, then demolished by torture, is never acquired again.'[16]

Anne Larkey had suffered this loss of faith. 'The person you are now is not the person you were before,' she said. 'You know that nobody is guaranteed tomorrow. When I think about anything ahead of me, I think, "If I'm alive . . ." It is like a Jekyll and Hyde thing. I trust nobody but myself. Sally was too trusting. You are not the same. You look the same, but inside you are changed. You go back and you torture yourself. Could I have done something? Should I have made her move from that house?'

Tears flowing, she said again: 'How did we come through it?' She spoke of all the young suicides and about having to go to give condolences to the bereaved parents. 'I just say, "I'm sorry,"' she said. 'I can't say any of those things that people say to try to be comforting. When you have been through it, you know there is nothing anyone can say that will make any difference at all.'

Her daughter, Anne Marie, came in with her little daughter. Anne smiled and reached out for the baby. Anne Marie looked concerned about the tracks of tears she could see on her mother's face. 'It was all such a terrible waste of innocent lives,' she said. 'And you know, it was going on in this area away back in the 1920s as well.' She began to talk about loyalist gangs from that period, some of them consisting of policemen. Sectarian murder had deep roots in North Belfast. Anne held up her hand. 'Stop,' she said. 'Don't go back to those times. We have had enough.' She smiled at her granddaughter and bounced her on her knee. 'We have, haven't we?' she said.

* * *

The loneliness of living with the memory of horror was an ongoing problem for Nathan Elliot, whose friend, James Morgan, was beaten and stabbed to death by loyalists in 1997.

I wrote to Nathan to ask him if he would let me interview him for this book. For a long time, he didn't reply, and when he did, he said he was torn. He was just back from a fortnight in Singapore, where he'd been taking part in a poker challenge. His parents wanted him to sign up for a postgraduate course, but he wasn't sure. He'd been on the point of heading off to Thailand a week before this, but had changed his mind on the way to the airport because he suddenly had a bad feeling about it. He was confused. He wanted to talk, but he was troubled about looking back at what had been a terrible time, one that had never, definitively, ended.

When we met, at his family's house looking out over the mountains he used to climb with James, he admitted he knew he'd been badly damaged. 'It was so gross and unbelievable,' he said. 'It was pure, unadulterated evil. It just seemed to come up out of nowhere. James's funeral was so overwhelming, and then just looking into his grave . . . just this black hole. It was pretty intense for three years or so. I tried not to think about it, but with a drink sometimes it would all come back with a vengeance. It just seems like such a waste. Such a complete waste. James was full of life. He wanted to do well at school. He was going to go to university. I'd say he'd have done something in computers. I'd say we'd still have been good friends.'

Nathan had gone to university in the north of England. He said it was hard to be among people who didn't know about the kind of things that had happened in Northern Ireland. When the subject came up, the conversation rarely went well. 'You'd just be full of anger, and you'd walk off. You'd think, "My mate was killed, what would you know?" People in England didn't understand any of it. People would ask you, "What's the matter with you people over there?" Then when you'd try to explain, they didn't really want to know. I remember one time trying to explain about James, but it was awkward and cringeworthy, and I decided not to talk about it again. It is impossible for people to relate to something like that.'

Nathan was very drunk one night and bumped into a man in a nightclub in Sheffield. The man turned on him violently and stabbed him. 'I was lucky – the stab wound was 5 mm from my lung. I might easily have died. All I could think was, "How many times did James get stabbed?"' He decided to return to Northern Ireland and enrolled at Queen's University in Belfast. 'Every so often I'd meet some of James's cousins or extended family. I regret that I didn't spend more time with his family at the time. It was just so painful. But I know that what I've gone through is nothing compared to what they have suffered.'

He said nobody had offered him counselling, and that he'd probably have refused it in any case. 'You just get through these things. You try not to think about it. You could never come to terms with it.'

Depression had dogged Alan Black since the Kingsmills massacre in 1976, though he is a remarkably good-humoured man. Having gone through the horrors of breaking his addiction to prescription drugs, he has not had recourse to them again. Anniversaries have been difficult. In January 2007, Richard Hughes had died, aged eighty-six. The death, thirty-one years after Kingsmills, left Alan feeling very much alone, the last survivor of the massacre. 'He was a quiet, kind and lovely man, and he and I came through that horrific ordeal,' he said. 'I went into a complete downer. I could feel myself going back to the old days of going to bed and crying and not being able to face the world.'

It aggravated and upset him that because he'd been caught up in a terrible incident, he was constantly being approached by journalists to comment on significant events in the peace process. 'I was just an ordinary bloke working in a mill who got shot,' he said. 'Now I get asked my opinion on all sorts of things, but I'm still just an ordinary, decent bloke. I was never a star. I just want to be anonymous.'

However, one thing he felt compelled to speak about was the Kingsmills massacre. 'I always feel it is a duty to talk for the boys who were murdered, to speak for those who aren't there to speak. They were decent men, harmless men. Their families have to take priority. For every one who died, so many others were hurt. There was one girl in one of the families and she was five when it happened and she has never spoken about it, ever. She just clams up.'

The assumptions other people make can make life difficult for survivors in other ways, too. A big, burly man with a scarred face, Derek Byrne has got used to people looking at him like he's bad news. After thirty-three years, the scars are well faded now, but there are deeper injuries which could kill Derek at any time. He has shrapnel all around his heart, too deeply embedded for the surgeons to operate. It is a miracle that he is alive. On 17 May 1974, at the age of fourteen, he was pronounced dead after the UVF bombed Dublin.

He couldn't feel any pain immediately after the bomb but has been in constant pain since. 'Still, twenty-four hours a day,' he said. 'I am meant to take two painkillers a day, but I take eight. There were times I'd take to alcohol as well, but it is no answer.

'At seventeen, I was being refused entry to discos. That stigma is still attached to me today – publicans just see the scars on your face. I've been putting up with it for so many years now, I just walk away. I think it is people on the outside who need rehabilitation. I was bitter, very bitter. I was frustrated. I fought with my friends. I'd just snap.'

He got a job at a bakery, and when it closed, he went to work on building sites. He took early retirement around 2005, fearing a heart attack. 'I flip sometimes,' he said. 'I just lose the head. I have a partner, Liz, and we've five children. I just snap. I mightn't speak to her for two whole weeks. I roar and bang doors. It is mental torture. It mightn't happen for six months and then it starts.'

Jim Dixon told me that the surgeons who treated him for his injuries after the Enniskillen bomb said it was a miracle he hadn't died. He was in constant pain, which could not be alleviated. Sometimes it became unbearable, he said.

Raymond Elliott had not been physically injured in the 1993 Shankill Road bombing but had been traumatised by taking part in the attempt to rescue people. 'Sometimes I wish I hadn't showed up that Saturday,' he said, bleakly. 'I still see what I saw that day every day. It doesn't get any better. A black veil just comes over you. My wife, Doreen, has got that she knows I'm having a bad day and to leave me be.

'I ask all the time, "Why me, Lord?" This has completely wrecked my life. I get annoyed when people tell me it is time to move on. There's days I just hope they pass. Sometimes I wonder if life is worth living.'

He pulled a bit torn from an envelope out of the back pocket of his trousers, a list of drugs with the times to be taken and the quantities, daytime and night-time. 'I don't want to be a walking zombie, but see those sleeping tablets? That is the strongest legal level they can give you and I'm still waking at four in the morning. I have to get up and wash my hands. I feel they are still full of blood.'

Facing the Enemy

'forgive us our trespasses, as we forgive those that trespass
against us . . . (the Lord's prayer, recited at Catholic and
Protestant funeral services)

Alan McBride agreed to take part in a public discussion on
'Dealing with the Past' in nationalist North Belfast early in
2007, and then spent the days before it worrying that the man
who murdered his wife would turn up. He avoided the remembrance ceremony immediately before the debate, because he
had a feeling Sean Kelly would be there.

Kelly is the man who, with Thomas 'Bootsy' Begley, planted
the IRA's Shankill bomb in 1993. He had written to the *Irish
News*, the paper read by Northern Ireland's nationalists,
expressing regret about those who died. Later, he claimed in an
interview for *Ardoyne, the Untold Truth* that on their way to
plant the bomb, he and Begley had repeatedly spoken about
their determination that no innocent civilians would be killed.
'There was absolutely no intention of killing innocent people
that day. We were talking about that even when we got out of
the car on the Shankill Road; we were saying, "Hope to God
that we get the right people here; hope to God there are no
innocent lives lost."'

Kelly repeated the IRA claim that its target was the leadership
of the UDA, which used a room above the shop. There was
meant to be time for the shoppers to escape. Kelly said the judge
who sentenced him to life in prison was wrong when he said it

was 'wanton slaughter'. The bomb exploded prematurely: 'There was nothing we could have done about it.'[1]

It was, of course, madness. The bomb exploded almost immediately after the pair entered the shop. There were no UDA men upstairs. It was like the 1975 bombing of the Bayardo Bar all over again – the intelligence was wrong. It was Alan McBride who'd drawn my attention to Kelly's account of the day. He told me he'd found the book by chance and had been bitterly disappointed by what he read there. It was denial, he'd told me. Kelly had concluded his piece by urging republicans to 'redouble' their efforts to reunite Ireland 'so that deaths like Bootsy's were not in vain'.

Kelly was released from prison under the Good Friday Agreement, after serving five years. He immediately became a constant presence at republican events, a thin, dark-haired figure with a pale face and watchful eyes. I'd approached him several times to ask him for a comment, but he always turned and walked silently away. Following a serious republican riot in Ardoyne, he was rearrested; prisoners released under the Agreement were on licence and could be returned to prison. The DUP claimed he had been involved in the riot; Sinn Féin said he was a steward, trying to keep the peace. Alan McBride commented to me that whatever impact Kelly's presence might have on the young nationalist rioters, the sight of him could hardly be expected to calm the young loyalists.

Graffiti on the Falls Road said, 'Free Sean Kelly', while graffiti on the Shankill Road said, 'Fuck Sean Kelly'. Sinn Féin campaigned for his release, pointing out he'd done his time and handing out leaflets that showed him as a family man, surrounded by his children. He was released again after a matter of weeks.

The discussion in which Alan McBride was to take part in 2007 was part of an impressive week-long programme called 'Respect', which aimed to address issues affecting the local community, including the aftermath of conflict. I went to the commemoration before the debate. It was held at a square in the middle of a redeveloped part of the area, surrounded by new, redbrick terrace houses. The open area had been turned into a garden of remembrance for local people who had been killed in the Troubles. The list engraved on the tall granite memorial wall was long. McGurk's Bar had been just down the road, and mother and daughter Philomena and Maria McGurk were near the top, along with the other thirteen people blown up in the bar in 1971.

One of the Sinn Féin speakers praised the IRA volunteers who had died over the years. 'They gave this community its self-respect,' she said. I saw Kelly, the familiar slight figure, standing in the shadows at the edge of the crowd, hands in the pockets of his parka jacket.

There was an attempt by the organisers to reach out to others whose names were not carved on the memorial but who had also died locally, soldiers and Protestants killed by the IRA. 'In war, all sides do terrible things,' said one of the speakers. 'The basis of respect is affording equal recognition to all who died.' Children came forward and placed lit candles at the memorial, 'in memory of all the families, everywhere, who have lost loved ones'. Someone played a lament on the tin whistle. I saw a couple of men approach Sean Kelly and speak quietly to him. 'Not a problem,' I heard him say.

The discussion was held in a hall up the road. Alan McBride gave what would in Protestant church gatherings be called his testimony. I had heard him do this several times, usually, like this, to a crowd that was largely nationalist and included many republicans. He had become well known and respected in these circles and had, the previous year, given the annual Bloody Sunday memorial lecture in Derry – again, largely based on the testimony of his own 'journey'.

After that event, in Derry's Guildhall, I had met Martin McGuinness. I said it was a pity so few Derry Protestants had come to hear Alan. 'He is a pioneer,' McGuinness said. Afterwards, Alan told me he had met with some disapproval when a photograph appeared in the local newspapers showing him with McGuinness at the reception in the mayor's parlour which followed the event, in which both were smiling broadly. Two years later, Ian Paisley would be appearing in similar photographs with McGuinness, but that had seemed impossible until it actually happened. McGuinness was right – McBride was a pioneer.

'We are screwed if we only think in terms of what happened to *our* people,' Alan said at the 'Respect' discussion. He described how his father had been in the UDA in its early days, before it started killing, when men like his father felt they needed to defend their areas. He was 'a lovely man, a beautiful man', Alan said. 'His heroes are the DUP.' His father had thought he was defending his people, he said. Alan had grown up believing that Catholics were the enemy and that they were ready to invade Protestant areas and put his people out. He recalled as a boy taking part in an angry picket of a new Catholic church.

He described how, after the death of his wife in the Shankill bombing, he had 'hounded' Gerry Adams and how he finally got Adams's letter claiming that 'no one was working harder for peace'. It was Kelly and Begley who carried the bomb into the shop, Alan said. 'They killed her, but they weren't responsible for the Troubles. I don't buy this line that we were *all* involved, that all of us have blood on our hands, but I do want to know, why did Sharon die?'

There had been a turning point. At the height of his anger, he had been invited by psychiatrist Oscar Daly to speak at a meeting in Scotland about post-traumatic stress disorder. The other speakers were two ex-prisoners, one loyalist and the other republican. Nervously, he had accepted. When they arrived in Scotland, the loyalist asked him would he go for a drink. Not wanting to be partisan, Alan had asked the republican if he'd join them.

At first, they talked about football, he said. 'But in the end we talked about our stories. After I told mine, the IRA guy touched my arm and said, "What happened on the Shankill Road was wrong and I, as an Irish republican, am sorry." That changed everything,' Alan said. 'He didn't add, "But you have to understand . . ." He didn't try to justify it or qualify it. That, to me, is the most important thing. People who committed murder have to take responsibility, not try to hide behind the fact that we were in a conflict.'

Then he talked about how anxious he had been in case Sean Kelly turned up at the 'Respect' discussion. He'd told me on the phone earlier that he had seen Kelly a couple of times that week: once when Alan was cycling down the Antrim Road from his work, and once in the supermarket. He wasn't ready to meet him, he told me. He didn't know how he'd deal with it.

But in the end, Kelly wasn't there, and it seemed as though Alan was almost disappointed. 'I thought he might be here tonight,' he told the audience. 'If you know him, maybe you could take this back to him.' He talked about reading Kelly's account of the bombing. 'He was making out it was an accident. I need people to look me in the eye and acknowledge it was wrong. I regret the loss of Thomas Begley. I respect his mother Mrs Begley's rights as a victim. Her sense of loss may be even greater than mine. My wife was an innocent. I don't know how I'd feel if Sharon had been responsible for the deaths of nine other people.'

A man spoke from the audience. He applauded Alan for 'coming into the lion's den'. Then he said, 'Alan, you said your wife was murdered, and I wouldn't argue. But when our people were killed, they never used that word. That's how you get the hierarchy of victimhood.' Another man said he didn't think that ordinary loyalists knew how ordinary Catholics had been treated. 'We were virtually prisoners in our homes,' he said. 'My son was shot by the Marines. They stopped me and asked me where he was. I said he was away. They said they'd get him in their own time. He was shot dead that night.'

Mike Ritchie, from the ex-republican prisoners' group Coiste, said of the IRA campaign: 'The UN recognises that people have a right to take up arms if the level of oppression under which they are living is too great,' he said. 'Self-defence is recognised in law. Alan spoke as an individual; republicans see themselves as a collective. This is a challenge for them – to tell personal stories and to hear them. They will find that difficult.' Ritchie had spoken in similar terms when he gave evidence at the Northern Ireland Affairs Committee hearings on dealing with the past in 2005. He said that republicans were unlikely to talk in any public forum about their individual involvement. They had thirty years of army discipline behind them and they would be more likely to speak in terms of what the IRA had done 'in relation to individual incidents'.

Asked about such individual incidents, republicans tended to adopt a passive voice. 'Terrible things happen in war,' was a favourite. I'd asked a friend to ask a former IRA man he knew who had been responsible for several killings if he would speak to me. The message that came back was that he didn't have any feelings about killing people, that those he'd killed were 'all Brits' and that he wouldn't talk about 'huggy stuff'. Oistin MacBride, whose brother Tony was an IRA man killed by the SAS, told me he had 'no problem with the issue of Tony being involved in stiffing'. This is the IRA jargon for killing. As a matter of fact, Oistin said, the level of 'stiffing' in South Derry should really have been higher. 'There was a war on,' he said.

The former unionist MP and UDR major Ken Maginnis had cast a similarly cold eye. After the SAS shot two IRA men he praised the operation but said, 'Two swallows do not make a summer.' Loyalist paramilitaries had fully absorbed the sectarianism that designated all Catholics as the enemy. Their hatred was expressed in such sayings as 'The only good Fenian is a dead Fenian' and in song lyrics like 'You've never seen a better Taig than with a bullet in his back.' A mural in the Maze prison summed up the attitude: 'Kill them all – let God sort them out.'

I went for a drink with Alan after the 'Respect' event. I asked him if he had intended to send a message to Kelly before he started. He'd always been so adamant that he wasn't ready to meet him. No, he hadn't, he said. He was quite shocked that he had done so. He'd just been so 'hyped up' in case Kelly was there, and then one of the organisers had told him just before the discussion that knowing Alan's feelings, they'd asked Kelly not to come. 'He said to me, "I had a word with Kells,"' Alan said. 'As if he was a mate of mine as well. That sort of hurt, knowing that these guys who I know and respect are that friendly with him. Kells, they call him.'

* * *

The question of meeting the enemy, those who had murdered someone you loved, had become inextricably bound up with the question of forgiveness through the person of Gordon Wilson because of his quiet and forgiving words after the death of his daughter, Marie, in the IRA's Enniskillen bomb in 1987.

In 1993, Wilson went to meet the IRA across the border in County Donegal. Although intensive negotiations were in fact going on behind the scenes between the British government and Sinn Féin, as far as ordinary people were concerned, no end to the unremitting horror of the conflict was in sight. Wilson pleaded with masked IRA operatives to end their campaign of violence. He told his wife he needed to confront them with the reality of what they had done before he faced his maker. She said that if he had kept his feelings bottled up, it would have killed him. The IRA rejected his appeal. He came home 'just pale and exhausted'.[2] The meeting took place under conditions of secrecy, but Wilson spoke publicly about it afterwards. Aileen Quinton, whose mother was one of those killed by the bomb, told me she felt 'contaminated' after he did this.

Wilson's 'forgiveness' of the IRA for killing his daughter won him admiration all over the world, with numerous peace prizes, a seat on the Irish senate and an endless demand for appearances on platforms and in television studios. Some of the other people bereaved in the bombing were dismayed and hurt by this. Jim Dixon, who had been critically injured, said he was 'full of righteous indignation'. The bomb was the work of Satan, a sin against God. Those who broke the law should be executed. Gordon Wilson had no right to forgive the bombers, he told me. 'God never forgave an evil man, God only forgives a repenting man.'

The local Catholic priest condemned the bomb in the strongest terms. Journalists were asking him what he would do if an IRA man admitted the bombing in confession at church. Confession was 'not a slot machine', said Monsignor Cahill. 'There is nothing automatic about forgiveness or reconciliation unless a person is prepared for a total change of heart.'[3]

However, some Protestants rejected such statements of solidarity. When a nun had come to try to help Mr Dixon's wife after the bomb exploded, Mrs Dixon sent her away, because she believed the Catholic Church was evil and supported the IRA. In 1972, Ian Paisley said the Provisional IRA was 'the armed wing of the Roman Catholic Church. Its real aim is to annihilate Protestantism.'[4]

One former RUC sergeant had survived an IRA attack

twenty-six years earlier but died in the Enniskillen blast. He and his wife were members of Paisley's Free Presbyterian Church. After he died, his wife found that he had marked a passage from the book of Proverbs in his Bible. 'These . . . things doth the Lord hate . . . hands that have shed innocent blood.'[5]

The fundamentalist attitude to IRA violence was laid bare in a series of bleak commentaries by the Free Presbyterian minister Ivan Foster, several of whose County Tyrone parishioners were injured in the bomb. Foster said the bomb was a message from God. It was God's punishment because too many Protestants were succumbing to ecumenism. Quoting the Old Testament, he wrote, 'Amos the prophet asked the startling question, "Shall there be evil in a city and the Lord hath not done it?"'[6]

God had allowed the Enniskillen bomb to happen because 'God will afflict a people who do not hearken to his word.' In condemnation of the evil ways of the Israelites, he had sent 'hunger, drought, blight, pestilence and war, Sodom-like destructions'. Protestants were becoming sickened by the attempts of certain clerics to promote unity. 'It is not good to eat too much honey,' say the scriptures.

Meanwhile, the cunning Catholic Church, known to Foster simply as 'Rome', was exploiting the ecumenists of Enniskillen. He described as 'effrontery' the holding in the town of a Catholic Mass for the dead, bereaved and injured. He was incensed that Gordon Wilson, along with a Methodist minister, had attended. 'Does he think his daughter is in purgatory?' he demanded. Protestants do not believe in purgatory, which is, according to Catholic teaching, the transitory place where souls are purified before going to heaven. Marie Wilson was with 'the Saviour who shed his blood for her redemption and needs no Romish Mass'. Foster urged evangelical Protestants to 'prepare to meet thy God'.[7]

The Reverend Ian Paisley also stressed that there was 'absolutely no forgiveness, none whatsoever, without repentance'.[8] In 1997, he preached at Drumcree that the 'cancer' that was destroying Ulster was ecumenism. In the same year, he once again equated Catholics, not just their Church but 'the entire pan-nationalist front', with the IRA.[9] Paisley famously claimed in 2004 that IRA decommissioning was not enough. They must also 'wear sackcloth and ashes'.

* * *

Kathleen Gillespie remembered seeing Gordon Wilson on television after the Enniskillen bomb in 1987 and saying to her husband, Patsy, who was watching with her, 'That man is either a saint or he has got himself into a corner he can't get out of.' Three years later, the IRA murdered Patsy by forcing him to become a human bomb. Kathleen had got to know Wilson, though she didn't warm to him. His words had been misunderstood, she said. 'He didn't really say he forgave them. He said he bore them no hatred.'

For her own part, Kathleen said forgiveness was not possible. 'I have publicly said I will hate the men who killed Patsy till the day I die,' she said. 'I can't forgive them. It isn't up to me; it was Patsy who was killed. Anyway, nobody has asked me to forgive them.'

Alan McBride had said something similar to me. He was close to and respected people who had supported the IRA. However, 'Forgiveness isn't really an issue for me. I am a Christian and I am interested in peace-building. I prefer to think in terms of being able to move on and let go. No one has ever asked me to forgive them. It isn't something I think about. My family would never forgive me if I forgave those who killed Sharon and her dad, and my family means a lot more to me than the IRA does.'

Alice Harper, whose father was shot dead by the British

army in 1971, said that after the Good Friday Agreement, a British paratrooper had come to a meeting in Belfast and asked people like her to forgive him. 'But he claimed he had never done anything wrong,' she said. 'So what were we supposed to forgive him for?' She struggled, though, because her mother had asked her children to forgive the killers of her husband and her son.

It was the IRA that had murdered Alice's brother, Bernard Teggart, in 1973. Alice said she accepted that the IRA had played a part in protecting her community from loyalists and the British army. However, it had, literally, labelled the child as an informer, hanging a sign around his neck with the word 'tout' scrawled on it before leaving him to die by the roadside. There was no deeper insult in the republican vocabulary.

Alice had campaigned tirelessly to get the IRA 'to tell me the truth, to clear my brother's name and to give us an apology'. It would help her family, she said in 2004, and above all, it would help her mother.

She got support later from the republican ex-prisoners' group Coiste, and in October 2004, the IRA issued a statement through the republican weekly paper *An Phoblacht*. It had carried out an investigation into the circumstances surrounding the fifteen-year-old's death, it said. 'At the time, no formal claim of responsibility for his death was issued. We can now confirm that Bernard Teggart was shot by the IRA. We offer our sincere apologies to the Teggart family for the pain and grief we have caused. The killing of Bernard Teggart should not have happened.' Alice said her family welcomed the statement. 'We have waited for the apology long enough,' she said. 'We are glad to get it.'[10]

Joseph McCloskey had overcome his urge to take revenge on Protestants for the loyalist murder of his grandfather, Joseph, in 1994, but the prospect of meeting his killers disgusted him. 'I still have a lot of hate for the people that did it,' he told me in 2007. 'I would hate to meet them. They don't deserve to be in the same room as me. They are pure evil.' He knew that some people could forgive, but he could not, he said. 'No way.'

Two IRA men were arrested after the bombing of Lord Mountbatten's boat in 1979. One was cleared and died some years later in a tractor accident. The other man was sentenced to life imprisonment, and after several attempts at escaping, he was released in 1998 after serving eighteen years. In the same year, John Maxwell, whose son, Paul, they had killed, had appeared on a platform calling for people to vote 'Yes' in the referendum on the Good Friday Agreement. He had already established himself as a campaigner for reconciliation, and it was a message that did not always go down well.

Shortly after the Enniskillen bomb in 1987, he had been asked to speak at a meeting about coping with the murder of his son. One of the things he said was that it helped to look at the context of the Troubles. 'I mean, you look back and you think, "If Paisley hadn't blocked every damn thing, Paul would still be alive,"' he told me. 'I've had people accusing me of not caring about Paul or other people killed by the IRA. I've met people who are so bitter that I feel like saying to them, "This is eating you up inside and it will kill you."'

John, who knew and was friendly with Gordon Wilson, said he was concerned for Wilson when he went to meet the IRA in 1993. 'I felt he returned very disillusioned,' he said. Wilson died in 1995. Nonetheless, after the man who had murdered his son was released, John wanted to meet him. He knew the town the man lived in, and he knew he had sons and a brother who was a solicitor. He also knew a priest who knew him. 'I tried to contact him through various channels,' John said. 'I wanted to get some idea of what he thought and why he did it. I wanted to ask him to justify it. But he obviously didn't want to. He never responded or sent any word.' John knew that such a meeting could have been traumatic. 'It would be dangerous for me to meet him,' he said. 'I could end up feeling very sore. But if he showed some sort of humanity or remorse . . .'

The poet Michael Longley had been moved by Gordon Wilson and spoke of other 'Homeric moments'. He wrote a poem about the occasion when a Methodist minister, who ran the Samaritans in Belfast, held a dying man in his arms and wrote a 'most eloquent tirade' against his loyalist killers, which appeared on the front page of the *Belfast Telegraph* that night. 'There have been other moments of grandeur,' Longley said. He mentioned the graveside oration given by Michael McGoldrick, whose taxi-driver son, also Michael, had been murdered by loyalists in support of the Orange Order's stand at Drumcree. The man had appealed to the killers to 'bury your pride as I bury my son'. The father got the news about his son's murder while he was on holiday in the mountains of Mourne. He said he fell down on his knees and prayed to God to forgive the killers.

Michael McGoldrick junior's wife, Sadie, had been pregnant with the couple's second child when he was murdered. She had kept out of the public domain, but having attended the trial of the loyalist who killed her husband, she agreed to make a short statement to the media. She came out of Belfast's Crown Court with a senior police officer. He said he would read out what she had written, and that afterwards she would not take any questions. Her statement said she was glad the murderer had been convicted, but that nothing would bring her husband back. At the end, a very experienced and normally very fine journalist thrust his microphone into her face. 'Do you forgive him?' he demanded. Her eyes filled with tears and she turned away.

The gang that killed Michael McGoldrick killed Sean Brown a year later. He was a respected GAA figure in Seamus Heaney's home town of Bellaghy. When Heaney heard the news, he was in Greece and had just visited the stadium at Olympia. He felt that the murder was 'a crime against the ancient Olympic spirit', which held that the athletic ideal was sacrosanct.[11]

Heaney contrasted Brown's involvement in drama and athletics, 'two of the great civilising activities of Greece', with the sinister violence of his killers. 'He represented something better than we have grown used to; something not quite covered by the word "reconciliation" . . .,' Heaney wrote.[12] It was apparent throughout the Troubles that loyalists and republicans sometimes targeted figures on the enemy side who were mainstays of their community. Sean Brown had worked hard to keep the mixed community in Bellaghy integrated.

The man who survived the IRA's Kingsmills massacre, Alan Black, said he had mixed feelings about forgiveness. He had no desire to know the names of those who carried out the massacre. 'It is quite possible that they might be people that I know to see, people who live near me even. I don't know how I could live with that,' he said. Like Sean Brown, he valued the fact that his village was mixed. He felt that people who had suffered a lot and lost people tended to be more forgiving than those that hadn't. 'I have a gut feeling that if you do wrong, you own up and apologise and then you can be forgiven . . .' He stopped. 'Well, no, not forgiven, but so you could say, "Well, I know where you were coming from and you were misguided."' He stopped again and shook his head miserably.

Eamon Collins' wife Bernie had similarly mixed feelings. 'People sometimes ask me, would you like to know who it is who did it? One part of me says, "Yes, name and shame them." Another part of me says, "What would happen if you knew some of them? How would you live with that?" Then I just think, "Leave it."' No one was ever charged with the murder of Eamon Collins in 1999, but it is widely believed that his killers were former IRA comrades. 'I had my feelings and suspicions but I didn't air them and I won't,' said Bernie. 'To be perfectly honest, I don't care. It doesn't make any difference.'

Newry has been designated a city, but it is a small enough town. Bernie meets republicans all the time, including many she knew well in the past. 'There are some who would say hello. There are others who ignore me. Some I just look through them as if they don't exist. I never confronted anyone. Part of me wouldn't let myself down to them,' she said. A lot of people live side by side with old enemies, she said. 'I have a friend who was shot six or seven times by loyalists. He lives a few doors away from the guy who set him up. That is how it was.'

For many people there was no question of speaking to the murderer of their loved one. Although his sidekick, Norman Coopey, was jailed, the loyalist who murdered James Morgan in 1997 was never prosecuted and continued to live just a few miles from the Morgans and from the home of Nathan Elliot, James's friend. Nathan had 'freaked' one day when the man got on the same bus as him and stared at him.

Nathan had moved to a flat in Belfast in 2007. He was working as a professional poker player. I called in on him. The flat was small and shabby, and apart from a computer and a television and a couple of photos, there was little sign of Nathan about it. He sat smoking on the sofa.

Whatever notion of revenge Nathan had entertained when he carried a hunting knife, it had passed. Another man, whose brother had been murdered, showed me one day a cleaver he had hidden at the back of a cupboard in his kitchen. He told me he used to drive at night to the killer's house and sit outside for hours with the weapon. He'd stopped, though. There is a Northern Irish word which well expresses this state of realising that there is nothing to be done but to put up with a bad state of affairs. It is the verb 'to thole', as in 'We'll just have to thole.'

When I met her, Kathleen Gillespie had recently gone to a faith healer because of a frozen shoulder and 'all sorts of illnesses and pains and rashes and anxieties'. A medical consultant had told her that these afflictions were probably stress-related and advised steroid treatment. She decided to try the healer first. 'He said he couldn't cure me,' she said. 'He said God couldn't cure me because I hadn't forgiven whoever had hurt me. He said I should write them a letter.' Her eyes flashed with fury. 'Maybe the steroid injection will work.'

Kathleen said she knew that she needed to try to 'let go of all the anger and hatred', but in the face of the loss of the man she had planned to spend the rest of her life with, she felt it was a tall order. 'We had been married twenty years, and we had a good life and we had three children and we had our own plans for when they'd grown,' she said.

She had, however, met with former members of the IRA. She had got involved with the Glencree Centre for Peace and Reconciliation in Wicklow, initially just meeting other people who had lost loved ones in the Troubles. 'At first the thought of meeting IRA people gave me attacks of flashbacks,' she said. But she had pushed herself. Meeting people from the organisation that murdered the man she loved was something she felt she needed to do, though it was tough explaining it to her family, she told me.

She attended a meeting at the centre which was addressed by a former IRA leader. 'The chairs were in a circle, but I grabbed one and sat myself down right in front of him,' she said. 'Nobody intimidates me. The facilitator asked me to move back into the circle. As soon as I got a chance I stood up and said, "My name is Kathleen Gillespie and I am the widow of Patsy

Gillespie, the human bomb. I am sure you know who I am talking about." I said, "Martin McGuinness has said my husband was a legitimate target. How can you explain that?" He talked rings around it and said nothing. You get nowhere.'

She understood why some people had joined the IRA. 'There's a lot of young fellows joined after Bloody Sunday in Derry, and I think they just got caught up in the glamour and excitement of it.' She'd joined a group in Glencree that included IRA women. 'They were saying they did the things they did for their community and their family. I said, "What about my family? My greatest fear was that my sons would seek revenge – thank God they've turned out all right. My life was ruined. What about my pain?" Of course, the tears were running down my face. The older woman said, "I'm sorry for the pain we caused you." But she didn't say she was sorry they had done it. It wasn't an apology.'

Kathleen said she had asked IRA people, 'Do you want me to forgive you? Are you sorry for what you've done? Have you any remorse?' She had not received any answers. She didn't respect the 'born-again' sort of loyalist killer, either. 'That's just another way of refusing to take responsibility,' she said.

Eventually, she had met Patrick Magee, who is known as 'the Brighton bomber'. He was part of the IRA gang that bombed the Grand Hotel in the English seaside town during the Conservative Party conference in 1984. The bomb killed five people, and Prime Minister Margaret Thatcher had a narrow escape.

After his release from jail in 1999, Magee had met with the daughter of one of those who died in the blast. Jo Tuffnall, who requested their first meeting, spoke about her reconciliation with the killer of her father in a BBC documentary shown in 2001. The pair shared a platform at a peace conference. Tuffnall said her seven-year-old child had asked if Magee was sorry. 'When I said yes, she asked, "Does that mean that Granpa can come back now?"' Tuffnall also described her own internal struggle between 'the side that wants to talk about reconciliation and the side that feels it is a betrayal'.[13]

Magee said that he often thought about his victims, although he did not say that he was sorry he had killed them. 'I deeply regret that anybody had to lose their lives,' he said. 'I have argued that the military campaign was necessary and equally now I would argue that it is no longer necessary. It's as simple as that.'[14]

Kathleen was not impressed by what she had seen and heard of Magee. 'I don't like him. There is a vacant look in his eyes. There is no remorse there. He is cold as a fish inside,' she said. However, what he said to her that day did in fact help her to move forward. 'He turned to me and said, "Patsy's death should never have happened. It was the worst thing the IRA ever did." There was a gasp around the table. Tears were falling down my face. I thought, "I don't like you but you have said what I believed for long enough." That was a turning point for me.'

There had been no such turning point for Vera McVeigh. She was plunged into rage and grief when she discovered in 1999 that her missing son, Columba, had been 'disappeared' by the IRA. It was believed that some of the IRA gang which abducted him in Dublin and brought him up to the Brackagh Bog in County Monaghan were from his own village, Donaghmore. She had heard Michael McGoldrick, the father of the taxi driver murdered over Drumcree, talking on the radio about forgiveness. 'A lot of nonsense,' she told me.

Gerry Adams has admitted that the IRA's practice of 'disappearing' people it had alleged were informers was wrong. He even called it a war crime. The IRA apologised. Some information was given, but much was withheld. A priest asked the McVeighs to pray for a dying IRA man who had Columba on his conscience. They were disgusted. 'No one came to our door with an open heart,' Eugene said.

Vera had nothing but anger for the murderers of her son. 'In God's own time he'll deal with them,' she said. 'And I hope they'll be trailing in bogholes and gutters and that they don't get away handy.' She was bitter about neighbours in the village who had never said anything to her over the years since her son disappeared. 'Every other house in this place is the three-letter word,' she said, meaning IRA. 'I know them. It is good to know people.' She said Sinn Féin people had never come to see her. 'They'd be afraid, daughter. They'd be shitting their trousers.'

She laughed wildly and then stopped. Striking her hand to her heart, she said, 'There is no forgiveness here. I'll take my chance with Peter when I get to the gates. That's my style. No forgiveness. I thank God I have a bit of religion in me. A good bit. I think of him. I pray for him. I have no call to pray for him. He's up there shining in heaven, and a whole lot of them will never see the road to it. The way I am with Columba is I have him here with me night and day. There is no question about that.' She sighed, a harsh, painful sigh. 'I feel the same way as the day he disappeared,' she said, again. 'And I know, looking out the window, they don't give a damn.'

In 2003, the body of the 'disappeared' Jean McConville was discovered on a beach in County Louth. One of her sons, Michael, told journalist David McKittrick that after the ravages of watching a series of unsuccessful digs for the body, he had a sudden revelation one sleepless night. 'For twenty-five years it was tearing me apart. It was ruining my life, hating them. Then I forgave them and that has changed me. I think I am a far stronger person now, a better person for it.'[15]

I got to know Father Dan Whyte because his parish in

Glengormley on the northern outskirts of Belfast was afflicted with loyalist gangs which continued to kill long after the 1994 loyalist ceasefire. I'd end up ringing him in the aftermath of these murders, mostly of young men.

Father Whyte had spent years in what he called 'the killing fields'. He remembered years when 'you were taking your life in your hands going out at night'. He spoke of his 'first blooding' and of his dread of hearing the doorbell in the night and going out to find a policeman with bad news. 'And it happened. I went out on a dark, lonely road, and there's a taxi with a man hanging out of it and his blood running into the gutter. Dead. Lured out, killed and abandoned. An indelible image. How could any human being do that to another? I had to go and tell his poor widow. There was a huge cross-community funeral.'

He was concerned that since Gordon Wilson's famous act of forgiveness, other people felt under pressure to behave in the same way, and then felt guilty when they could not. This was certainly true. I once heard a woman interviewed on the radio. She was asked what she felt about a multiple murder in her town. 'May God forgive them,' she said, piously. Then her tone grew fierce. 'And may they rot in hell.'

'I am not sure we are meant to forgive instantly,' Dan Whyte told me. 'But we are required to forgive.' He said the issue was surrounded by misunderstanding. 'Forgiveness has a bad name. It is a minefield. It is not about forgetting or denying or condoning what happened, and it isn't some namby-pamby thing which betrays the murdered person. It is the overcoming of injustice with good, and it isn't about how deserving of forgiveness the other person is or whether they have repented or asked to be forgiven.'

It was not a matter of a 'grim obligation', he said; it was 'a gift freely given'. However, it was utterly problematic. 'One of the terrible ironies of unjust suffering is that if the suffering person fails to extend forgiveness, then their own humanity is compromised. Until they forgive, they are not free, they remain prisoners of those that hurt them.'

People imagined that forgiveness implied giving up on justice, he said, but that was not so. 'You must also pursue justice,' he said. 'Justice is different from mercy. Justice demands retribution. That isn't inimical to forgiveness.' You could forgive someone and still do your best to see them sent to prison, he said. If people weren't convinced by the moral arguments for forgiveness, he said, they should consider this: 'There is no revenge so complete as forgiveness.'

I asked him what some of the biblical sources on forgiveness were. He laughed. 'Och, you're not going to bring religion into this, are you?' he said. 'The gospel is always asking us to do impossible things. Love your enemy? For God's sake! You need God's grace to do that.'[16]

Jude Whyte did not have 'God's grace'. He was an atheist. However, after the sudden death in 2007 of the Progressive Unionist Party leader, David Ervine, Jude wrote a remarkable tribute to him in the Belfast nationalist daily paper, the *Irish News*. Ervine had been in the UVF in his youth and had been jailed for transporting a bomb. In the 1990s, he had worked hard to try to move the UVF away from violence and to cultivate political activism among working-class Protestants.

Latterly, he had railed against the 'hamster wheel of violence' and against those who had used young men as cannon fodder, keeping them in a state of paranoia and fear, stoking old sectarian fires. Once, during a fierce Drumcree week in the late 1990s, I went to him to ask his views on the latest apocalyptic warning from Ian Paisley. 'He says this is Ulster's darkest hour,' I said. Ervine raised his eyebrows, stroked his moustache and sighed theatrically. 'Again?' he said.

Sometimes he caused grave offence. He told Peter Taylor on the BBC programme *Loyalists* that the UVF's Dublin and Monaghan bombs in 1974, which killed thirty-three people, were a matter of the UVF 'returning the serve' after the IRA's Bloody Friday. But he was a force for good, and I liked Ervine. He was passionate and brave about the peace process. I was grateful to him, too, for he'd stood up for my book *Northern Protestants* when it came under attack from some unionists. He died of a massive heart attack, a stroke and a brain haemorrhage.

In the article, Jude described how as a member of a Catholic family living in a predominantly Protestant part of Belfast during the Troubles he had come to 'fear and loathe the UVF in equal measure'. He said the first UVF commander he met told him it was his duty to kill as many Fenians as possible. This man later died from drug addiction.

'It was against this background and the fact that the UVF had bombed our home on two occasions, murdered my mother Peggy, murdered six people in the local bar and God knows what else, that I met David Ervine in 2003,' he wrote. Jude was teaching courses on community relations and conflict resolution, and 'unlike many politicians from the larger parties', Ervine agreed to speak on many occasions to different groups of students.

In one of the early classes, a woman asked Ervine to explain why the UVF murdered her husband in cold blood. 'He responded like no politician I have ever heard before,' Jude wrote. 'He said sorry, nothing more, nothing less. They were terrible times, he said, and if as a young man he had the opportunity to kill Catholics, he would have done so without reservation. There were no buts, ifs, maybes or any other mitigation. It was wrong then and it is wrong now.'

Ervine had explained that the UVF's policy was 'to murder

the easiest targets possible to instil fear and terror in the Catholic community and put pressure on the IRA to stop their campaign'.

Jude said he found Ervine not just non-sectarian but anti-sectarian. 'The last time I saw him,' he wrote, 'he had somehow found out that the UVF had been responsible for the murder of Mum. After a very emotive session with the students he collared me and apologised in a way that will live with me forever.'

Jude pointed out that his mum was fifty-three when the UVF murdered her. Ervine had 'left this world' at the same age. 'Two people who were reared within half a mile of each other but from different planets. Imagine writing an obituary for a loyalist politician who was part of an organisation who wrecked your life and your family,' he concluded. 'Such is the north, such is peace, such was Ervine.'[17]

It was twenty years since I'd last seen Jude, at a funeral in 1987. I emailed him when I read his piece. I told him I thought it would help others with difficult and conflicting feelings. We arranged to meet after Ervine's funeral two days later.

The funeral was huge. I stood outside on the footpath across the road from the East Belfast Mission where the service was held. It was relayed via loudspeakers to those outside. The road was packed with men in black suits and white ties, some with red-hand badges, many with tough faces. Ervine's brother, Brian, spoke first. This was not a funeral but a celebration of his brother's life, he said. David 'had the guts and the courage to climb out of the traditional trenches', he said.

The metaphor was telling. The UVF had been set up to oppose Home Rule, but when Gusty Spence and his gang revived it in the early 1960s, the then Northern Ireland prime minister, Terence O'Neill, banned it and called it a 'criminal conspiracy' which bore no relation to the original UVF, many of whose members fought and died in the First World War.

Loyalist paramilitary bands have avoided prosecution over the years by claiming their banners related to the 'old' UVF.

After it was over, Ervine's widow, Jeanette, stood in the porch of the mission and the dignitaries filed out, paying their respects as they passed. Meanwhile, the men on the road were forming into military lines to follow the cortège. Suddenly, it was Sinn Féin leader Gerry Adams who was hugging Jeanette, before walking down the steps of the church, flanked by other senior republicans. The men on the road fell silent and their heads turned as one towards Adams. In the past, they'd tried to kill him. They stared after him until he got into his car and was driven away. No one jeered. No one moved.

It was good to see Jude again. He still lived in West Belfast. We had dinner, and then Jude said we should go down to the Casement Club for a drink. The club was in the grounds of Casement Park, the big GAA stadium which had been occupied by the British army in the early days of the Troubles.

A couple of Jude's friends came over. 'I suppose you were at your UVF friend's funeral today,' one of them said to him with a sneer. 'No, I wasn't,' Jude said. 'I was working.' 'But you would have been otherwise,' the man persisted. Jude shrugged. 'He murdered your mother,' the man said. 'He was the bomber.' 'Well, he wasn't,' Jude said. 'But if he had been I'd still forgive him ten times over.'

I asked the man why he claimed Ervine was Peggy Whyte's killer, something that had never been suggested and for which there was no evidence. He drew himself up. 'IRA intelligence,' he said. Afterwards, I asked Jude if he minded such things being said. 'Not from him – he's a family friend – but there will be others who will tackle me for what I wrote,' he said. We talked about how it was a sign of the times that a man in a bar could start boasting about being in receipt of 'IRA intelligence'. Such idle claims could have led to an early death in the not so distant past.

Jude described the day Ervine spoke to him about Jude's mother's murder. 'He said to me, "I think you and I need to have a yarn, mate." He said, "I'm very sorry about your mother and the cop. I can't turn the clock back, mate. They were terrible times." Then he put his arms around me. I felt a ton had been taken off my shoulders.'

Jude knew well that Ervine wasn't just about 'huggy stuff'. He'd asked him about another recent post-ceasefire murder presumed to have been carried out by former UVF men. 'I'd just handed him a cup of coffee,' Jude said. 'He said, "Oh yes, we knew who did it but we couldn't bang them till we found where they dumped the body." Then he said, "Is there sugar in this coffee?" I said, "No, but there will be, very soon."'

Ervine and Jude had got on well. Jude felt that they had a growing friendship. Sport is sectarianised in Northern Ireland. Jude planned to bring Ervine to a GAA match at Casement Park, and Ervine was going to take him to a soccer match at Windsor Park in South Belfast. 'His death deprived me of a way out. I saw him as a conduit out of this darkness,' said Jude. 'I felt elated getting to know him. I felt he could help me. I feel more vulnerable now that he is gone.'

After the UVF stated in 2007 that it would put its guns aside but would not hand them over to the decommissioning body, Jude and I were on a radio panel together. Callers were demanding that the authorities clamp down on armed loyalist organisations. Several spoke angrily about the notion of forgiveness. 'Everyone has to do things their own way,' Jude said to one man. 'You don't have a monopoly on suffering.'

* * *

In March 2006, the BBC broadcast a series of television programmes called *Facing the Truth*. Archbishop Desmond Tutu, who had headed South Africa's Commission on Truth and

Reconciliation, chaired a series of encounters between people bereaved or injured in the Troubles and people from the organisations responsible.

'We pray that the wound will be opened, cleansed and a balm or ointment poured over it so that there will be a healing that will redound to the blessing of all of the people of this land,' said Tutu at the start. God, he said, had enlisted their participation.

I had read and admired poet Antjie Krog's book about the South African Commission, *Country of My Skull*, and knew that she felt passionately that the process depended utterly on Tutu's Christian spirit. But in the BBC programmes I found him patronising, manipulative and overbearing.

The final programme concerned Dermot Hackett, a thirty-seven-year-old bread-delivery man from County Tyrone. He was married with a child and very involved in charitable work. He was Catholic, but he sang in a choir which was mostly made up of Protestants.

In 1987, his wife, Sylvia, was pregnant. They were happy, except that the RUC had taken to harassing Dermot. Local SDLP politicians had protested to the police that they were risking setting him up as a target for paramilitaries. The IRA could have decided he was helping the police, while loyalists could have decided he was in the IRA.

One morning, Dermot was driving his Mother's Pride van on his rounds when a car pulled up alongside him. A gunman began to shoot, and didn't stop until he had emptied the clip on his sub-machine gun. Dermot died slumped over the steering wheel.

A year later, UDA man Michael Stone launched an audacious attack on mourners at the funerals in Belfast of three IRA volunteers who had been controversially shot in Gibraltar by the SAS. As the coffins were being lowered into their graves, gunfire

and explosions were heard, and Stone was seen firing indis-
criminately with a handgun and throwing hand grenades while
running down through the cemetery. Several young men ran
after him, catching him just as he reached the M1 motorway.
They had beaten him unconscious by the time the RUC arrived
and took him away.

Stone had killed three men. Three days later, mourners at
one of their funerals set upon two British army corporals, beat
them almost to death and then shot them. The soldiers, in an
unmarked car and plain clothes, were observing the funeral
from a side street. A woman I knew who lived with her IRA
partner next to where they were shot told me that for weeks
afterwards, when it rained you could still see their blood in the
puddles. 'Not very nice,' she said.

Stone was convicted of the Milltown murders, and he also
admitted killing three other men, including Dermot Hackett.
He became a loyalist celebrity. Another loyalist told me that
young paramilitaries used to ask him to get locks of Stone's
trademark long black hair for them. He got out of jail under the
Good Friday Agreement, and it became clear that he was
unwilling to leave the limelight.

He launched a career painting lurid abstracts, which sold
well, and wrote an autobiography which led to him being interviewed on the main TV chat show in the Republic. So it was no
surprise that he agreed to take part in the televised meeting
with Sylvia Hackett, her daughter and her late husband's
brother, Roddy. For her part, Sylvia wanted to use the opportunity to clear her husband's name. The UDA had claimed he was
an IRA man and that it had intelligence to prove this.

The interviews appeared to take place in the library of a
country mansion, with mahogany furniture and portraits and a
fireplace. The Hacketts came in first, and Sylvia and her daughter, Robina, both sobbed. The heavy footfall of Stone was heard

approaching. 'Do be calm,' beamed Tutu. 'We understand.' Sylvia said she had a few questions for Stone. Why did he do it? Who was behind it? Why was Dermot targeted?

Breaking down again, she asked, 'Why did you destroy me?' She had almost lost her home, as her mortgage was not insured. She lost a huge amount of weight, which endangered her pregnancy. Her mother died soon after the murder. 'The shock never left her face.' Her husband was a good man, Sylvia said. 'He was the best.' Stone insisted the UDA had acted on intelligence that the victim was an IRA organiser. Robina fled the room sobbing.

Tutu intervened. 'Will the truth help you?' he asked Sylvia. 'If it is the truth,' she answered. 'I'd even shake hands with you,' she said to Stone, 'if I get the truth only. But how will I know I'm getting the truth?' Tutu smiled at Stone. 'Thank you, Michael, for your patience,' he said, inviting him to speak. Stone spoke with some swagger about his time in prison, the 'university of terror', and of his motivation: 'It was vengeance.'

The killing of Dermot Hackett was 'nothing personal', he said. 'He was a soldier, I was a soldier.' The Hacketts exchanged disgusted looks. He then denied he was the killer. While he agreed he was morally responsible, he had not actually fired the fatal shots, he said. He'd only said he did to get a young man off and to get the security forces off the case.

Tutu mentioned the expectation that people taking part in these encounters would speak 'the gospel truth'. Stone preened. 'I'm a lot of things, but I'm not a liar,' he said. The UDA would not have insulted him by sending him to kill an innocent man, he said. 'I don't wish to come across as hard-hearted or a psychopath,' Stone said, though it was far too late. He had come across as both. 'I'm known as the cemetery killer. You feel like Freddy Krueger [a fictional undead serial killer].' He admitted he knew all along it was wrong to take a life. He wasn't seeking redemption.

Sylvia said she felt sorry for his children. 'I pray for you. I forgive you. I can face my man above – I hope you can face yours,' she said. Stone said he appreciated her forgiveness, and that she was a better person than he was. Sylvia was overwhelmed again by her grief and sobbed on her brother-in-law's shoulder. We heard a muffled, 'I'm lost.'

Then Tutu came back in with his celebrity smile. The show was nearly over; now for the grand finale. 'We have reached an extraordinary moment here,' he said. 'Michael has spoken of regret and asked for forgiveness. There was, earlier on, what Sylvia said about shaking hands. That must come from yourselves, but perhaps it is God who is present at this moment. There is need for healing on both sides.'

Sylvia stood up, reached out and shook Stone's hand. Then she snatched back her hand and sobbed, 'Oh my god, oh my god,' and ran from the room screaming.

Tutu went on with the show. 'You've done something that didn't seem possible,' he said to Stone and to the brother of the man he'd murdered. 'We are deeply humbled . . . and we pray God will bless you . . . It is only because there are people like yourselves that there is hope.'[18]

In November of the same year, Stone made the headlines again. Up at Stormont, the DUP and Sinn Féin were supposed to be engaged in a piece of pre-election choreography, with the former nominating Ian Paisley as first minister and the latter nominating Martin McGuinness as deputy first minister. The meeting had already turned to farce when Stone made a dramatic appearance, apparently armed with a gun, a knife and a smoking bomb. 'No surrender!' he yelled, charging across the marbled hall towards the chamber. Security guards disarmed him and he was taken away by the PSNI. He would later claim he'd been inspired by a television comedy show about

Northern Irish politics and that it was all just a piece of performance art.

Sylvia Hackett was disgusted. She said this episode had led her to question everything Stone had said on *Facing the Truth*. 'I don't believe any of it now,' she said. This had been a publicity stunt and, she now felt, so had the meeting with her. 'I hope they lock him up and throw away the key.'[19]

Gerard McErlane, whose brothers, John and Thomas, were murdered by loyalists in the 1970s, had watched the BBC programme, riveted and appalled. The next morning, he called a radio show on BBC Northern Ireland. Presenter Stephen Nolan was inviting people to respond to the TV programme, and Gerard was the first caller taken. He said the horror that seemed to overwhelm Sylvia Hackett when she took Michael Stone's hand had come from the evil that emanated from Stone. Nolan asked him what he would have done. I asked Gerard what he had said. 'I think I said I would have cut his throat,' he said. 'I got taken off air and they didn't let me on again.'

He had. I listened to a tape of the programme. He was followed by a furious woman whose brother-in-law had been shot dead by the IRA, while her husband and children had also been shot but not killed. They were a security-force family. She said she would never forgive, never, ever, 'if they crawled on the stones in front of my house till their knees are bleeding'. She, too, had been moved to violent feelings by Stone. 'I'd have reached for him,' she said. 'They'd have had to pull me off him.'[20]

3

Hierarchies of Victims

Gerard McErlane was deeply frustrated at not being given a chance to speak again on the radio programme, not least because he had not been able to tell the story of the murders of his brothers. He hadn't meant to say what he'd said, he told me; anger had got the better of him. He badly wanted people to know about his brothers. He believed nobody cared about them. He believed there was a hierarchy of victims: his brothers, working-class Belfast Catholics from an area that supported the IRA, had been murdered by loyalists. They were at the bottom of it.

He was not alone in this view. It had been expressed at the event at which Alan McBride had spoken about needing killers to take responsibility, and had received powerful corroboration from the former Metropolitan police chief, Sir John Stevens, when he reported in 2003 on his lengthy inquiry into collusion between the security forces and loyalists. He said he had analysed how the RUC dealt with intelligence from its agents about threats against individuals, his aim being 'to determine whether both sides of the community were dealt with in equal measure'. His conclusion: 'They were not.'[1]

The following year, the police ombudsman, Nuala O'Loan, strongly criticised the RUC's investigation into the loyalist murder of GAA official Sean Brown in 1997. The murdered man's son told me that 'right from the start of the RUC investigation, we just felt that the attitude was, "He was just another Catholic. What does it matter?"'[2]

Anne Larkey, whose nephew had been killed and his mother raped and left for dead, told me that the people of Ardoyne were regarded as 'less than human'. It didn't matter if they were murdered, and it was assumed that they must have deserved it, she said.

Early appeals for an end to violence from those who had suffered got lost in the clamour for war. Patsy McGurk made an eloquent statement of forgiveness immediately after he had lost his wife, daughter, friends, home and business in a loyalist bomb in 1971. He also said he was praying for those responsible, and he called for there to be no retaliation. However, British intelligence sources were meanwhile busy telling lies, putting it about that this was an IRA 'own goal'. The IRA was busy planning its revenge.

McGurk's appeal was ignored. Sixteen years later, Gordon Wilson spoke with similar grace about the loss of his daughter in the Enniskillen bomb. Wilson's great spirit made him world famous; McGurk's had long since been forgotten.

I first met Gerard McErlane at a conference in Belfast organised by the campaigning and support group Relatives for Justice in 2005. Most of the people taking part had lost relatives in the conflict, and many were from a republican background. 'Remembrance quilts' made by bereaved relatives were displayed around the walls of the dingy lounge on the edge of West Belfast. Each square commemorated someone. Squares which included Armalites were side by side with others that had teddy bears or motorbikes. I was chairing one of the discussion panels, and Gerard spoke up from the audience. He was disgusted, he said, that there had been such a furore in the media about the murder of Robert McCartney and so little about people like his brothers. He was white and shaking. He was applauded.

We met for coffee on the Falls Road not long after this. 'It is only from my mother's death four years ago, after twenty-eight years of hell, and this McCartney thing that I've opened my mouth,' Gerard said. 'After the McCartney thing, I was livid. Every party in the country, from the DUP to Sinn Féin, condemned it. Those sisters were flown all over the world, brought to the White House in limousines, interviewed on every television programme. Thirty-one years after my brothers were murdered, I haven't even got as far as Dublin.'

Gerard's brothers, John and Thomas, were murdered by loyalists in 1975. Robert McCartney was murdered in a Belfast bar thirty years later, in January 2005, after he intervened in a row between his friend and a group of men which included some who had been active in the IRA or Sinn Féin. Some of these people had just returned from commemorations in Derry of the Bloody Sunday massacre in 1972. The killing was brutal and protracted: McCartney was knifed and beaten to death with sewer rods outside the bar.

Republicans, with skills presumably well honed during the 'armed struggle', then efficiently cleaned up the scene to remove forensic and CCTV evidence. When police arrived at the homes of suspects in the nationalist enclave of Short Strand soon afterwards, they were met by rioters. Sinn Féin duly issued a press statement complaining about heavy-handed police tactics and harassment.

In December 2004, the DUP leader, Ian Paisley, had made his demand for the IRA 'to wear sackcloth and ashes'. Sinn Féin said it would not be humiliated; within weeks, one group of IRA men killed Robert McCartney, another carried out a massive bank robbery, and the IRA was seen to humiliate itself. Republicans denied the robbery and were defensive about the murder.

*

The murder of Robert McCartney, a father of two from the Short Strand, did attract massive publicity. It was condemned by the British, Irish and US governments. McCartney's sisters and fiancée mounted a powerful and moving campaign to bring his killers to justice. Sinn Féin was badly damaged and came under fierce pressure. Some of those in the bar had been elected representatives; others were members and supporters.

Some republicans sneered at the McCartneys for meeting US president George Bush, even though he was possibly the most powerful man in the world and Gerry Adams had been happy to shake his hand, too.

Almost no evidence was offered to the police; over seventy people claimed they were in the bar's toilet during the incident. Sinn Féin had not at this time agreed to support the post-Good Friday Agreement PSNI. It was reported that the IRA had privately offered to shoot those responsible. The family rejected this idea with disgust – it was justice they wanted, not revenge. The cartoonist Ian Knox portrayed Gerry Adams and Martin McGuinness reading a newspaper. 'I mean,' says an anxious McGuinness, 'it would be unreasonable to expect us to sign up to a policing system that was less than perfect! Wouldn't it?' Adams ponders the question, stroking his beard. The front-page headline on the *Daily News* reads, 'We'll shoot them for ye, missus.'[3]

Gerard agreed that the McCartneys had every reason to be angry and to fight for justice. 'Robert McCartney's murder was wrong,' he said. 'But dozens of innocent people from the Short Strand were murdered and tortured over the years, and their deaths have just been swept under the carpet. There was no one to sympathise, let alone offer to shoot someone. Maybe it is just jealousy or hurt, or is it the unfairness – were my brothers' lives not worth as much as theirs?'

* * *

The McErlane brothers had been murdered when the conflict was at its worst. Over two hundred people were killed in 1975, and more than three hundred had been killed the year before. Murders had become horribly mundane, and people were numb with the endless horror. Robert McCartney, however, was murdered thirty years later, at a time when the conflict was seen to be over. The brutality of his killers was more shocking because the times were peaceful.

But there was more to it than that. From the 1970s on, the defeat of the IRA was seen by the British and Irish governments and by unionists as the most urgent priority for peace. The notion that loyalist violence was a reaction to republican violence was largely accepted without much examination, other than by northern nationalists and republicans. Suggestions that the British colluded with loyalist paramilitaries were often dismissed as IRA propaganda.

Over the long killing years, attempts to suggest that the conflict was more complicated, by reference to parties other than the IRA who were engaged in violence, were seen as 'whataboutery'. The practice of 'whataboutery' – deflecting attention away from an atrocity carried out by your 'own side' by referring to an enemy atrocity, as in, 'Yes, that was bad, but what about . . .?' – was, in fact, common on all sides. Writing about the violence was fraught. The late distinguished journalist Mary Holland was disparaged by some as a 'fellow traveller' of the IRA when she argued that demonising republicans would not help end the conflict.

By 2005, a deal to restore the power-sharing executive in Belfast was tantalisingly close, with the IRA widely regarded as an obstacle to peace, even by Sinn Féin. The outrageous murder of Robert McCartney inevitably provided powerful ammunition to those in politics and the media who believed the IRA could now, finally, be pushed off the stage once and for all.

The DUP was to the fore in condemning the McCartney murder, claiming that it proved Sinn Féin were unfit to govern. However, when, in November 2007, a nineteen-year-old South Armagh man called Paul Quinn was beaten to death in a cattle yard in County Monaghan, with his heartbroken parents saying they had 'no doubt at all' that the IRA was responsible, the party had a very different attitude. One of the first politicians to re-assure unionists was the deputy leader of the DUP, Peter Robinson, who said he had been told that the murder was not sanctioned by the leadership of the IRA.

There had been no suggestion that the murder of Robert McCartney was sanctioned either, and no suggestion that either murder was politically motivated. The difference was that by this stage, Robinson was Minister for Finance in the new exec-utive at Stormont, in partnership with Sinn Féin, and it was not in the DUP's interests to see republicanism brought into disre-pute. The Irish Taoiseach, Bertie Ahern, likewise rushed in to say that the murder was 'not paramilitary but pertained to feuds about criminality'.[4] Under pressure from the family, he later stated that he did not believe Paul Quinn was a criminal. However, there was none of the clamour that had surrounded the McCartney murder, despite a valiant campaign by the Quinn family, to which the McCartneys lent their support. It simply was not politically expedient.

Political expediency bruised the widow of a policeman in the Republic when the issue of whether or not his killers should be released from prison under the terms of the Good Friday Agreement arose. Ann McCabe's husband, Detective Garda Jerry McCabe, was shot dead during a botched IRA armed rob-bery in County Limerick in 1996. Four men were jailed in the Republic for his manslaughter. The Irish government stated that they did not qualify for early release and strong personal assurances were given to Ann McCabe that they would serve out their sentences. This caused outrage among the families and colleagues of members of the security forces who had been killed by the IRA in the North. The killers in their cases had already walked free, and inevitably, they were wounded by the implication that the murders of their loved ones were seen as less appalling.

Under pressure from Sinn Féin to do a deal and give the McCabe killers early release in return for republican concessions during a late stage of the peace process, the Irish government wavered. The writer and columnist Fintan O'Toole wrote that for the politicians, the McCabe killing had become 'a political weapon, deployed with occasional sincerity, but with increasing degrees of cynicism and opportunism'.[5]

Ann McCabe campaigned hard to hold Taoiseach Bertie Ahern to his word. She confronted Sinn Féin president Gerry Adams during a St Patrick's Day event in New York in 2006 and demanded that he condemn the murder of her husband. In a moving interview with journalist Kathy Sheridan, McCabe said she felt she had been 'a pawn in the peace process'.

Northern police widows backed her, she told Sheridan. They had failed to stop the release of the killers of their husbands and they rejected the hierarchy of victims, but they identified with Ann McCabe's brave and lonely stand. 'I have met those people on numerous occasions and they are 100% behind me,' she said.[6]

Many from the unionist community did not consider that IRA members who were killed were entitled to be called victims at all. In 1982, the RUC killed three IRA men in what would become a highly controversial 'shoot to kill' incident in Lurgan, County Armagh. Lord Justice Maurice Gibson acquitted three policemen charged with the murders. The judge said he considered the killers 'absolutely blameless' and indeed he commended their 'courage and determination'. They had brought the three dead men 'to justice, in this case the final court of justice'.[7]

(Controversy over the shootings led to the Stalker Inquiry. Solicitor Pat Finucane represented the widow of one of the IRA men in legal proceedings but was murdered before they concluded. In 1987, the IRA murdered Lord Gibson and his wife, Cecily, blowing up their car as they drove across the border into the North after a holiday.)

The book *Ardoyne, The Untold Truth* was published in 2002 by a group of community activists to commemorate ninety-nine people from the area who had been killed there between 1969 and 1998. Based on more than three hundred interviews with families and friends of the victims, it sets out to record the experiences of a 'much maligned and marginalised community'. The authors contend that 'to compound personal and collective grief, sections of the media have ... given less than equal recognition to all victims ... they have demonised and labelled Ardoyne a terrorist community, thus implying ... that the community got what it deserved'.[8]

The British had added insult to injury in 1997 by appointing former senior civil servant Sir Kenneth Bloomfield as Victims Commissioner and Adam Ingram as Minister for Victims, as well as Minister for the Armed Forces. Many of the Ardoyne dead were killed by British soldiers. Bloomfield's report, 'We Will Remember Them', is accused of taking a hierarchical approach, with nationalists and republicans seen as being 'undeserving' victims.[9] The effect of this, the authors argue, is that while the Good Friday Agreement was meant to herald 'a new era of equality', the report had 'sowed anew the old seeds of ostracism'.[10] Mark Thompson of the group Relatives for Justice also made this point before the Northern Ireland Affairs Committee in 2005.

In a fierce preface to the book, poet and academic Seamus Deane deplores the 'ravenous media' which had helped the British government to 'portray the conflict as the war of a legal state on terror' and to conceal the reality that 'Northern Ireland is a criminal state' whose legal system was 'founded upon terror'.[11] Deane says the book is 'an instance of what the truth sounds like'.[12]

The book is a powerful account of a community's neglected suffering, but it is no more the whole truth than other accounts about which it is exceedingly critical. Alan McBride's grief over the IRA's murder of his wife and nine others in the 1993 Shankill bomb was compounded by the interview in the book with the surviving bomber, Sean Kelly, which, he felt, was a denial of the truth and an evasion of responsibility.

In her book on truth recovery after conflict, the academic author Marie Breen Smyth forensically examines the workings of the 2004 Northern Ireland Affairs Committee (NIAC) at Westminster and finds considerable evidence of a bias towards hearing the experiences of victims from the unionist community. The committee initially consisted of Conservative and Labour MPs, along with three unionists and one nationalist. The chairman, Michael Mates, seemed to assume, Smyth shows, 'that there has been very little violence on the part of the state' and that such violence was not the concern of the committee. Smyth suggests that since more than 20 per cent of the deaths of Catholics were due to the security forces, and since most of those killed by the security forces were Catholic, 'the chairman's interpretation of the brief is puzzling'. His attitude associates him, she says, 'with a denial of the experience of that community'.[13]

On a Saturday afternoon in 1993, the IRA, with a callous disregard for human life, placed a bomb near shops in the centre of

Warrington, in Cheshire. Inevitably, the result was tragic. Two children, Tim Parry, twelve, and Jonathan Ball, three, died in the explosion. There was a huge outpouring of grief and anger all over the UK and in Ireland. There was saturation coverage in the media of the events in England, and also of a new peace movement which was started in response in Dublin, with rallies, marches and speeches on the theme of 'never again'.

Colin Parry, the father of Tim, wrote a book. He had been asked many times what made the Warrington bomb different from other IRA atrocities. 'My answer has always been that the people of the Republic woke up from their passive acceptance of violence for the first time since 1969,' he writes.[14]

For an article in an Irish newspaper, I interviewed a number of parents of children who had been killed before the Warrington bomb. All of them expressed their deepest sympathy for the families of Jonathan and Tim. 'May God give them the strength to go on,' said one mother. 'My heart goes out to them,' said another.[15]

However, there was hurt, too. The first child to die in the Troubles, Patrick Rooney, was hit by a stray police bullet in 1969. His father, Cornelius, described the bullets flying through the thin walls of the family home in the Divis flats, and how he went to lift Patrick from his bed. 'His brains had been blown out. His blood was running down the wall,' he said. 'We thought Patrick's death would have brought peace.' A government report had found that the actions of the RUC were 'wholly unjustifiable'. Patrick's mother, Alice, asked, 'Why didn't the South come out when our boy was killed?'[16]

Others asked similar questions. Before the Warrington bomb more than a hundred children, including small babies, had been killed as a result of the conflict in Ireland. Marian Walsh, whose teenage son, Damien, was murdered in Belfast by loyalists five days after Warrington, said her family had said prayers for the English children at Damien's funeral. She knew the agony their families were experiencing. However, she added that there had been almost no reaction to the death of her son from the Republic. No planes full of flowers, no front-page headlines. Just a couple of cards from individuals.

Damien's uncle wrote a letter to the *Irish Times* in which he said that the family did not want to score points. 'Every single life is unique and precious,' Sean Loughlin said. 'There must be no discrimination in our reactions to murder, which is always the supreme evil.'[17]

There had, of course, been a huge wave of revulsion against violence in 1976, when Anne Maguire's children were killed. Writing thirty years later about the formation of the Peace People in response to those deaths, journalist Fionnuala O'Connor noted that days later, when a soldier shot twelve-year-old Majella O'Hare in Whitecross, South Armagh, her death had 'little resonance'. The Peace People did not march through Whitecross. It was clear, O'Connor said, that while the Peace People wanted all violence to end, 'the IRA was their main target'. After making a mildly disparaging comment about the organisation in an article at that time, she was spotted at a Belfast rally by the co-founder of the Peace People, Betty Williams. 'Fucking Provo!' Williams shouted. She apologised a year or so later.[18]

Ann McCann, whose younger brother had been murdered by loyalists in a random sectarian shooting in 1973, had joined the Peace People when it started, and by 1993, she was working as the organisation's administrator. She gave her full support to the new 1993 peace movement in Dublin, and she deplored the Warrington bombing. She said she hoped Sinn Féin would now 'cut its ties' with the IRA. However, she told me she did feel uneasy about the scale of the reaction in the Republic. 'I don't mean to be insulting, but it appears there is a lot of apathy in the South about what is happening in the North,' she said. Referring to the other children who had been killed, she said, 'It is as if we are on another planet.'[19]

The then president of the Republic of Ireland, Mary Robinson, addressed this disquiet with characteristic tact and graciousness when she performed the official opening of the Warrington Project, the precursor of the Warrington Peace Centre. She spoke about the way the community in Warrington had made 'a common purpose of their suffering, and a common purpose of their healing'. She had been deeply impressed, as had many other people in Ireland.

'But we must understand that there are many people in . . . Northern Ireland, Catholic and Protestant, who are deeply hurt and pained that the attention so rightly given to the tragic deaths and injuries in Warrington has not been matched by similar attention to their loss and suffering,' she said. There were communities 'locked in the midst of recurrent, brutalising violence' which was met with indifference because it had become routine. She asked that the 'spirit of Warrington should pay tribute to their endurance, should include their suffering and try to understand their pain'.[20]

The concept of the 'wave of revulsion' was explored by columnist Roy Greenslade in 1999, when he analysed why the murder, two years previously, of fifteen-year-old Bernadette Martin and the trial of her murderer, which had just ended, had got so little attention in the British media. After all, it was 'the kind of Romeo and Juliet story which usually sets tabloid pulses racing'. The fact that she was killed on the same day as fashion designer Gianni Versace only partly explained the indifference, he felt.

A month before Bernadette's death, two RUC constables had been murdered by the IRA in Bernadette's town. 'It was front-page news and the lead story on BBC TV and radio. Almost every paper wrote leading articles of condemnation. Quotes were sought from political leaders in Britain, Ireland and the USA,' Greenslade wrote.

Referring back to the Warrington bombing and the media response, Greenslade concluded that waves of revulsion were created by media coverage. Surveying the coverage of Troubles murders in the British media, Greenslade found that a 'hierarchy of death' had been constructed. 'In the first rank – getting the most prominent coverage – were British people killed in Britain; in the second, members of the security forces, whether army or RUC; in the third, civilian victims of republicans, including prison officers; in the fourth, members of the IRA or Sinn Féin, killed either by the security forces or loyalist paramilitaries; and in the fifth rank, garnering least coverage, were the innocent victims of loyalist paramilitaries.' Murders by the IRA got 'the full treatment', while murders by loyalists were 'virtually ignored'.[21]

After the murder by loyalists of reporter Martin O'Hagan in 2001, Greenslade commented that if the killers had been from the IRA, 'his dastardly death would have dominated the front pages for weeks regardless of Afghanistan'. Instead, 'Sefton the horse – injured in the 1982 Hyde Park bombing – got bigger and more headlines.'[22]

In Ireland, too. I had covered O'Hagan's murder for the *Sunday Tribune*. He was the first reporter to be killed and it happened late on a Friday. I expected the story to be on the front page, but it was not.

British journalists have, however, carried out important investigations in connection with the Troubles in Ireland. The campaign to free the 'Birmingham Six' and 'Guildford Four' – Irish people wrongly convicted and jailed for life for carrying out IRA bombing atrocities – could not have succeeded without this work. In Northern Ireland, there is a Catholic daily and a Protestant daily, and their stories about victims of the Troubles tend to reflect that. However, the *Irish News* and the *Newsletter* have, on occasion, joined forces to campaign against violence.

There has undoubtedly been a failure in the Irish media to give due attention to the lives lost in the UK as a result of the Troubles. Relatively little was written about the victims of the Birmingham and Guildford bombs, or about casualties like Inan Ul-haq Bashir, killed by the Canary Wharf bomb with which the IRA ended its 1994 ceasefire in 1996. The twenty-nine-year-old Londoner ran his family's news kiosk. His funeral at Croydon mosque was scarcely noticed by Irish journalists busy analysing the implications of the end of the ceasefire, which was restored in 1997. British soldiers killed in the North got only the most perfunctory media coverage.

* * *

Money caused bitterness and resentment. Some people got large compensation payments from the Northern Ireland Office (NIO) after a murder, while others got very little. If the person killed had any connection with paramilitarism, their family was not even entitled to apply. Gerard McErlane said that his mother had refused to use the compensation she was given after the murders of her sons. She called it 'blood money'.

The vast costs run up by the Bloody Sunday inquiry were mentioned with some bitterness by a lot of Protestant victims. Merle Eakin, who'd lost her child when the IRA bombed Claudy, a few miles from Derry, six months after Bloody Sunday, said that Claudy was a 'forgotten massacre', while millions were being spent on finding out what happened on Bloody Sunday.

The DUP MP Jeffrey Donaldson also referred to the huge cost of the Bloody Sunday inquiry and said, in 2007, that the government was creating a hierarchy of victimhood by paying for this while cutting funds to the Historical Enquiries Team (HET), which was looking into more than three thousand murders.

No one was ever going to feel that a large compensation payment made up for the loss of someone they had loved, but derisory payments caused deep offence. Billy Eakin, Merle's husband, remembered the day he went into Derry to meet someone from the NIO to try to sort out compensation towards rebuilding the house and the shop. 'They insulted me,' he said. 'I walked back up towards the Guildhall crying so hard if I'd met Merle I wouldn't have known her.' The family was given £58 compensation. They were told they wouldn't have Kathryn to support, so they would be better off than before. Billy said he regretted cashing the cheque. 'I should have kept it to show how people were treated.'

The headline in the Northern Irish *Sunday News* on 29 May 1972 read: 'My wife was worth nothing, says angry widower'. The story told of a man awarded just £250 compensation for the loss of his wife, the mother of his eight children. This was to cover funeral expenses. She was shot by British paratroopers on the day internment without trial was introduced, in August 1971. On the same day, a teenage girl who got a black eye in an incident not linked to the conflict was awarded the same amount.

The man had suffered a nervous breakdown and a heart attack since his wife's death. He told the court that a week after his wife died, two Saracens had pulled up outside his house. A soldier got out, playing on a trumpet the pop song that went 'Where's your mama gone, chirpy chirpy cheep cheep . . .'[23]

Alice Harper's father, Danny Teggart, was standing in the same group of people during the internment-night shooting, and he, too, was shot dead. Alice had told me that the soldiers had sung the same song to deride her. She spoke at a meeting in Belfast in

2007 to commemorate the 'Ballymurphy Eleven', those killed in the area in the two days following internment.

She told me the relatives had wanted the meeting, organised by Relatives for Justice as part of the annual West Belfast Festival, because the truth had to be told about what was really a massacre. 'They were innocent people and they are forgotten people,' she said. One of the relatives of those killed said the people had been shot down like dogs. The families wanted an independent inquiry, and for a start, an apology from the British army.

A woman who was a tiny child when her mother was murdered, and didn't remember her, said she hadn't missed her until she grew up and had her own daughter. Then she began to dream that she was running after her mother but could never see her face. She'd gone to mediums and fortune-tellers and counsellors in search of a memory of her. In the end, she realised she would never find what she was looking for, although she did have a photograph. This was shown on a screen behind her at the meeting, a little girl in a yellow dress on the knee of her smiling, red-headed mother. It reminded me of the lines from Louis MacNeice: 'My mother wore a yellow dress/Gently, gently, gentleness.'[24]

An elderly woman spoke from the audience. She wept as she told about how a man was shot outside her home. She had gone over to the dying man and tried to hold a cloth to his head 'to keep the blood from going'. An ambulance arrived, and people were carrying the man onto it when a soldier shouted, 'Halt.' The woman was between the soldier and the ambulance. 'I stood and I faced the soldier and I said, "Go ahead, shoot,"' she said. 'Then I heard a voice saying, "Calm yourself, ma'am," and this officer put his hand on my shoulder. I said, "How can I calm myself while that man's life blood is running away?"' The man died in hospital. The old woman wept. 'I am sorry for his family, but I want them to know that everything possible was done for him and he was an innocent man.'

A Quaker from England who'd moved to Ballymurphy to work in its new community centre was remembered. He'd been a pioneer in the sort of youth work Terry Enright had gone on to do. On 11 August 1971, he'd been inside the community centre with a crowd of local people while intense shooting was going on outside. He tied a white flag to a brush and attempted to go out. The army shot at the flag, a man told the meeting. Later on, the youth worker insisted on attempting to bring bread and milk out to people in the houses around the centre. There was a confrontation with some soldiers and he walked away, but collapsed a short distance up the road and died. He had suffered a massive heart attack.

A man who had been shot and injured by the army told how someone had gone to get the local priest, Father Hugh Mullan, who had spent the day pleading with loyalists to stop attacking Catholic homes in the area. The priest had made his way across the waste ground where the man was lying. He was waving a white Babygro. The image chillingly brings to mind the famous one which followed it, when, the following year, the same regiment of soldiers shot dead thirteen unarmed civilians in Derry on Bloody Sunday and Father Edward Daly was photographed waving a white handkerchief as he helped carry one of the fatally wounded men off the street. Father Mullan gave the last rites to the man, and then the paratroopers shot the priest dead.

Alice Harper was at the meeting, along with members of her family. Each of the families of the dead had chosen a piece of music to be played in memory of their loved one. Alice had chosen 'Danny Boy' for her father, his favourite song. It is in the voice of a person who knows that they are going to die and who asks a loved one to kneel on their grave and pray for them. It imagines them being reunited after death.

When I went to talk to Alice after the meeting, she was full of conflicting emotions. There was pride that her father had been honoured and that the truth had been told about his death. There was fury because, the week before the meeting, in August 2007, the British army had formally pulled out most of its remaining troops from Northern Ireland, and commentators and politicians had, since then, been paying tribute to the soldiers who'd died and praising the army for the restraining role it had played. 'They killed my daddy and then they said he was a gunman. I hate them,' Alice said. 'I'll never forgive them.'

Another woman said if the paratroopers had been reined in after what they did in Ballymurphy during those few days in 1971, Bloody Sunday would never have happened. But she said she didn't hate them, as it would be a waste of her life. Alice Harper shook her head. Even though her mother had asked her to forgive them, she said she couldn't do it. 'I can't help it,' she said. 'I hate them.'

After General Sir Robert Ford, the British commander of land forces in 1972, gave evidence to the Savile Inquiry into Bloody Sunday in London in 2003, some of the relatives of the dead heard that he had cancer. One woman told film-maker Margo Harkin of her reaction. 'Well, I hope it eats him and the last days of his death he's screaming in pain and the fourteen people that were killed are haunting him,' she said, her voice shaking with rage. 'For the lies he told in there today.'[25]

4

Law Ceased to Exist

It was painful for Eugene Reavey to watch his mother going to funeral after funeral in her constant grief for her murdered sons. It became agonising after Ian Paisley stated in Parliament that Eugene was an IRA man responsible for the sectarian massacre at Kingsmills, the sole survivor of which was family friend Alan Black.

Local security-force personnel had put it about that Sadie Reavey's was an IRA family and that her sons had been killed because they were themselves killers. Eugene had felt ashamed and impotent because he was unable to protect his mother from the harassment she suffered because of this. Paisley's claim seemed to corroborate the slur.

Since the murder of his three brothers in 1976, Eugene had wanted to find out why his family was targeted for slaughter, and since 1999, he had wanted to clear the family's name. His mother was getting old. After she began to suffer from the delusion that she herself was a murderer and that she was going to be punished for it, he began to feel a desperate sense of urgency about these tasks.

That was in 2003. In the same year, DUP MP Jeffrey Donaldson said he had evidence that Gardaí from the Irish Republic had colluded with the IRA in the murders of Protestants in South

Armagh. He said 92 per cent of IRA murders in the area were unsolved, and that this was 'a travesty of justice'. There had been an inadequate security response 'both in providing reasonable protection for law-abiding citizens and in pursuit of justice', he said.

He was accompanied by Willie Frazer, head of the victims' group Families Acting for Innocent Relatives (FAIR). Frazer said Protestant victims in south Armagh had received 'pitiful' compensation compared with nationalists.[1]

The DUP leader never retracted his allegation against Eugene Reavey. On the thirtieth anniversary of Kingsmills, in January 2006, Donaldson and Frazer attended a memorial service, and Frazer used the occasion to say he would that day hand over a dossier to the Historical Enquiries Team that would prove who was responsible for the massacre and also prove that they were responsible for numerous other murders as well.

The HET had been set up by the PSNI's Chief Constable, Hugh Orde, in 2005, because the PSNI was inundated with demands for inquiries into Troubles murders. His job was to police the future, he said; the HET would review more than 3,000 murders committed in the past.

The plan was to start with the earliest murders and work chronologically. However, because a number of families, including the Reaveys, had taken proceedings to the European Court of Human Rights, the British government was keen that these cases should be dealt with swiftly, so they were taken out of sequence. The case made was that the British had failed to investigate properly the allegations made in 1999 by ex-RUC man John Weir in relation to the murders of the Reaveys and others.

Eugene spent more than thirty hours with HET investigators. Three months after Frazer said he was handing over his dossier, the head of the HET, Detective Dave Cox, had tea with

Sadie Reavey and some of her surviving children, including Eugene. Cox told Mrs Reavey that he wanted to reassure her that he had examined all the available intelligence material from the period around the murders of her sons and that there was 'no trace of any credible material' that would link them to any paramilitary organisation or illegal activity. 'They were, as you have always known, entirely innocent victims of senseless sectarian violence,' he said. He also apologised to her on behalf of the PSNI for the 'appalling harassment' her family had been subjected to in the aftermath of the murders 'at the hands of elements of the security forces'.[2]

Eugene was greatly moved by the apology, but sadly he wasn't sure if his mother had entirely understood. 'I think it might have come just a wee bit too late for Mummy,' he said. 'She's worn out.'

* * *

After Ian Paisley named him as an IRA man in Parliament in 1999, Eugene Reavey had gone to the RUC's then chief constable, Ronnie Flanagan. Flanagan told him the source of Paisley's 'information' was not the RUC, but he speculated that it might have emanated from local security-force sources at Glenanne. 'He said in the past that had been known to be a very dangerous source,' Eugene said.

The Pat Finucane Centre (PFC) in Derry is a human-rights group named after the murdered solicitor. It had set up a Recovery of Living Memory Archive to research loyalist murders in the South Armagh area. The PFC had trawled through news cuttings and official papers, and they'd interviewed witnesses to attacks, people who had been injured and many of the bereaved.

They had established that a gang made up of loyalists and members of the security forces, in various 'permutations', had been responsible for multiple murders, including those of the Reavey brothers. Alan Brecknell, whose father was murdered by the gang, began to work on an elaborate diagram based on reported ballistics evidence from the attacks. What emerged was a complex and sinister web which showed the same weapons turning up again and again in the killings. Weapons used to kill Alan's father were also used to kill Eugene Reavey's brothers. They found out that UVF arms had been found on RUC reservist James Mitchell's farm in 1978 and that he had been convicted of storing them. This was the farm Eugene used to visit as a poultry adviser.

A former RUC officer responded to a PFC request for information. He had investigated some of the incidents and said that he knew members of the security forces had been working with local paramilitaries. He said he had been obliged to 'watch his front as well as his back' at work. On one occasion, he said, he had provided RUC colleagues with witness descriptions of a suspect for the preparation of a photofit. When he next saw the man he believed to be the suspect, he had changed his appearance, suggesting that a police source had tipped him off.

In response to commitments made to victims in the Good Friday Agreement, the government of the Irish Republic set up a Victims' Commission in 1999. The PFC and other human-rights groups, notably Justice for the Forgotten, the group representing those hurt and bereaved by the Dublin and Monaghan bombs, pressed the commission to help those bereaved by the Glenanne gang and other combinations of loyalists, soldiers and policemen. A year later, a commission of inquiry under a former Irish High Court judge was set up to look initially into the Dublin and Monaghan bombs of 1974, and then into related terrorist atrocities.

In its submission to the inquiry, the PFC suggested that the handling of some of the cases which came before the courts in the late 1970s and early 1980s indicated the complicity of senior police officers, the Office of the Director of Public Prosecutions and the judiciary. Victims identified killers but they were never charged, or charges were made and then inexplicably dropped. Witnesses were not called or even told trials were happening. In one case, a man who said a gunman had aimed at his heart but had in fact seriously wounded him in the stomach was not told the policeman who shot him, Billy McCaughey, was to be tried. The then Lord Chief Justice, Lord Lowry, had heard the case and accepted McCaughey's claim that he shot the man in the leg merely to hurt him, giving the policeman a suspended sentence. Charges of attempted murder against two others were dropped.

The reports published by Mr Justice Henry Barron in 2003 and 2006 made sombre reading. They confirmed that ex-RUC officers John Weir and Billy McCaughey were credible witnesses, despite also being convicted murderers. This finding was echoed by the European Court of Human Rights in 2008, when it found in relation to John Weir that his allegations were serious and plausible.

Barron found that the farm of James Mitchell was the hub of a loyalist gang which included members of both the RUC and the UDR, and the gang was involved in multiple murders, including the Dublin and Monaghan bombings and the murders of the Reaveys and others in South Armagh.

'The security forces in NI knew that Mitchell's farm was a centre for illegal activities from as early as January 1976, and probably for some time before that,' the 2006 report states. 'Yet these activities were allowed to continue unhindered until the arrest of William McCaughey and others in December 1978.'[3]

The Reavey family used to leave their front-door key in the

lock. They did not know that a gang of heavily armed sectarian killers, including policemen and soldiers, had its base a couple of miles away.

James Mitchell had only ever been prosecuted for keeping loyalist paramilitary weapons on his premises, for which he got a suspended sentence. Interviewed by the RUC in 2000, Mitchell said his place had been a calling house for British soldiers since the Second World War. They came for tea, he said. I decided to call on him. He still lived with Lily Sheils, who had been his poultry keeper in the days of the Glenanne gang. She had admitted to the police that she sat in the back of one of the cars used in a murder, pretending with one of the men to be a courting couple.

I drove through the tiny village of Glenanne, where the stone ruins of the old UDR base still stand. The IRA blew it up in 1991. The house and sheds at Mitchell's farm were on the side of a steep hill, down a long lane. One of the gateposts had a stone hen on it, the other an eagle. The house was shabby, the yard untidy. The front door was open. I was standing pressing the bell when James Mitchell came across the yard behind me from his car. He had been at church. He was carrying a glossy programme for a twenty-fifth anniversary gospel service. I walked back to meet him and extended my hand, immediately regretting the conventional gesture. I introduced myself and told him I was writing a book and wanted to talk about what had happened in the area.

He shook my hand, reluctantly. His mouth, when he spoke, was full of rotten teeth. 'What happened around here was terrible and it should never have happened, but sure all that is all settled now,' he said. 'I lost a lot of friends. But I am still here, and I am still walking about, as you can see. I don't want to talk to any of you reporters or writers or whatever you call yourselves.'

I said that terrible allegations had been made against him, and asked him if he wanted to give his side of the story. 'It's all lies what has been said about me,' he said. I asked him whether he would like to tell the truth, then. A look of disgust crossed his face. 'Sure you won't print the truth,' he said. I asked about the Glenanne gang. 'There was no such thing,' he said.

I pointed out that Lily Sheils had made statements admitting her involvement in certain events. He got really angry then. 'Sure they can make you say anything,' he said. 'Didn't they murder a boy there was only buried today there?' He was referring to nineteen-year-old South Armagh man Paul Quinn, who had been beaten to death a few days before this. His family claimed the IRA was responsible. This had been denied by Sinn Féin, which, in keeping with the new way of things in Northern Ireland, had condemned the murder and called on anyone with information to give it to the Gardaí or the PSNI.

I asked Mitchell who he was saying had carried out the murder. 'The IRA,' he said. 'But it wasn't the IRA that got Lily Sheils to make a statement,' I said. 'It was the RUC.' 'Get away out of this,' he said, beginning to walk away from me towards his house. 'You'll get nothing here.'

* * *

Perhaps more disturbing than what Mr Justice Barron did find was what he could not. The British authorities, despite an assurance of support from the then prime minister, Tony Blair, had refused to co-operate. When Barron requested security documents, his letters were initially ignored. Then he was told there were some 68,000 potentially relevant files, but in the end, 'no copies of any original documents were forthcoming'. The scope of his inquiries was, Barron said, limited as a result.

Barron commented that 'the moral ambivalence inherent in covert intelligence work was compounded in Northern Ireland by the ambivalent attitude of many in the security forces towards loyalist paramilitary groups and their activities'. The 'real enemy' was the IRA. 'The expression "My enemy's enemy is my friend" had already been developed into a philosophy of counter-terrorism by British army strategists . . . One of the main advocates of this approach, Brigadier Frank Kitson, was a brigade commander in Belfast from 1970 to 1972.'[4]

He quotes a UDR commander who, in 1972, said that he would probably take no action against a member of the regiment who was also in the UDA. Irish army intelligence personnel were aware, Barron notes, of 'close links' between RUC Special Branch officers and loyalist paramilitaries, and were also told that the British military had reservations about the RUC because they knew it had been 'penetrated by the UDA'.

A distinguished panel of international witnesses headed by Professor Douglass Cassel went on to examine seventy-six loyalist murders from this period, and found that in seventy-four of them there was compelling evidence of security-force collusion.[5] Cassel, who acted as a legal adviser to the UN Commission on the Truth for El Salvador, said he had been 'deeply shocked' by what he had learnt, in particular the extent to which superior officers appeared to know about and condone these activities.

Powerful confirmation of this situation had also come to light in 2003, when a team of researchers including Alan Brecknell found a document in the Public Records Office in London. 'Subversion in the UDR' had been prepared for briefing the 'joint intelligence committee at Westminster' in 1973. It advised officials that a significant number of UDR soldiers were also involved in loyalist paramilitary groups. UDR soldiers were also training loyalists in the use of arms. The UDR was the main source of weapons and ammunition for 'the most violent of the criminal sectarian groups in the Protestant community'.[6]

The nationalist MP Seamus Mallon, who as deputy first min-

ister in 1999 had protested when Ian Paisley called Eugene
Reavey an IRA man, told the Barron Inquiry that in South
Armagh in the mid-1970s 'the overall situation was that law
ceased to exist. There was no viable authority. Good senior
police officers were vulnerable. The government approach was
to close your eyes and get on with worrying about winning the
war.'[7]

Eugene told me that when the HET detectives came to review
the murders of his brothers, he had been able to unburden his
soul to them. 'You couldn't have trusted the RUC,' he said. 'You
couldn't have let them past the door. After our boys were shot,
Anthony went to our good Protestant neighbours' house. Those
people were never even interviewed. Any evidence the RUC got,
they'd have burnt it.'

* * *

All this was certainly consistent with the picture painted in a
remarkably revealing book written by one of the RUC men who
was part of the Glenanne gang. In 2004, journalists Vincent
Kearney and Brendan McCourt from BBC Northern Ireland
were investigating the gang's activities for a documentary, when
they found a slim paperback called *From Palace to Prison*, by
Gary Armstrong.

Described on its cover by DUP politician the Reverend Willie
McCrea as a 'thrilling story', the book was published in 1991 by a
small religious press in England. While on remand in prison
awaiting trial for the kidnap of a Catholic priest, along with
members of the UVF, Armstrong had been 'saved', a frequent
enough occurrence for loyalist prisoners. It had also happened
to Robert 'Basher' Bates. As a born-again Christian, Armstrong's
concern was to spread the word of his salvation in an effort to
save the souls of others.

His book is a testimony. It tells how a clever boy from a poor,

rough family deals with various humiliations by becoming a
'hard man'. Eight years before RUC man John Weir's shocking
confession, Armstrong confirms that he was part of the RUC's
Special Patrol Group in South Armagh and that this was a
group of about forty men 'who were just as venomous and militant as I was'.

He loved mounting checkpoints. They were part of a
'vendetta', he says. 'Roman Catholics . . . were fair game . . . my
hatred was running amok . . .' They were frustrated, though, by
having to work, however loosely, within the law: 'We knew who
the terrorists were and although we would torture them, beat
them and intimidate them we could never convict them.'

This, he says, was why he and others decided to join forces
with 'the Protestant terrorist organisation'. He describes his
'growing appetite for IRA hunting' and talks about 'terrorising
the terrorist' and passing information to loyalists about IRA
men. He says it wasn't just the SPG. His 'terrorist friends' told
him that when the RUC arrested them, they would give them
details of 'IRA hitmen'; the detectives would assure them that if
assassinations took place, police investigations into them would
be 'far from exhaustive'.

Nor were SPG officers prosecuted for most of their excesses.
Armstrong's account supports that of his RUC colleague, John
Weir, on this point: blind eyes were turned, until Constable
Billy McCaughey broke down in 1978 and confessed.

After his conviction for the kidnap, Armstrong's lawyers had
told him to expect to spend several years in prison. But to his
astonishment, Lord Chief Justice Lowry 'seemed to be trying to
rationalise the irrational and justify the unjustifiable', and
showed compassion and understanding of 'the tremendous
pressure we had been under'. Armstrong got a two-year suspended sentence.

Former members of the gang, including Armstrong, were

confronted by the team from BBC Northern Ireland's investigative programme *Spotlight* but refused to discuss their past. Before the book had come to light, the RUC had, at Mr Justice Barron's request, attempted to interview Armstrong. He said the 'alleged events' into which Barron was inquiring happened in an era which, for him, 'is now buried and forgotten . . . I am not prepared to resurrect any part of it.' He expressed fury that the RUC was wasting its resources in this way, 'especially with so many heinous IRA crimes still on the books', and he blamed this situation on the 'pernicious Belfast Agreement [the term used by some unionists for the Good Friday Agreement]'.[8]

After his release from jail, Armstrong became a travelling preacher, giving testimony 'all over Ulster' about his sin and his salvation. He was, by his own account, much in demand. His metaphors are interesting. He compares the sinner coming before the throne of God on judgement day with his experience of facing the Lord Chief Justice in court. The mercy shown by Lord Lowry is like God's mercy, and indeed, when Lowry had pronounced sentence, Armstrong had shouted in court, 'Praise the Lord!'

However, the unsaved need expect no mercy, Armstrong warns. The Great Judge will send them to 'the most indescribably awful and injurious place'. He quotes the Bible: 'Depart from me, ye cursed!'

The authorities had information implicating Armstrong in the attack on the Rock Bar, near Keady, but he denied involvement and was not charged. The gang made their getaway in a police car, and in an interview with author Toby Harnden, Billy McCaughey describes how several of the RUC men involved in the Rock Bar attack 'were back in the station in time to get the emergency call'.[9]

Armstrong describes events remarkably like those of that night in his book. He does not name the pub and says of his own role simply that he was there. The bombing becomes a metaphor. The aim was 'to cause maximum injury and devastation', he says. But, though the fuse was lit, the bomb failed to go off: 'Unfulfilled potential!' It was the tragedy of the contemporary church, he says, this 'unfulfilled potential'. By contrast, he thanks God for 'the day he lit the fuse in my life ... how I long for the bomb to wreak havoc to the principalities and powers around me'.[10]

When he was in prison in 1966, Ian Paisley wrote about the preaching of the gospel. It was charged, he said, 'with the dynamic of heaven' and 'dynamite to be displayed in all its mighty potency must have the fuse and the fire. When the fuse of true prayer is set alight with the fire of the Holy Ghost and thus the gospel dynamite is exploded, what tremendous results occur.'[11] As Tom Paulin notes, three years later the UVF planted the bombs that blew Terence O'Neill from power. 'Puritan metaphor has a habit of becoming literal,' he writes. Forty years after his jail term, when an Orange parade had a minor restriction placed on its route through a Catholic part of Belfast, Paisley warned that 'this could be the spark that lights a fire there will be no putting out'. A serious riot followed.

*   *   *

When Eugene Reavey went public with the apology from the HET, Willie Frazer, of Families Acting for Innocent Relatives, was incensed. Under the headline 'Just Never Proven Guilty', FAIR claimed the HET had 'joined the chorus of hand-wringing apologists who row up to sing the praises of the Reavey family'. All were mistaken. 'Their words are meaningless and hollow for they can never assure innocence; all they can do is point to a lack of legal convictions.'[12]

Anthony, Brian and John Martin Reavey were dead, so they couldn't be brought to court. They 'no longer have to worry about earthly justice'. However, Frazer continued, the people of South Armagh who knew them knew better. 'After all, innocent until proven guilty has been afforded to hundreds of killers who continue to roam our streets thanks to the failure of the police and to date the HET to bring them to justice . . .'[13]

FAIR went on to reason that if, 'as some allege', local security-force members were involved in the murders of the Reaveys, 'Why would those who had access to security-force intelligence choose a family of innocent men in the heart of South Armagh when they had the choice of actual republican terrorist targets, their details and files?' It then answers its own question: 'The more suspicious would assume that the Reavey family featured in such security-force files and were obvious targets for such alleged rogue members.' In any case, the HET would shortly be investigating the Kingsmills massacre, and 'it would have been more prudent of them to have considered the evidence we wish to present before fully exonerating the Reavey brothers'. FAIR went on to accuse the HET, 'like every other agency', of showing a 'partisan approach' to victims. According to FAIR, the bias was against Protestants.

* * *

I went to see FAIR's Willie Frazer in the small South Armagh town of Markethill. I arrived early, so I called into the offices of the other victims' group in the town, SAVER/NAVER, which stands for South Armagh (and North Armagh) Victims Encouraging Recognition. The woman who founded it, Reetha Hasson, used to be involved in FAIR but had become unhappy with its politics and had left. Its offices were in a house on the main street. There were smiling women in the reception area, scented candles on the windowsills and a poster about colonic irrigation on the noticeboard in the hall.

The new group, Reetha told me, focused on helping people

to recover from the tragedies they'd faced in the Troubles and to go on to live fulfilling lives. Its slogan was 'We are victims of the past but we are not prisoners of the past.' Reetha had been in the UDR and was based at its barracks in Glenanne. She knew nothing about collusion with loyalists, she told me. The people she knew had joined the security forces to serve their country.

SAVER/NAVER was building a peace and memorial garden at the back of its building. It ran courses and trips and had developed strong links with a group working on peace studies at the University of Limerick in the Republic. Reetha gave me a book called *A Legacy of Tears – 30 Years of Protestant Suffering at the Hands of Irish Republican Terrorists in South and North Armagh: 1969 to 1999*. Most of the stories in it were about members of the security forces murdered by the IRA.

Willie's headquarters had a very different feel. The men working in the offices did not smile, and Willie talked to me in a large, untidy room which had old RUC and UDR uniforms and guns all around it, along with photographs and prints of military operations. They were putting together a museum, he told me. He was preoccupied and angry because the deputy leader of the DUP, Peter Robinson, had just sent him a letter in which he'd suggested that Willie was more interested in politics than in supporting victims, and that the victims didn't want him to represent them anyway. Robinson had cited Willie's poor showing when he had stood in elections.

Willie was busy gathering in letters of support from other like-minded victims' groups. The falling out with the DUP had happened because Willie saw the DUP coalition with Sinn Féin at Stormont as the ultimate betrayal of his father, Bertie, and his circle. Willie had put Robinson's letter up on the website. 'Peter could not tie the boots of my father . . . that paid the ultimate sacrifice,' he wrote.[14]

FAIR's slogan is 'Help us to tell the truth.' I asked Willie why he persisted in claiming that the Reaveys were IRA men, when everyone else said it was nonsense. I'd been told that after his brothers were murdered, the IRA had approached Eugene, wanting him to get involved. He had refused. One day, Eugene showed me a framed certificate, signed by Princess Diana. 'I have a daughter with special needs,' he said. 'She got this award, and we went to London to receive it from Diana. The IRA came to this house and told me we weren't to go. I told *them* where to go.'

But Willie insisted that the truth would come out eventually and that FAIR would be vindicated for its claims about the Reaveys. Like the DUP, he was adamant that there were 'innocent' victims and those who had no right to be called victims because they were perpetrators and terrorists. He expressed the view, shared by ex-RUC man John Weir, that Captain Robert Nairac was playing loyalists and republicans off against each other. He believed his father and his colleagues in the UDR and RUC had been sacrificed in this dangerous game, a game in which Nairac, ultimately, also lost his life.

In 2003, Willie's own application for a weapon for personal protection was turned down because the police said they had 'reliable intelligence' that he 'associated with loyalist terrorist organisations'. He denied it, although he did believe they had played a role in defeating the IRA. 'Obviously, I'm not saying anyone has a right to kill innocent Catholics,' he had told me. 'But if the security forces had been allowed to do their job, there would never have been any need for the loyalist paramilitaries . . . You take the UDR thing in South Armagh. You take a UDR man. He is in fear of his life. He knows who these boys are. He has the information. He knows the government won't do anything about it. What does he do? He passes it on to the loyalist paramilitaries.'[15]

* * *

Collusion, according to Sir John Stevens, was evidenced in many ways. 'It ranges from the wilful failure to keep records, the absence of accountability, the withholding of intelligence and evidence, through to the extreme of agents being involved in murder,' he said. He had found all of these elements in Northern Ireland. The former head of the Metropolitan Police was speaking at the launch in Belfast of the report into his third inquiry in 2003.[16]

Stevens had begun this inquiry in 1999, after the human-rights group British and Irish Rights Watch had produced a convincing report alleging collusion in the murder of solicitor Pat Finucane. In 1989, the UDA had defended the murder of another man by revealing that it had been given security-force documents which claimed he was involved in the IRA. Stevens found that the leaking of such information was widespread, and more than fifty people were prosecuted.

In 2003, more prosecutions were anticipated: Stevens said he had sent more than twenty files to the Director of Public Prosecutions, some of them relating to the British army's agent-handling unit in Northern Ireland, the Force Research Unit (FRU), the RUC's Special Branch and MI5. He published only a brief overview of his inquiry, giving rise to the myth that a damning report running to thousands of pages had been withheld.

His task had proved daunting. Throughout all his inquiries, he said, he had been obstructed by elements of the RUC and the army. The FRU had destroyed evidence, leaked evidence to loyalists and tipped off suspects. His offices were destroyed in an arson attack, which was, he said, not properly investigated. He noted his 'considerable disquiet' over the failure of the MOD to provide documentation when he requested it.

Despite all these obstacles, he found that the murder of Pat Finucane could have been prevented and should have been detected. So could the murder of Protestant student Adam Lambert, killed in 1987 after being mistaken for a Catholic. This attack was believed to have been in revenge for the IRA's Enniskillen bomb.

Stevens found that senior RUC officers had briefed Home Office minister Douglas Hogg before he said in Parliament that certain solicitors were 'unduly sympathetic to the IRA'. The comments were 'not justifiable' and the minister was compromised, he said. A confidential British army document written a few weeks after Hogg's statement records that an agent named Brian Nelson was becoming better organised: 'He is currently running an operation against selected republican targets.' Days later, Finucane was murdered.

Informers and agents had been allowed to operate without controls and to take part in terrorist crimes. Nationalists whose lives were known to be in danger were not warned or protected. Crucial information was withheld from senior officers. Important evidence was neither exploited nor preserved.

As a result of Stevens' investigations, one of the gang responsible for Finucane's murder was tried, acquitted because of lack of evidence and later shot dead by the UDA. He had told journalists that he was an intelligence agent and had given details of the security forces' manipulation of loyalist gangs. A second member was convicted of the murder. He told a journalist that it was the RUC Special Branch, for which he worked, that had suggested to the UDA that it should murder Finucane.

A retired detective called Johnston Brown subsequently published a shocking and revealing book in which he described how his attempts to investigate murders, including that of Finucane, had been thwarted by Special Branch. He had made a tape recording of a UDA man confessing to Finucane's murder, only for Special Branch to doctor the tape and remove the confession. When detectives strayed into cases which involved intelligence agents, it was known as going 'into the dark', he said.[17]

Since Pat Finucane's murder, his family has run a powerful campaign for an independent inquiry, and they appeared to have won this battle when, in 2004, retired Canadian judge Peter Cory carried out an examination of the evidence in relation to a number of controversial killings. This process was part of the peace negotiations, and the British government agreed beforehand that they would implement the judge's recommendations. However, when Cory called for an inquiry into the Finucane murder, Tony Blair thwarted it by rushing through a new law which gave the government significant power to limit the scope of any inquiry. Cory subsequently stated that 'no self-respecting judge' would preside over such an inquiry, and the Finucanes said they would have nothing to do with it.

In 2007, the families of several victims of UDA killings in which there appeared to have been collusion, including the Finucanes, received a hand-delivered letter from the Public Prosecution Service. It informed them that there were to be no prosecutions of any police or army personnel following on from the files Lord Stevens had submitted. One woman was told that while one policeman had given the UDA the gun which was subsequently used to kill her son, he could not be prosecuted because he was only following orders given by a more senior officer, and he could not be identified because of an absence of records.

The lack of records was proving to be a serious problem for the Historical Enquiries Team as well. 'The military have a policy of destroying records after thirty years,' said the head of the HET, Dave Cox. 'Records up to and including those from 1975 were destroyed in January 2005 – three months before we were set up, at which point we asked them to suspend the practice.'

To make matters worse, a 'gentleman's agreement' between the RUC and the British military police meant that the latter took statements from soldiers up until 1975. 'They weren't exactly rigorous, and the courts have already ruled them inadmissible in one case,' said Cox. 'Our friends in the Pat Finucane Centre call them tea and sandwiches investigations.'[18]

5

Making Peace with the Past?

After seven dramatic years as the North's first police ombudsman, Nuala O'Loan was convinced that what was needed to bring a proper end to the Troubles was an independent truth-recovery process. 'We must ensure that we leave no reason to justify the resurrection of the Troubles,' she said. 'We need to take our courage in both hands. Truth can cause pain and shock – but it doesn't destroy people.

'The traditional Irish way of dealing with grief is not to talk. There have been families here where someone has been killed and the decision has been taken – "We will never speak of this." That closes people down and then maybe twenty or thirty years later the trauma manifests itself in ways that people don't understand.'[1]

O'Loan's office was set up as one of the pillars of the new policing regime under the Good Friday Agreement, but as she finished her term in 2007, she said she suspected that the authorities got more than they bargained for when they appointed her. 'I think they expected a little woman,' she said.

Instead, they got a formidable one. She found out that Special Branch had failed to tell the RUC prior to the Omagh bomb in 1998 of two warnings that the Real IRA was planning a major bomb attack, and she said the RUC's investigation of the bombing, in which twenty-eight died, was seriously flawed.

The then chief constable, Ronnie Flanagan, said she had mis-understood everything, and that if what she said was true, he'd publicly commit suicide. Ulster Unionist security spokesman Ken Maginnis compared her to a suicide bomber, while former Secretary of State for Northern Ireland Peter Mandelson claimed she was inexperienced and gullible.

In 2007, after a fifty-nine-day trial, the case against the one man charged with the Omagh bombing collapsed and he was acquitted. Mr Justice Weir criticised the police harshly, saying that there had been 'deliberate and calculated deception' in their evidence. Relatives called for a public inquiry.

O'Loan had exposed fundamental failings in the investigation of the murder of GAA official and community leader Sean Brown. The DUP said she was out to 'blacken the name of the RUC'. But it was her Operation Ballast report of 2007 that really rocked the foundations of the state, not least because the matters it dealt with were recent and only emerged because of the tenacity of one bereaved father, Raymond McCord, who refused to drop his quest to find out who murdered his son, Raymond, a minor figure in the UVF, in 1997, despite threats from loyalist paramilitaries and the inaction of the authorities. He brought the case to O'Loan.

It did not take long for O'Loan and her investigators to realise that this was a very dirty story with more than one victim. However, when she went to the Secretary of State to look for more money so that she could give the case the resources it required, her request was refused. The Operation Ballast inquiry was severely delayed, and although some money was eventually released, O'Loan never did get as much as she needed and had to take investigators off other cases to do the work.

'I had expected anger,' said O'Loan. 'Actually, it was very peaceful and calm. It was a sad and gentle occasion.'[2] She was describing the meeting she had to call in 2007 of the families of ten people murdered by the UVF in North Belfast in the 1990s. She had to tell them that she had found out that the UVF leader who killed Raymond McCord junior had also been involved in the murders of their loved ones. He had also attempted at least ten other murders and had carried out armed robberies, assaults and punishment shootings. He had been involved in drug dealing, extortion, hijacking, intimidation, conspiracy to murder and making death threats. He had done these things with the knowledge of the police because 'Informant One', whose name is Mark Haddock, was an agent of the RUC's Special Branch.

Haddock was protected at every turn by the police. Even after he confessed to the murder of a woman he was freed without charge. He was 'babysat' through 'sham interviews'. After one double murder, he was arrested. He asked police for a razor and was given one. His custody photograph was taken after he shaved off his beard, meaning he no longer matched the witness's description of the killer; in any case, there was no identity parade.

This incident reminded me of what the police officer in South Armagh had told relatives of some of those killed by the Glenanne gang. He had supplied a description of a suspect to colleagues, but the next time he saw the man, the suspect had made changes to his appearance.

After O'Loan published the Operation Ballast report, some former police officers said she had behaved criminally and called for her resignation. Unionist politicians were dismissive. However, surveys throughout her tenure showed that she was also strikingly popular and trusted by all sides of the community. 'Calling me a suicide bomber was extremely dangerous,' she said. It could have been interpreted by some as a 'call to arms'. She received several warnings from the police about threats to her life.

Protestants in the north of Ireland had seen the police as 'theirs', she said; to criticise them was regarded almost as 'treason'. She said the families of republicans who had been killed were particularly likely to feel that 'nobody cares'. She had been shocked by what her inquiries into hundreds of cases had revealed. 'For a long time the authorities said there was no war but now they are saying that this was a war and that was how things had to be. I can accept that with the Troubles the police found themselves in untrodden territories and that they were fighting a terrorist war – but the absence of proper management is inexcusable.'[3] Dave Cox, head of the HET, told me that the level of disorganisation and the lack of systems in the RUC in the early years of the Troubles were 'staggering'.

A deeply religious Catholic, O'Loan liked to quote from a book by Cardinal Bernardin: 'Like Jesus, we will love others only if we walk with them in the valley of darkness, the dark valley of sickness, the dark valley of moral dilemmas, the dark valley of oppressive structure and diminished rights.'

'I have been told on several occasions that I would destroy the peace process,' she said. 'It has been a clear case of trying to shoot the messenger. The fact is, I have a job to do. We have asked the people to sign up to a constitutional process and the rule of law. If the government doesn't uphold these, it will be discredited, the police will be brought into disrepute, and the canker will regenerate.'

* * *

In 2006, a remarkable group called Healing Through Remembering published a report called 'Making Peace with the Past'. Written by Professor Kieran McEvoy of Queen's University in Belfast, the report is the result of several years of discussions involving an unusually disparate group of people, including loyalist and republican 'ex-combatants', members of the security forces, academics, human-rights activists, civilians who had lost relatives in the Troubles, and others.

They came up with five options for truth recovery. These were: drawing a line under the past; internal investigations by organisations which participated in the conflict; community-based projects; a truth-recovery commission; and a commission for historical clarification.

McEvoy points out that surveys have shown that the general public in Northern Ireland sets no great store by truth commissions. Academics Patricia Lundy and Mark McGovern, who have done extensive and important research in this field, found in 2005 that while just over 50 per cent of people said they thought a commission might be a good idea, with Catholics more likely than Protestants to think so, 85 per cent agreed it might not necessarily get at the truth. A striking 92 per cent of those surveyed said they would not trust the British government to run such a commission, and this included 95 per cent of Catholics, and more surprisingly, 89 per cent of Protestants. However, the authors caution that those surveyed might have had limited awareness of what a truth commission might involve.

The 'Making Peace with the Past' report documents previous attempts to deal with the aftermath of wars. It warns against the danger of blaming individuals who carried out gun and bomb attacks, while leaving unexplored the social and political context in which the violence occurred. 'Put simply, an exclusive focus upon naming the 18-year-old paramilitary who carries out a sectarian or racist murder obfuscates the role of the sectarian or racist demagogue who inspired him to take up an AK47 or a machete in the first place,' writes McEvoy.

Jude Whyte, whose mother was blown up by the UVF, agreed

with this. Calling for an amnesty and a truth commission, he said that it was 'hypocrisy to blame some average Joe that went and planted a bomb'. In the hierarchy of blame, he said, First Minister Ian Paisley was far higher up. He recalled seeing Paisley at a rally in Ballymena in 1981, 'standing in a field surrounded by 500 men holding legally held arms'. British cabinet papers from 1977 released in 2008 revealed that officials had discussed arresting Paisley for conspiracy because he 'associated with paramilitaries' and had their support.[4]

McEvoy also suggests that while the rule of law nominally applied to all during the conflict, 'de facto cultures of impunity' were allowed to develop, 'most notably in the intelligence services and elements of the police involved in collusive activities with loyalist paramilitaries'.[5] Citing Michael Ignatieff, McEvoy says that for its advocates, 'Truth recovery exposes the myth of blamelessness.'[6]

* * *

The DUP rejected the idea of a truth commission outright. It was, according to MLA Arlene Foster, 'the last thing Northern Ireland needs'. Speaking at a discussion in Derry in 2004, Foster, who became a minister in the power-sharing government of 2007, said her party favoured the appointment of a victims' commissioner instead. However, she added that such a commissioner would deal with funding 'genuine victims rather than the current government policy of funding former terrorists and ex-prisoners' groups'.

When the Secretary of State did appoint Bertha McDougal as interim victims' commissioner, nationalists reacted angrily, and the High Court found the Northern Ireland Office had acted improperly, since the DUP was the only party consulted about the appointment. McDougal's husband was a police reservist who was murdered by the INLA. The appointment of her successor was also embroiled in controversy. In 2008 it was announced that McDougal was to return as one of four commissioners. One of the others was Patricia MacBride, a sister of Tony, the IRA man shot dead by the SAS.

'On this island, people tend to have very long memories,' wrote former UVF man Martin Snodden in a report on a discussion held by loyalist ex-prisoners on the subject of truth commissions. 'Once someone is branded as having done something seen to be wrong, their children and even grandchildren may have to live with the long-term legacy of those past actions.' Loyalist paramilitaries were particularly vulnerable to such a process, 'for they have never enjoyed the same level of legitimacy in their community as republicans', he argued.

Even though they took up arms because the state failed to protect them against armed republicanism, he wrote, 'experience has shown that pro-state paramilitaries typically have more difficulty justifying their actions than those who disguise theirs with the language of a "liberation struggle against a colonialist regime"'.

Loyalists rejected this version of the conflict, seeing it instead as a fight between the pro-state unionist community and the anti-state nationalist community. The latter 'gave birth to, nurtured and sustained the republican campaign'. It was, therefore, 'culpable' in the eyes of loyalist paramilitaries. However, the latter were 'stigmatised for carrying their campaign to the community they regarded as the real enemy, for which the republican armed groups were the cutting edge'. A truth-recovery process would write loyalists off as 'criminal gangs who operated on the fringes of the pro-British community'. Why, then, would they participate in it? The 'abject and true remorse' that loyalist paramilitaries offered their victims as they announced their ceasefire in 1994 should not be misconstrued.

If there was a further attempt to force a united Ireland on them, loyalists 'would not hesitate to respond with armed resistance'. Snodden articulated the common unionist belief that republicans were 'skilful in the art of propaganda'. They would abuse a truth process, and loyalists would end up as the scapegoats. There was nothing in it for them.[7]

* * *

Alan McBride, whose wife, Sharon, was killed by the IRA's 1993 Shankill bomb, had, for the first few years afterwards, shared the view that republicans would simply use a truth commission for propaganda. However, his views had changed. He was involved in Healing Through Remembering and believed that finding out the truth involved more than just identifying those who carried out the killings. 'As much as I hate Begley and Kelly [the IRA bombers] for what they did, I can't blame them for the conflict,' he said. 'They were part of an environment that shaped them, as I was.'

When he read the 2005 *Ulster at Crisis Point* newspaper, he was horrified. 'Blood was pouring from it,' he said. The publication, a special edition of the local Belfast paper, the *Shankill Mirror*, introduced the 'Love Ulster' campaign. In a heavily symbolic piece of drama for the television cameras, the papers were brought ashore from boats at Larne, in County Antrim – a re-enactment of the landing of the illegal guns with which Edward Carson's UVF intended to fight Home Rule. Among those unloading the bales of papers at the harbour were leading figures from loyalist paramilitary organisations. The spokesman for the campaign was a former DUP election candidate.

The paper narrated the Troubles as if it was one long IRA onslaught. It included photographs of the incinerated bodies of some of the twelve victims of the IRA's La Mon Hotel firebombing in 1978 and the bodies of the three men who died after the INLA opened fire on the congregation at Darkley in 1983. There were mutilated bodies and bloodstained floors and pavements. There was an account of the Teebane slaughter in 1992, when eight Protestant building workers in a van were killed by a landmine as they went to work at a British army base. There were accounts of the Kingsmills massacre, of Bloody Friday in Belfast. The grief, pain and anger of the victims and their families was described, and it was vivid and heart-rending. Alan McBride could not read the section on the Shankill bomb. 'I still have to protect myself from the details,' he said. 'I could not bear to know certain things.'

It saddened him, he told me, that there was no acknowledgement that the unionist community had caused grief and pain as well. The Catholic community featured in the paper almost entirely as IRA murderers. This sort of one-sidedness was, he felt, perpetuating conflict.

The story the paper told was of the Protestant people as the innocent victims of a genocide which nobody else had noticed. There was an appeal for the 'unionist family' to reunite to fight the common enemy. One article referred to those who were trying to push the Protestant people of Northern Ireland 'into the sea'. The destruction of the B Specials was lamented, as was the disbandment of the UDR.

This call for ethnic solidarity had been the mindset of the 'Drumcree warriors', those who believed the only way to settle the North's difficulties was for the British to wipe out the IRA, or if they continued to refuse to do so, for there to be a full-scale civil war, with Britain arming the loyal Protestants of the unionist family, united behind the Orange Order. It was the thinking of those who felt profoundly threatened by the peace process and its outcome, the Good Friday Agreement. It was the outlook of those who saw the Agreement as, to use Ian Paisley's words, 'a partnership with the men of blood'.

Later in the summer of 2005, the 'Love Ulster' campaigners and other unionist victims of the Troubles came to Dublin for a march. Several dissident republican groups called for their supporters to join a protest against it. The Northerners got off their bus on Dublin's main city centre thoroughfare, O'Connell Street, and held up their banners and placards, demanding that their dead be remembered. The Gardaí were unprepared for what followed, with a violent rabble launching an attack on the marchers. Some of them, their faces wrapped in tricolours, ripped up cobblestones from around the statue of Charles Stuart Parnell to throw at their countrymen and women. The self-styled republicans matched the marchers' 'Remember Kingsmills' placards with their own 'Remember Bloody Sunday' ones.

They yelled at the worried-looking Gardaí, 'You fucking Brit-loving bastards, protecting fucking Protestants. You should be ashamed to be Irish.' And, 'Bang, bang, Jerry McCabe,' a hateful reference to the controversial IRA murder of the Irish detective during an armed robbery. Displaying the crudeness of their political knowledge of unionism, they shouted, 'If they like England so much, tell them to go back.' Hardline unionists of a particularly narrow mind would revert to this stunted reasoning when nationalists complained about the Northern state or spoke of aspiring to a united Ireland: 'If they like the Free State so much, why don't they go and live there?'

After the unionists abandoned their 'Love Ulster' march, the 'republicans' shouted after their buses: 'We won!'

This ill-conceived march and the outrageous attack upon it saw the dead summoned up to fight in an undignified battle. The confrontation exemplifies the practice of what the critic Edna Longley has called 'remembering at'. It is a sort of coat-tailing which Longley also calls 'rhetorical history'.[8]

In the summer of 2007, Sinn Féin also attempted to marshal the dead for political advantage when it led a 'March for Truth' to a rally in the centre of Belfast. British collusion with loyalists was denounced, and bizarrely, the families from the various victims' groups which backed the march were accompanied by people dressed in paramilitary uniform, including masks, and carrying guns, presumably fake ones.

The march was led by people carrying photographs of the men who died on the IRA's 1981 hunger strike and was, indeed, declared to be in memory of them. This meant that in order to show solidarity with the victims of collusion, people had to accept the notion of the heroic IRA championing the cause of justice. It was a cynical exercise. The march was led by the Sinn Féin president, Gerry Adams, who had urged people to 'wear a black ribbon for truth'. He said that some of the victims were calling for a truth commission and that Sinn Féin would 'look carefully' at this idea.

During a late phase of the peace process, Sinn Féin had signed up for a piece of legislation that allowed IRA men and women who were 'on the run' from the authorities in the North to return home without prosecution. The law would also allow members of the security forces accused of collusion to escape prosecution. However, victims' groups and the SDLP fought against it, and it was dropped. Sinn Féin was embarrassed. The party was trying to recover its moral authority with victims from hard-hit nationalist areas. The 'March for Truth' was clearly meant to reassure them that they had not been left behind once Sinn Féin took power at Stormont. Adams would have felt it was safe to sound as though he supported such a notion, confident that it wouldn't happen; the British had gone to extreme lengths to make clear their attitude to truth recovery by their blocking of inquiries and inquests.

Jane Winter, director of British and Irish Rights Watch,

which had played an important role in monitoring, investigating and exposing human-rights abuses, told me she regarded Sinn Féin's involvement in the march as 'total hypocrisy'. The only people who really wanted a truth commission, she said, were some of the victims.

The Sinn Féin president's commitment to the truth about the past being excavated was in any case doubtful. After all, the man most people believe to have risen to the top of the IRA and to have led it through the worst years of the Troubles has always flatly denied that he was ever even in the organisation.

However, John Finucane, the son of the murdered solicitor Pat Finucane, said the march showed the determination of the victims of collusion not to give up on the demand for the truth. He asked the question: 'Can it really be defined as our past when it continues to dominate our present?' The 'poison of the past' would 'infect the future' if it was not dealt with, he said.[9] In 2008, several groups that largely represented nationalist and republican families stated that they would campaign for a truth commission.

That same year, there was an undignified display of tit-for-tat remembering at Stormont. Sinn Féin declared its intention to hold a commemoration for Mairead Farrell in the Long Hall. She was an IRA volunteer shot dead by the SAS in Gibraltar while on a botched bombing mission. The DUP was outraged and retaliated by proposing that the Long Hall be used for an event to commemorate members of the SAS who had been killed in Northern Ireland.

*   *   *

The Finucane family had won powerful international support for its campaign for a full-scale independent inquiry. Pat Finucane's widow, Geraldine, said she was concerned that a truth commission might not be rigorous enough.

The family of the other person named by Sir John Stevens in his report as a victim of collusion, along with Pat Finucane, had a strikingly different attitude. Adam Lambert was a Protestant who was killed because the UDA assumed, given that he was working on a building site in nationalist West Belfast, that he was a Catholic. He was a nineteen-year-old student who had just returned from travelling around Europe.

'We haven't forgotten Adam, and if we could have him back we'd go to the ends of the earth,' said his mother, Ivy Lambert, a retired schoolteacher from Ballygawley, County Tyrone. 'We mourned him and we still miss him terribly. But we have effected closure. We have accepted he is gone, with as much grace as we can. Adam wouldn't have wanted us to live in the past or destroy ourselves with bitterness. We have a good outlook.'

I interviewed her in 2003, after the Stevens report was published and sixteen years after her son's murder. 'What Sir John Stevens said doesn't worry me at all. I have the utmost admiration for the police, and we have brought up our family to respect authority and the security forces. Otherwise, you'd have anarchy. We live near the border, and a lot of young men were shot dead in their beds by the IRA. The police were under great pressure. Mistakes were made. Adam was murdered the day after the Enniskillen bomb. We heard Gordon Wilson on the radio that morning making his historic statement about bearing no ill will for the killers of his daughter. We little knew that by five in the evening, we'd be in the same boat.

'Adam was killed by loyalists who wanted revenge. The police came and told us. They were very supportive. It was complete and utter devastation, a terrible pain in the heart. We knew so little about the circumstances and there were things that didn't add up, but we keep all those things at a distance,' said Ivy. 'People who won't let go lose sympathy. You have to move on.

We support the peace process and we want a bright future for the young.'[10]

*   *   *

Bernie Collins, whose husband Eamon was murdered in 1999, probably by former IRA comrades who considered him a traitor, had no doubts. 'What this country needs is a no-holds-barred truth commission to investigate what happened during the Troubles,' she said. 'The IRA, UDA, UVF, UDR, MI5, MI6 – and the FBI, might I add – should all take part. It is going on nine years since Eamon was murdered and I still haven't had an inquest because it is still an "open" police case. His death has still not been registered. It would help to get all that sorted out. It's unfinished. It is still hanging over me.'

The inquest was finally heard in 2007. Coroner John Leckey and state pathologist Jack Crane agreed it was one of the most brutal and grotesque murders they had ever encountered. The pathologist described the considerable force that had been required to stab Collins repeatedly in the skull. He had also been stabbed in the back and severely beaten. The coroner said he hoped the 'sub-human thugs' who carried it out would be caught.

Bernie's concerns were different. 'I'd like to know how it happened. Could I have intervened and made a difference? Part of you, as a human being, still wants to know why. There are so many possible whys.'

She also wondered with some bitterness why Eamon was killed while others were let go. His 'boss' on the 'nutting squad' which 'tried' and executed those it found to be informers was Freddie Scappaticci. In 2003, journalist Greg Harkin had sensationally exposed him as the long-term IRA informer known as 'Stakeknife'. Scappaticci must have been an invaluable source for his British handlers, and if the use of informers on the loyalist side is anything to go by, he may well have been directed by them as to who was to live and who was to die. He had presided over the interrogations and murders of numerous 'touts' and had debriefed IRA volunteers after countless operations. Sinn Féin and its supporters pretended to dismiss the story, but their narrative of the conflict, with its clear-cut heroes and villains, was undermined. Scappaticci had denied everything and then quietly left the country, and is now believed to be living in Italy.

'Why was Scap let go and Eamon was not?' asked Bernie. 'Why was Denis Donaldson killed? Who decides what makes the difference?' Donaldson ran Sinn Féin's administration during the first executive at Stormont, and was arrested and accused of spying in 2002. These events, known as 'Stormontgate', led to the collapse of the first power-sharing government set up after the Good Friday Agreement.

When charges against Donaldson were dropped, he was released from jail and posed, smiling, on the steps of the parliament building with Sinn Féin leaders. A few days later, however, I got a terse call from the Sinn Féin press office. They were rounding up journalists for a press conference in a Dublin hotel. Donaldson was to be expelled from the party. 'Why?' I asked. 'Because he was a tout,' replied the press officer. Sinn Féin announced that he had confessed that he had been spying for the British since the 1980s. Donaldson disappeared. Then, in 2006, his murdered body was found at his isolated holiday home in Donegal.

* * *

For some people, the past they'd learned to live with would suddenly change, a narrative they'd learned to bear suddenly lurching off into a whole new set of possibilities, none of them comforting. When I met her in 2006, Kathleen Gillespie told me she'd had a very hard summer. Her friend, the SDLP MLA Mary

Bradley, had arrived at her house one morning with a newspaper to show her. There, all over the front page, was a report that the Gardaí in Donegal had known in advance that some sort of attack on her home was planned by the IRA. It revealed that a week before Patsy's murder, a Donegal woman with IRA connections had been found by the Gardaí to have a map with the Gillespies' street marked on it. The report also claimed that the 'human bomb' idea had been thought up by the British government as a way of discrediting the IRA and then fed to the organisation through a double agent. It said the leader of the gang that murdered Patsy Gillespie was closely related to a leading figure in Sinn Féin.

Kathleen didn't know whether to believe this conspiracy theory or not, and elements of it seemed far-fetched. However, she did know that there were elements of the investigation of her husband's murder which did not make sense. She had found out that a few hours after the bomb, six people were arrested in a house in Donegal, just across the border from Coshquin. They were released soon afterwards and later took a case for unlawful imprisonment to the European court, which they won. She learnt that a coat which appeared to match the one worn by one of the IRA men who took Patsy, and which she had described in detail to the police, was found in the house.

'It feels like a violation,' said Kathleen. 'For sixteen years I blamed the IRA for Patsy's death. I'd found my own way of going forward with that. I mean, you expect the IRA to do bad things. Then you are hit in the face with the idea that the government was involved, that they sacrificed their own employees, soldiers and civilians. The question that has been raised is, did the government collude through MI6 with the IRA in order to discredit the IRA? And the thing is, if it is true, it worked for them – the whole of Derry turned against the IRA.

'It was like starting all over again. To have this thought put in your mind, that the government was willing to use an innocent man as a weapon . . . it's unthinkable. It's all gone to pot. My trust in authority has all gone. I actually needed counselling, which I never had to have before. I went into WAVE [the victims' group] and I burst out crying, and I said, "I need help." I got the most wonderful woman and she stayed with me for three solid hours.

'After Patsy's death, the police and army were very helpful to me. Now, I think of all those top-brass people that used to come and all those services and ceremonies I went to . . . The first one was soon after the bomb, and I was afraid the soldiers' families would think Patsy had been connected with the IRA and they'd blame me. I was shocked they were so friendly and so nice. I met some of the soldiers who survived, too. I presented two big Tyrone crystal bowls to the army. At the back of my mind now I'm wondering, did they know? Were they laughing up their sleeves?'

The Historical Enquiries Team was to investigate Patsy Gillespie's murder, while British and Irish Rights Watch had also written a report on it and was demanding answers to a number of difficult questions. The implications were potentially devastating not only for Kathleen but for the families of the five soldiers who also died. One father, Brian Bethell, told me he wasn't angry with the IRA for killing his son. 'That is what they do. Paul was a British soldier. He was the enemy,' he said. 'I expected the loss of a soldier, though I mourn the loss of my son. But the idea that those with a duty of care towards him neglected their duties and helped the IRA . . . that has destroyed my faith. It has made me a complete cynic.'

* * *

In 2000, Herbert Cunningham was carrying out some building

work on a church in Derry. The priest had put *Lost Lives* on display on a lectern. The book was displayed in a similar way in other churches across Northern Ireland. It was an appropriate act of reverence towards the magnificent, Bible-sized chronology of the 3,720 victims of the Troubles.

Herbert's younger brother, Henry, had been murdered in 1973, when a gang ambushed the van in which the brothers were travelling. 'I went up to the lectern to check that Henry's name was there,' Herbert told me. 'There it was printed that it was the UVF that murdered him. Nobody had ever told us that. We were dumbfounded.'

This was a staggering revelation. 'We didn't even know when we went there that Glengormley was a strong loyalist area,' said Robert, another of the brothers who was with Herbert and Henry in the van that was ambushed that day. He said the family now assumes the UVF just saw the Donegal registration and saw it as 'just a matter of getting a wheen of [a few] Catholics'.

The family had spoken out after this, angry that they had been kept in the dark. A local schoolteacher told them his teenage students were amazed to learn that something so terrible had happened to a local boy and that they had never heard about it before. It was important to the brothers to feel that Henry was at last being acknowledged as a lost member of the Donegal community.

Henry's brothers were galvanised into an angry determination to find out more. 'We know we'll probably never get who did it,' said Robert. 'But we want to know at least somebody was looking about it at the time. They held the inquest within a matter of weeks and it looks like the inquiry went nowhere.

'We'd like to know how soon they knew it was loyalists. Years and years have gone by now and nothing ever happened. Sometimes we feel we've let Henry down, waiting so long. It is bad enough the RUC and the politicians in the North, but our own government seems to have done nothing at all, and they are duty-bound. Henry was an Irish citizen.'

The brothers visited the Pat Finucane Centre in Derry, where they were put in touch with the Historical Enquiries Team. At a first meeting, they were impressed by the sympathetic and polite attitude of Dave Cox's team. They are full of praise for the centre. It was a welcome contrast to the neglect they'd experienced before.

'Henry's lost. It maddens us how we've been treated. We'd like to bring this to an end. We don't want to be dwelling on it for all time,' said Robert. 'We have to let people know that even if the people who did it have forgotten about it, we haven't,' said Herbert. 'We want justice. My mother said to me one time, "Murder is a thing that never lies – it'll come up some time." She felt it wouldn't come up in her lifetime, but she said it might in mine.

'The Irish government did plenty when the IRA murdered the brother of those McCartney sisters. They made fish of one and flesh of the other. In July, a Sinn Féin TD [member of the Dáil, the Irish Parliament] asked the Minister for Justice about our sense of hurt and abandonment. The reply was that a comprehensive search of Irish documents from the time was conducted and nothing was found.'

The family had been political innocents. 'I tell you, we have got our eyes opened this last couple of years,' said Robert. 'There is not a night I go to bed that what happened that night isn't in front of my eyes as plain as yesterday,' said Herbert. 'It is justice we are after,' said Robert. 'We'd go to the ends of the earth.'

In 2008, the HET informed the Cunninghams that their investigation was complete. Most of the records were missing, so it was impossible to establish what had happened in the case.

The police officer in charge had since died. However, what they could say for certain was that one of the guns used to shoot Henry Cunningham had been 'stolen' from a Territorial Army base in Lurgan.

Such robberies were not uncommon, and there is evidence that the authorities knew or suspected that in many cases local members of the security forces facilitated them. The day after Robert Cunningham discussed the HET report with me, Paul O'Connor of the Pat Finucane Centre showed me some declassified secret documents from British military archives. The theft, which included the sub-machine gun used to murder Henry Cunningham, is recorded beside the comment, 'UVF have claimed responsibility. Collusion is strongly suspected.'[11] The Cunningham family was left angry and disappointed. The full truth had not emerged and justice, it still seemed, would not be done. 'It's a disaster,' Robert said.

* * *

Others, too, had lived with the stigma of false history. In 1974, a man from Newry died in a bomb blast near a British army checkpoint in South Armagh. The British army claimed he was an IRA man who was killed when his own bomb exploded prematurely, something the IRA did not deny. His shocked and bewildered family lived for thirty-two years with the fact that he was seen by many people as a terrorist who brought about his own death while out on a mission to kill others.

In 2006, under pressure from the family, the IRA issued a statement. It had carried out an investigation, it said. The man had been used as an IRA human bomb. The target was a British army patrol, but the bomb had exploded prematurely. In the statement the IRA admitted that by failing to tell the truth about the incident at the time, it had caused the family 'considerable heartache'. It offered its 'sincere apologies'.

When a fourteen-year-old schoolgirl was shot dead outside her home in Derry's Bogside in 1973, the IRA blamed the British army. Local people suspected this was untrue, but the IRA even claimed to have shot a soldier in retaliation. The family persisted in demanding the truth, and in 2005 the IRA admitted that it had shot the child, apologising and acknowledging that its failure to accept responsibility sooner had added to the family's pain.

Inquiries that did not fully expose the truth could cause more harm than healing. The British government reacted to Irish outrage over Bloody Sunday in 1972 by setting up a tribunal of inquiry chaired by Lord Widgery. It exonerated the soldiers. Bishop Edward Daly, who as a young priest had been photographed holding up a white handkerchief as he helped carry one of the dead off the street, said in 2000 that the Widgery tribunal had been 'the second atrocity'.

6

Setting Memory in Stone

'Well might the Dead who struggled in the slime
Rise and deride this sepulchre of crime.'
                                              Siegfried Sassoon[1]

One night in 1992, a young man approached the war memorial
in Enniskillen. It had been adapted the previous year to commemorate the people blown up there by the IRA in 1987. The
bronze plaque on its base had these words inscribed on it: 'In
remembrance of 11 of our neighbours who were killed in a terrorist bomb . . .' Above it, eleven bronze doves had been placed
around the stone plinth which held the single bronze soldier of
the original memorial commemorating those who died in the
First and Second World Wars. The young man took a hacksaw
and cut one of the birds from the plinth. Then he walked away.

There had been talk of a garden of remembrance on the
bomb site, but the Catholic Church, which owned the ground,
rejected this. The bomb had gone off in the old reading rooms
on the banks of the River Erne, facing the cenotaph. In the end,
it was decided to build a college there and to put a memorial
around the cenotaph. The decision had not been a great success.
The memorial stands in the middle of a busy road with no space
to sit or even stand in contemplation. The building, named after
former US president Bill Clinton, looks cramped in the small
site, and its role as an education centre has not been developed.

The memorial is unpopular with the relatives of some of the
victims of the bombing. 'My mother would have disapproved,'

Aileen Quinton told me. Her mother, Alberta, was one of those killed by the bomb, although Aileen objected to the use of the word 'killed'. 'She didn't fall in a war. She was murdered . . . It used to be such a dignified memorial. Now it's like a still out of Hitchcock's *The Birds*.' She also disliked the idea that her mother was represented by 'a creature', and said that when the dove disappeared, 'I like to think that was Mum escaping.'

Alberta Quinton had served as a nurse in the Women's Royal Air Force during the Second World War. Remembrance Sunday was important to her, she'd told her daughter, because it gave people time to mourn. There had been no time to do so during the war.

Aileen felt that the trustees of the memorial fund had 'vandalised' the original and that it was wrong to 'play down the truth' of what had happened. She said that every time she has to pass the cenotaph, she turns her face away. The young man who took the dove felt the same. The memorial insulted the memory of people he had loved and lost. This was his protest.

James Mullan, whose elderly parents, James and Nessie, were killed in the bomb, was also opposed to this 'tampering' with the original cenotaph. He had been in London during the controversy about the memorial and had stood for a while at the war memorial in Whitehall. 'It was so simple, no ornamentation,' he told journalist Denzil McDaniel. 'I thought I should bring the people from Enniskillen over to see it.'[2]

In his book *Sites of Memory, Sites of Mourning*, Jay Winter describes the Whitehall memorial, by Sir Edwin Lutyens, as a 'work of genius' because of its simplicity. The role of a war memorial is to bring the dead of the war into history, he writes. This one goes beyond the political and conventional architectural forms, 'to express existential truths too often obscured in the rhetorical and aesthetic fog of war and its aftermath . . . It says so much because it says so little.'[3]

The architect Richard Pierce, who designed the Enniskillen memorial, had stated in his proposal that 'the bomb turned that bronze soldier from a provincial war memorial in a West Ulster market town into an international symbol of the triumph of ordinary decent people over cold-blooded terrorism'.[4] One of the trustees who chose the design, a Presbyterian minister, said that, morally, he agreed that what had happened on Remembrance Day 1987 was murder. 'But when you have it set in stone and in memorials it seems to have an emotive connotation of anger and bitterness that I think should not be conveyed.'[5]

Monuments to the victims of the Troubles inevitably have emotive connotations, and many are contentious. A dispute about the wording on a plaque also overshadowed the unveiling of the design for a memorial to the victims of the Omagh bomb. Some of the families wanted there to be reference to 'dissident republicans'. Others wanted no physical memorial at all, favouring a memorial scholarship instead. Others kept the silence they had maintained since the atrocity in 1998.

In 2007, on my way to a press conference at which Mr Justice Barron would launch the report on his inquiry into the failings of the Garda investigation into the 1974 Dublin–Monaghan bombs, I drove past the memorial to the loyalist atrocity. It is a plain, polished slab of black granite, which stands at the end of Talbot Street, in Dublin's city centre. There is a list of the dead carved on the stone, but no surrounding garden or even a plinth. It is a most inconspicuous monument. That day, a man was sitting on a bench near the stone, crying.

Some of the survivors of the bombing and the relatives of the dead believe that this inconspicuousness is symbolic of how little care the Irish Republic has shown for those who died. Derek Byrne, who came close to being on the list of the dead, was angry about it. 'It shouldn't be there, outside a public house on a side street. I pass here regularly and I see people drinking cans of beer and urinating against that memorial,' he said. 'There should be a fitting tribute.' This, he said, should be out on the main thoroughfare, O'Connell Street, which is already lined with monuments 'for everyone to see'.

I live in the Republic, and when I drive north, I cross a bridge in the next small town to mine. There is an engraved stone on the arch of the bridge which commemorates two local men 'brutally done to death by British forces during the war of independence'. Wilhelm Verwoerd, who has written extensively about truth and reconciliation processes, has described his reaction to a plaque he saw in Cork. This commemorated one of the heroes of the 1798 rebellion and included the words, 'If I could grasp the fires of hell in my hands, I would hurl them in the face of my country's enemies.'

Verwoerd comments that this vengeful cry chilled and disturbed him, since it was intended to inspire new patriots and its spirit was utterly destructive. It reminded him of the necklacings in his native South Africa. He suggests that implicit in such a message is a 'moral forgetfulness' which needs to be countered by 'inclusive moral remembrance'. People need to be able to 'see the face of their former enemies', he writes.[6]

Gordon Wilson did not want his daughter, Marie, commemorated on a monument that spoke of murder. To the rest of the world, Wilson represented the spirit of Enniskillen. To some, in his home town, he was a source of resentment – the acceptable face of victimhood, the good victim who made others look bad. Twenty years on, Aileen Quinton was able to laugh about it. 'I'm the bad-ass victim,' she told me. She returned to her home town for the anniversary, but stayed away from the memorial.

* * *

The director of Kilmainham jail in Dublin has said that the building was so contentious that it had to fall into almost irrevocable ruin before it was possible to resurrect it as a museum. The British executed the leaders of the 1916 Easter Rising there, but the use of the jail by the new Irish authorities to house prisoners on the losing side of the civil war left an even deeper legacy of bitterness.

When it was announced that the Maze prison near Belfast was to be demolished, republicans proposed that a section of it be preserved to build a 'museum of conflict transformation'. During 2006, the Northern Ireland Office facilitated visits to the now empty prison. Laurence McKeown agreed to take me around this bleak place where he had spent sixteen years of his life and where he had almost died on hunger strike in 1981.

It was vast, 360 acres in total. The prison buildings were collapsing. Grey corrugated iron, concrete and rusting razor wire were all around. Tough grass had pushed up through the tar on the empty roads and exercise yards. It was spring, and a few cherry trees were in bloom, incongruously beautiful. 'Those weren't there in 1981,' said Laurence. Inside, there was grey lino and magnolia paint going black with mildew. Narrow iron beds. 'This is Bobby's cell,' Laurence said, with reverence. The cell had later been adapted for use by prisoners at risk of self-harm.

He showed me the broken metal chair where he'd sat in the yard outside the hospital, taking the sun while he was dying. 'Some people did go crazy here,' he said. 'One of the doctors committed suicide.'

Prison officer Dessie Waterworth was completely against the proposed museum. 'Put the bulldozers in and grind it to dust,' he said. 'We live in history. Remember 1690. Remember 1916. Remember the hunger strikes. No, let's not. Let's forget.'[7] The victims' group FAIR claimed republicans intended to turn the jail into a shrine to the IRA. It issued a statement claiming it had proof that republicans were lying when they denied this. 'In a recent visit by victims to the Maze, we discovered rosary beads, Mass cards, crucifixes and candles . . . the Maze has *already* become a shrine to republican murderers!' FAIR had published a booklet about the crimes the ten hunger strikers who died had allegedly committed. 'What about the history of the ten men massacred beside a minibus in South Armagh . . .?' it demanded.[8]

The UDA used Remembrance Sunday in 2007 to try to demonstrate that it was making a historic shift. It had come under pressure, particularly from women, after a teenage boy killed himself after taking drugs he had bought from the organisation in one of its heartlands, Tiger's Bay, in North Belfast. This was where young Glen 'Spacer' Branagh, a member of the UDA's youth wing, had lived before, on Remembrance Sunday, 2001, he was killed by his own bomb.

The favoured inscription on the graves of loyalist paramilitaries was 'Here lies a soldier.' Also popular was the self-serving claim that 'his only crime was loyalty'. Loyalist paramilitaries held ceremonies for their dead on Remembrance Sunday, and this insistence that loyalists had served the British Crown and that their fallen were among the 'Glorious Dead' was a source of deep embarrassment to the authorities.

The UDA had refused to disarm. Jackie MacDonald, who was known as the South Belfast brigadier of the UDA, was the main speaker on Remembrance Sunday 2007. Flute bands led the way to a UDA memorial set into an end-of-terrace wall. Poppy wreaths were laid, and MacDonald said, 'We have to get rid of the criminality. The drug dealers must go. If you can't shoot 'em, shop 'em.' The bandsmen in their traditional blue uniforms departed, carrying their drums and flutes, and the men in black suits walked away to the strains of 'What the world needs now, is love sweet love . . .' In its heyday, the UDA's anthem was Tina Turner's 'Simply the Best'.

*

The republican tradition is replete with stirring graveside orations, notably Padraig Pearse's from 1915: 'The fools, the fools, they have left us our Fenian dead. Ireland unfree shall never be at peace.'[9] The cult of the martyr has been a powerful engine for the 'armed struggle' for centuries. On the twenty-fifth anniversary of the IRA's 1981 hunger strike, Sinn Féin laid on an elaborate programme of commemorative events.

The centrepiece was a rally. 'A generation remembers,' said a banner, as ten children carried photographs of the men who died through West Belfast to a rally at the Casement Park stadium. The two British corporals captured at a 1988 IRA funeral near by had been dragged into the park before they were killed.

The parade took an hour to pass. There were middle-aged men and women dressed in brown blankets, the garb they'd worn as young protesting prisoners. Most of the ex-prisoners marched in black trousers, white shirts and black ties. There were hundreds of them. Some wore paramilitary gear, with dark glasses and black berets. There was a big banner with the Bobby Sands line: 'Our revenge will be the laughter of our children.'

People carried posters, some of which said, 'Thatcher – wanted for murder'. There was a British army Saracen with a banner on its roof: 'We murdered Irish children from these.' One band was led by a man in black beating a drum with '*Tiochaidh ar la*' (our day will come) written on it and a painted gunman in a mask. Another, from Glasgow, had a drum on which 'Ireland unfree shall never be at peace' was printed.

In the park, the ex-IRA people formed ranks on the pitch. Speakers praised 'ten heroes in a proud tradition' and spoke of courage and sacrifice and martyrdom. White doves were released from ten boxes on the grass. They fluttered off into the Belfast sky. The singer Frances Black sang a Bobby Sands poem set to music by Christy Moore. 'I believe all the spirits of the men who died are here with us today and I believe they'll join us when we sing with our hearts and souls,' she said.

Then it was time for the Sinn Féin president, Gerry Adams. He launched straight into a poem by Sands: 'There's an inner thing in every man,/Do you know this thing my friend?/It has withstood the blows of a million years,/And will do so to the end.' This thing 'hung bleeding on the cross', it 'marched with Wat the Tyler's poor' and 'stormed the old Bastille', and its 'heart was buried in Wounded Knee'. Adams finished his recitation: 'It is "the undauntable thought", my friend,/That thought that says, "I'm right!"'[10] The crowd erupted into cheers and applause.

Adams listed the hunger strikers and then shouted: 'Thank you for being right!' He spoke of the years of peace talks in Downing Street and elsewhere. 'I often think our side of the table is rather crowded,' he said. 'There's Bobby behind us and Francis Hughes, there's Mairead [Farrell], and Maire Drumm.' These were all IRA figures who died in the conflict. With these ghosts behind it, Adams said, the republican movement must look to the future. 'We need to have the confidence to take political power,' he said.

* * *

There were other ghosts, though, haunting the rally. They had played a major role in the events to which Adams was referring, but they were not 'right', according to his interpretation of Sands, and they were absent. 'They have sold out the people for penny loaves and homes in Donegal,' said the angry man on the radio. 'And where is the money coming from for the so-called leadership to do this? The British exchequer. The British government is the enemy of the Irish people. We spent thirty years trying to bring down this monster of a sectarian regime. They brutalised us, tortured us, kept us in slavery. I'm still in my prison cell, until I wake up.' Now Sinn Féin was pleading to be let into Stormont, he said.[11]

This was the voice of Brendan 'The Dark' Hughes, once an IRA legend. He was the man who led the IRA hunger strike of 1980, the one which ended in confusion, with one young IRA man in a coma and on the point of death. There had been rumours of a deal, and Hughes had sent word to the hospital wing: 'Feed him.'

It was a Sunday afternoon in January 2007, and I was on my way to a commemoration for an IRA volunteer killed by the SAS in South Armagh in 1977. Momentous things were happening in the peace process. Sinn Féin was about to sign up to an agreement to support the police service. Far more than decommissioning, this was the real proof the war was over. Hughes was being interviewed on the radio as I drove through the windy, mucky roads around Crossmaglen.

The PSNI was just the same as the RUC, Hughes said. Those who were about to support it were nothing more than collaborators. The war was over, 'But I wouldn't condemn anyone who resumed it in the future.'[12] This was strong talk from an old warrior.

Flocks of small birds flitted across the fields. This used to be the poor country celebrated in Patrick Kavanagh's poetry. Now, big new red-brick houses rose proudly out of the boggy land, many of them with high walls and grand security gates. Some of these were undoubtedly financed by the fuel laundering and smuggling that were rife along this stretch of the border.

There was a lorry set up as a platform, with chairs and loudspeakers, in the middle of an old clachan, a cluster of ruined stone cottages. I parked in the mud at the side of the road. The memorial was enclosed like a small suburban back garden with tall clipped leylandii. A narrow concrete path ran down to a

Celtic cross. 'In proud and loving memory of Vol. Seamus Harvey, killed on active service at this spot on 16th January 1977. *Fuair sé bás ar son saoirse na hÉireann* [He died for the freedom of Ireland].'

Gradually, the cars and SUVs arrived, lining the ditches. A young Sinn Féin steward asked me to move my car. Why? I asked. It would get crowded, he said, and it would be in the way. I said I couldn't see how it would be in the way. 'God forbid anything would happen to it or anything,' he said. 'A wing mirror broke or the like.' I reversed it awkwardly through the growing crowd.

I approached a group of men sheltering from the cold breeze against the wall of one of the cottages and introduced myself. 'Did you hear Brendan Hughes on the radio?' I asked one of them, a hard-faced man with a woollen hat pulled down low over his forehead. He was of an age to remember the hunger strikes. 'No,' he said. 'He says you've sold out,' I said. 'Does he now?' said the man, coldly. 'What did you say his name was?' 'Brendan Hughes,' I said. 'The Dark.' 'Who is he? Must be a Belfast man with a name like that,' he said, and turned his back to me.

We could hear the procession coming. There was a piper playing a lament, and then the banners appeared around the corner. The first one remembered 1923. The one for Seamus Harvey had painted on it: 'We sent our vision aswim like a swan on the river. The vision became a reality. Winter became summer. Bondage became freedom.' One of the banners had the legendary Irish hero Cuchullain on it, with the raven on his shoulder. Another had an explosion embroidered onto it.

The banners were carried by young people in black and white uniforms, and they marched to military orders in Irish from a young woman. The IRA was still recruiting, though it was thirteen years since its ceasefire. A young man had been killed 'while serving his community' a couple of years earlier. As they halted at the platform I saw another banner: 'Life springs from death and from the graves of the patriots.' Someone called through the microphone for the elected representatives to take the platform, and they filed up importantly.

A local councillor said the growth of the party was down to people like Seamus Harvey. 'He and his comrades took on the British army and took them to their knees. Some of the British regiments will never forget their time here,' he said, smiling proudly. I thought of ex-British soldier John Moore, in his wheelchair, reading about Irish history.

Wreaths of green, white and orange artificial flowers were laid by relatives and comrades of the dead man. A woman said a decade of the rosary in Irish. A young woman read South Armagh's 'roll of honour', a list of its IRA dead, and another sounded, with excruciating difficulty, the last post.

Then there were whoops and cheers for Gerry Adams, the president, smiling in his green wool coat. He praised the 'fearsome name of South Armagh', whose people had built dolmens and cairns and standing stones and high crosses. These stones had a story to tell, of magic, mysticism and romance, he said. He spoke of the many battles there had been to control this area, of Cuchullain, the Gaelic clans, Cromwell, British garrisons, the Fenians and the 'Staters'.

The British army was one of the best equipped in the world. It had used violence, torture, murder and harassment. 'But armed aggression was met with armed resistance. The men and women of South Armagh had boldly and gallantly resisted occupation,' said Adams. As for young Harvey, 'None of us should glamorise war,' he said, 'but the stories of his deeds are the stuff of legends.' I thought of the Kingsmills massacre of 1976. One of the guns used that day had, a year later, also been used by Seamus Harvey and his comrades in the ambush which led to his death.

Now it was time to look to the future, Adams said. The same courage as was shown in war had been shown in the search for peace, he said. The republican struggle was still about a united Ireland. 'It is about making the proclamation of 1916 a reality.' Republicans owed it to their patriot dead to take part in this stage of the process.

As I waited to get back to my car, I watched a group of young men folding up the banner they'd been carrying. It read, 'Whether on the scaffold high or in the battlefield, the noblest place for man to be is where he dies for man.'

Brendan Hughes had become disillusioned with such heroic rhetoric and had gone public with his feelings towards the end of 2006. In an interview with the *Irish News*, he described how he had almost lost his sight as a result of damage done during the hunger strike. He was not unique, he said. Hundreds of ex-prisoners were suffering. 'If not physical problems there are men with mental problems, alcohol problems, depression, trouble holding down a job or a relationship,' he told the paper. He said he knew there were those who criticised him for calling off the protest.

'If the truth be told, and I have never said this before,' Hughes told reporter Allison Morris, 'not one of those men was prepared to die.' He said that before the young man who almost died went into a coma he had said, 'Dark, don't let me die,' and, said Hughes, 'I promised him I wouldn't.

'They were putting him onto a stretcher to take him to the hospital. We thought an agreement was on the table and I just shouted up the corridor, "Feed him," and with those two words the first hunger strike was over. I weighed about five stone at the time. You could smell the rotting bodies in the hospital ward. I was very conscious of the smell of my own body eating itself.

'There are men still suffering in silence today. The recent

commemoration events to mark the twenty-fifth anniversary of the hunger strike didn't even touch on that terrible legacy.'

Dissenting voices were not tolerated by the current Sinn Féin leadership, he claimed. 'Painting murals on walls to commemorate blanketmen after they have died a slow and lonely death from alcohol abuse is no use to anyone. I would hate for young people now to have this romanticised version of the events of that time and what went on in the prison. The truth is so very far removed from that, and I suppose I'm living proof of that.'[13]

Hughes lived alone in Divis Flats. He died in early 2008, aged fifty-nine.

The family of an INLA man who died on the hunger strike also protested about Sinn Féin including him in its commemorations, pointing out that the IRA had threatened to kill him not long before he was jailed.

After the commemoration, I asked for directions for the journey from the Celtic cross in the hills behind Crossmaglen to Belfast. I was told to go straight across the junction called Ford's Cross, beside the hunger-strike memorial – big white stone crosses laid out in the form of an 'H', with plaques and finely maintained gravel. Beyond it, I crossed through mountains and over a lake, and then I was in Camlough.

I saw the square, the Sinn Féin office, the shop, the school, and there, opposite the school, a house, handsome, painted a bold pink that would hold the sunlight. Roofless. Charred. This was Eamon Collins's house, the house he'd written about in the closing lines of his book, *Killing Rage*. Describing his plans to return to the old family farmhouse with his wife, Bernie, and their four children, he said: 'I want to see my children there, laughing and playing. The anger and hatred this place has seen may in time be forgotten, if not forgiven. I do not want much else more.'[14]

He was not to get that much. I thought of the line from Sands so favoured by republicans: 'Our revenge will be the laughter of our children.' The IRA burnt the house down and then they murdered Eamon Collins. The ruin stands there, a monument to anger and hatred and revenge.

* * *

It was from Camlough that British soldier John Moore had escorted back the dead bodies of four of his comrades after their Saracen was blown up by the IRA in 1981. He remembered local youths throwing stones and jeering. Days later, the IRA hunger striker from Camlough, Raymond McCreesh, died in prison and John had watched his funeral through binoculars from the hills above the village.

It was two months after McCreesh's demise that John had his own brush with death, in the IRA ambush in which his friend, Gavin Deane, was killed. John lay critically injured while 'Deano's' funeral was taking place and had always felt the need to pay his respects. He described the anniversary, 16 July, as 'my Remembrance Day'.

In 2002, he persuaded his wife, Steph, to drive him back to South Armagh. 'We drove through all the areas,' he said. 'We went into a notorious pub in Crossmaglen. I'd been in there before with a beret on and a rifle. There was a guy helping a blind man up the steps, and he offered me a hand, too. We had a drink and he was watching us. When we went to leave, he followed us out. I asked him to take a photograph of us at the memorial!'

John showed me the photograph, a smiling man in a wheelchair with his smiling wife; behind them, the bronze phoenix that rises from the flames in the square in Crossmaglen, in memory of all the IRA fallen. 'If only he knew,' said John. He might have had a fair idea, I suspected. The memorial was designed by a Breton sculptor, and soon after it was erected in the 1970s, the British army reversed a Saracen into it. It is one of the few IRA monuments in pride of place in a Northern Irish town, the place more often occupied by a war memorial to those who died for Britain in the world wars.

Stephanie drove John to the place on the border the army had known as 'Hotel 24', where the ambush took place. The scrapyard in which the soldiers had been hiding was still there. 'It brought up all sorts of intense emotions,' said John. 'There was security on the scrapyard, so I couldn't go in. It is dangerous around there – bodies have been dumped in those fields. But I had to pay homage to Deano. I left a single flower there.' It was something, the flower, but John said it wasn't enough. 'I really need to get back in there, into the actual scrapyard where it happened. That is the holy grail for me.' On their way back to the airport, they drove through Ford's Cross. 'That's where the big aggressive memorial to the hunger strikers is,' he said. 'I remember the graffiti about McCreesh: "My brother is not a criminal." But there will never be anything there to remember Deano.'

In September 2007, John sent me an email to tell me that he was 'really pleased' because 'at last there is to be official recognition of Deano with a memorial dedicated to all the men and women of the UK armed forces . . . killed on duty or as a result of terrorist activity since the Second World War'. John was making the journey to the National Memorial Arboretum in Staffordshire, where the memorial would be dedicated in the presence of HM Queen Elizabeth. 'I'm sure it will be an emotional time for me when I see Deano's name for the first time,' he wrote.

John had an intense need to pay his respects to Deano in a ceremonial and communal way that would honour the soldier's death. He was filled with a sense of responsibility towards his lost friend. He carried Deano's name and his story, which was otherwise not to be heard. In *Sites of Memory, Sites of Mourning*, Jay Winter suggests that rituals at war memorials, especially the reading out and touching of engraved names, provide a way of 'passing through mourning, of separating from the dead and beginning to live again'. War memorials are there 'to help in the necessary art of forgetting'.[15]

There is a small black plaque at the side of the road at Coshquin, near Derry, that commemorates Patsy Gillespie, the IRA's human bomb, though the plaque does not say that; it simply says that he died there. The names of the five soldiers who died along with him are not listed. Brian Bethell, whose son was one of them, remembered the memorial service that was held at the scene. 'It was very cold, bare trees and an awful lot of crows. There was a table in the road with a brass cross on a white table-cloth. It was very stark. I saw all the faces of Paul's friends in their uniforms. There were press men, too, and I said to Paul's mum, Gloria, "The people who did this will be watching. If you cry, I'll divorce you."'[16]

While he was at the scene of the bombing, Brian noticed a small triangular flower bed with a lamp post in it at the entrance to the estate in which houses were damaged by the explosion. 'Every time I go to Ireland, I take poppy seeds and I plant them there. Welsh poppies. I'm a gardener by trade.' Brian paused, his face sad. Then he turned cynical momentarily. 'It is probably so I can tell people like yourself that I can add something – something that regenerates in a place which was once very bleak.' He said it was the soldiers who erected the plaque to Patsy Gillespie. 'If you put a plaque up for the soldiers, it would be wrecked.'

There is a memorial to the soldiers in Liverpool and in Palace Barracks in County Down, but Brian was determined that since his son died in the uniform of his country, his name was going to be commemorated properly, on the cenotaph in his home town. 'I felt very keenly that in a few years, no one will remember the soldiers who died in Northern Ireland. I rang up the British Legion and said, "Why isn't Paul's name on the cenotaph?" They said, "He didn't die in a war. It wasn't a war in Northern Ireland." I was incensed. I found a law and I quoted it to them. I wrote to the Queen, the Queen Mother, Mrs Thatcher.

'Eventually, a man from the council got back to me and said, "OK." So Paul's name was put on the war memorial, the first name since the Second World War. It doesn't mention Ireland. His name is there under "other conflicts". I think they were afraid IRA supporters would wreck it otherwise. There have been about fourteen others since.' Brian had got involved in the Northern Ireland Veterans' Association. He said relatives in Ireland needed to understand that for the families of soldiers it is a case of 'different wound, same pain'.

In 1995, John Bruton became the first Irish Taoiseach to acknowledge neutral Ireland's debt to the Allied forces and also the role played in the fight against fascism by thousands of Irish people in the British forces. Three years later, Ireland's President Mary McAleese and Britain's Queen Elizabeth travelled to Flanders, where they jointly inaugurated a round tower in memory of the Irish casualties of the First World War. When Alex Maskey became Belfast's first Sinn Féin lord mayor in 2002, he laid a wreath on Remembrance Sunday at the cenotaph at City Hall in memory of those killed in the British army at the Battle of the Somme. The DUP said it was an insult to the dead, but it was widely seen as a gesture of healing.

In her account of the IRA bombing that led to the death of her father, Lord Louis Mountbatten, her son, Nicholas Knatchbull, her mother-in-law, Lady Doreen Brabourne, and Paul Maxwell at Mullaghmore, County Sligo, in 1979, Lady Brabourne mentions that the family had their little dog with them that day when they sailed. The dog was picked up in the sea the next day, dead. 'She's buried over there, under a little cairn at Classiebawn, with her name on a stone and the date,' she said. 'That's the only memorial to that whole occasion. A little dog's grave, just in the corner of the castle grounds.'[17]

* * *

Those who tried to commemorate their dead in hostile places often found that the murderous violence meted out to their loved one was not yet fully spent. Hazlett Lynch, whose RUC brother was murdered in an IRA ambush at Ardboe, County Tyrone, described what happened when he brought his parents to see the place where their son had died.

'The wee nest the IRA guys had made themselves was still there. We had police with us, armed to the teeth. There was a housing estate beside it and women came out to their doors and cheered and clapped and celebrated that these three men had been taken out. I can still see my mother's face when she heard that and knew that other human females could lower themselves to that depth. That was hurtful. Boy, that was hurtful.' The family left a wreath at the scene, but when Hazlett went back soon afterwards, he found it had been torn up and scattered about the roadside.

Hazlett ran a victims' group in Tyrone. 'West Tyrone is only ten minutes from the border,' he said. 'We were the third-worst-hit area outside Belfast and South Armagh. The RUC was still a civilian police force that worked alongside the army, and 82.5 per cent of the UDR personnel who were murdered were off duty – civilians in terms of the Geneva Convention. But as far as the Provos were concerned, they were legitimate targets.'

He took me to visit a graveyard in nearby Castlederg, a small, dismal town of the sort that perfectly illustrates Yeats's lines: 'Great hatred/Little room.' Around these parts, the conflict was terribly intimate. 'We had men murdered by people they shared their lunch box with,' said Hazlett.

We drove along the narrow country roads in his big, sleek car. 'I would refer you to Romans 13, verses 1 to 7,' he said. '"The powers that be are ordained of God . . . they that resist shall receive to themselves damnation./For rulers are not a terror to good works . . . But if thou do that which is evil, be afraid; for he beareth not the sword in vain; for he is the minister of God, a revenger to execute wrath upon him that doeth evil."'

Hazlett said that the trouble in Northern Ireland was that the authorities had refused to act to crush the IRA; they had, in fact, done everything to 'appease' the terrorists. I asked him what he thought about unionists who said that in these circumstances the loyalist paramilitaries had a role to play, as the 'gloves-off' wing of the security forces. He sighed. 'Yes, well, there is this level of schizophrenia in all of us. Sometimes you wish they had done a better job. But not on innocent people.'

At the graveyard, we walked up and down the straight avenues of graves, shiny black granite stones, many of them including in their gold inscription 'Murdered by terrorists.' All Protestant names: James, Norman, Charles, Heather, Elma, Dessie . . .

'There's a wedding photograph, and three out of the four in it are lying here now,' said Hazlett. 'The groom, the best man and the bridesmaid. All UDR.' He told me that one man had lost seven members of his family.

He stopped at another stone. 'That man was blown to bits at his home. What they couldn't gather up, the crows ate.' And at another. 'That was a most cowardly murder. His nephew survived the bomb but has serious psychological problems.' He was going to show me an IRA memorial out on the border, but in the end he didn't have time. 'It is a Celtic cross – totally offensive. It is to two IRA men blown up by their own bomb. I wouldn't drop a lot of tears for them.' He named a few local IRA men, one of whom had been 'taken out' by the SAS. 'That was one killer taken off the scene,' he said.

Northern Ireland has hundreds of plaques and monuments to those who died in the Troubles. Memorials describing the heroism of those commemorated go down badly with the families of their victims. Jim McCabe, whose wife Nora was shot dead by the RUC, said he was infuriated every time he heard reference to the 'gallantry' of the police.

In 2002, the IRA erected a memorial to Tony MacBride and two other young IRA men, Kieran Fleming and Joe McManus, on a roadside near the border village of Belleek in County Fermanagh. MacBride was shot by the SAS during a failed ambush of the RUC, while Fleming drowned as he tried to swim across a flooded river in the same incident. McManus was shot by a UDR man in self-defence after the IRA had lured the man, a part-time dog warden, out to a lonely border road supposedly to deal with a dog. The UDR man was seriously injured but survived.

The placing of the memorial stone caused offence to local Protestants because it was very close to the spot where the IRA had killed two Protestant men, civilian workers at a police station. There were protests from local unionist and SDLP politicians, and from some of the relatives of the dead men. A major row erupted within Sinn Féin about it, with some republicans agreeing that the placing of the stone had been insensitive, if not provocative.

A short time after it had been unveiled, the memorial stone was vandalised. The next thing the MacBride family heard, it had been demolished. Oistin MacBride, Tony's brother, showed me the statement the family had issued when they got this news. They spoke of their 'great sadness and anger' at this 'callous and cruel act', accusing local unionist and SDLP politicians, as well as the *Irish News*, which had written an editorial on the subject, of creating a 'climate of marginalisation and hostility' that had led to the destruction of the 'simple stone'. No offence had been intended.[18]

The stone was replaced by Sinn Féin at another spot along one of these winding border roads, but local republicans were vague about its whereabouts. I saw plenty of new stones, embossed with the figure of a gunman, placed along roads and in housing estates to commemorate local IRA men who died in the conflict. In one border village, I was directed to a bridge which connected the two sides of the border. The British army had blown it up, along with a lot of other border crossings. A flimsy footbridge had been erected in its place, and one night two local men returning from the pub had fallen into the river and drowned. There was a plaque remembering them as victims of the British.

Some monuments were meant to threaten. The village of Pettigo was cut in two by partition, so that Pettigo remained in Donegal, in the Republic, and Tullyhomman was in Fermanagh, in the North. The village had been the scene of a battle between the IRA and the British in the war of independence in the 1920s, and a statue commemorating IRA soldiers known as 'The Quiet Man' was positioned so that the IRA men's guns were pointing across the border into the North. The message was clear: the North was yet to be liberated. In 1987, on the day of the Enniskillen bomb, the IRA also attempted to bomb a Remembrance Day commemorative event in Tullyhomman.

In 2006, a Belfast man whose son had been killed by loyalists – assisted, he believes, by the UDR – objected to plans to erect a large memorial to UDR soldiers in Lisburn town centre. He said it would insult the memory of his son, who was shot on his way to Mass and whose little daughter was blinded in the attack. Sinn Féin supported the objection, stating that such a monument would be 'deeply insulting to the many victims of this unionist militia'. If such monuments had to be put up, Sinn Féin went on, they should be inside military bases or in 'non-contentious areas'.[19]

In 2007, Craigavon council agreed to allow a memorial bench to LVF killer Mark 'Swinger' Fulton be put up in its municipal graveyard. Fulton died in prison, apparently as a result of suicide. The SDLP accused unionists of 'utter blindness' and reminded them of the 'string of murders' for which Fulton and his gang were responsible, including that of a council employee. 'It is an obscenity,' said MLA Dolores Kelly.[20]

Monuments are frequently wrecked or defaced. A memorial to eight workmen blown up by an IRA landmine at Teebane crossroads in County Tyrone in 1992 was frequently vandalised until it was completely destroyed in 1996. The rebuilt monument is still attacked periodically.

After fifteen-year-old Michael McIlveen was beaten to death in Ballymena in 2005, local teenagers turned the wall against which he was beaten into a shrine. After the flowers died and the soft toys were taken away, spray-painted messages were written by his friends in his memory. A year later, someone came in the night and flung paint over them.

In the same week, someone smashed up an IRA Celtic cross in South Armagh. Sinn Féin denounced this desecration, which was probably carried out by republicans who saw the peace process as a sell-out. 'All monuments, all places of reflection and remembrance should be left alone and treated with respect,' the statement said.

In 2007, families of those killed in the IRA's Claudy bomb woke to the news that the memorial in the village had been seriously vandalised. The bronze statue shows a young girl kneeling in pain, holding her hands to the side of her head. It depicts eight-year-old Kathryn Eakin, while on a low stone wall around the statue there are plaques to each of the nine who died. 'We were hurt and disgusted,' said Merle Eakin, Kathryn's mother. 'This wasn't casual vandalism. It took a lot of effort. It has to have been planned.'[21]

* * *

Funerals throughout the Troubles were bombed, shot at and prevented from proceeding. In 1977, loyalists planted a car bomb near the home of an IRA man who had been shot dead by British soldiers. The bomb exploded as mourners were preparing to leave the house, killing two young men.

The IRA used the dead several times as a lure for the security forces – booby-trapping bodies, for example. In 1987, in Derry, it murdered a Protestant man who worked in one of the prisons as a part-time instructor in leather work. Then it placed a bomb in his car, which killed two policemen. The Catholic bishop, Edward Daly, said this showed 'a degree of inhumanity and lack of respect for both the living and the dead which is hard to comprehend'.

The previous day, the bishop had banned paramilitary funerals from church grounds in the city after a pitched battle between the police and the IRA at the funeral of an IRA man. This was followed by the IRA's traditional firing of a volley of shots over the grave. Bishop Daly said this was an act of desecration and it was only by 'some stretch of their own imaginations' that those who cheered and applauded it could be called Christians.

Nor were the Troubles' dead allowed to 'rest in peace' in graveyards. UDA killer Michael Stone infamously launched a gun and grenade attack on the thousands of mourners who had turned out for the funerals in 1988 of three IRA members killed by the SAS in Gibraltar. Mourners had to take refuge behind tombstones, and three were killed. An IRA bomber had, in 1983, hidden behind a gravestone in the city cemetery in Derry, waiting for a British army patrol to pass. He then detonated a bomb, killing a soldier.

In the summer of 2001, loyalists in North Belfast began a particularly vicious 'protest' over an annual Catholic ceremony in a 'mixed' council graveyard. The cemetery at Carnmoney held the graves of many victims of the Troubles. The leader of the Shankill Butchers, Lenny Murphy, was buried there, under a stone engraved with 'Here lies a soldier.' His gravestone had been vandalised in 1989. On 'cemetery Sunday', it was the practice of Father Dan Whyte to perform a blessing of the Catholic graves, with hundreds of people gathering to take part. In 2001, a local loyalist leader complained to the council that holy water had been splashed on his car. Loyalists burnt down Father Whyte's church and put a bomb among the Catholic graves in the cemetery. Within months of the murder of a young Catholic postman, his tombstone was wrecked, prompting his girlfriend to say, 'Daniel is dead. What more do these people want?'[22]

In 2003, families of the dead arrived for the ceremony to find a distraught Father Whyte in the middle of smashed and paint-splashed tombstones and scattered wreathes. Meanwhile, like lost souls howling at the cemetery gates, a crowd of UDA supporters hurled abuse, blew whistles and honked horns to drown out the priest's voice. They carried placards which read, 'Let our dead rest in peace.' In 2005, the loyalists yelled that they would dig up the 'Fenian graves' and 'piss on them'.

The mother of a young Catholic man who had died as a result of a sectarian beating and who was buried in the cemetery told me in 2003 that she felt sorry for those taking part in the grotesque protest 'and their mummies who reared them'. It was a beautiful summer's day, she pointed out. 'They could have been out walking in the mountains. They are wasting their lives with hate.' While local Protestant clergy offered immediate support to the beleaguered Catholics, one local unionist politician suggested that Father Whyte 'had an agenda' because he hadn't painted out the letters 'KAT', meaning 'Kill All Taigs', from the door of his church. Father Whyte pointed out wearily that he was tired of painting the letters out. 'All I know is that this kind of performance has to stop or we are all in danger of losing our soul,' he told me. 'We are getting to be beyond outrage.'

* * *

Soon after I moved to Belfast in 1981, I went upstairs on a bus and saw, painted on the back of the seat in front of me, '13 dead but not forgotten – we got 18 and Mountbatten.' This tallying of scores – the thirteen killed by the British on Bloody Sunday, 1972, against the eighteen soldiers and the British establishment figure in 1979 – was common. Victims who were revered in their own community were mocked in enemy areas. West Belfast was still in mourning for Bobby Sands, but on a wall near where I lived in the south of the city someone had painted up: 'We'll never forget you Jimmy Sands!'

The poet Michael Longley wrote of his horror when he came upon a 'ghastly and inaccurate' piece of graffiti which referred to his friend, the magistrate Martin McBirney, and a judge. Both men had been shot by the IRA in 1974. Written on the wall, he saw: 'The two judges. Ha! Ha! Ha!'[23]

The murals in loyalist and republican parts of Belfast are now an established part of the tourist trail, with red open-topped buses crawling up and down the Shankill and the Falls. During the Troubles, they played a significant and sometimes menacing role in communities. They contained political messages, warnings and threats, and they marked out paramilitary territory. Republican ones tend to celebrate martyrdom, whereas loyalist ones tend to celebrate killing. Both employ high, heroic language painted in antique script. Loyalists love muscular 'warriors', and while Cuchullain has traditionally been claimed as a precursor to republican 'freedom fighters', in the 1980s loyalists 'reclaimed' him. He was, the murals imply, the first Ulster Freedom Fighter.

A favourite figure in areas dominated by loyalists is the Grim Reaper, often featured in the background of murals dominated by 'Eddie' from the cover of an album by the heavy-metal band Iron Maiden. The big, menacing figure in paramilitary uniform, with a skull face and a gun, strides out from a background of burning buildings and mayhem. In some cases there are crosses, too, with the names of republicans on them. The image was also a popular UDA tattoo.

A few years ago, I went to interview a young Chinese couple who had been attacked by loyalists in their rented home in South Belfast. At the end of their street, there was a Grim Reaper mural with the accompanying rhyme: '. . . so when you are in your bed at night and hear soft footsteps fall, Be careful it's not the UFF and the Reaper come to call.' The UDA carried out hundreds of 'doorstep killings'.

Banners were another way of parading killers as heroes. In 1980, former policeman Billy McCaughey, who, as a member of a UVF gang, had been convicted of the sectarian murder of a Catholic, presented a banner to one of the loyal orders. A local SDLP representative said that by parading with it, the Apprentice Boys had 'defiled' the streets of Derry. After the murder of former Shankill Butcher and Orangeman Robert 'Basher' Bates in 1997, the Orange lodge to which he had belonged added his name to a banner 'in fond memory of our fallen brethren'. One of the relatives of those murdered by Bates's gang said, 'It hurts the memory of those that the

Butchers killed.'[24] In 2007, the DUP defended a band named after a UVF bomber, pointing out that GAA clubs were named after republicans.

Academic and writer Bill Rolston, who has made several valuable collections of photographs of paramilitary murals, states that in the early days of the Troubles, there were surprisingly few depictions of armed loyalists. 'This changed after the signing of the Anglo-Irish Agreement between London and Dublin in 1985,' he writes. After that, 'military iconography came to predominate'. This was at a time when Ian Paisley was rallying loyalists and threatening to form an army, the so-called 'Third Force', to oppose the Agreement.

Rolston points out that the loyalist mural tradition goes back to the beginning of the twentieth century, with celebrations of King Billy at the Battle of the Boyne. 'Given their exclusion [from the unionist state],' he writes, 'nationalists did not paint murals . . . the streets and public places were unionist.'[25] It was the hunger strikes which precipitated the use of walls to deliver highly charged political messages to communities that were then engaged in extensive street protests.

Rolston commented to me that after the ceasefires of 1994, loyalist murals 'actually got heavier and more threatening'. This was a time of great confusion within unionism, with peace seen as imminent surrender and therefore somewhat threatening. In republican areas, the murals became more taken up with political issues. 'The murals impacted on solidarity in communities,' Danny Devenney told me. He is one of the best-known republican mural painters.

His most famous image is of Bobby Sands, which is on the wall of Sinn Féin's headquarters on the Falls Road. Reproductions of the image have tended to be cropped in recent times, for the mural is taken from a prison photograph, and the man with his arm draped over Sands' shoulder is Denis Donaldson, who led Sinn Féin's administration at Stormont, before being exposed as a British spy in 2005, banished and murdered.

On the Shankill, a mural glorifying sectarian massacres by loyalists was removed in 2000 by a former loyalist paramilitary turned politician who was deputy mayor of Belfast. This symbolic gesture of reconciliation followed protests from relatives of some of those killed in the events portrayed after they had seen a photograph of it in the *Irish News*. Some local youths came to jeer as the politician painted over the mural. One of the relatives praised his action. 'I was devastated when I saw that terrible mural,' she said. 'At least this makes me feel there is good on both sides of the community.'[26]

By 2005, there was a concerted move to get the gunmen off the walls. 'We have to de-paramilitarise the culture,' former UVF man 'Plum' Smith told me. Taking down the murals was part of that. 'The ones that are memorials will stay,' he said. We drove through the side streets off the Shankill, passing three memorials in a row, portraits of murdered loyalists. 'One of those men was killed by the British army, one by republicans and one by loyalists during a feud,' Smith said.

A newish mural showed images of IRA bombs on the Shankill from 1971 to 1993. The caption says, 'Thirty years of indiscriminate slaughter by so called non-sectarian Irish freedom fighters.' Another showed the UVF as 'the people's army', from its formation to resist Home Rule in 1912, to the emergence of its political wing, the Progressive Unionist Party, in the 1990s. The party's leader, David Ervine, who died in 2007, is seen pointing towards a sign that says 'Peace'.

A 1983 mural in East Belfast showed a UVF man beside a local British soldier who had been awarded the Victoria Cross in the First World War. In 2006, in South Belfast, a Grim Reaper had been removed from a wall facing a primary school. Loyalists replaced it with a portrait of a local British soldier who was awarded the Victoria Cross in the Second World War. He was a Catholic.

In the summer of 2007, Gerry Adams unveiled a mural in West Belfast that was a copy of Picasso's *Guernica*. David Ervine's son Mark was one of the painters, and Adams was joined by Jeanette Ervine, David's widow. Adams quoted Picasso's comment on the original Spanish Civil War painting: 'I clearly express my abhorrence of the military caste which has sunk Spain in an ocean of pain and death.'

* * *

All that was left of Kathleen Gillespie's husband, Patsy, after the IRA turned him into a human bomb in 1990 was, she said, 'a piece of a grey zip with a bit of flesh attached'. There was no body to be identified, no open coffin. 'I have a phobia now which comes up when I go to a wake and someone wants me to see the body in the coffin,' she said. 'I am jealous that others can have that chance to say goodbye.'

Others have experienced similar anguish. One woman whose husband was shot in the face by loyalists in 1977 told me that she had not been allowed to see her husband's body. She felt this had been wrong. 'I didn't need to see his face,' she said. 'I would have known his hands and his feet.'[27]

There is a vast additional dimension of distress and grief for the families of those who were 'disappeared' in the course of the Troubles. Vera McVeigh spent twenty-three years waiting for her son, Columba, to come home after he went missing, aged nineteen, in 1975. Then she found out the IRA had murdered him and buried his body in a bog. She spent the last nine years of her life pleading with the IRA to tell her where he was.

Vera died in May 2007, aged eighty-two. Her death struck a poignant note in a week which saw the restoration of power sharing at Stormont, the tone set by images of Sinn Féin's Martin McGuinness and the DUP's Ian Paisley smiling from ear to ear. There had been no peace for Vera, no smiles to mark the end of a long, hard journey.

She was buried under a gravestone which bears the names of her late husband, Paddy, and of Columba. It was after learning of his murder that she had Columba's name engraved there, but her longing to bury his body in the family grave was unfulfilled. Among the first to offer their condolences to the McVeigh family were the new first and deputy first ministers, Paisley and McGuinness.

The IRA told the Independent Commission for the Location of Victims' Remains only that Columba McVeigh's body was in Brackagh Bog. Her son, Eugene, had accompanied his mother to one of the searches that followed. 'It was harrowing and weird to see her there in that desolate place,' he told me. Vera herself had got a water diviner involved. She had given him a garment that had belonged to Columba, and he had marked out on a map where he believed the body was buried. She said the police had not searched that spot.

After the searches proved fruitless and were called off, Father Denis Faul, who had given Vera enormous support over the years, offered to consecrate the bog. 'I wouldn't let him,' Vera told me. 'Sure he is in a grave. He's in Brackagh Bog. If he is got, sure what good will it be? They'll take him out of one hole and put him in another.'

However, this was not always her view, and her family said she continued to hope against hope to the end of her life that she would be able to give Columba a Christian burial. She died full of rage at the injustice that had been done to her son and to her family. Eugene, a cameraman, had filmed the opening of mass graves in Bosnia. He described the wailing and sobbing of the women as they identified their loved ones. That night, he'd got drunk, thinking about his mother and the time he'd stood with her at the dig at Brackagh Bog.

In 2006, the National Museum in Dublin displayed bodies which had recently been unearthed, some 2,000 years after they had been buried in Irish bogs probably located, archaeologists believed, on the edges of territorial areas. One of them had hair that still shone in bright amber waves. Their skin, black as the turf in which they'd lain, was smooth and supple. Another had the elegant, unblemished hands of a man who never laboured. One was headless, and there were signs that all had suffered violent, ritualistic deaths.

The McConville family, whose mother, Jean, was 'disappeared' in 1972, got her body back thirty-one years later. Her adult children were able to identify the jumper she had been wearing as they clung to her and the IRA dragged her away.

Journalist Gerry Moriarty movingly described the 'typical Irish wake' at her son's house, the night before the funeral. 'There was a steady stream of mourners throughout the night, and all were welcomed. Jean McConville's coffin was in the sitting room, a photograph of the mother of ten beside it. There were candles around the coffin and vases of flowers. You could have a cup of tea . . . You could touch the coffin, say a little prayer, hope that the demons of thirty-one years would be banished.' Stories were swapped, both sad and happy, and there was a 'true feeling of peace' in the house.[28]

At her funeral in Belfast, Bishop Patrick Walsh said the family had 'waited, wounded and scarred with grieving and restless hearts'. A priest compared the murder to the actions of the Nazis and called it 'our most shameful example of the moral corruption and degradation that violence generates in the human spirit'. It had 'dehumanised' her murderers.

In his classic story from an earlier phase of the Irish conflict, *Guests of the Nation*, Frank O'Connor describes the IRA's killing of two English soldiers and their burial in a bog. One of the volunteers who had been guarding the soldiers before orders came to kill them is shattered. He suddenly feels remote from everything around him. The story ends, 'I was somehow very small and very lost and lonely like a child astray in the snow. And anything that ever happened to me afterwards, I never felt the same about again.'[29]

A 2007 BBC documentary about the disappearance of British army captain Robert Nairac included an interview with a man who had been brought by the IRA to the scene of Nairac's assassination. He was told to pretend to be a priest and to say the last rites. He did so. Thirty years on, he told television reporter Darragh McIntyre, 'I am absolutely ashamed. I'm disgusted at myself.'[30]

Another of Vera McVeigh's sons, Oliver, vowed after she died that he would take up his mother's quest. 'I just hope the people who refused to come forward are proud of themselves,' he said.[31]

The IRA claimed that Jean McConville, Columba McVeigh and most of the other 'disappeared' were informers, known on the streets as 'touts'. Throughout the Troubles, warnings were painted on walls in both republican and loyalist areas – 'Touts out', 'Touts will be shot' or naming names – which would often be followed by the hasty departure of that person from their home. In 1987, the IRA murdered one of its former members, claiming he was an informer. His hooded, naked body was dumped on the border. His hands were tied and he had been shot in the head. Gerry Adams had this to say of the dead man: '[He] . . . like anyone else living in West Belfast, knows that the consequence for informing is death.'[32]

By stark contrast with the way the 'patriot dead' were buried with great ceremony, the body of an informer would be treated with ostentatious disrespect. I remember the funeral, shortly before the IRA ceasefire, of a young woman murdered for being an informer. Women who had been her friends sat in a cafe along the route of the cortège, smoking and watching impassively as the small band of loyal family members and friends passed by on the Falls Road. Some years later, I was told that the Protestant farmer who had found the woman's body on her land had returned to the spot to plant a rose bush there.

* * *

Some families have chosen to commemorate their loved one with a living memorial. For the funeral of Nicholas Knatchbull, Lord Mountbatten's family asked that instead of flowers, donations should be made to the National Society for the Prevention of Cruelty to Children, to provide cross-community holidays for children from Northern Ireland. His mother said that while everyone would remember her father – 'the whole world knew of him' – Nicholas 'could easily have been forgotten' and she wanted to 'keep his memory alive'.[33] Nicholas's schools also started funds in his memory. The family donated a prize to the Gordonstoun student who showed the best example of service to the community. 'It's a solace to think that because of Nicky there's a little bit of good happening in the world,' Countess Mountbatten said.

After the IRA's Enniskillen bomb in 1987, large sums of money were donated to an appeal fund, and its trustees set up the 'Spirit of Enniskillen' bursary. This enables fifty young Northern Irish people each year from both Catholic and Protestant backgrounds to travel to other countries in which there had been ethnic conflict. They do work which 'encourages leadership . . . in respecting and accepting diversity'.[34] The Canadian government set up a 'Marie Wilson Voyage of Hope' scheme, which sends teenagers from Fermanagh to Canada, where they stay with families.

The Enniskillen bomb had a profound impact on John Maxwell, who had returned to his job as a teacher in the town soon after the IRA murdered his fifteen-year-old son, Paul, in the 1979 bomb that killed Lord Mountbatten. 'I was sitting here,' he said, as he sat at the table in his lovely house overlooking Lough Erne. 'I heard the bomb. I'd always felt I should do something to improve society, and this was the catalyst. I got up off my backside and got involved in setting up an integrated school. I was brought up in a segregated school and had very little contact with Catholics. I felt that was part of the problem here.' Like most Northern Irish towns, Enniskillen had Catholic schools and Protestant schools. The cross-community 'Enniskillen Together' group was the moving force in getting the integrated primary school opened. There is now an integrated secondary school also. 'The success of the schools has been a great pleasure to me,' said John.

People made generous gestures to ensure that the goodness they remembered in the victim was perpetuated: colleagues of a British soldier blown up by the IRA in Belfast in 1972 built a children's playground in his memory in Hong Kong; a man whose wife was one of those burnt to death in the IRA's La Mon Hotel atrocity in 1978 went to help build a village for homeless children in the Philippines; and after the sectarian murder of an eighty-seven-year-old Protestant man and his fifty-year-old daughter in Belfast in 1980, a memorial fund was set up to help build a hospice in North Belfast.

The parents of Tim Parry, one of the children killed by the IRA's Warrington bomb in 1993, set up a Foundation for Peace and the Warrington Peace Centre, a big, bright, modern building in the town, which lies near Liverpool. The foundation runs peace projects for children from around the world and also ran a six-year project called Legacy for 'GB victims, survivors and veterans of the NI Troubles'. Many former soldiers have begun to meet and talk with Irish people, including ex-IRA combatants, thanks to the project.

Soon after Belfast youth worker Terry Enright was murdered by the LVF in 1998, one of the young people he'd been working with came to see his parents, Mary and Terry senior. He had an idea. 'Terry saved me,' he said, and he told them he and some of the other young people wanted to continue his work. The Terry Enright Foundation was set up, with Terry's parents on its board.

Terry had revitalised the Mourne Challenge – a demanding walk in the Mourne mountains – and had got a lot of young people to do it. After his death, it was renamed the Terry Enright Challenge. Mary showed me a bog-oak trophy given in his name to the winner of the challenge. It was inscribed: 'If all the brown leaves of the forest were gold, if all the bright waves were of silver, Terry would give them all.' The GAA club for which he had played also honoured his memory by renaming its pitch after him.

'It is very important, especially for his children, to give them something to live up to. It is all about his ethos,' said Mary. She and Terry showed me a plaque inscribed in Irish: '*Mol an oige agus tiochaidh si* – praise the young and they will flourish.' 'It was all about keeping him alive, in a way,' said Mary.

7

Broken Things

'In the dark times,
will there also be singing?'
Bertolt Brecht

After a week of funerals, there was a memorial service in the centre of Omagh for the twenty-eight who had been killed by the Real IRA's 1998 bomb. Down the street, police were still sifting through the rubble. The hospital was full of the injured, and some among the huge crowd outside the town hall were bandaged up or on crutches.

From the moment Juliet Turner began to sing, a profound silence fell. 'You can have my heart/If you don't mind broken things/You can have my heart/If you don't mind these tears . . .' she sang in her local accent, her heart in her voice, broken, sorrowful, but also full of solace, the Bible's balm in Gilead.

Thousands of people were there, and millions watched on television across the world. 'Broken Things', by American singer-songwriter Julie Miller, is based on Psalms 34 and 42. It had seemed that no comfort could be found; that it could seemed like a miracle.

'I don't think I have ever experienced anything like it,' David Bolton told me. As director of the Northern Ireland Centre for Trauma and Transformation, he was one of the organisers of the ceremony and was standing behind the singer. 'You could see people's faces in the crowd. It said everything that needed to be said.' He said it was like Gordon Wilson's interview after the

Enniskillen bomb. 'It offered a way through the tragedy. It saved lives.'

Turner later recorded 'Broken Things' as part of an album, the proceeds of which went to a fund for victims of the bomb.[1] She told me she could not fathom the depth of the people's response that day. 'It wasn't me,' she said. 'It was the power of music for healing . . . that sense of a mysterious God.'

* * *

That the right words at the right time could perhaps save lives has been something understood by many bereaved people over the years of the Troubles, when they have used the brief, grief-stricken moments they had in the public eye to appeal for 'no retaliation'. The importance of such appeals is not diminished by the fact that the killers may already be on the road. It is impossible to measure the force of hidden restraints.

Poetry, according to William Carlos Williams, may be despised by those preoccupied with events, but is also essential: 'It is difficult/to get the news from poems,' he wrote, 'Yet men die miserably every day/for lack/of what is found there.' Michael Longley referred to Primo Levi, who survived Auschwitz and wrote about it for the rest of his life. 'The most important thing he did was to remember,' he said. 'To bear witness when memory was being obliterated.'[2]

After Longley read his poem 'The Ice-Cream Man' on the radio, he received a letter, which he showed me. Its author signed herself 'The Ice-Cream Man's Mother', and she was writing to thank him. 'I do appreciate very much that someone outside our family circle remembered my son John,' she wrote. 'May God bless you.' The short poem opens with a list of the ice-cream flavours Longley's child would 'rhyme off' before 'They murdered the ice-cream man on the Lisburn Road/And you bought carnations to lay outside his shop.'[3]

'Getting that stunning letter was one of the most important events in my life,' Longley told me. Some time later, he was in a bookshop in Belfast when a man took his elbow. 'He told me he was the ice-cream man's brother and that his mother had died of a broken heart on the anniversary of her son's murder,' said Longley.

He had also received a letter from John Maxwell, whose son had been murdered. 'He wrote to me about "Ceasefire",' he said. 'He told me he had turned to poetry himself.' Maxwell had told me that the poem struck a chord. His own attempts at poetry were a way of mourning the waste of his boy's potential.

'Ceasefire' is about the moment in Homer's *Iliad* when Hector has been killed and his father, Priam, goes to Achilles to ask for his body. Achilles is moved, and the old enemies weep together. The poem ends: 'I get down on my knees and do what must be done/And kiss Achilles' hand, the killer of my son.' Longley was proud of 'Ceasefire' but said that he had his own reservations about it. The poem was published in the days after the IRA announced its ceasefire in 1994. 'There is perhaps something a bit middle-class and presumptuous about the poem,' he said. 'It went down well with politicians and priests. But who am I to say people should forgive? A man came up to me in the street shortly after it was in the paper and he said, "I admired your 'Ceasefire' poem but I'm not ready for it."'

There is an ambiguity to the poem, and as Longley pointed out, 'It is about a ceasefire, not about peace.' However, Longley worried that the poem might have been 'too symmetrical' and wrote 'All of These People' as, he said, 'a corollary, or a correction'. This poem opens with a question: 'Who was it who suggested that the opposite of war/Is not so much peace as civilisation?' It then celebrates civilised people who have been killed.[4]

Longley lost a close friend when the magistrate Martin McBirney was shot dead by the IRA. 'He was a wonderful man,' he said. 'A very good QC, very erudite. He was a Labour man, an all-Ireland man, and as a barrister he defended the early civil-rights protesters. He wrote programmes for Radio Three on subjects like the influence of music on Tolstoy. He used to test us on his "Round Britain" quiz. He used to empty the fridge of food and drink. We loved his visits.'

Longley's elegy to McBirney is in a powerful series called 'Wreaths', and it is a cry against the wanton destruction of a civilised man. 'He was preparing an Ulster fry for breakfast/ When someone walked into the kitchen and shot him:/A bullet entered his mouth and pierced his skull,/The books he had read, the music he could play.' The poem ends with the dead man's wife in her grief damaging his piano.[5]

Also in the 'Wreaths' sequence is 'The Greengrocer', who was shot 'serving even the death dealers' as he got organised for Christmas. Longley imagines the Three Wise Men calling in at the shop for gifts to bring with them to a small house on the Shankill or the Falls: 'Dates and chestnuts and tangerines.' This man was, Longley told me, a Catholic who was doing well in a Protestant area, and for this he was targeted by loyalists. The last in the sequence is 'The Linen Workers', about the ten Protestants who died at Kingsmills. Longley suggests a ruined Communion scene, the bread and wine spilt along with the dead men's personal belongings.

Professor Edna Longley (the poet's wife) has written that these poems contain 'unresolved images', with 'Christ stuck between heaven and earth', and that their 'denial of elegiac consolation also functions as a critique'. There is the suggestion, in the Northern Irish context, she suggests, 'that Christianity has not so much failed as never been tried'.[6] Longley himself said that 'elegies brim with the remembered liveliness of the dead. They are a celebration as well as a lamentation.' He saw the brevity of most of these elegies as a kind of tact, 'a touch and no more'.

Longley has said that because of the Troubles, the poet's role had unavoidably been more public than was usual. Poems like 'Ceasefire' and Seamus Heaney's 'Cure at Troy' became part of the narrative of the peace process, with Van Morrison's song 'Days Like This' as its soundtrack. John Montague's 'A Response to Omagh' was first published on the front cover of a news magazine containing reports on the bombing in its immediate aftermath.

Longley said he believed in the wartime slogan 'careless talk costs lives'. This was used by both security forces and paramilitaries as a warning to the public. 'To write carelessly and self-indulgently . . . could have terrible consequences,' he said. He described the good poetry that emanated from Northern Ireland, as opposed to the 'Troubles trash', as having the same qualities as the language of the Good Friday Agreement, which 'depended on almost poetic precision and suggestiveness to get its complicated message across'.[7]

When the prisons were full of paramilitaries, Longley took part in the prison-education programme, teaching poetry appreciation to loyalists. Walking in the funeral cortège for David Ervine, the former UVF man and leader of the Progressive Unionist Party, I saw on a wall near his office in East Belfast a UVF mural with lines from the Siegfried Sassoon poem 'Suicide in the Trenches'. The poem was painted in the old-fashioned script favoured by loyalist muralists: 'You smug-faced crowds with kindling eye/Who cheer when soldier lads march by,/Sneak home and pray you'll never know/The hell where youth and laughter go.'

Longley has written about his father's time as a British army officer during the First and Second World Wars, and linked his experiences with the Troubles. He reminds us that Belfast has seen casualties before, as in an image of the bodies of children laid out in swimming pools after the German bombing of the city, and that Wilfrid Owen's 'the pity of war' is a constant. 'Wounds' begins with the Ulster Division at the Battle of the Somme, with 'a boy about to die/Screaming "Give them one for the Shankill!"' and ends with 'a shivering boy' who shoots a man in his living room. 'To the children, to a bewildered wife,/I think "Sorry Missus" was what he said.'[8]

The 'sacrifice at the Somme', as it was known, was seen by many Northern Protestants as their side of a covenant with Britain. Frank McGuinness's poetic play *Observe the Sons of Ulster Marching Towards the Somme* is a searing exploration of the heart and soul of an old soldier, Pyper, a survivor of the battle, a leader who led his men to their deaths. 'Dear Lord . . . Did you intend that we should keep seeing ghosts?' he demands. 'It was the first sign that your horrors had shaken us into madness.'[9]

As in McGuinness's black tragicomedy *Carthaginians*, which is set in a graveyard in Derry after Bloody Sunday, the living implore the dead to help them. Pyper joined the army in order to die, to become a hero. He is torn between believing in the patriotic sacrifice made by his comrades and the sense that they acted, like him, out of an inherited hatred, a lust for blood. His final soliloquy ends with a plea to God for salvation, a plea which turns, with terrible inevitability, into a battle cry: 'I love their lives. I love my own life. I love my home. I love my Ulster. Ulster. Ulster. Ulster. Ulster . . .'[10]

The play was culturally important because, on one level, it saw a gay playwright exploring Irish masculinity in war, while on another, an Ulster Catholic addressing the possibility that loyalism is about love of country can be seen as a reconciliatory act in itself. One production of the play in Dublin during the peace process was attended by Northern unionist politicians, along with the Republic's minister for foreign affairs, with smiles all round for the cameras – another symbolic moment.

McGuinness was inspired to write the play in 1985 while

standing at the war memorial in Enniskillen, County Fermanagh. Two years later, after the IRA bombed the Remembrance
Day ceremony there, he returned to the town full of rage and
grief. He wrote an article for the *Irish Times* about this journey.
It is a journalistic account with the intensity of poetry, a painful
reflection on what it is to be Irish. He describes the ancient
stone statues on Boa Island, in Lough Erne, near Enniskillen.
'These faces have never released their secrets,' he writes. He then
describes the beautiful face of his friend, who is driving him, a
man who had not been back to the North since Bloody Sunday:
'His face is set in stone.'

He describes the different Protestant churches in the town,
all of them with funerals going on. He praises Gordon Wilson,
who, without being asked, forgave. 'His was the hand which
raised us to our feet when we should have been on our knees
with shame and grief.'

Those who were being remembered when the bomb was detonated had fought in the First World War 'with such courage
even the enemy never forgot'. In the Second World War they
fought Nazism. 'Eleven are dead at the hands of a movement
who willed Hitler to victory in that same war. Let no one forget.
Let no one excuse.' He sets against this the 'sixty years of discrimination' suffered by Northern Catholics. 'The bomb did
not discriminate,' is his bleak comment.[11]

The article is all the more powerful for appearing on a newspaper page alongside reports of the political reactions: a
demand from the Secretary of State for the passage of the extra-
dition act by the Dáil; a call from the SDLP's Seamus Mallon for
human compassion and forgiveness to be translated into political terms; a statement from Cardinal Tomas O'Fiach about
'how fragile is the cohesion of our two communities'. There was
also a photograph of the three daughters of William and Nessie
Mullan at their parents' funerals.

*

In his book about mourning and the commemoration of the dead after the First World War, Jay Winter writes about Abel Gance's film *J'Accuse!*, made between 1918 and 1919. The film features the dream of a wounded soldier-poet in which the mutilated dead rise from the battlefield and march as bloodied ghosts back to their villages.

They discover that petty life has resumed. Their wives are with other men, their businesses have been taken over. Their sacrifice has meant nothing. The villagers are terrified into mending their ways. Winter comments that by making the dead central figures in this vision of war, Gance 'turned it from a celebration of patriotic certainties to the exploration of eternal themes of love, death and redemption'.[12]

The late Stewart Parker's last play, *Pentecost*, is a magnificent and deeply moving exploration of these themes in the context of the Northern Irish conflict. It is also immensely funny, full of shafts of bleak, black Belfast humour. First performed in 1987, it is set during the Ulster Workers Council Strike of 1974.

Marian and Lenny have separated, their marriage having blossomed during the brief life of their baby, Christopher, and foundered over his death. Lenny's friend, Peter, has returned from England and is suffering from what he calls 'exilephilia', the opposite of homesickness. Marian's friend Ruth has run away from her violent policeman husband. All are lost souls, prone to outbursts of rage and bitterness. All are around the age at which Christ was crucified.

Their salvation comes, bizarrely, through the ghost of Lily, the old lady in whose house they shelter from the thuggish mayhem on the streets outside. Marian has gone to live there. It is to be her refuge. The others drift along after her. It is the last house on a ruined street, caught between enemy areas. A staunch Protestant with deep historic and personal grievances against 'Fenians', Lily at first appears in order to tell Marian, a lapsed Catholic, to get out.

However, as Marian pieces together the story of Lily's life, she breaks through this harshness, and in the end, a tenderness born of shared loss enters into their exchanges. On Pentecost Sunday, there is a row about the meaning of the events on the streets. Ruth is outraged by Prime Minister Harold Wilson's famous denunciation of the strikers and their unionist supporters as sectarian and anti-democratic 'spongers'. Peter calls the strikers 'pigbrain mobsters and thugs' who are engaged in 'root and branch fascism'. Ruth and Peter end up making love on the sofa in Lily's front parlour.

Peter imagines Christ appearing in Belfast, 'in the middle of the marching ranks of the Ulster zealots, watching at the elbow of the holy Catholic nationalist as he puts a gun to a man's knee, a man's brain . . .' Lenny says that what Christ would do is expunge religion 'until the people could discover no mercy except in each other, no belief except to believe in each other, no forgiveness but what the other would forgive, until they cried out in the dark for each other and embraced their own humanity . . .' Marian speaks of how she hated life after her baby's death, and how she denied 'the Christ in him' which is now absorbed into the Christ in her. 'We have got to love that in ourselves,' she declares. 'In ourselves first and then in them. That's the only future there is.'[13] It was a radical message in the darkest of times and it continues to resonate.

Glenn Patterson's novel *That Which Was* contains a poignant dream about the return of the dead. The novel opens with a biblical quote: 'In those days there was no king in Israel: every man did that which was right in his own eyes.'[14] The book is a subtle exploration of the challenges faced by the individual in a society in which communal ideas about morals seem to be shattered or too seriously undermined to be relied upon.

Memory is also unreliable, and people can be haunted by the terror of what they might have done, though they might, historically, be innocent. Reality shades into nightmare, and dreams are full of memories and sorrow.

In the book, Avery, a minister at odds with his congregation, has a dream about a former girlfriend, murdered years before. In it, he was in a bus station waiting for her. 'He knew . . . she was dead, but thanks to negotiations, which he understood without having to articulate, the Troubles dead were being allowed home for the weekend. Temporary release. The station was full of people clutching photographs, bits of old clothing, soft toys, letters, newspaper cuttings.'[15]

An empty bus pulls in with a 'Limited Stop' sign on the windscreen. The people in the waiting room surge forward and there are sounds of tearful reunions. 'The dead were materialising as though from contact with the bus station air. They looked like they had been on a particularly hectic holiday, weary, but full of stories.' He tries, but fails, to find Joanna, and then, suddenly, the bus is reversing out of the station. Avery hears an unknown woman's voice behind him: 'You obviously didn't want badly enough.' But when he turns, no one is there.[16]

The playwright Michael Duke deals with the return of the dead in his uneven but moving 2004 play *Revenge*. A father is set against the marriage of his son, whose first bride, it emerges, was killed in an explosion that left the son with injuries from which he has not recovered. The couple want the new bride to carry a fragment of the dead woman's wedding dress as a gesture of healing.

'Healing,' says the father. 'It's nothing, only betrayal.' The father is encouraged in his bitterness by an old woman, who brings on a chorus of the dead. The old woman urges him towards revenge, and the chorus chants the one ominous word: 'Remember.'

The father is reconciled to the new marriage, but the old woman curses him. 'Don't look to me for comfort . . . Hearts were nailed on the trees of every roadside in Ulster and nobody remembers.'[17]

'Remember' was the word the poet John Hewitt dared not use in his 'Neither an Elegy nor a Manifesto', a sombre meditation on the Troubles dead in which he urges that thoughts of those already dead should act as a restraint on all parties. The poem has an air of stoic resignation to it.

Hewitt says he will not list the dead, as there are too many. However, the title *Bear in Mind These Dead* was used by Malcolm Sutton for his 1994 index of deaths from the conflict. This was a hugely ambitious project for one author to undertake, and it was followed in 1999 by *Lost Lives*. This huge, sorrowful and brilliant book, written over several years by David McKittrick, Seamus Kelters, Brian Feeney and Chris Thornton, provides brief histories of all the dead and has been updated several times.

The journalist Nell McCafferty described the book as 'the print equivalent of Picasso's *Guernica*'. The SDLP politician John Dallat told one of the authors he had seen a man in a bookshop staring grimly at a stack of the books. Dallat told him it was good. The man replied, 'I'm buying five.' He was from a security-force family.

In his introduction to the book, David McKittrick, the respected Ireland editor of the *Independent*, wrote about the 'intrinsic power' of the facts, for all that they were dispassionately presented. 'The words we have written may read like journalism,' he wrote. 'But readers will quickly become aware that between the lines lie much grief and tragedy.' The authors, 'like most other people', hoped the Troubles were drawing to a close. 'We also hope that anyone tempted to think of resorting to violence will find in these pages more than 3,700 reasons to think again.'

When the death toll was standing at less than half that, there had been an attempt to shock people into contemplating how many had died. It was a week after the murder, by the Shankill Butchers, of a young member of the Witness for Peace group. He was a songwriter, and at a ceremony in his memory, his sisters sang one of his songs while 1,662 small white crosses – one for each of the victims up to that date – were planted in the grounds of Belfast's City Hall.

* * *

After the murder of her father, her mother-in-law and her son by the IRA, Countess Mountbatten comforted herself that terrorists were a species apart; Northern Irish writers know well that this is not so. Bernard MacLaverty's *Cal* is a sympathetic portrait of a young man from a small, bitter town. Without political convictions, he gets caught up in the IRA and then falls in love with the widow of the RUC man he helped to murder. Loyalists drive him from his home. There is no escape. The novel ends as Cal's past is about to catch up with him, and such is his sense of shame that he is 'grateful that at last someone is going to beat him to within an inch of his life'.[18]

The late journalist Mary Holland considered that many in the Irish Republic made a grave mistake by failing to recognise that paramilitaries were part of both republican and loyalist communities in the North. They expressed deeply rooted communal fears and aspirations, and they had considerable support. Some of her columns are as passionate and demanding as literature.

She was at the funerals of the IRA volunteers shot dead by the SAS in Gibraltar in 1988 and described how one man's widow, in a green coat, stood oblivious as grenades flung by UDA man Michael Stone exploded around her in the cemetery. Two days later, at the funeral of one of those killed by Stone at the earlier funerals, Holland witnessed the crowd dragging two

British soldiers from their car and beating them before dragging them off to be shot dead by the IRA. One of the soldiers was wearing a jumper of the same shade as the coat worn two days earlier by the widow, she noticed, 'vivid as tropical birds against the grey of the Belfast sky and the dark clothes of the mourners'.[19]

The piece is a cry of horror-stricken conscience. 'How did we let it happen?' she demands. 'He passed within a few feet of myself and dozens of other journalists. He didn't cry out, just looked at us with terrified eyes as though we were all enemies in a foreign country who wouldn't have understood what language he was speaking if he called out for help.'[20]

She says that whenever in future she sees that shade of green, she will have to ask herself why she did not make some gesture to show the young man he was not 'utterly alone in a hostile country'. Such a gesture might, she feels, have turned the crowd from a lynch mob back into individual human beings again. But no one made it.

However, Holland refused to join the clamour of those calling the people at the funeral 'bestial' and 'barbaric'. This was, she wrote, a community in a 'state of nervous crisis'. The blame for what happened lay with the crowd, but also with 'the rest of us who have left this community increasingly abandoned in recent years'. It was an unpopular message, but Holland was presaging the philosophy behind the peace process. In another column she writes that 'we all recognise some act of grace which moves the situation forward'.[21]

Her own willingness to write against the tide had within it such grace. When she died in 2004, the poet Seamus Heaney and the former SDLP leader John Hume paid tribute to her role in shaping the North's recent history. At her funeral, I remembered seeing her walking once along the street from her office during a bad time in the North. She looked exhausted, ravaged.

It reminded me of W. H. Auden's line about Yeats: 'Mad Ireland hurt you into poetry.'

* * *

War poetry has often emphasised the gulf that divides the domestic from the battlefield, but in the Northern Irish conflict the violence invaded normal life. Some died in gun battles but most did not. People were shot as they sat at home eating breakfast, as they drove their children to or from school, as they fed cattle in the fields, as they had a drink in the pub. They were blown up in hotel ballrooms and shops.

In Ciaran Carson's poems, fear is never far below the surface of everyday life. 'Last Orders' has the poet entering a Belfast pub, one of those that used to have steel cages around them to stop bombers. 'Squeeze the buzzer on the steel mesh gate like a trigger, but/It's someone else who has you in their sights . . .' Allowed in, he looks around, wondering if it is true that 'Taig's written on my face'. In his fear, acting casual, he suddenly realises that while he is afraid of the company of these strangers, one of whom is 'looking daggers at us/From the Bushmills mirror', they too are afraid – of him – and wonder if he has come to kill them.[22]

Padraic Fiacc addresses the impossibility of the friendly gesture in 'Enemy Encounter'. The poet is dumping leaves when he comes upon a British soldier 'perched hiding . . . like a lonely little winter robin'. The poet says 'something bland to make him grin', but the soldier does not smile. 'I am an Irishman, and he is afraid/That I have come to kill him.'[23]

Yet home has had a powerful allure. Even in the worst days of the Troubles, people who left, sometimes in real fear for their lives, returned because they could not bear to be elsewhere. John Hewitt wrote 'An Irishman in Coventry' when he was living, with a strong sense of having been exiled, in England. A fragment of Irish music heard as he passes a pub brings back to him the memory of 'the sick, guilt-clotted legend/of my creed-haunted, godforsaken race'. In language reminiscent of Louis MacNeice in 'Autumn Journal' a generation before, he recalls a people whose minds are fed on 'glittering fables/which gave us martyrs when we needed men . . .' But the poem ends with the longing for home: 'Yet like Lir's children, banished to the waters,/our hearts still listen for the landward bells.'[24]

Derek Mahon's poem 'Rage for Order' lends its title to poet Frank Ormsby's fine anthology of 'Poetry of the Northern Ireland Troubles'. In his introduction to the book, Ormsby quotes from the poem: 'Somewhere beyond/The scorched gable end/And the burnt-out/Buses there is a poet indulging his/Wretched rage for order/Or not as the case/May be, for his/Is a dying art/An eddy of semantic scruple/In an unstructurable sea.' Ormsby says the book celebrates what the speaker in the poem 'at first dismisses . . . but later concedes – the values of art in times of violence'.

He describes the 'journalistic pressure to produce a kind of war poetry' and says that most poets resisted. Paul Muldoon deals humorously with the question in 'Lunch with Pancho Villa'. The Mexican revolutionary has harsh words for the poet. 'Look, son. Just look around you./People are getting themselves killed/Left, right and centre/While you do what? Write rondeaux?/There's more to living in this country/Than stars and horses, pigs and trees,/Not that you'd guess it from your poems./Do you ever listen to the news?'[25]

The Troubles tend to feature obliquely in Muldoon's work. In one poem, a hunger striker who has been taken off his fast is on a kidney machine in the hospital, while the narrator gets tests done for sexually transmitted diseases. In another, bombs go off elsewhere in the city, while he is chatted up in Lavery's Bar.

However, Muldoon does occasionally confront questions concerning the writer and war directly, as in '7 Middagh Street'. He has short shrift for Yeats's famous question about the Easter Rising. 'As for his crass, rhetorical/posturing, "Did that play of mine/send out certain men (*certain* men?)/the English shot . . .?"/the answer is "Certainly not."'[26]

In an interview for the book *Ardoyne, The Untold Truth*, Sean Kelly, the IRA man who survived after planting the Shankill bomb in 1993, describes Thomas 'Bootsy' Begley, the bomber who died in the atrocity. 'His favourite poem was by Seamus Heaney,' Kelly says. 'It's a poem about taking the hard road to freedom; he had that poem on his bedroom wall.'[27] Kelly would not speak to me, and Begley's parents said they had no memory of the poem being on the wall. Heaney suggested it may have been his 1966 poem 'Requiem for the Croppies', which is about the persecution and slaughter of Irish rebels by the British during the 1798 rebellion: 'Terraced thousands died, shaking scythes at cannon/ . . . They buried us without shroud or coffin/And in August the barley grew up out of the grave.'[28]

'I stopped reading that poem in the 1970s when it would have been taken as coded support for "the armed struggle",' Heaney told me. However, he added that it had been set to music and recorded on several patriotic albums. 'So did it help send out . . .?'

Immediately after the 1993 bombing, journalist Brenda Power had interviewed Begley's parents, and they allowed her to look into their son's room. She didn't mention a poem, but she did notice a book. It was *The Shankill Butchers* by Martin Dillon.

* * *

Seamus Heaney was living in the North when the Troubles erupted. He has written about how this transformed his task as a poet, making him embark on a 'search for images and symbols adequate to our predicament . . .' He felt it was imperative 'to discover a field of force in which . . . it would be possible to encompass the perspectives of a humane reason and at the same time to grant the religious intensity of the violence its deplorable authenticity and complexity'. He had a political understanding of what had erupted in 1969. It was, he wrote, 'the tail end of a struggle in a province between territorial piety and imperial power'.[29]

He left the North to live in Wicklow in the 1970s, describing himself in 'Exposure' as 'neither internee nor informer;/an inner émigré, grown long-haired/And thoughtful; a wood kerne/Escaped from the massacre . . .'[30] (The 'wood kerne' were dispossessed Irish Catholics who hid in the woods and had fought against the Protestant planters since the sixteenth century.)

In 1979, during the IRA's no-wash protest in the Maze prison, Danny Morrison, Sinn Féin's director of publicity, was travelling on the Dublin to Belfast train when he spotted Heaney and approached him. 'I said to him, "Are you going to do anything?"' Morrison told me. 'This is an incredible situation.' Heaney told him he was writing a poem about Count Ugolino. In Dante's *Divine Comedy*, Ugolino is one of the souls to speak. He was starved to death in prison in the thirteenth century for his political activities. Morrison's intervention was counterproductive. 'I had contemplated dedicating "Ugolino" to the prisoners on the dirty protest,' Heaney told me. 'But after the encounter – when support was being more or less levied – my attitude changed.'

He writes about such a meeting in 'The Flight Path'. The republican figure 'goes for me head on', demanding: 'When, for fuck's sake, are you going to write/something for us?' To which the poet replies,' . . . If I do write something,/Whatever it is, I'll be writing for myself.'[31]

'Station Island', the long title poem of Heaney's 1984 collection, narrates a pilgrimage to St Patrick's Purgatory on Lough Derg, on the Donegal–Fermanagh border. The poet fasts and meditates there, and is assailed by the souls of the dead. He meets the nineteenth-century writer William Carleton and tells him, 'I have no mettle for the angry role,' and that he was not tuned to 'that harp of unforgiving iron/The Fenians strung.'[32]

Heaney meets a man who, we can surmise, is William Strathearn, the 'Good Samaritan' grocer murdered by loyalists, including policemen Billy McCaughey and John Weir, who came at night pretending they needed pills for a sick child. Strathearn, whom Heaney had known as a young man, relates what happened, the way he recognised the men and the way his wife was afraid. Then he jokes with the poet about their youth, and Heaney sees him as he was then, 'the perfect, clean, unthinkable victim'. The poet surprises himself by saying: 'Forgive the way I have lived indifferent –/forgive my timid circumspect involvement.' But Strathearn replies: 'Forgive/my eye . . . all that's above my head.' Then 'a stun of pain' goes through him and he fades from the poet's sight.

A second cousin, the victim of a sectarian assassination, is less forgiving. The boy accuses the poet of choosing to stay in the company of poets while he, 'your own flesh and blood', was 'carted' home, dead. The poet pleads with him, 'I was dumb, encountering what was destined,' but the boy will not relent. 'You confused evasion and artistic tact.' He accuses his Protestant killer directly, 'but indirectly, you/who now atone perhaps upon this bed/for the way you whitewashed ugliness and drew/the lovely blinds of the Purgatorio/and saccharined my death with morning dew.'

The poet is then spoken to by a dead hunger striker, presumably Francis Hughes, 'laid out with a drift of Mass cards/At his shrouded feet.' To him the poet says, 'Unquiet soul, they should have buried you/In the bog where you threw your first grenade,/Where only helicopters and curlews/Make their maimed music . . .' The poet rebels, weary of his knowledge of 'broken covenants', full of sudden hatred for all that he was born into.

Danny Morrison was not satisfied. In a book published in 2006 to mark the twenty-fifth anniversary of the hunger strike, he castigates the journalists who succumbed to a 'climate of intimidation' in which the IRA was seen as evil, the British as good and unionists as misunderstood. As for the writers and poets, Morrison says their response to the plight of the prisoners was a 'deafening silence'.[33]

Describing the writings of Bobby Sands, who led the hunger strike and was the first to die on it, he says Sands demanded to know where were those who were meant to 'express in culture some defence of the oppressed'. Many of them were 'more than eloquent' in condemning the IRA but 'lost their voices'[34] when it came to condemning the British.

He quotes a Sands poem: 'The men of Art have lost their heart,/They dream within their dreams./Their magic sold for price of gold/Amidst a people's screams./They sketch the moon and capture bloom/With genius, so they say./But ne'er they sketch the quaking wretch/Who lies in Castlereagh.' (Castlereagh was the RUC's notorious interrogation centre.) Apart from an 'honourable minority', Morrison asserts, 'they simply sat on or sniped from the fence while throwing their hands up in theatrical despair at the "intransigence" of all sides'. His honourable minority includes the Wolfe Tones, a band noted for fervent ballads unambiguously celebrating the deeds of the IRA.

Morrison is particularly contemptuous of Heaney for the way he 'self-consciously struggles with a sense of guilt' in 'Station Island'. He snipes that after Heaney asks the murdered

Strathearn for forgiveness, 'he is told there is nothing to forgive – which must be very reassuring'.[35]

Heaney had written about the complexities of his own silence and his unhappiness, at times, with it. He returns to what he describes as one of his constant themes, 'that idea of poetry as an answer', quoting the Greek poet George Seferis, who said that poetry was 'strong enough to help'. He describes the pressure on poets from Northern Ireland 'to be true to the negative nature of the evidence and at the same time to show an affirming flame, the need to be both socially responsible and creatively free'.[36]

Morrison's anthology contains only work which is broadly sympathetic to the hunger strikers, including the lovely Christy Moore song which begins, 'The time has come to part, my love . . .' and ends, 'The flame he lit while leaving is still burning strong,/By the light it's plain to see the struggle still goes on.' In a passionate commentary on the song, Moore writes that he will sing it for as long as he lives. 'I will give it an airing each time I encounter those who seek to demean and trivialise the fallen men and their families.'[37] Poet Medbh McGuckian writes of how the 'shock and shame' of the hunger strike 'pierced the verbal atmosphere'.[38]

The writer Padraig O'Malley notes in his study of the hunger strike, *Biting at the Grave*, that Sands' sense of Irish history was heavily influenced by the American author Leon Uris's *Trinity*, a sentimental work of romantic fiction about Ireland's fight for independence. Sands would recite long passages of the book to fellow prisoners. 'It is a paean to blood sacrifice . . .' writes O'Malley. 'Bad history but powerful propaganda.'

He quotes one of the characters: 'No crime a man commits on behalf of his freedom can be as great as the crime committed by those who deny him freedom . . . the British have nothing in their entire arsenal of imperial might to counter a single man who refuses to be broken. Irish words, Irish self-sacrifice and ultimately Irish martyrdom are our weapons . . .' As O'Malley comments, 'Fact and fiction reinforced each other . . . fantasy fed the heart.' This is a reference to the lines from Yeats: 'We had fed the heart on fantasy, heart's grown brutal on the fare.'[39]

According to Edna Longley, who edited his *Selected Poems*, Paul Durcan is the pre-eminent poet from the South of Ireland to respond 'painfully and continuously' to the Ulster Troubles. Longley, a penetrating critic, is also deeply politically engaged, with an intense dislike of contemporary Irish republicanism and its culture. She criticises Declan Kiberd, who edited the contemporary poetry section of the *Field Day Anthology of Irish Writing*, for rejecting Durcan's political poems and for his statement that the poets have had 'remarkably little to say' about politics. 'This may simply mean', Longley remarks, acidly, 'that they don't say what Kiberd wants to hear.'[40]

Durcan has a passionate hatred for the IRA and brings to his poetry a sense of the history of the Republic, reminding us of the origins of some members of the late-twentieth-century elite in the violent excesses of the Irish civil war in the 1920s. His elegy to those killed in the Miami Showband massacre is lovely and poignant. Politically, though, his work is sometimes confused. He has written several elegies to the victims of what were, in fact, loyalist atrocities, but even in those poems, it is the IRA that he savages.

'In Memory of Those Murdered in the Dublin Massacre, May 1974' ends with the brutally surreal fantasy of an old cleaning lady who would 'make a fine explosion now, if you were to blow her up; . . . For a free Ireland.' The Dublin massacre was the work of the loyalist UVF.[41]

Durcan is sometimes inclined to rant. He wrote the long

poem 'Omagh' in the immediate aftermath of the 1998 bomb, employing a series of litanies to try to convey the scale of the horror, listing separately the names of the places the victims came from, their ages and their names. It accuses Sinn Féin leader Gerry Adams of hypocrisy for condemning the bomb and ends: 'I cannot forgive you.'

The poem is too loose, too emotional and too long, and it has the air of having been spilt out unworked. This is writing as therapy. Interviewed by writer Theo Dorgan, Durcan said that after an event like the Omagh bomb, 'my only way to cope with it is to write my way through it or out of it'.

There are, in fact, a great many writing projects and story-telling groups set up specifically to help people through the trauma of having been bereaved or otherwise hurt by the Troubles. The writings which people treasure are not always those which are of the most literary value. Talking to members of the family of Sean Brown, murdered by loyalists in 1997, I mentioned Seamus Heaney's tribute. The family had been pleased by this, but they were equally proud of the poem a twelve-year-old Protestant girl had written. It ended, 'Sean was a very good neighbour and a/very good friend too./All the love in my heart goes out to his family.' This poem was read at Sean's funeral.

Merle and Billy Eakin liked the ballad James Simmons wrote about the Claudy bomb, with its lines about their daughter, eight-year-old Kathryn. However, it was lines written by a neighbour that they chose to have engraved on her memorial: 'This golden child/her passing/epitomising sorrow/beyond belief/beyond endurance . . .'

The Eakins were young when their child was killed. When I met them in 2007, they were old, finding it hard to climb the steps to their daughter's grave, but with their grief still raw. Billy began to quote from 'Ode to the Fallen' by Laurence Binyon,

'They shall not grow old, as we that are left grow old . . .' He began to cry and his voice faltered. Merle took up the poem: 'Age shall not weary them, nor the years condemn . . .' They finished it together, tears on both their faces. 'At the going down of the sun and in the morning,/We will remember them.'[42] Merle Eakin died in 2008.

One poem, Alan Gillis's 'Progress', written at the end of the Troubles, imagines them not happening:

> 'They say that for years Belfast was backwards
> and it's great now to see some progress.
> So I guess we can look forward to taking boxes
> from the earth. I guess that ambulances
> will leave the dying back amidst the rubble
> to be explosively healed. Given time,
> one hundred thousand particles of glass
> will create impossible patterns in the air
> before coalescing into the clarity
> of a window. Through which, a reassembled head
> will look out and admire the shy young man
> taking his bomb from the building and driving home.'[43]

'The Disentanglement of Life and Death'

On 8 May 2007, the Reverend Ian Paisley made his inaugural speech as first minister of Northern Ireland. He spoke of those who had died in the conflict: 'Today we salute Ulster's honoured and unageing dead – the innocent victims, that gallant band, members of both religions, Protestant and Roman Catholic . . . all innocent victims of the terrible conflict,' he said. 'In the shadows of the evenings and the sunrise of the mornings we hail their gallantry and heroism. It cannot and will not be erased from our memories.'

He went on to quote from King Solomon: 'To every thing there is a season, and a time to every purpose under heaven. A time to be born and a time to die . . . A time to kill and a time to heal . . . A time to love and a time to hate. A time of war and a time of peace.' Northern Ireland had come to its time for peace, he said. 'Today we have begun to plant and we await the harvest.'[1]

These were remarkable words from the man who may well have been in the mind of the editorial writer who warned readers of the *Belfast Telegraph* in 1966 against listening to those who had been 'sowing dragon's teeth' since it could now be seen 'how terrible the harvest can be'. This was after loyalists had begun their murderous campaign. In the years that followed, Paisley and his followers had often balefully predicted that bitter harvests would be reaped. The DUP's Reverend Willie McCrea had done so after Sinn Féin's Martin McGuinness defeated him in the elections to Westminster in 1997. Loyalists murdered Sean Brown ten days afterwards. Ten years later, Paisley was standing beside McGuinness as he spoke, with the former IRA man taking his place as deputy first minister. While many were moved by what seemed to be an amazing change of heart, others had deep reservations.

'There are no winners in war,' said Anne Larkey, whose nephew was made to witness the rape of his mother before he was shot dead in 1972. 'I am glad it is over but it kind of annoys me to see Mr McGuinness and Mr Paisley all smiles and the best of friends on the television. Why did it take them thirty-five years? Now they say it is over – forget it. Do they tell you how to do that? You are not a computer that you can just wipe the screen. I can't undo what happened to my nephew and to my sister. I can't just say, "I never buried young David."' Anne believed she had been irrevocably damaged. She was just glad that all of her children had survived the killing years.

Eugene Reavey was still waiting for Paisley to apologise for putting it on the record of the Houses of Parliament that he was a mass murderer. Others wonder if Paisley is still using the term 'innocent victims' to distinguish them from others still designated by the DUP leader as terrorists and therefore not victims at all.

Many former members of the security forces felt betrayed and abandoned. Less than a year before the inauguration at Stormont, Paisley had commemorated the ninetieth anniversary of the Battle of the Somme with the claim that 'No unionist who is a unionist will go into partnership with the IRA–Sinn Féin . . . it will be over our dead bodies that they will ever get there . . .'[2]

Former RUC man Bill Harpur had believed him and was bitter and furious. He had spoken about his brother's murder by the INLA to the Historical Enquiries Team, but he had no hope of justice. 'I'll be as old as Methuselah by the time they get to my family,' he said. Hazlett Lynch, who ran the victims' group to which Bill belongs, described the new Northern Ireland assembly as a 'political mess' which had devastated the 'victims of terrorism'. They were McGuinness's victims, he said, but now if they wanted government assistance, they would have to turn to McGuinness himself. It was their 'worst nightmare'.[3]

Lynch said, however, that these victims would remain defiant. They would refuse to 'go with the flow', as some victims, who had surrendered, had done. Instead, they would 'stand up for what they believed in and many died for'.[4]

Alan McBride is the editor of the newsletter in which Hazlett Lynch wrote about his dismay. He said he respected his views, though he did not share them. 'I am hugely optimistic,' he said. 'Totally optimistic. Paisley and McGuinness are a good double act.' He had recently become the manager of the WAVE victims' centre in Belfast, and said he was inspired by the people he had met there. 'They are incredible. It is a privilege to work with them.'

WAVE occupied a handsome Victorian mansion in North Belfast, and we were talking in its huge drawing room, looking out over trees and a conservatory. It wasn't a mile from the narrow streets of Ardoyne and Tiger's Bay, and it was even closer to a house which had recently been sold at auction. The *Irish News* had used the story as its front-page lead, under the headline, 'Fourteen people were murdered in this street but now one house is worth £800,000.'

There are sixty or so victims' groups, many of them with substantial state funding. I asked him if there was a risk that people could get stuck in the role of being victims. 'Yes,' Alan said. 'We always have to have an eye to people having exit strategies. When the time is right, we need to be prepared to leave the stage. But we are needed for the foreseeable future. We are working with second-generation people now. There's dealing with the past and there is peace-building for a shared future.'

Stewart Parker had imagined a future in which people reached across sectarian divisions to embrace their own humanity. Such relationships did exist before and during the conflict, and there were many who nurtured them quietly in communities and families. There were wonderful gestures. The Chapman brothers, Reginald and Walter, were standing on either side of Richard Hughes at Kingsmills in 1976 when the gunman demanded that 'the Catholic' identify himself. Fearing that their workmate was going to be shot, they each held their hand out to him to hold him back. As it turned out, the killers were from the IRA, and it was the Chapmans and eight other Protestants who were murdered that night.

Sometimes during the conflict a gesture was enough to save a life. The father of a British soldier who was blown up by the IRA told me about an incident in which the IRA had made a man drive a car with a bomb in it. One of the IRA gang tipped the driver off that the courtesy light would trigger the bomb. He told him not to open the door and to get out of the window instead. 'That's the only IRA man I have any love for,' the soldier's father told me. 'He had some sense of humanity.'

Sometimes it wasn't. The bomb a UVF man was planting outside Peggy Whyte's house in 1983 exploded prematurely and he collapsed, seriously injured, on the path to her door. Peggy came out and comforted him until the ambulance came. The following year, the UVF bombed the house again and this time Peggy was killed.

That sense of humanity was deeply appreciated when it made

an appearance in the middle of a situation of mutual hatred. Nora MacBride's IRA son, Tony, had been on a mission to kill RUC men when the SAS shot him dead in 1984. The RUC behaved with hostility and aggression at the funeral, but one officer saluted. Nora was grateful for this sign of respect for the dead, and remembered it with pride because it had honoured her son.

The mother of a Catholic girl who was murdered by the loyalist friend of the girl's Protestant boyfriend told me that sometimes, when she goes to her daughter's grave, there is a small bunch of fresh flowers there. She said she knows they have been left there by the mother of her late daughter's boyfriend. The gesture means a lot to her.

Alice Harper recalled with warmth the young soldier who put his arms around her mother and wept with her as he told her that the body of her son had been found. The child had been killed by the IRA, but the soldier also acknowledged that Bella Teggart had already suffered the loss of her husband at the hands of the British.

Alan Black, the sole survivor of the Kingsmills massacre, set great store by respectful gestures. He told me that a few years ago, he had found out that a friend of his was working with Ann Carlin, the nurse who had known 'the magic words' that made the difference between him living and dying after the attack: he had decided to let go and die; she would not let him, reminding him that his little daughter, Karen, needed him to live.

Alan had arranged to meet Ann, along with some other friends. 'We had a drink and we had a good laugh,' he said. After they left the pub, he bought a bouquet of flowers and sent someone into the pub to give them to her.

In 2006, Alan teetered on the edge of depression after the death of Richard Hughes. 'But people are good,' said Alan. 'I was in a bar in Newry, and people were coming up to me wanting to talk about Richard, and I didn't want to, and a man came over to me and said quietly, "Alan, you are getting skundered here. ['Skundered' means aggravated, annoyed, sickened.] Come over to us in the corner.'"

Hughes, aged eighty-six, was buried in his Manchester United blazer. At his funeral, Alan took a seat in the body of the church. When Bernadette Hughes, the dead man's wife, saw him, she asked him to come up and sit with her at the front. A television reporter who had filmed the funeral and interviewed Alan later sent him a video of it.

Alan had also quietly shown solidarity to Eugene Reavey and his family after Eugene was falsely accused by Ian Paisley of involvement in the Kingsmills massacre, simply by being seen with them. He was still exceptionally close to his own daughter, Karen. She and her partner lived within sight of his house in Bessbrook, County Armagh. I was meant to come to the house to interview him on a Friday night in summer, but he rang to say that there was to be a big Orange parade through the village, and I'd be better coming the following morning.

When I arrived, it turned out he'd been at a family party at Karen's house until all hours. His son's wife, Jackie, rang. There was much banter about the party and about the bands that had passed by the house. 'Did it make you proud to be a Prod?' Alan joked. Afterwards, he explained that Jackie is a Catholic. She and Karen were close friends.

'I just love them to bits,' he said, warmly, adding that his sons were great, too. He'd been in a pub in Newry with one of them not long before, and a man had swaggered up to them and said, by way of introduction, 'I'm a republican.' 'Really?' said Alan's son. 'Active or armchair?' Alan said the whole bar burst out laughing.

Alan said he was an ordinary man, and he regretted having become 'part of the history of the Troubles'. He knew that at his funeral, Kingsmills will be mentioned, but he accepted that this was how it was. He was grateful to be alive, and grateful to the families of those who had died for letting him know, when he felt guilty, that they were glad he had survived. Bessbrook had survived, too, as a mixed community. Its huge army base, where former British soldier John Moore had been based, was about to be turned into a housing estate.

Alan was a long-distance lorry driver. 'I love to get into my lorry with the rain beating down on the windscreen and my dog, Shankly, on the seat beside me and my music on the CD, turned up good and loud,' he told me. 'I love stopping at all-night garages.' Shankly was a Jack Russell terrier, named after the legendary Liverpool manager. He sat watchfully by his master's side as we spoke. Alan had a framed photograph of the dog sitting up in the lorry, with mountain scenery in the background, the two of them on the road. Alan sighed. 'I lost a lot of good friends in the Troubles, a lot of them Catholics,' he said. 'But you couldn't let it destroy you.'

*　*　*

Alan Black's life was saved by the thought of his child. Many who were bereaved in the Troubles have spoken about how it was their children, or their grandchildren, who saved them from despair and even from suicide. When John Moore was left severely paralysed after an IRA ambush in 1981, he was told he would probably never be able to have children. 'It didn't bother me until I met Steph and we got married,' he told me.

Steph had been his girlfriend when she was fourteen and he was seventeen, before he joined the army. When they met again, he had been in a wheelchair for three years. 'She says I ran away and was wheeled back,' he said. 'I couldn't be without her. She is unbelievable. She took me on knowing all the problems. How many women would take on a man like me?'

When they got together, one of the things Steph had to accept was that she was unlikely ever to be a mother. However, the couple refused to give up hope. 'The doctors devised a way of using electric shock to get me to ejaculate under general anaesthetic, and then I had to inject Steph,' John said. 'It worked first time! In April 1995, two embryos were turned into Toby and Jack. They were born a minute apart. The doctors were delighted. Having the boys has moved me on a lot.'

John Maxwell's marriage had broken up not long after the IRA murdered his son, Paul, in 1979. He married again and for years, he said, his new wife, Marian, was the only person he could talk to about Paul. The couple had two more children. They went to the integrated primary school which John had helped to found after the Enniskillen bomb. 'A thing I found hard was that when my new son Robbie was around the age Paul was when he died, he looked a bit like him, and he'd act a bit like him sometimes, too. It was almost as if Paul was there again. But I was able to talk to Robbie about it and he was fine about it,' he said.

Timothy Knatchbull, whose twin, Nicholas, then aged fourteen, had also been killed in the bombing, had come to visit John a few years ago. When John had been told on the day of the blast that his son was wounded but still alive, he had rushed to the injured child's side, only to find that it was Timothy who had survived and not Paul.

'It was very emotional to meet Tim,' remembered John. 'We talked about that day. He is married and has kids of his own now. I find it helps to concentrate on the other kids, and I have grandchildren now, too. I have kept some of Paul's things: his rugby ball, his cricket bat. I kept some of the newspaper cuttings as well.' He gestured to a table covered in family photos, and Paul was there, too.

*

When an RUC man shot dead Norah McCabe in 1981, her husband, Jim, was left with three children under the age of seven. Looking back, he felt keenly how much they must have missed their mother, and he was a harsh judge of his own parenting skills.

He didn't realise that as they grew up, people were saying hurtful things to his children. They heard rumours he had got a lot of compensation and that he had gone off with other women. 'I didn't talk to them,' he said. 'I was arrogant – I assumed I knew best.'

He is proud of his children, though, and cautiously allows that he may take some credit. 'I tried not to instil hatred in them,' he said. 'I couldn't have blamed them if they'd grown bitter and joined the IRA, but they didn't.' His son, Paul, had recently returned to live in Belfast after many years abroad. 'I felt so guilty about the past,' Jim said. 'But we have talked now.'

Jim felt that too many young Catholics who were doing well in post-conflict Northern Ireland had no idea of what things were like for Catholics before the conflict erupted and during the worst years of the Troubles. 'They just take it for granted that they can get whatever jobs they want and make money and live in nice houses,' he said. 'They don't know what a terrible place this was. They don't know what people died for.'

His children were trying to open their father up emotionally. 'My daughter called her daughter after her mother,' he said. 'Norah. She's four now. There's a mural about the people murdered by plastic bullets on the Falls there, and when she passes it she waves up and says, "Hi, Granny Norah, keep smiling!"' He smiled.

In her big, bright house looking out beyond Newry to the Mourne mountains, Bernie Collins shudders when she has to talk about the past. 'Looking back, it was an awful dark era we grew up in,' she said. 'In 1969, I was nine. Our whole lives have been caught up in violence and harassment and discrimination and deaths. I am just so glad the children now don't have to live with that. Since Eamon's death, I don't take any interest in politics.'

Now in a senior position in the health service, she has been able to provide well for her children. 'I feel I have done a lot with my life in the last seven years,' she said. 'I've achieved a lot. I've a good post. The family is reared. They have done well. That is more of a fitting tribute to Eamon than engaging in slanging with his killers.

'As the years go on, you don't want to go back there. It is not as if I don't think of Eamon every day, but you have to get on with life. It is so precious and so short. You should live it. You shouldn't live in death.'

Jude Whyte, whose mother had been murdered by loyalists, said that he believed that if the dead wanted anything for the living, he was sure that it was 'for them to be happy'.

* * *

Kathleen Gillespie told me that she sometimes reflected on how her experience of life had changed in the aftermath of her husband's murder by the IRA. After several anguished years of denial, she had finally had to come to terms with the bleak fact that Patsy was dead. She had children. She had grandchildren. She had to go on.

She had got involved in support groups and victims' groups, and she had done many things that she could never have imagined in her former life as a part-time check-out worker in a supermarket near her home in Derry.

'We never went on holidays, because Patsy wouldn't fly,' she said. 'Soon after his death, I went on a pilgrimage to Italy, because although Patsy wasn't religious, he did believe in Padre

Pio. I've been to America. I brought my daughter to Greece. I've done courses and spoken at meetings all over the place. I've been interviewed on television. Sometimes I travel to conferences and things, and sometimes I travel with former combatants. Sometimes I wake up at night and think, "How could you do that?" But I know Patsy wouldn't want me to be lonely or sad. I've had two long-term relationships. I just have to get on with the life I have.'

The man who runs the Northern Ireland Centre for Trauma and Transformation, David Bolton, believed strongly that 'there are people who soar above the experience of victimhood' and that 'post-traumatic growth', such as Kathleen described, was to be celebrated. He had spoken about this at the opening of the centre in 2002. No one would choose to go through tragedy and loss, he said. However, if the person afflicted had the ability to hope and to struggle, transformation was possible. 'Beyond life's experiences of great distress, loss and injustice, beauty and wonder can be found,' he said.

Bolton had been a middle manager in the local social-services team in Enniskillen in 1987. When the IRA's Remembrance Day bomb exploded, he saw the grief and the devastation and realised that the social services, despite nearly twenty years of the Troubles, had failed to develop ways of helping individuals and communities to cope.

'We might as well have been in Surrey,' he told me. It was partly to do with the way people avoided conflict by not talking about what was going on in Northern Ireland. 'There was this gripping silence which prevented us from addressing the needs of our clients,' he said. 'It immobilised us.'

He became involved in working on strategies for such situations and was able to apply some of these in the aftermath of the Omagh bomb in 1998, when he headed the trauma team within the local health trust. The Centre for Trauma and

Transformation offered therapy to people suffering from post-traumatic stress disorder (PTSD).

According to Bolton, many victims of the Troubles had learnt, perforce, to live with terrible things in ways that were perhaps unhealthy or destructive. Sometimes a parent whose child was murdered might become obsessed with the lost child and neglect the needs of the remaining children. 'People sometimes end up living in the shadow of a lost person,' he said.

The therapy encouraged people to reappraise their lives and strike out in new directions. 'It is a message of resurrection, the experience of new life after a psychic death,' said Bolton. However, he did not underestimate the immensity of what people were suffering. 'As workers here we are often moved and also outraged. People here have had to carry such awful things in their head. Sometimes you meet someone and there is just a sadness on them.' He quoted Erich Maria Remarque's novel *All Quiet on the Western Front*: 'All these things that now, while we are still in the war, sink down in us like a stone, after the war shall awaken again, and then shall begin the disentanglement of life and death.'

Bolton and I spoke about the intimacy of many Troubles murders, neighbours murdering neighbours in what would otherwise be known as 'close-knit' communities. 'The sense of betrayal in such situations is profoundly hurtful,' Bolton said. People often focused on the symbolism of the breaking of bread. The priest at the funeral of the young Michael McIlveen in Ballymena had spoken about how the Catholic teenager had shared his last meal, a takeaway pizza, with a Protestant friend.

When a death occurs in Northern Ireland the warmth and solidarity of neighbours towards the bereaved family is normally striking. Everything is done to bring comfort. However, during the Troubles, when a person was murdered, and murdered because they were identified as a combatant, the solidarity was shattered.

Nora MacBride experienced hostility after it came out, through his death, that her son had been in the IRA. Her grandchildren had not lived through such harsh times, and Nora did not want them hurt by past enmities. While we were talking at her house, with a black-and-white photo of Tony looking down from the wall, one of Nora's granddaughters came in with her friend, two glossy-haired teenagers. They went into the kitchen and were laughing and chatting. Nora became uncomfortable. She began to whisper, and then she got up and closed the door. 'That wee girl is a Protestant,' Nora explained to me. 'She's a lovely wee girl. I don't know how much she knows about our family.'

Darren Graham was a three-week-old baby when the IRA ambushed and murdered his father, Cecil, a UDR man, while he was visiting his wife and baby son at the home of his parents-in-law. Catholic neighbours neither helped the dying man nor offered condolences to the bereaved family.

Darren's mother refused to let her son's life be poisoned by bitterness. She brought him up as a Protestant, but he was frequently brought to family events in the Catholic church. 'I never paid much heed,' he told me. Now that he was an adult, he said most of his friends were Catholics, but the mother of his two-year-old daughter, Brooke, was Protestant. 'Touch wood, there's a heaven and I'll be going to it,' he said.

From childhood, he had lived with his mother in a mixed housing estate in Lisnaskea. She let him go to both the Protestant and the Catholic youth clubs, and it became obvious from an early age that he was talented at sports. The Protestant headmaster of the state school he attended allowed him out early to play Gaelic football at the Catholic school.

By the time he was ten, he was a star on the GAA pitch, and the family has a thick book full of photos of the smiling boy in winning teams. 'As well as the Gaelic and the hurling, I was into soccer, rugby, golf and anything else you could mention,' he said. 'I won any cups and medals I could win. Sport is my religion.' He said the Protestant side of his family was as proud of his achievements at hurling and football as the Catholic side.

He played for the Lisnaskea Emmets team. However, in 2007, Darren dramatically quit. In the middle of a game, he suddenly flung his shirt at the referee and walked off the pitch. The story he had to tell was a shocking one. For years, he had been subjected to persistent sectarian abuse. He was called a 'black cunt' and an Orange one ('black Protestant' is an abusive label unrelated to skin colour). He was told that Protestants had no right to be on 'our' pitches. Worst of all, there were shouts of 'Remember what happened to your da.'

It was done, Darren said, to put him off his game, and it sometimes succeeded. But what hurt even more was the fact that referees and GAA officials somehow never managed to hear the insults. He'd get angry and upset, and he'd get booked.

He didn't walk away; he demanded an apology from the GAA and a commitment to dealing with this unacknowledged problem. His integrity was obvious. He did this as much for others as for himself. And he succeeded. The GAA did the right thing and apologised unreservedly. It also committed itself to dealing with the problem, promising that sectarian abuse would no longer be tolerated.

Darren returned to his team, which is named, as it happens, after Robert Emmet, who was hung, drawn and quartered by the British in 1803 for his part in leading the 1798 Irish rebellion. In his speech from the dock, Emmet had said he was going to join the other 'martyred heroes' and demanded that his epitaph should not be written until Ireland was liberated.

Darren laughed when I asked him if he knew about Emmet. 'All I know about him is he was a Protestant,' he said. 'And I only know that because I read it in the *Fermanagh Herald* last week in an article about this row with me.' He did not dwell on his own family history either. 'My father was killed when the Troubles were at their height,' he said. 'I came of age when they were dying away.'

'Sport is what will bring us together now. If I was out being sectarian, I'd be no better than the fellow that pulled the trigger on my father. The people that shouted the abuse at me are bigots. They are trying to keep all that going, passing the hatred to another generation, leading on and leading on and then someone gets hurt and retaliates.'

In the spring of 2006, a slim sixteen-year-old boy with dark hair and just the beginnings of a moustache stood up to speak at the launch of a mural against racism painted by children from nationalist and unionist working-class communities in North Belfast. 'I would see myself to be a young loyalist from the Shankill,' he said. 'By loyalist, I mean loyal to my community, not paramilitary, not running about shooting people and causing mayhem.' He spoke inspiringly about the need for reconciliation. This was at a stage when the DUP was still refusing to share power with Sinn Féin, with many people doubting they ever would.

'I grew up hating Catholics,' he said. 'That was my attitude. I thought someone in a Celtic shirt was in the IRA. I didn't see the bigger picture. Then I got involved in a local community organisation, and now I chair the Belfast City Youth Council. Through that, I met a young Catholic from Ardoyne. I never had a chance to meet a person like that before. I would like him to be able to visit me on the Shankill, and me to be able to visit him in Ardoyne. We can't do that yet. Gerry Adams and Ian Paisley aren't going to change that – we are.'

We met for old-fashioned milky coffee a week or so later, in a cafe on the Shankill Road. Robert Bates wore his dark suit and was courteous and formal with the young waitresses, who seemed affectionately bemused by him. Out on the street, boys his age were wearing tracksuits and baseball caps.

'My grandfather was a born-again Christian who lived for God and was dedicated to peace. I remember him as a loving person and a real family person. I remember a party during the peace process, and there is a picture of me and him at a bouncy castle. The night we heard he was killed we were on holiday in Turkey and we got a phone call. I remember crying my eyes out. I was seven. I remember walking down the Shankill Road with a rose in my hand and Dr Paisley taking the funeral. It was about what my grandfather had become, not what he was before.'

What Robert's grandfather was before was Robert 'Basher' Bates, one of the Shankill Butchers. At his grandson's age, he was already a violent troublemaker, and his career as a killer was about to begin. He was released from jail in 1996 and murdered by a relative of one of his victims, a rival loyalist, in 1997.

Thirty years on from the horrific nights of the Shankill Butchers, young Robert Bates didn't like questions about his grandfather's brutal past. He claimed the Troubles had been exaggerated by journalists, and he was particularly scornful of Martin Dillon's book about the Butchers. 'I read a lot,' he said. 'I read the way other people watch TV. That book is pathetic. I know terrible things happened but it is blown out big time.'

I said, uncomfortably, that the book was based on the facts. There was the trial, the judge's remarks about the depravity of these crimes, his grandfather's confession to ten murders . . .

Robert was impatient. He pointed out that he'd only agreed to meet me to talk about the work he was doing now. 'The media just want to dwell on all that. I won't justify murder and I never will, never have, but there was a war going on. My community suffered a lot at the hands of the republican community and the republican community suffered a lot at the hands of mine.'

His grandfather had told him he had seen the carnage after the IRA bomb which killed one of his relatives. I said I was sorry for pushing him about his grandfather. He smiled. He wasn't offended. 'Don't worry,' he said. 'You couldn't cut me with a knife.' I winced.

After 'Basher' Bates's former gang leader, Lenny Murphy, was murdered, the mass murderer's mother said in an interview, 'My Lenny wouldn't have hurt a fly.' It was clear that Robert Bates junior was also in serious denial about what his grandfather had been. However, his own dedication to cross-community ideals was admired and respected by the nationalists with whom he had worked. He was obviously inspired by the grandfather he had known, and he was being supported and encouraged by men from the UVF ex-prisoners' group, EPIC. 'I've seen a lot of changes,' he said. 'When I was growing up, my father used to bring me to visit my granda in jail. Then there was all the peace work going on. Ceasefires, the Good Friday Agreement, the prisoners coming out of jail. You have to focus on positive things.'

During the conference at which I'd met him, Robert had chatted with Gerry Adams, with whom he had already been in contact over litter problems on the Shankill, which was, as Robert pointed out, in the Sinn Féin leader's constituency. It was during the dinner after this conference that some Shankill community activists walked out because of the presence of Sean Kelly, the Shankill bomber. Robert had stayed. 'You have to remember, there were loyalist killers there, too,' he told me.

Having suffered the loss of both her father and her brother, Alice Harper had learnt in this most painful of ways to look after people who were suffering. She had always been a rock of support for her mother and had made a career out of her gift for looking after others. 'I looked after the dying. I seemed to be able to bring something to them,' she said.

She had looked after her mother for many years, and helped look after several other family members who had been traumatised by the terrible events of 1971 and 1973. She said that her family always asked her father and her brother to watch over them at difficult moments in life.

Bella Teggart died in 2005, aged eighty. 'She was ill for a long time,' said Alice. She had made her mother's final years as tranquil as she could. Bella's husband and son had died violent and lonely deaths. Their photographs were on the wall beside her bed, a child and a still young-looking man. As the elderly woman approached her last days, Alice made sure she was surrounded by her loved ones and that all was hushed and peaceful. 'The night she died, our ones were all sitting talking in the room. I shushed them. I said, "My mummy has passed away. Let her be." Loud noises can bring the dead back. You have to be quiet. We had the window open to let her soul go.'

When I met him, Joseph McCloskey was back home in Belfast and the house was buzzing with excitement as the last-minute preparations were made for his twenty-first birthday party. He was living in Leeds with his English girlfriend, Lauren, and 'making good money' working on the roads. He would have loved his grandfather, Joseph McCloskey senior, to have met Lauren. 'I'm a good judge of character, and I think my granda would have liked her,' he said. 'Every one of us has a wee gold chain with his photo on it.' He was wearing the locket, and he pulled it out to show me a smiling man with slicked-back hair. 'People say, "Is that Elvis?"' he said.

It was easy for the loyalists who murdered Joseph McCloskey senior in 1994 to get at him: the family, like many others in

Belfast, follows the tradition of leaving the key in the front door. The priest at his funeral had spoken about the 'open door that let in the men of darkness'. The key was in the door of Joseph junior's father's house, where we met. Friends and family came and went, talking excitedly about the party. 'It is to show that anyone is welcome,' Joseph said. His granny locked her door now, he said, sadly. 'It still haunts her, what happened.'

Joseph was enjoying his life in England, but he had said he would always come home. 'You can take the boy out of Belfast, but you can't take Belfast out of the boy,' he said. 'No matter where I go I'll always come back.' Now that he was older, people had started telling him what his grandfather was like. 'They say he was a gentleman,' he said, with pride.

'I still don't talk much about my own feelings, but I do think I've learnt from what happened to Granda.' He had become a good listener, he said – 'I like to think that people will come to me if there is anything wrong.' He was in a bookshop with a friend, when his friend picked up Brendan Murphy's fine collection of photographs, *Eyewitness*, and in it found the photograph – used on the cover of this book – of Joseph, aged eight, at his grandfather's funeral. 'I was chuffed, like,' Joseph said. 'If I have kids of my own, I'll show it to them and talk them through the Troubles,' he said. 'I'll tell them not to be bitter.'

Glossary

Alliance Party Set up in 1970 as an attempt to provide a cross-community alternative to traditional nationalist and unionist parties, though it supports the union with Britain. Attracts small numbers of mainly middle-class voters.

Apprentice Boys One of the 'loyal orders' set up to commemorate the thirteen Protestant apprentices who shut the gates of Derry against the army of King James, leading to the Siege of Derry in 1689. Every year they burn an effigy of Lundy, the governor who favoured a compromise to end the siege.

B Specials Set up in 1920 as the Ulster Special Constabulary, an auxiliary force to back up the Royal Ulster Constabulary. Armed, entirely Protestant and with extensive powers, it was feared and hated by nationalists. It was abolished in 1970 and much lamented by unionists. Many of its members immediately joined the new Ulster Defence Regiment.

British Army Troops were sent into Northern Ireland in 1969 to support the beleaguered RUC in the face of widespread rioting. Initially welcomed by nationalists, internment, systematic ill-treatment and brutal behaviour by the Parachute Regiment and others soon alienated them. British troops killed over three hundred people, half of them civilians.

More than a quarter of a million soldiers served in Northern Ireland over the thirty-eight years of their deployment, which ended in 2007. More than seven hundred soldiers were killed, mainly by the IRA.

Collusion Refers to collaboration between the security forces and illegal paramilitary organisations through the use of agents and the passing of confidential information. A growing body of evidence is emerging to show the practice was widespread, particularly between loyalist paramilitaries and elements of the local security forces.

Combined Loyalist Military Command (CLMC) An umbrella group formed in 1991 to represent the main loyalist paramilitary organisations. It announced the loyalist ceasefire of 1994, and fell apart soon afterwards.

Dáil Éireann The lower house of the parliament of the Irish Republic, in Dublin. Public representatives are known as TDs. The head of the government is called the Taoiseach. The upper house is the Seanad, or Senate.

Democratic Unionist Party (DUP) Founded in 1971 by the Reverend Ian Paisley, who has led it since then. It overtook the Ulster Unionist Party to became the dominant unionist party after the collapse, in 2002, of the first executive set up under the Good Friday Agreement. The DUP opposed the agreement, but after negotiating modifications to it, in 2007 Paisley became first minister in a new executive in Belfast, with Sinn Féin's Martin McGuinness in the joint and equal position of deputy first minister.

Drumcree A small Church of Ireland church in Portadown, County Armagh, which in the mid-1990s became the focus of annual violent clashes between the Orange Order, the authorities and local nationalists over an Orange parade along a disputed route through a Catholic area. Unionist leaders supported the Orangemen.

Fenians A term of sectarian abuse used against Catholics by a bigoted element of the Protestant community. Its origins are in the Fenian Brotherhood, a militant republican body founded in the nineteenth century. 'Taig' is used in a similar way.

Fianna Fáil Literally 'soldiers of destiny'. One of the founding parties of the Irish Republic, and the dominant one.

Gaelic Athletic Association (GAA) Large and almost exclusively Catholic sporting and cultural organisation with 'cumainn' (clubs) in parishes all over Ireland. Regarded with suspicion by many unionists. Until 2001, members of the North's security forces were banned from joining. The abolition of this rule was opposed by most Northern GAA clubs.

Garda Síochána Known as the Gardaí, the routinely unarmed police force of the Irish Republic.

Good Friday Agreement Political settlement reached on 10 April 1998 after lengthy negotiations involving the British and Irish governments and Northern Irish political parties. The talks were chaired by former US senator George Mitchell in Belfast and were preceded by at least six years of what became known as 'the peace process'. The Agreement kept Northern Ireland within the United Kingdom but acknowledged an Irish dimension.

An assembly of 108 'Members of the Legislative Assembly' (MLAs), all designated unionist, nationalist or 'other', was led by a ministerial executive, headed by a first minister from the majority unionist community and a deputy first minister of equal standing from the minority nationalist community. The Northern Ireland Office retained responsibility for key areas, including justice and security.

A large majority of citizens of the North and the Republic endorsed the Agreement, but nationalists liked it better than unionists, and the DUP opposed it. The first assembly was led by the Ulster Unionist Party and the SDLP but collapsed acrimoniously in 2002.

Historical Enquiries Team (HET) Police investigations team set up by the chief constable of the Police Service of Northern Ireland in 2006 to re-examine all deaths which occurred as a result of the security situation in Northern Ireland between 1968 and the signing of the Good Friday Agreement in April 1998. A 'White Team' was set up to look at deaths in which there were allegations of collusion.

Irish National Liberation Army (INLA) A breakaway paramilitary faction of the Official IRA. Formed in 1974, it gained a reputation for ruthlessness and for feuding. Its political wing is the Irish Republican Socialist Party (IRSP), which has never been popular with voters.

Irish Republican Army (IRA) Usually refers to the Provisional IRA – *Óglaigh na hÉireann*. Known to the British as PIRA (colloquially the 'Provos' or the 'Ra'), it emerged after a split in the IRA over the use of arms in defence of nationalist communities in the North in 1969. Its youth wing was Fianna Éireann.

The IRA had its origins in the Easter Rising of 1916, and it aimed to end British rule in Ireland and form an Irish Republic consisting of the whole island of Ireland. By 1969, it was largely dormant.

The Provisionals rearmed and engaged in an intense campaign of violence lasting until its ceasefire in 1994. This lapsed after problems in the peace process, but was reinstated in 1997. The other faction, the Official IRA, retained its Marxist ideology. It engaged in violence, but called a ceasefire in 1972. Known colloquially as the 'Stickies', the organisation continued to feud with the Provisionals and the INLA.

The PIRA decommissioned its weapons in 2005. It was responsible for almost half of all the deaths in the conflict, and almost three hundred of its volunteers were killed. Criminal activities continued after the ceasefires.

Long Kesh The name of the prison where thousands of paramilitaries were held throughout the years of the conflict. Although it was renamed the Maze in the mid-1970s, republicans use the old name. The prison was closed in 2000.

Loyalist Volunteer Force (LVF) Paramilitary group which broke away from the UVF, which was on ceasefire, in 1996 and resumed sectarian killings in support of the Orange Order at Drumcree. Joined forces with elements of the Ulster Defence Association in opposition to the Good Friday Agreement, using *noms de guerre* including Red Hand Defenders and Orange Volunteers.

Northern Ireland The name given to the six counties in the north-east of Ireland which remained British after the partition of the island in 1920. The remaining twenty-six counties became known as the Free State and then the Republic of Ireland. Nationalists and republicans have tended to use 'the North' or 'the Six Counties' to designate the northern state.

Northern Ireland Office (NIO) Set up as a government department by the British government in 1972 after it prorogued the unionist government at Stormont in Belfast. Headed by the secretary of state for Northern Ireland.

Orange Order Exclusively Protestant body set up in the late eighteenth century to ensure Protestant solidarity across the class divide. In the nineteenth and twentieth centuries, it opposed Irish nationalism and republicanism. Consisting of local 'lodges', the highlight of its year is the 12th of July celebration of King William of Orange's victory over King James at the Battle of the Boyne in 1690. Its insistence on marching with bands through Catholic areas has led to riots, disturbances and deaths during times of conflict, from its establishment to the Drumcree years. 'Orangie' and 'Jaffa' are sectarian terms of abuse against Protestants.

Peace Lines Latterly known as 'interfaces', these are barriers which still divide Catholic and Protestant areas, particularly in North and West Belfast. Originating from barricades put up by local people in the early days of the conflict, the British army reinforced and extended them with corrugated iron and barbed-wire fences. In later years these were replaced by high brick walls with gates which can be locked or opened depending on local levels of strife. Riots across the interfaces were common throughout the conflict.

Police Service of Northern Ireland (PSNI) Replaced the Royal Ulster Constabulary in 2001 under the recommendations of the Patten Report. The PSNI is meant to achieve a balance of 50 per cent Catholic membership and is answerable to a cross-community policing board. Complaints about police conduct can be brought to the police ombudsman.

Progressive Unionist Party (PUP) Small left-leaning party set up to lead the paramilitary Ulster Volunteer Force into politics, arguing that traditional unionism had exploited working-class Protestants. At its peak, after the signing of the Good Friday Agreement, it had just two MLAs.

Real IRA (RIRA) Dissident republican group which broke away from the Provisional IRA in 1997 because it opposed the peace process. There is also the Continuity IRA, a smaller body. The RIRA was responsible for the post-Good Friday

Agreement Omagh bomb atrocity. It is politically close to the 32 County Sovereignty Movement.

Royal Irish Regiment (RIR) British army regiment set up in 1992 after the Ulster Defence Regiment and the Royal Irish Rangers merged.

Royal Ulster Constabulary (RUC) The armed and almost exclusively Protestant police force set up in 1921, along with an RUC reserve force. Under emergency legislation introduced at this time, it had extensive powers and was feared and distrusted by nationalists, particularly after it used violence against civil-rights protesters and mistreated internees and paramilitary suspects. A substantial number of RUC personnel joined to serve the whole community fairly, but members of its Special Branch, which dealt with intelligence, were found by the police ombudsman in 2006 to have colluded with loyalists.

Over three hundred policemen and women were killed in the conflict, mostly by the IRA. The RUC was awarded the George Cross for courage in 1999. It became the Police Service of Northern Ireland in 2001.

Sinn Féin The dominant nationalist party in the North, it is a thirty-two-county party with seats in the Dáil also. Although it has seats at Westminster, its MPs do not sit there. The party was founded in Dublin in 1904, but its current leaders, party president Gerry Adams and the deputy first minister, Martin McGuinness, emerged from the Provisional IRA in the North, a source of grievance to unionists.

Social Democratic and Labour Party (SDLP) Founded in 1970, the party emerged from the civil-rights movement and represented the majority of Catholic voters in Northern Ireland until it was eclipsed by Sinn Féin after the collapse of the first assembly formed under the Good Friday Agreement. Led by

John Hume from 1979 until 2001. The party played a leading role in establishing the peace process.

Special Air Service (SAS) A special unit of the British army which was involved in controversial undercover operations in Northern Ireland.

Stormont Built for the original unionist government of Northern Ireland, it is now the seat of the Northern Ireland Assembly.

Third Force A loyalist militia set up in 1982 and backed by the DUP, the Third Force claimed the security forces needed its help to defeat the IRA.

Ulster Defence Association (UDA) The largest loyalist paramilitary organisation, it was set up as a vigilante body to defend Protestant areas in 1971. It was the muscle behind the Ulster Workers Council Strike of 1974, which brought down the Sunningdale Agreement on power sharing. Using the cover name of the Ulster Freedom Fighters (UFF), the UDA killed over 430 people, mainly Catholic civilians. Members of the UDA were initially allowed to be members of the Ulster Defence Regiment, and many were. It claimed it existed only to react to republican violence, and was legal until 1992. Its youth wing was called the Ulster Young Militants. A political wing, the Ulster Democratic Party, was short lived. The UDA called a ceasefire in 1994, but killings continued sporadically. It survives as a criminal organisation.

Ulster Defence Regiment (UDR) Largely Protestant, locally recruited British regiment set up in 1970 after the abolition of the B Specials, who joined en masse. The UDR had a 'bad name' with nationalists, and elements of it were close to loyalist paramilitaries, providing them with guns and information, and even joining forces with them. However, many

UDR soldiers were not involved in such activities. UDR soldiers in rural areas were particularly vulnerable to IRA attack, and over two hundred were killed. The IRA also killed off-duty and ex-UDR personnel.

Ulster Unionist Party (UUP) The party which ran Northern Ireland from 1920 until 1972, when the British government prorogued its powers and set up the Northern Ireland Office. Traditionally, its politicians and leaders were from the landed gentry.

It discriminated shamelessly against Catholics. Prime Minister Terence O'Neill belatedly attempted to reform the state at the start of the civil-rights movement, but opposition to his efforts, led by Ian Paisley, led to his resignation. Elements of the UUP joined the militant Vanguard movement during the 1970s and were close to loyalist paramilitaries. The UUP was the dominant unionist party until it split over aspects of the Good Friday Agreement. It was overtaken by the DUP, which resoundingly defeated it in elections to the 2007 assembly.

Ulster Volunteer Force (UVF) Loyalist paramilitary organisation which carried out the first murders of the Troubles in 1966. It modelled itself on the UVF set up by unionists to resist Home Rule for Ireland in 1912. It was linked to the smaller Red Hand Commandos and has a youth wing called the Young Citizens Volunteers. Carried out murders in collusion with elements of the security forces, especially in mid-Ulster. Developed a small political wing in the 1990s (see PUP). The organisation called a ceasefire in 1994 but killings continued, mostly linked to loyalist feuds, particularly with its breakaway faction, the LVF.

Ulsterisation British policy of giving primacy on dealing with security matters back to the local security forces in the mid- to late 1970s.

Acknowledgements

I am deeply grateful to all of the very many people who helped me, above all those who talked to me about the murders of their loved ones, exploring painful memories with brave honesty.

I am also grateful to my good friends for their support and encouragement, especially Madeline McGahern.

Thanks to all of those who read and commented on drafts, or parts of drafts, of the book, especially my editor at Faber and Faber, Neil Belton, who has been both rigorous and patient; also to Ian Bahrami, Brian Feeney, Hilary Bell and Alan Brecknell. Thanks to Brendan Murphy for the cover photograph and to Katherine Armstrong, who went many extra miles for this book.

Thanks to Nick Perks and all at the Joseph Rowntree Charitable Trust for their interest and generosity. I could not have written this book without the grant they provided.

My love and thanks, as always, to Mike, Madeleine and Caitlin. Without them, I couldn't write at all.

Notes

Introduction

1. *Guardian*, 2 June 2007.
2. W. G. Sebald, *Austerlitz*, Penguin, 2001, p. 395.
3. Alexandra Fuller, *Scribbling the Cat*, Picador, 2004, p. 250.
4. Primo Levi, 'Our Nights', in *If This Is a Man*, Abacus, 1987, p. 66.
5. Primo Levi, 'The Grey Zone', in *The Drowned and the Saved*, Abacus, 1989, p. 26.

PART I: THE KILLING YEARS
Chapter 1

1. *Belfast Telegraph*, 27 June 1966.
2. John Hewitt, 'The Coasters', *A Rage for Order*, Blackstaff, 1992, pp. 49–51.
3. Michael Longley, 'Wounds', *Cenotaph of Snow*, Enitharmon Press, 2003, p. 13.
4. *Belfast Telegraph*, 11 August 1971.
5. *Irish Times*, 22 December 2007.

Chapter 2

1. Quoted in Malachi

O'Doherty, *The Telling Year*, Gill and Macmillan, 2007, p. 99.

2. David McKittrick and David McVea, *Making Sense of the Troubles*, Blackstaff, p. 79.

3. Louis MacNeice, 'Autumn Journal XVI', *Collected Poems*, Faber and Faber, 2007.

4. Quoted in David McKittrick, Seamus Kelters, Brian Feeney, Chris Thornton and David McVea, *Lost Lives*, Mainstream Publishing, p. 219.

5. Ardoyne Commemoration Project, *Ardoyne, The Untold Truth*, Beyond the Pale Publications, 2003, p. 127.

6. Ibid., p. 131.

7. Ed Moloney, *Hidden History*, Penguin, 2002, p. 81.

8. O'Doherty, p. 20.

9. Ardoyne Commemoration Project, p. 132.

10. Kevin Myers, *Watching the Door*, Lilliput, 2006, p. 96.

11. McKittrick *et al.*, p. 218.

12. James Simmons, *A Rage for Order*, Ed. Frank Ormsby, Blackstaff, 1992, p. 95.

13. Padraic Fiacc, *Missa Terribilis*, Blackstaff, 1986, p. 25.

Chapter 3

1. Eric Bogle, 'My Youngest Son Came Home Today', sung by Mary Black, *Collected Mary Black*, Dara Records, 1984.

2. Quoted in David McKittrick, Seamus Kelters, Brian Feeney, Chris Thornton and David McVea, *Lost Lives*, Mainstream Publishing, p. 401.

3. Padraig Fiacc, 'Wee Lads', *Missa Terribilis*, Blackstaff, 1986, p. 41.

4. Tom Paulin, in *A Rage for Order*, Blackstaff, 1992, p. 120.

5. Richard O'Rawe, *Blanketmen*, New Island, p. 141.

6. Martin Dillon, *The Shankill Butchers*, Arrow, 1989, p. 27.

7. Padraic Fiacc, 'Crucifixus', from *Missa Terribilis*, p. 21.

Chapter 4

1. *Irish Independent*, 27 May 1974, p. 22.

2. Susan McKay, *Northern Protestants*, Blackstaff, 2000, p. 190.

3. Quoted in Toby Harnden, *Bandit Country*, Hodder and Stoughton, 1999, p. 138.

4. Paul Durcan, 'The Minibus Massacre – The Eve of the Epiphany', *The Selected Paul Durcan*, Blackstaff Press, 1982, p. 94.

5. Michael Longley, *Cenotaph of Snow*, p. 22.

Chapter 5

1. Francie Brolly, 'The H-Block Song', quoted in *Nor Meekly Serve My Time*, compiled by Brian Campbell, Beyond the Pale Publications, 1994.

2. Alf McCreary, *Tried by Fire*, Marshal Pickering, 1986, p. 49.
3. Ibid., p. 53.
4. Quoted in David McKittrick, Seamus Kelters, Brian Feeney, Chris Thornton and David McVea, *Lost Lives*, Mainstream Publishing, p. 794.
5. Denis O'Hearn, *Nothing but an Unfinished Song*, Pluto Press, 2006, p. 271.
6. Richard O'Rawe, *Blanketmen*, New Island, p. 113.
7. Bernadette Devlin McAliskey, *Britain and Ireland – Lives Entwined II*, British Council Ireland, p. 126.
8. Interview with author.
9. O'Rawe, p. 141.
10. Quoted in David McKittrick and David McVea, *Making Sense of the Troubles*, Blackstaff, p. 144.
11. Seamus Heaney, 'Frontiers of Writing', in *The Redress of Poetry*, Faber, p. 187.

Chapter 6

1. Michael Longley, *Cenotaph of Snow*, p. 21.
2. Quoted in John Lindsay, *Brits Speak Out*, Guildhall Press, 1998, p. 45.
3. Chris Ryder, *The Ulster Defence Regiment*, Methuen, p. 143.
4. Ibid., p. 143.
5. Eugene McCabe, from 'Heritage', in *Heaven Lies About Us*, Jonathan Cape, 2005, p. 104.
6. Chris Ryder, *The UDR*, p. 199.
7. Colm Tóibín, *Bad Blood*, Vintage, 1994, p. 100.

Chapter 7

1. Padraig Pearse, 'The Mother', *Plays, Stories and Poems*, Talbot Press, 1966, p. 333.
2. Oistin MacBride, *Family, Friends and Neighbours*, Beyond the Pale Publications, p. 105.
3. Oistin MacBride, document shown to author.
4. Louis MacNeice, 'Autumn Journal XVI', *Collected Poems*, Faber and Faber, 2007, p. 137.
5. Padraig Fiacc, 'Intimate Letter 1973', *Missa Terribilis*, Blackstaff, 1986, p. 34.

Chapter 8

1. Paul Brady, 'The Island', *Back to the Centre*, Mercury Records, 1986.
2. Denzil McDaniel, *Enniskillen, the Remembrance Sunday Bombing*, Wolfhound, 1997, p. 131.
3. Quoted in David McKittrick and David McVea, *Making Sense of the Troubles*, Blackstaff, p. 164.
4. McDaniel, p. 72.

5. Jonathan Bardon, *A History of Ulster*, Blackstaff, 1992, p. 777.
6. Frank McGuinness, *Irish Times*, 13 November 1987.
7. Bardon, p. 773.
8. Quoted in McKittrick and McVea, p. 195.
9. Quoted in David McKittrick, Seamus Kelters, Brian Feeney, Chris Thornton and David McVea, *Lost Lives*, Mainstream Publishing, p. 1,349.

Chapter 9

1. Susan McKay, 'The Valley of Death', *Sunday Tribune*, 3 August 1997.
2. Ibid.
3. Ibid.
4. Ibid.
5. Ibid.
6. Ibid.
7. Ibid.
8. *Irish News*, 2 February 1998.
9. *Irish News*, 12 June 1997.
10. Interview with author.
11. Reprinted in the *Burning Bush*, July/August 1997.

Chapter 10

1. Jackson Browne, 'After the Deluge', recorded by Moving Hearts on *Moving Hearts*, 1981.
2. Good Friday Agreement, p. 21.
3. Quoted in 'A Bomber Loyalists Will Find Difficult to Forgive and Forget', Susan McKay, *Irish Times*, 20 July 2005.
4. BBC Northern Ireland newspages, 11 May 2000.
5. *Irish News*, 26 July 2000.
6. Seamus Heaney, from 'The Cure at Troy', *A Rage for Order*, p. 318.
7. John Montague, 'A Response to Omagh', *Smashing the Piano*, Gallery Books, 1999, p. 77.
8. Eamon Collins, *Killing Rage*, Granta, 1997, pp. 282–3.
9. Ed Moloney, 'Why Collins Died', *Sunday Tribune*, 31 January 1999.
10. Collins, p. 252.
11. Quoted in David McKittrick, Seamus Kelters, Brian Feeney, Chris Thornton and David McVea, *Lost Lives*, Mainstream Publishing, p. 1,049.

Chapter 11

1. Susan McKay, 'A Wee Boy Given a Man's Job', *Sunday Tribune*, 8 June 2003.
2. *Irish News*, 2 December 2006.

3. *Irish News*, 28 March 2007.
4. Susan McKay, *Northern Protestants*, Blackstaff, 2000, p. 240.
5. 'Don't Let This Happen Again', *Irish News*, 9 May 2006.
6. Susan McKay, 'Something Has Got to Be Done to Stop This Madness', *Irish Times*, 13 May 2006.
7. Ibid.
8. Ibid.
9. Ibid.
10. Ibid.
11. Ibid.
12. Ibid.
13. Ibid.
14. Susan McKay, *Irish Times*, 18 May 2006.
15. Ibid.
16. Ibid.

PART II: AFTERMATH
Chapter 1

1. Ryszard Kapuscinski, 'When There Is Talk of War', *Granta* 88, 2004.
2. David McKittrick, Seamus Kelters, Brian Feeney, Chris Thornton and David McVea, *Lost Lives*, Mainstream Publishing, p. 1,382.
3. *Irish Times*, 5 February 1994.
4. Interview with author.
5. McKittrick *et al.*, p. 383.
6. Ibid., p. 268.
7. *Irish News*, 7 April 2007.
8. Oistin MacBride, *Family, Friends and Neighbours*, Beyond the Pale Publications, p. 64.
9. Quoted in McKittrick *et al.*, p. 819.
10. Interview with author.
11. Ibid.
12. Julia Orange, 'Plight of the Single Twin', *The Times*, 1 May 1989.
13. David McKittrick, 'The Night They Took Our Mother Away', *Independent* magazine, 25 September 2003.
14. Sharon O'Neill, 'The Poyntzpass Killings – 8 Years On', *Irish News*, 1 March 2006.
15. Ibid.
16. Quoted in Paul Bailey's introduction to Primo Levi, *The Drowned and the Saved*, Abacus, 1989, p. xii.

Chapter 2

1. Ardoyne Commemoration Project, *Ardoyne, The Untold Truth*, Beyond the Pale Publications, 2003, p. 490.

2. Denzil McDaniel, *Enniskillen, the Remembrance Sunday Bombing*, Wolfhound, 1997, p. 152.

3. Ibid., p. 72.

4. Quoted by Andy Pollack in 'Fear God and Keep Your Powder Dry', *Irish Times*, 21 December 1996.

5. Proverbs 6:16–17, quoted in McDaniel, p. 58.

6. Amos 3:6.

7. 'The Burning Bush', November 1987, *www.ivanfoster.org*.

8. Pollack, 'Fear God and Keep Your Powder Dry'.

9. Susan McKay, *Northern Protestants*, Blackstaff, 2000, p. 147.

10. *Irish Times*, 15 October 2004.

11. Seamus Heaney, letter to the *Irish News*, 14 May 1997.

12. Ibid.

13. *Looking the Brighton Bomber in the Eye*, BBC TV News, 13 December 2001.

14. David McKittrick, Seamus Kelters, Brian Feeney, Chris Thornton and David McVea, *Lost Lives*, Mainstream Publishing, p. 997.

15. David McKittrick, 'The Night They Took Our Mother Away', *Independent* magazine, 25 September 2003.

16. Interview with author.

17. *Irish News*, 10 January 2007.

18. *Facing the Truth*, BBC TV, March 2006.

19. *Irish News*, 25 November 2006.

20. BBC Northern Ireland, Stephen Nolan radio show, 7 March 2006.

Chapter 3

1. Stevens Report, Overview and Recommendations, Sir John Stevens, London Metropolitan Police Service, 2003, p. 11.

2. Susan McKay, 'Police Ombudsman to Publish Damning Report on Sean Brown Murder Investigation', *Sunday Tribune*, 18 January 2004.

3. Ian Knox, *The Hand of History*, Brehon Press, 2005, p. 54.

4. Susan McKay, 'A Terrible Retribution', *Irish Times*, 17 November 2007.

5. Fintan O'Toole, 'Leave Jerry McCabe in Peace', *Irish Times*, 21 February 2006.

6. Kathy Sheridan, 'Reluctant Campaigner', *Irish Times*, 3 June 2006.

7. Quoted in David McKittrick, Seamus Kelters, Brian Feeney, Chris Thornton and David McVea, *Lost Lives*, Mainstream Publishing, p. 920.

8. Ardoyne Commemoration Project, *Ardoyne, The Untold Truth*, Beyond the Pale Publications, 2002, p. 1.

9. Ibid., p. 3.

10. Ibid.

11. Ibid, pp. xiii, xiv.

12. Ibid., p. xv.

13. Marie Breen Smyth, *Truth Recovery and Justice After Conflict*, Routledge, 2007, p. 113.
14. Wendy and Colin Parry, *Tim, an Ordinary Boy*, Corgi, 1994, p. 179.
15. Susan McKay, *Sunday Tribune*, 28 March 1993.
16. Ibid.
17. *Irish Times*, 3 April 1993.
18. Fionnuala O'Connor, *Irish Times*, 11 August 2006.
19. *Sunday Tribune*, 28 March 1993.
20. Wendy and Colin Parry, p. 306.
21. *Guardian*, 1 July 1999.
22. *Guardian*, 29 October 2001.
23. *Sunday News*, 29 May 1972.
24. Louis MacNeice, 'Autobiography', *Collected Poems*, Faber and Faber, 2007, p. 200.
25. *Bloody Sunday, A Derry Diary*, Besom Productions, 2007.

Chapter 4

1. *Irish Times*, 6 August 2003.
2. Letter from the HET, quoted to author by Eugene Reavey.
3. Interim Report on the Report of the Independent Commission of Inquiry into the Bombing of Kay's Tavern, Dundalk, published by the Joint Committee on Justice, Equality, Defence and Women's Rights, Houses of the Oireachtas, Dublin, 2006.
4. Barron Report, 2003, p. 225.
5. Quoted in the Report of the Independent International Panel on Collusion, 2006, p. 77.
6. 'Subversion in the UDR', p. 9, available at www.patfinucanecentre.org.
7. Barron Report, 2006, p. 119.
8. Barron Report, 2003, p. 157.
9. Toby Harnden, *Bandit Country*, p. 139.
10. Gary Armstrong, *From Palace to Prison*, New Wine Press.
11. Quoted in Tom Paulin, *Writing to the Moment*, Faber and Faber, 1996, p. 36.
12. 'Just Never Proven Guilty', 15 July 2007, FAIR website, www.victims.org.uk.
13. Ibid.
14. See Latest News, www.victims.org.uk.
15. Susan McKay, *Northern Protestants*, Blackstaff, 2000, pp. 193–4.
16. Stevens Enquiry 3, London Metropolitan Police Service, 2003.
17. Johnston Brown, *Into the Dark*, Gill and MacMillan.
18. Interview with author.

Chapter 5

1. Interview with author.
2. Ibid.

3. Ibid.

4. *Irish News*, 9 January 2008.

5. Kieran McEvoy, *Making Peace with the Past*, p. 30.

6. Ibid., p. 98.

7. 'Truth Recovery', Progressive Unionist Party document, *www.pup-ni.org.uk*.

8. Edna Longley, 'Commemoration, Elegy, Forgetting', in *History and Memory in Modern Ireland*, Ed. Ian McBride, Cambridge University Press, 2001, p. 231.

9. *Irish News*, 17 August 2007.

10. Interview with author, 2003.

11. Pat Finucane Centre archives.

Chapter 6

1. Siegfried Sassoon, 'On Passing the New Menin Gate', in Jon Stallworthy, *Anthem for Doomed Youth: Twelve Soldier Poets of the First World War*, Constable, 2002, p. 81.

2. Denzil McDaniel, *Enniskillen, the Remembrance Sunday Bombing*, Wolfhound, 1997, p. 139.

3. Jay Winter, *Sites of Memory, Sites of Mourning*, Cambridge University Press, 1995, p. 104.

4. McDaniel, p. 136.

5. Ibid., p. 138.

6. W. Verwoerd, *Towards Inclusive Remembrance After the Troubles, A South African Perspective*, IBIS working paper 35, p. 1.

7. Interview with author.

8. www.victims.org.uk.

9. www.easter1916.net/oration.htm. *The Complete Works of P. H. Pearse*, Phoenix, 1917, pp. 133–7.

10. Bobby Sands, 'The Rhythm of Time', quoted in Denis O'Hearn, *Bobby Sands, Nothing but an Unfinished Song*, Pluto Press, 2006, p. 253.

11. Interview on RTE radio programme *This Week*, 21 January 2007.

12. Ibid.

13. *Irish News*, 6 October 2006.

14. Eamon Collins, *Killing Rage*, Granta, 1997, p. 371.

15. Jay Winter, p. 115.

16. Interview with author.

17. Alf McCreary, *Tried by Fire*, Marshal Pickering, 1986, p. 43.

18. MacBride family statement, issued 9 May 2002.

19. Sinn Fein press statement, 23 August 2006, *www.sinnfein.ie/news*.

20. SDLP press release, 2 October 2007.

21. Interview with author.

22. David McKittrick, Seamus Kelters, Brian Feeney, Chris Thornton and

David McVea, *Lost Lives*, Mainstream Publishing, p. 1,505.
23. Michael Longley, *Tuppenny Stung*, Lagan Press, 1994, p. 60.
24. McKittrick *et al.*, *Lost Lives*, p. 1,412.
25. Drawing Support 2, Bill Rolston, *Beyond the Pale*, p. i.
26. *Irish News*, 26 July 2000.
27. Susan McKay, *Northern Protestants*, Blackstaff, 2000, p. 83.
28. Gerry Moriarty, 'McConville Family Finds Peace After a Wait of 31 Years', *Irish Times*, 31 October 2003.
29. Frank O'Connor, 'Guests of the Nation', reprinted in *The Hurt World*, Ed. Michael Parker, Blackstaff, 1995, p. 25.
30. BBC NI, *Spotlight, The Hunt for Captain Nairac*, 19 June 2007.
31. *Irish News*, 10 May 2007.
32. McKittrick *et al.*, *Lost Lives*, p. 1,072.
33. McCreary, *Tried by Fire*, p. 53.
34. McDaniel, *Enniskillen*, p. 140.

Chapter 7

1. Juliet Turner, *Across the Bridge of Hope*, White Records, 1998.
2. Interview with author.
3. Michael Longley, 'The Ice-Cream Man', *Cenotaph of Snow*, Enitharmon Press, 2003, p. 29.
4. Ibid., p. 45.
5. Ibid., p.22.
6. Edna Longley, 'NI, Commemoration, Elegy, Forgetting', in *History and Memory in Modern Ireland*, Ed. Ian McBride, Cambridge, p. 252.
7. *Thumbscrew* 12, 1989, www.poetrymagazines.org.uk.
8. 'Wounds', *Cenotaph of Snow*, p. 13.
9. Frank McGuinness, *Observe the Sons of Ulster Marching Towards the Somme*, in *Frank McGuinness, Plays 1*, Faber and Faber, p. 97.
10. Ibid., p. 196.
11. 'All Is Changed after Enniskillen', *Irish Times*, 13 November 1987.
12. Jay Winter, *Sites of Memory, Sites of Mourning*, Cambridge University Press, 1995, p. 17.
13. Stewart Parker, *Pentecost*, in *Stewart Parker, Plays 2*, Methuen, 2000.
14. Judges 17:6.
15. Glenn Patterson, *That Which Was*, Penguin, 2004, p. 107.
16. Ibid.
17. Michael Duke, *Revenge*, Tinderbox Theatre Company publication, p. 57.
18. Bernard MacLaverty, *Cal*, Vintage, p. 154.
19. Mary Holland, 'Could Any of Us Have Shouted Stop?' 23 March 1988, reprinted in *How Far We Have Travelled, The Voice of Mary Holland*, Ed. Mary Maher, Townhouse, 2004, p. 48.
20. Ibid.

21. Ibid., 'Putting the Past Behind to Give Peace a Chance', p. 157.

22. Ciaran Carson, *Belfast Confetti*, Gallery Books, 1989, p. 46.

23. Padraic Fiacc, *Missa Terribilis*, Blackstaff, 1986, p. 35.

24. John Hewitt, 'An Irishman in Coventry', *A Rage for Order*, Blackstaff, 1992, p. 282.

25. Paul Muldoon, 'Lunch with Sancho Panza', *A Rage for Order*, Blackstaff, p. 129.

26. Ibid., p. 213.

27. Ardoyne Commemoration Project, *Ardoyne, The Untold Truth*, Beyond the Pale Publications, 2003, p. 489.

28. Seamus Heaney, 'Requiem for the Croppies', *Door Into the Dark*, Faber and Faber, 1969, p. 24.

29. Seamus Heaney, 'Feeling into Words', in *Preoccupations*, Faber and Faber, 1980, pp. 56–7.

30. Seamus Heaney, 'Exposure', *North*, Faber and Faber, 1975, p. 66.

31. Seamus Heaney, 'The Flight Path', *Opened Ground*, Faber and Faber, 1998, p. 412.

32. Seamus Heaney, 'Station Island', *Opened Ground*, Faber and Faber, 1998, p. 242ff.

33. Danny Morrison (Ed.), *Hunger Strike*, Brandon, 2006, pp. 9–10.

34. Ibid.

35. Ibid.

36. Seamus Heaney, 'Frontiers of Writing', in *Redress of Poetry*, p. 191.

37. Danny Morrison (Ed.), pp. 9–11 and 21–2.

38. Ibid., 'The Desire for Freedom', p. 192.

39. Padraig O'Malley, *Biting at the Grave*, Beacon Press, 1990, pp. 55–6.

40. Edna Longley, *The Living Stream: Literature and Revisionism in Ireland*, Bloodaxe, p. 26.

41. Paul Durcan, *Collected Poems*, p. 53.

42. Laurence Binyon, 'Ode to the Fallen', from *The Winnowing Fan: Poems of the Great War*, Elkin Mathews, 1914.

43. Alan Gillis, 'Progress', *Somebody, Somewhere*, Gallery Press, p. 55.

Chapter 8

1. Newsletter, 9 May 2007.

2. Quoted in *Village*, 3 August 2006.

3. Hazlett Lynch, 'Thrown in Any Towels Lately?', *WAVE Newsletter*, January 2008, p. 8.

4. Ibid.

ff

Faber and Faber – a home for writers

Faber and Faber is one of the great independent publishing houses in London. We were established in 1929 by Geoffrey Faber and our first editor was T. S. Eliot. We are proud to publish prize-winning fiction and non-fiction, as well as an unrivalled list of modern poets and playwrights. Among our list of writers we have five Booker Prize winners and eleven Nobel Laureates, and we continue to seek out the most exciting and innovative writers at work today.

www.faber.co.uk – a home for readers

The Faber website is a place where you will find all the latest news on our writers and events. You can listen to podcasts, preview new books, read specially commissioned articles and access reading guides, as well as entering competitions and enjoying a whole range of offers and exclusives. You can also browse the list of Faber Finds, an exciting new project where reader recommendations are helping to bring a wealth of lost classics back into print using the latest on-demand technology.